STORIED
INDEPENDENT
AUTOMAKERS

Great Lakes Books

*A complete listing of the books in this series
can be found online at wsupress.wayne.edu*

STORIED
INDEPENDENT
AUTOMAKERS

Nash, Hudson, and American Motors

Charles K. Hyde

WAYNE STATE UNIVERSITY PRESS
DETROIT

Library of Congress Cataloging-in-Publication Data

Hyde, Charles K., 1945–
Storied independent automakers : Nash, Hudson, and American Motors /
Charles K. Hyde.
   p. cm.
Includes bibliographical references and index.
ISBN 978-0-8143-3446-1 (cloth : alk. paper)
1. American Motors automobiles—United States—History. 2. Nash Motors
Company—History. 3. Hudson Motor Car Company—History. 4. American
Motors Corporation—History. 5. Nash, Charles Warren, 1864–1948. 6. Auto-
mobile engineers—United States—Biography. I. Title.

TL215.A44H93 2010
338.7'6292220973—dc22
2009011989

∞

Designed and typeset by Anna Oler
Composed in CaseStudyNo1 and Fairfield

To the memory of John A. Bluth (1932–2009),
fellow automotive historian and friend.

Contents

Tables

Preface

This book is rooted in my research on the history of the Chrysler Corporation, which resulted in a book published in 2003. While poring over documents in the DaimlerChrysler Historical Collection for several years, I noticed a section of the archives filled with boxes of materials on Nash Motors, the Hudson Motor Car Company, and American Motors. These documents came to the Chrysler Corporation after its purchase of American Motors in 1987. In this case, as is true with most corporate takeovers, "to the buyer go the company records." The story of American Motors, formed with the merger of Nash and Hudson in 1954, is part of Chrysler's history as well. I also learned that no serious scholarly business histories existed for any of these three independent automakers. All three companies were important automakers in their own right. Their early successes and eventual failures as small independent producers are important stories that need to be told.

My initial book manuscript was far too long, with far too many details, to be turned into a reasonably sized (and reasonably priced) book. As a result, I trimmed roughly one-quarter of the original manuscript, but without eliminating any key characters, products, or events from the narrative. Those who might want more details will find an unabridged copy deposited at the National Automotive History Collection located in the Skillman Branch of the Detroit Public Library.

The work of automotive historians depends on the assistance and cooperation of many archivists and librarians. I owe a great debt to Brandt Rosenbusch of the DaimlerChrysler Historical Collection for graciously granting access to largely unprocessed materials on Nash, Hudson, and American Motors. Similarly, I found the collections of the National Automotive History Collection (NAHC) of the Detroit Public Library to be invaluable.

Mark Patrick and Barbara Thompson cheerfully guided me through the NAHC's collections. A bevy of individuals and institutions helped me navigate through widely scattered materials relating to Charles W. Nash and Nash Motors: Michael Madden at the Flint (Michigan) Public Library; Jeff Taylor at the Sloan Museum in Flint; David White at the Scharchburg Archives at Kettering University in Flint; the staff at the Southwest Branch of the Kenosha (Wisconsin) Public Library; Cynthia Nelson at the Kenosha History Center; and Dee Grismud, reference archivist at the Wisconsin Historical Society in Madison. The archival staff at the Bentley Historical Library at the University of Michigan, which holds the papers of Roy D. Chapin, Roy D. Chapin, Jr., and George W. Romney, was especially cordial.

I owe a special thanks to Jack Miller, who allowed me to use the extensive collection of Hudson images held by the Ypsilanti Automotive Heritage Museum in Ypsilanti, Michigan. I would also like to thank Leroy Cole for giving me access to his private collection of automotive history materials. Two anonymous readers who reviewed the manuscript for Wayne State University Press offered many valuable and constructive suggestions. I would also like to thank the following individuals who carefully read all or part of this book in draft form: John A. Bluth, Tom Bunsey, Bill Chapin, Jim Dworschack, Bob Elton, Don Loper, Ed Ostrowski, Jack Miller, Ken Poynter, and Vince Ruffalo. Their encouragement and assistance has improved this book considerably. Any errors that remain are my sole responsibility.

Abbreviations

BHL   Bentley Historical Library, University of Michigan, Ann Arbor, Michigan
DCHC   DaimlerChrysler Historical Collection, Detroit, Michigan
JMC   Jack Miller Collection, Ypsilanti Automotive Heritage Museum,
         Ypsilanti, Michigan
NAHC   National Automotive History Collection, Detroit Public Library, Detroit,
         Michigan
SA/KU   Richard P. Scharchburg Archives, Kettering University, Flint, Michigan
SM   Buick Gallery and Research Center, Sloan Museum, Flint, Michigan

Introduction

The "Big Three" American automakers (General Motors, Ford, and Chrysler) dominated the U.S. auto industry by the late 1920s and further tightened their dominant grip when most remaining independent automakers did not survive the Depression. Substantial producers such as Hupp, Pierce-Arrow, Franklin, Auburn, Willys-Overland, Durant Motors, and others could not match the production and marketing economies of scale enjoyed by the Big Three. Two of the survivors, the Studebaker Corporation and the Packard Motor Car Company, merged in 1954 to form Studebaker-Packard, which made automobiles until 1966. The Studebaker and Packard company histories are well chronicled in several outstanding scholarly studies.[1] The failed effort of Henry J. Kaiser and Joseph W. Frazer to start a new automobile company, the Kaiser-Frazer Corporation (1945–55), showed the difficult challenge of starting a new automobile company in the postwar era.[2]

Historians have written dozens of competent corporate histories of the Big Three, but the independent automakers are largely ignored in general histories of the American automobile industry. Academic historians have focused on the "winners" in the competitive automotive industry—Ford, General Motors, and Chrysler. Serious automotive historians including E. D. Kennedy, John B. Rae, and James J. Flink treat the competitive outcome as inevitable. The smaller companies that eventually lost out to the giants and went out of business are consigned to an historical scrapheap and are largely forgotten. Their numerous contributions to automotive engineering, styling, and marketing are forgotten as well. One exception is Charles Edwards, who published a detailed study (1965) of the postwar struggles of the independent automakers to survive.[3]

The same can be said of the stories of the men who led the independent automakers. Biographies of Henry Ford are legion, and other leaders of the Big Three, such as Billy Durant, Alfred P. Sloan, and Walter Chrysler, are the subjects of serious biographies.[4] In sharp contrast, biographers have not written about the pioneering leaders of Nash Motors and the Hudson Motor Car Company, including Charles Nash, George Mason, and Edward Coffin. One exception is the J. C. Long biography of Roy Chapin.[5]

Several authors, including John Conde and Patrick Foster, have compiled valuable pictorial histories of Nash, Hudson, and American Motors, which focus almost entirely on the automobiles they produced. These are useful books for the general reader and for collectors of classic cars but add little to our understanding of the complexities of the American automobile industry during the first half of the twentieth century. This study focuses on the business history of these firms and is intended to fill in at least part of the missing story of the independent automakers.[6]

This volume will examine the individual histories of Nash Motors (1916–54) and the Hudson Motor Car Company (1909–54), which survived long enough to merge in 1954 to form the American Motors Corporation (AMC), the "last independent" in the industry. American Motors achieved some success against its larger competitors primarily by concentrating on the production of compact cars. American Motors survived into the 1980s by allying itself with Renault, but it struggled to earn profits and in 1987 Renault sold AMC to the Chrysler Corporation. Several useful guidebooks to the Nash, Hudson, and American Motors products exist, but there is no serious business history of these automakers.

The Walter P. Chrysler Museum in Auburn Hills, Michigan, has a wall display outlining the complex "family trees" of the Chrysler Corporation. The combined "business genealogies" of Walter P. Chrysler and the Chrysler Corporation, when Nash, Hudson, and AMC are added, include most substantial twentieth-century American automakers other than Ford, the various components of General Motors, and Studebaker-Packard.

Tracing the "tangled tendrils" of the interconnections among the early American automobile pioneers and their companies is a challenge to automotive historians. Charles W. Nash was the president of General Motors and Walter Chrysler's boss before Nash lost a battle with William C. Durant, resigned his presidency, and established Nash Motors. Chrysler also left General Motors following disputes with William C. Durant and soon helped rescue the Willys-Overland Corporation. American Motors bought Kaiser Jeep, the surviving remnant of Willys-Overland, in 1970, and Jeep was the main impetus for Chrysler's purchase of AMC in 1987. Roy D. Chapin, Howard E. Coffin, and Frederick O. Bezner were the key men who worked at the Olds Motor Works in Detroit until 1906, when they founded Thomas-Detroit, which evolved into Chalmers-Detroit, which in turn later merged with Maxwell to become the birthplace of the Chrysler Corporation. They established the Hudson Motor Car Company while at Chalmers, but then left Chalmers to concentrate on running Hudson. The Chrysler Corporation purchase of American Motors in 1987 reunited the various pieces of Walter P. Chrysler's illustrious automotive career.

This book will attempt to explain the successes and failures of these independent automakers (Nash, Hudson, and American Motors) over their lengthy existence. Each survived because of engineering, styling, or marketing innovations that helped distinguish their products from those of the Big Three and allowed some success in the market. This study will also attempt to uncover the particular strategies that allowed these small independents to survive and sometimes prosper in an industry dominated by enormous firms that enjoyed economies of scale in styling, engineering, tooling, marketing, and sales. Finally, this book will analyze the ultimate failure of the independents to survive.

U.A.W. Local 602
2510 W. Michigan Ave.
Lansing, MI 48917

Hall: (517) 372-4626
Fax: (517) 372-6909
www.local602.org

Bill Reed
President

Kevin Baker
Vice President

Scott Smith
Recording Secretary

Doreen Howard
Financial Secretary

Rick Martinez
Shop Committee Chair

 11

GM Benefit Center - Fidelity (800) 489-4646

Health/Life Pensions PSP Service Time SUB Sick Leave

Workers Comp/Unemployment Rep.	(517) 492-5756
Benefits Office (LDT)	(517) 721-3817 or 3818
EAP (Family & Work Program)	(517) 721-3841
Chaplain	(517) 449-3321
Security	(517) 721-3900
Skill Center	(517) 721-3844
GM Call-In System	(800) 222-8889
GM Payroll	(866) 245-5957
GM Vehicle Purchase Program	(800) 235-4646
GM Service Parts Customer Center	(800) 433-6961
GM Legal Services	(517) 887-2800

ONE

The Thomas B. Jeffery Company, 1902–16, and Its Bicycle Heritage

When the fizz and fireworks cease to sizz and splutter in the automobile business and the trade settles down to the normal level, it is fairly safe to say that the firm of T. B. Jeffery & Co. of Kenosha, Wis., will be found well up on the list of the fittest who have survived.

Motor World, 2 May 1901

In August 1916, Charles W. Nash bought the Thomas B. Jeffery Company, an automaker since 1902, changed the company name to Nash Motors, and introduced the Nash nameplate the following year. The Jeffery firm, a manufacturer of the popular Rambler automobile, had its roots in bicycle making but had achieved its greatest success in manufacturing automobiles. For Charles Nash, the Jeffery firm was an attractive target for a buyout.

Thomas Buckland Jeffery was born on 5 February 1845 in Stoke, Devonshire, England, the second of five children of Thomas Hellier Jeffery, a letter carrier, and Elizabeth Buckland Jeffery. Thomas B. Jeffery apprenticed with a scientific instrument maker in Plymouth, Devonshire, before emigrating to the United States in 1863 at age eighteen. Jeffery settled in Chicago, where he first worked for others making telescopes, microscopes, and other scientific instruments and then established his own business making patent models for inventors applying for U.S. patents. Thomas B. Jeffery was far from an overnight success in America as a manufacturer and itinerant inventor. He struggled for fifteen years before riding the "bicycle craze" sweeping the country and finding success as a bicycle manufacturer.[1]

Thomas Buckland
Jeffery (1845–1910).
Courtesy DCHC.

From Bicycles to Automobiles, 1881–1902

Jeffery visited his native England in 1878 and became infatuated with a popular English bicycle known as the "penny farthing." In 1879 he assembled a bicycle he dubbed "The American" from parts shipped from England to Chicago. In 1881 Jeffery convinced an old classmate from his youth, R. Phillip Gormully, to become his business partner, and the resulting firm, the Gormully & Jeffery Manufacturing Company, became one of the largest American bicycle makers of the 1890s. This was a logical partnership, bringing together Gormully's business skills with Jeffery's inventive and mechanical talents.[2]

First, a few words about the development of the bicycle industry in the nineteenth century. Pierre Michaux of Paris introduced the first modern bicycle, which he called a "pedal velocipede," in 1867. A second French inventor/manufacturer, Pierre Lallement, successfully patented the basic bicycle in the United States in April 1866. (Lallement had developed a bicycle prototype in Paris between 1863 and 1865, when he emigrated to America.) His patent drawings were almost identical to Michaux's first bicycle. Initially, Lallement was unable to interest American manufacturers in producing his bicycle and in 1868 sold the patent rights.[3]

R. Phillip Gormully.
Courtesy DCHC.

Enter Albert A. Pope, a small-time Boston manufacturer of tools and supplies for the shoe manufacturing industry. After seeing bicycles in action at the 1876 Centennial Exposition in Philadelphia, he began making a high-wheel English bicycle in his Boston factory in 1877 and simultaneously purchased the Lallement patent, which was valid for another six years. Pope manufactured 12,000 bicycles by 1880 and had back orders for another 2,500. He profited from the sales of his own bicycles and from royalties he collected from other manufacturers.[4]

Gormully and Jeffery established bicycle production in their Chicago factory in 1881 and introduced several bicycle models, including the American Ideal, the American Challenge, and the American Safety, all high-wheel Ordinary models. They misnamed the American Safety, since a "Safety" bicycle had two wheels of equal size. Their success brought the threat of a patent infringement lawsuit from Albert Pope, which convinced Gormully to sign a licensing agreement, under which Gormully & Jeffery could only produce bicycles for the youth market. They were essentially limited to manufacturing tricycles, while Pope kept the lucrative high-wheel adult bicycle segment to himself. After the Lallement patent expired in the fall of 1883, Pope permitted companies like the Overman Wheel Company and Gormully & Jeffery to make high-wheel bicycles under license.[5]

Albert Pope continued to collect royalties after the Lallement patent had run out because he owned multiple patents and was willing to employ an army of attorneys to prosecute violators. When threatened by rival patent holder A. H. Overman (manufacturer of ball bearings), he fashioned the "Treaty of Springfield" with Overman in 1886, effectively creating a Pope-Overman cartel. Shortly after that, Gormully & Jeffery declared their independence from Pope and stopped paying royalties.

In the June 1886 issue of *The Wheel, A Journal of Cycling,* the Gormully & Jeffery Manufacturing Company featured five models in large advertisements—the American Ideal, Challenge, Safety, and Champion, all high-wheelers, and the American Ideal Two Track Tricycle. These models were the "Ordinary" bicycles of the time, with front wheels ranging up to fifty inches in diameter. Pope brought eight lawsuits against Gormully & Jeffery but in 1887 lost all of them. Gormully & Jeffery, along with other American bicycle makers, were finally free of Pope's thicket of patent claims.[6]

With Albert Pope's restrictions on their ambitions out of the way, Gormully & Jeffery became the second largest American bicycle manufacturer (after Pope) by the late 1880s. Bicycle design changed fundamentally in the 1880s, setting off a boom in bicycle popularity. The high-wheel Ordinary bicycle was extremely difficult and dangerous to operate. Small bumps or obstacles sent the rider over the front wheel, often causing him to hit his head on the ground or on some fixed object. Riders and their detractors alike simply called this result a "header."

A new bicycle design emerged between 1884 and 1890 and soon made the Ordinary obsolete. The new design, simply known as the "Safety," featured front and rear wheels of equal size, sprocket-and-chain drive, with power to the rear wheels, and a braking system. Pneumatic tires, which became practical only in the early 1890s, replaced the hard rubber tires of the Ordinary and provided greater comfort and speed.[7]

Gormully & Jeffery catalogs illustrate the introduction of Safety models and the gradual disappearance of Ordinary bicycles from their offerings. Their 1889 catalog cover shows a Great Plains Native American standing next to his dead horse killed by an arrow to the neck. It is not entirely clear who killed his steed, but the cover shows the warrior mounting a Gormully & Jeffery Ordinary bicycle, thus adopting a more modern means of transportation. The 1891 catalog repeats the scene, but with the Native American mounting a Rambler Safety bicycle.[8]

Gormully & Jeffery prospered in the 1890s following the collapse of Albert Pope's efforts to control bicycle manufacturing. They produced only Safety models starting in 1893 under the generic name Rambler. Bicycle production exploded and competition reduced prices and profits. Gormully & Jeffery advertised a base price for their bicycles of $80 in 1897, only $60 in April 1898, and a mere $40 a year later. In 1898, Albert G. Spaulding, manufacturer of sporting goods and bicycles, convinced Pope and forty of the largest American manufacturers to form a cartel, the American

Gormully & Jeffery catalogue, 1891.
Courtesy DCHC.

Bicycle Company (ABC). In 1899, Jeffery and Gormully sold their bicycle business and tire company to ABC for what *Motor World* characterized as "a princely sum." The bicycle cartel struggled and in 1902 went into receivership.[9]

Thomas B. Jeffery and son Charles experimented with gasoline-powered automobiles several years before they left the bicycle business. Charles Jeffery convinced his father to attend the *Chicago Times-Herald* automobile race held in Chicago in November 1895, and this sparked the elder Jeffery's interest in automobiles. Father and son built three experimental vehicles in Chicago and two more in Kenosha, Wisconsin, before manufacturing an automobile for sale in 1902. They fabricated their first car at their bicycle factory on North Franklin Street in Chicago in spring 1897 and Thomas Jeffery dubbed it "the Rambler." It had a one-cylinder gasoline engine designed by the elder Jeffery (he was now fifty-two) and produced five horsepower.[10]

Thomas Jeffery made no further progress with the automobile until 1899, when he encouraged Charles to improve his first design. The younger Jeffery (age twenty-three) developed an improved carburetor, which he patented in his father's name.[11]

Thomas Jeffery and his first experimental Rambler (1897). *Courtesy DCHC.*

He also designed and built two more experimental cars, a runabout and a stanhope model, both with two-cylinder, five-horsepower engines. ABC exhibited both cars in 1900, first at the First International Automobile Exhibition and Tournament (also known as the Inter-Ocean Tournament) in Chicago in late September. The "tournament" included competitive testing of cars on a hill climb and a crude dynamometer. ABC also displayed the two cars at the first national automobile show at Madison Square Garden in New York in November 1900.

The "bicycle trust" announced in October 1900 that it would focus on automobile manufacturing and devote four or five factories exclusively to automobiles. Before bringing his cars to New York, Charles Jeffery drove both from Chicago to Milwaukee, gaining some notoriety. These automobiles were notably different from the others on display in New York in that they had two-cylinder engines (versus one-cylinder) and had left-hand steering with a tiller. The press called the two automobiles "Ramblers" or "G. & J. gasolene [*sic*] vehicles."[12]

Charles Jeffery's move from bicycle manufacturing to automobiles was by no means uncommon in the late 1890s and early 1900s. Albert Pope, whose Pope Man-ufacturing Company produced the Columbia bicycle, was perhaps the most famous manufacturer to make this transition. Hiram Maxim, who served as the chief engineer for Pope Manufacturing in the late 1890s, argued that the bicycle was an important psychological predecessor to the automobile because it allowed its manufacturers (and users) to think about personal transportation *not* involving the horse.[13]

A substantial number of early automobile industry pioneers had roots in the bicy-cle industry: Edgar and Elmer Apperson, who ran a large bicycle repair shop in Kokomo, Indiana, partnered with Elwood Haynes to make the Haynes-Apperson automobile; John and Horace Dodge manufactured the Evans & Dodge bicycle in the 1890s; Charles and Frank Duryea manufactured bicycles in Springfield, Mas-sachusetts, before assembling their first car; the Peerless Company of Cleveland made bicycles before introducing the Peerless automobile; the George N. Pierce Company of Buffalo, New York, built bicycles before evolving into the Pierce-Arrow Company; the White Motor Company of Cleveland began as the White Company, a successful manufacturer of sewing machines and bicycles; John North Willys began his career by operating a large bicycle retail store in Elmira, New York, before enter-ing the automobile industry; and Alexander Winton was a successful bicycle manu-facturer in Cleveland before launching the Winton Motor Carriage Company in 1897. These are only the most famous successful automobile pioneers with bicycle industry roots. A comprehensive listing would include scores more.[14]

Thomas B. Jeffery, Automaker, 1902–10

Perhaps because of the positive reception the Ramblers received in New York, Tho-mas B. Jeffery bought a factory in Kenosha, Wisconsin, forty miles north of Chicago, in December 1900. He paid ABC $65,000 (including $10,000 for machinery) for a factory formerly used to manufacture Sterling bicycles. Jeffery also launched a new firm, Thomas B. Jeffery & Company, at the same time. He encouraged his two sons to take control of separate spheres of the company, with Charles T. Jeffery operating the commercial side of the business and Harold W. Jeffery managing the factory. The *Kenosha Evening News* initially speculated that Jeffery, who held many patents on sew-ing machines, would use the factory to make that popular product. Two trade journals reported in December 1900 that Jeffery would have an automobile into production in sixty days. For his part, Jeffery was cagey and refused to reveal his plans.[15]

Charles Jeffery developed two additional experimental cars (Models A and B) in 1901, both equipped with steering wheels on the left side of the vehicle, a radi-cal departure from the standard tiller in the middle. Both had two-cylinder engines mounted in the front of the vehicle, also an unconventional design. A small workforce of fifty-six built the experimental cars. Two brothers from Indiana, Frederick and August Duesenberg, came to Kenosha to road test these experimental vehicles. They drove them all around Wisconsin, sometimes pulling farm wagons to test the strength of these models. A company letterhead in 1901 had the address, "The Sterling Works, Thomas B. Jeffery & Co., Hydro-Carbon Automobiles, Kenosha, Wis."[16]

A correspondent from *Motor World* visited Thomas Jeffery at his Kenosha factory sometime in early 1901 and reported on the development of the new automobile. The visitor noted the unconventional location of the two-cylinder engine at the front of the vehicle, with the gasoline tank at the rear. He also praised the novel carburetor, the use of a steering wheel, and the easy access to all major mechanical components from above or the side, eliminating the need to work on the car from underneath. He also pointed out that Jeffery used a nearby half-mile horse-racing track to test his new vehicles.[17]

However, when Thomas Jeffery introduced his first production Ramblers (Models C and D) in early 1902, they had conventional designs, with one-cylinder eight-horsepower engines mounted under the driver and a center-mounted tiller. Introduced in March 1902 at the Chicago Auto Show, the Model C runabout carried a low price of $750. The Model D stanhope differed from Model C only because it came equipped with a leather top and side curtains and cost $825. Jeffery assembled 1,500 cars in 1902, making him the second largest producer in the United States, right behind Ransom E. Olds.[18]

1902 Rambler factory assembly department. *Courtesy DCHC.*

The first Ramblers were an instant success, receiving gushing praise in the automobile trade literature. *Motor World* described the Rambler exhibited at the Chicago Auto Show in early March 1902.

> Its low price, $750, almost warrants one in expecting something infinitely inferior to the reliability [*sic*]. The vehicle is plainly a high class one. Design, workmanship and finish all make for the same end and it is impossible to long resist the conviction that here is a rare value for the money. A light, but not too light runabout is the Rambler. Yet ample strength, ample power, have been incorporated in it too. The Jeffery thoroughness and ingenuity saw to this; the Jeffery brain could not have conceived anything not thoroughly well done.[19]

Advertising for the new car was straightforward. The first Rambler advertisement in the *Saturday Evening Post* proclaimed, "Simplicity–Durability–Reliability are the three cardinal virtues in motor-carriage construction. You will find them in their highest development and efficiency in the Rambler Touring Car." The ad listed the price of $750 and urged interested parties to order a free catalog. The first Rambler catalog, which showed the Model C, listed the important mechanical features found in the new offering. The vehicle had battery ignition and came with two sets of batteries, with the second set available when the first lost power. The (crank) starting system featured automatic spark advance (an industry first), which prevented the crank from kicking back on the operator. The one-cylinder engine would power the carriage to a top speed of eighteen miles per hour. The catalog also pointed out that the design allowed for easy accessibility to the mechanical workings.[20]

The early Ramblers sold to the public were tough, reliable cars. Thomas Jeffery entered his cars in several early automobile endurance contests and they performed well. In the summer of 1902, a Rambler entered a 100-mile endurance contest sponsored by the Chicago Automobile Club and finished sixth behind cars that carried prices ranging from $1,300 (Franklin) to $5,000 (Columbia). The Automobile Club of America sponsored a "New York to Boston and Return Reliability Run" of 488 miles, which ran from 9–15 October 1902. A Model C Rambler driven by Arthur Gardiner successfully finished the course at an average speed of 14 miles per hour.[21]

Thomas Jeffery and his company remained stubbornly independent from the mainstream automakers. After the successful introduction of the Rambler in 1902, he became embroiled in a battle with the Association of Licensed Automobile Manufacturers (ALAM), which tried to collect royalties from every American automaker based on its ownership of the Selden patent (1879). Founded in March 1903, ALAM

had most of the automobile makers in the fold by August 1903. The two most important exceptions were Jeffery and Henry Ford. ALAM wooed Jeffery, but he refused
to concede the legitimacy of the Selden patent, just as he had earlier resisted Albert
Pope's efforts to control bicycle manufacturing. He said privately, "it is easier to fight
a patent than to break a contract." In October 1903, Jeffery assured Rambler owners
that his company "will defend to the utmost any action for infringement brought by
the Association of Licensed Automobile Manufacturers against users of the Rambler
automobile in any part of the United States." ALAM decided to ignore Jeffery, aware
of his previous legal successes against the Pope bicycle patent claims, and aimed its
legal guns against Ford.[22]

One leading automotive trade journal, the *Motor World*, noted in early September
1903 Jeffery's well-deserved fame as a formidable fighter against restrictive patents:
"Mr. Jeffery, as everyone knows, is a seasoned warrior so far as concerns patent litiga-
tion. As pioneer builders of bicycles, he and his then partner, the late R. P. Gormully,
waded early and often and long and up to their necks in the intangible gore of a dozen
patent battles. . . . They upset a couple of so-called master patents and made it possible
for any one to build bicycles who cared to build them."[23] A month later, *Motor World*
predicted that ALAM was on the brink of suing both Ford and Jeffery, but the association left Jeffery alone. In early October 1903, the Jeffery company announced its lineup
of seven models for 1904, openly defying the owners of the Selden patent.[24]

ALAM's battle with Ford slowly wound its way through the courts, with Ford eventually victorious in January 1911. Jeffery attended the Selden patent trial held in New

1903 Rambler Model E. *Courtesy DCHC.*

Rambler in 1909 mid-winter endurance run. *Courtesy NAHC.*

York in May 1909 in which ALAM won an important victory against Ford. Thomas Jeffery continued to contest the Selden patent, and his company never joined ALAM or paid royalties. Sadly, he died before Ford's triumph over ALAM and the Selden patent. Charles T. Jeffery appreciated Ford's perseverance and sacrifice in fighting the Selden patent and contributed $10,000 to help Ford with his legal expenses.[25]

Thomas B. Jeffery believed that ALAM members discriminated against his cars and his company at every opportunity. Thomas Jeffery & Company entered two of its 1903 Ramblers in an endurance run that began on 7 October 1903 and was supposed to go from New York City to Buffalo, then on to Cleveland, ending in Pittsburgh. Held under the auspices of the National Association of Automobile Manufacturers (controlled by ALAM), most of the race took place during torrential rains that washed out bridges and often made the roads impassible. Most of the competitive cars were large expensive models costing upward of $7,000 and weighing twice as much as the Ramblers, which were regular production models costing $750. Thirty-four automobiles started the race.

One Rambler (Number 18), driven by Arthur Gardiner, finished the race ahead of all of the competitors. The Rambler and a car costing $5,000 both arrived at the garage in Buffalo after the midnight deadline, which the race organizers had publicly waived. The Rambler beat the other car and arrived under its own power, while a team of horses pulled the expensive car into the garage. The judges disqualified the

Rambler and awarded the gold medal to the expensive car, which they also should have disqualified. The Jeffery company published a booklet, *A Little History or A Test of Endurance*, exposing this injustice. The booklet claimed that the judges unfairly enforced the rules to prevent Jeffery, an independent automaker with a $750 car, from beating one of their own.[26]

Although Jeffery did not join ALAM, he began making cars that more closely resembled the large cars offered by the elite auto companies. The 1903 Rambler Model E sold for $750 and was largely unchanged from 1902, but with one exception. The model came equipped with a tiller early in the year, but with a steering wheel at the end. A stanhope version (Rambler Model F) sold for $800 and came with a steering wheel. Rambler production for 1903 was 1,350 units. The 1904 models grew in size and price, but production jumped to 2,342 units. The company kept one-cylinder Rambler Models G ($750) and H ($850), but added a two-cylinder Rambler Model J roadster ($1,000) and a pair of two-cylinder touring cars, Rambler Models K ($1,200) and L ($1,350). The one-cylinder cars disappeared in 1905, replaced by touring cars priced at $1,200 and $1,650, with a limousine offered at $3,000. This upscale mix worked for the Jeffery company, which produced 3,807 cars that year. Jeffery was the third largest producer in the American automobile industry in 1904–6.[27]

Jeffery offered its first four-cylinder engines in 1906 and experienced a drop in production to 2,765 units that year. Four Rambler models came with two-cylinder engines and ranged in price from $1,200 to $1,650, while the four-cylinder offerings included two touring cars, priced at $1,750 and $2,500, and a limousine at $3,000. By the 1908 model year, the least expensive Rambler cost $1,200 and the limousine $3,250. In contrast, the 1909 Model T Ford touring car carried a price of $850. The company sold two-cylinder Ramblers for the last time in 1909 and the 1910 Ramblers, all four-cylinder cars, ranged in price from $1,800 to $3,700. Production reached 3,597 units in 1908, dropped to 1,963 in 1909, and then recovered slightly to 2,243 the following year. The Jeffery company equipped the 1909 models with a spare tire mounted on a fifth wheel, the first automaker to do so. The others offered their customers a tire repair kit. After initially making lightweight, inexpensive vehicles, the Jeffery company successfully transformed the Rambler into a mid-priced car.[28]

Part of Rambler's success resulted from the work of Edward S. Jordan (1882–1958), who joined the Jeffery company in 1907 and revolutionized the automaker's advertising campaigns. He changed Rambler advertising from a straightforward mechanical description of the car to an approach that emphasized the emotional appeal of the car. He developed slogans such as "June Time Is Rambler Time" and "The Car of the Open Road." Jordan worked for the Jeffery company as secretary, advertising manager, and general manager. He left Jeffery in early 1916 to launch

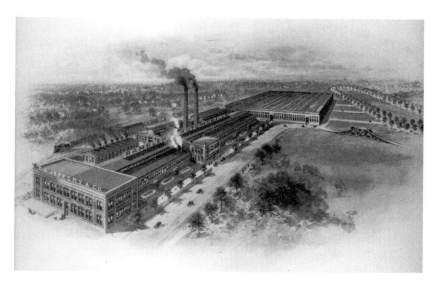

Rambler plant in 1904. *Courtesy DCHC.*

his own firm, the Jordan Motor Car Company, which produced Jordan automobiles from 1916 to 1931. The Jordan Playboy model was the most famous.[29]

Little information exists about the Rambler factory in Kenosha. Given Thomas Jeffery's manufacturing experience and expertise, it comes as no surprise that observers described the Kenosha plant as up-to-date and efficient. The automotive journal *Motor* visited the Jeffery plant sometime in 1904 and published a lengthy article about the facility in January 1905. The original Sterling bicycle factory was a single building 700 x 100 feet (70,000 square feet) and sat on a site of 7.5 acres, but the plant in 1904 occupied 33.5 acres and appeared to have at least 300,000 square feet of floor space.

The plant also featured a banked half-mile cinder test track with an incline that every Rambler had to negotiate several times before the company shipped it to the customer. One side of the incline had a 30 percent grade, while the other side had three grades of 20 percent, 30 percent, and 40 percent, respectively. This was the earliest dedicated test track at an automobile factory. Dodge Brothers built a test track next to its factory in 1915, but Ford Motor Company did not have a test track until 1936. Testing prototypes and new cars on public streets was the usual practice for decades.[30]

Motor claimed that the plant employed more than a thousand men in 1904 and would likely employ upward of 2,000 in 1905. The complex produced nearly all the Rambler parts, except tires, the spark coil, and wooden parts. The trade magazine did not indicate if this self-sufficiency was necessary because of the location of the plant, remote from the major components manufacturers in Michigan, Ohio, and Indiana, or if this was the result of a conscious manufacturing strategy on the part of Thomas Jeffery.[31]

Thomas B. Jeffery & Company published a twenty-three-page booklet in 1907 showing the Rambler factory and the various fabricating and assembly operations. The plant provided a half-million square feet of floor space sitting on forty-five acres. A large illustration shows a remarkably modern factory consisting almost entirely of single-story, steel-framed buildings with sawtooth roof monitors, which would provide ample natural lighting. An article on wooden body-making at the Kenosha factory published in 1911 claimed that they made 92 percent of all the Rambler parts in-house, including the bodies for the Rambler touring car. The Kenosha plant was as large and up-to-date as any of the contemporary Michigan auto plants, a reflection of Thomas B. Jeffery's manufacturing ability.[32]

Thomas B. Jeffery died suddenly from a heart attack on 2 April 1910 at the Grand Hotel in Pompeii, Italy, at age sixty-five. He was vacationing in Europe with his wife, Kate, and had reported that he felt reinvigorated from the vacation. He left an estate worth approximately $5 million, which was divided among his wife and three children.[33]

Thomas B. Jeffery was a quiet, reserved man who shied away from the various trade organizations and clubs that attracted his fellow automakers. He had learned "the art of listening" better than "the art of speaking." He seldom shared his views with others. In remembering his grandfather in a letter written in 1946, Jeffery Carqueville recalled that "Every worker, from the humblest on up knew he could come right into Mr. Jeffery's office and talk things over if he had any grievance. He kept a million dollars in cash on reserve in the bank in case of any emergency, so his men could always be paid, or in case of a panic, etc. He did not use tobacco in any form, drink or use profane language, was extremely honest in all things and was always a very healthy and robust man."[34] Thomas B. Jeffery was an inventor and manufacturer of bicycles and automobiles who enjoyed great success and prominence in both industries. Only Albert Pope could claim a similar record.

Charles T. Jeffery at the Helm, 1910–16

Following the death of the company founder and following his wishes, Thomas B. Jeffery & Company was incorporated as the Thomas B. Jeffery Company on 10 June 1910. The Jeffery family owned the entire capital stock of $3 million. Charles T. Jeffery took control of his father's business and transformed it into a much larger company with a growing focus on truck production. The Rambler model lineup changed only marginally in 1911 and 1912 from the offerings of 1910. The Jeffery company introduced a new four-cylinder touring car, the Rambler Cross Country, as a 1912 model. A major shake-up in the Rambler lineup took place in 1913, when Charles Jeffery reduced the eleven body styles and four chassis available in 1912 (prices ranging from $1,650 to $4,200) to a single chassis and five choices of bodies, with prices ranging from $1,875 to $2,750. They sold the 1913 models as the Rambler Cross Country and increased production considerably, from 2,243 units in 1910 to 4,435 in 1913. Charles Jeffery also decided to replace the Rambler marque with "Jeffery" in honor of his father.[35]

In a six-page advertisement in *The Automobile* in late October 1913, Charles Jeffery announced and explained the change in the nameplate: "The unquestioned position of this company, and of its product in the world at large, is due to the energy, ability and life work of Thomas B. Jeffery. To the end that his name may remain in the memories of men, we have named our new car the Jeffery. We believe it to be entirely worthy of the name we have given it."[36]

Charles Jeffery introduced two new car lines for 1914, the four-cylinder Model 93, which ranged in price from $1,550 to $2,350, and the Model 96, a six-cylinder automobile with list prices from $2,250 to $3,700. The advertisement in *The Automobile* proclaimed that the Jeffery Four was "A Remarkable Car at a Remarkable Price—$1,550" and described its features in detail. The Six received a half page and fainter praise. The Jeffery company claimed that its dealers had already ordered half the production of cars planned for the 1914 model year.[37]

Both of the new offerings for 1914 sold well, but the four-cylinder car had the greatest demand, largely because it was a remarkably high-quality car for $1,550. Anticipating an upsurge in sales, the Jeffery company enlarged its factory and added new machinery including an electric spot welder to weld body panels together, a press with a capacity of 1,500 tons, multi-spindle drill presses, and a host of other machinery. The company continued to produce most of its parts internally. Sales in March 1914 were double the record of a year earlier. By year's end, production had reached 10,417 automobiles. The Jeffery company also produced trucks, which will be discussed later in this chapter.[38]

The 1914 models underwent few changes for 1915. The Jeffery company introduced a new four in 1916 (Model 462), which sold in a roadster and touring car version for only $1,000, and a four-door sedan with a price tag of only $1,165. An advertisement in the *Saturday Evening Post* announcing the new model proclaimed that the company was "Establishing a New Standard of Value at a $1000 Price." *The American Chauffeur* described the model's innovative high-speed motor: "It runs smooth as oil. It is as quiet as an electric motor. It is as fast as an express train. It pulls like a farm tractor. It saves gasoline. It saves oil." A Jeffery Four brochure for 1916 described the model as "America's Standard Automobile at a Thousand-Dollar Price." This brochure portrayed the car on the front cover with three upper-class women and no men present, with a fourth woman at the wheel on the back cover. In contrast, a 1916 Model T Ford touring car sold for only $360, but the Model T was already outdated by then. A better contrast would be the Oldsmobile offerings for 1916, a four-cylinder touring car priced at $1,095 and an eight-cylinder model at $1,295. Buick's six-cylinder touring car ($1,020) would be comparable to the Jeffery model.[39]

In January 1916, the Jeffery company took a full-page advertisement in the *Chicago Examiner* explaining that the surge in demand for its cars had kept the factory operating at full capacity and it was not able to keep up with the flood of orders. The company had hired an additional 2,000 workers in the previous year, was hiring another 200 in 1916, and could promise timely deliveries of its passenger cars. Jeffery assembled 4,608 automobiles in calendar 1916, an impressive accomplishment considering the company's focus on truck production for the combatants in World War I.[40]

The Jeffery company first produced vehicles for commercial use when it introduced the 1904 Rambler Type 1 Delivery Wagon, which was nothing more than a panel truck body placed on a Jeffery automobile chassis. The Jeffery company also sold ambulances and fire trucks, which all used an automobile chassis. Jeffery introduced a new line of trucks at the Chicago Automobile Show in 1912, including one-ton and 1 1/2-ton capacity trucks, available with a variety of bodies. These had

1915 Jeffery delivery truck. *Courtesy NAHC.*

heavy-duty frames and semi-elliptic springs. A catalog of the Jeffery truck offerings in 1914 showed two basic truck chassis, a 3/4-ton ($1,300) and a 1 1/2-ton ($1,650). Customers could then purchase a wide variety of bodies, including a stakes platform, screened express body, open delivery body, and a panel delivery body, all at additional cost. The catalog also featured the Jeffery Quadruple Drive truck, selling for $2,750 for the basic chassis. Most 1914 Jeffery trucks had pneumatic tires for the first time, replacing solid rubber tires. They still had four-cylinder engines and the steering wheel on the right side. A new line of 1915 Jeffery trucks had the steering wheel on the left side.[41]

The Jeffery Quad, first sold in 1914, was an innovative truck design with all four wheels driving, steering, and braking. The Quad had a four-cylinder engine and solid rubber tires. The origins of this remarkable truck are murky, but the Jeffery company did not invent four-wheel-drive technology. Two Wisconsin blacksmiths, Otto Zachow and William Besserdich, who were brothers-in-law, operated a thresher repair shop in Clintonville, some fifty miles west of Green Bay. They started selling REO automobiles in 1906 and became interested in improving motor vehicle traction on rural roads.

In 1908 Zachow patented a double-Y universal joint which made four-wheel drive practical. After having problems producing a functional vehicle, Zachow and Besserdich sold their interest to a group of investors who established the Four Wheel Drive Company in 1910. Although this company produced prototypes that the U.S. Army tested successfully, the government did not order any trucks. Starting in 1914, the company sold four-wheel-drive trucks to the British and the Russians for use in the war. The U.S. government first bought Four Wheel Drive Company trucks in 1916 for the Mexican campaign against Pancho Villa. Following the U.S. entry into World War I, the U.S. Army immediately ordered 3,750 trucks. The Four Wheel Drive Company managed to turn out 10,000 trucks in 1918 by licensing other companies to manufacture their trucks, including the Mitchell Motor Car Company of Racine, Wisconsin and the Kissel Motor Car Company of Hartford, Wisconsin.[42]

The precise chronology of how the Jeffery company developed the Quad cannot be determined with certainty. Beverly Rae Kimes claims that one of Charles Jeffery's friends, who was in the U.S. Army, approached him in 1911 about building a four-wheel-drive truck. Jeffery asked a young engineer with his company, Martin Winther, to study the problem. Winther secretly bought a truck from the Four Wheel Drive Company and drove it to Kenosha, where he and his fellow engineers examined the truck and concluded that they could produce a superior design on their own. The Jeffery company introduced the Quad in 1913 and manufactured 5,578 of them in the first year, selling mostly to the French and Russian governments.[43]

Brigadier General John J.
Pershing with his 1916
Jeffery Quad during the
Pancho Villa expedition in
Mexico. *Courtesy DCHC.*

Jeffery Quad stake truck,
winter 1916. *Courtesy
DCHC.*

Other sources, including two booklets the Jeffery company published, suggest that the Kimes chronology places events at least a year before they actually occurred. According to the company's publication, *The Jeffery Quad,* U.S. Army officers visited the Jeffery plant in Kenosha sometime in 1912 and asked the engineers to design a truck that would "go anywhere a four-mule team would go." The factory delivered its first experimental Quad to the army on 15 September 1913 and the first Quad for civilian use in April 1914. The army rigorously tested the first Quad and urged several modifications in the design, including replacing the original wooden spoked wheels with steel disc wheels.[44]

Another booklet, *The Story of the Jeffery Quad,* suggests that production did not get underway until early 1914 and that by January 1916 the Jeffery company had built more than 3,000 Quads. The production figure Kimes cites for 1913 (5,578 units) was the Jeffery company's production of trucks that were not Quads. The production of Quads for 1914 and 1915 combined was perhaps 3,000 units. We will never know exactly how many Quads were built at Kenosha because the Jeffery company and then Nash Motors lumped all truck production together. Starting in 1913, Jeffery and Nash were among the largest truck makers in the United States. Jeffery also built a prototype armored version of the Quad, which the army tested at its Rock Island (Illinois) Arsenal in June 1915.[45]

Charles T. Jeffery sailed for Europe on 2 May 1916, planning to visit European automakers on a fact-finding tour. He left New York City on the *Lusitania*, which a German U-Boat sank five days later with the loss of nearly 1,200 souls. Charles Jeffery was not among the unfortunates; he survived in the Atlantic for four hours before being rescued by a trawler. This was a life-altering experience and he lost much of his enthusiasm for the automobile business as a result. In mid-July 1916 Charles Jeffery announced the sale of the Thomas B. Jeffery Company to Charles W. Nash and Lee, Higginson & Company. Charles Jeffery retired at age forty and spent the next two decades of his life visiting England, sailing, promoting various charities, and pursuing other interests. Charles Nash quickly transformed the Jeffery company and its products, which will be the subject of the next chapter.[46]

Thomas Jeffery's company was a significant pioneering automaker that remained among the top ten producers from 1902 through 1908, despite its modest numbers by later standards. The larger and more costly Ramblers were as popular as the earlier, less-expensive offerings and the Jeffery company remained among the top fifteen automakers in output in 1911–14. During his tenure as head of the Jeffery company, Charles T. Jeffery increased automobile production, but more important, he entered the truck market in a serious, substantial way starting in 1913. The development of the successful Jeffery Quad continued this new focus. After 1914, the company's automobile production made it a minor, marginal producer in an industry increasingly dominated by Ford, Willys-Overland, Buick, Studebaker, Chevrolet, Cadillac, and others. Dodge Brothers, for example, produced 45,000 automobiles in 1915, their first full year in operation.[47]

Table 1.1 illustrates the Jeffery company's overall performance in manufacturing automobiles and trucks. The company's small size was a competitive disadvantage in an industry of large firms with extensive national dealer networks and national advertising campaigns. Its relative isolation from the automobile industry's major parts suppliers located in Michigan, Ohio, and Indiana may have been a competitive disadvantage as well. None of this mattered to Charles W. Nash, who arrived in Kenosha in August 1916 and soon put his personal stamp on the company that would bear his name.

Table 1.1. Jeffery Company Production of Automobiles and Trucks,
Calendar Year, 1902–16

	Automobiles	Trucks	Total
1902	1,500	–	1,500
1903	1,350	–	1,350
1904	2,342	–	2,342
1905	3,807	–	3,807
1906	2,765	–	2,765
1907	3,201	–	3,201
1908	3,597	–	3,597
1909	1,692	–	1,692
1910	2,273	–	2,273
1911	3,000	–	3,000
1912	3,550	–	3,550
1913	4,435	5,578	10,013
1914	10,417	3,096	13,513
1915	3,100	7,600	10,700
1916	4,608	2,117	6,725

Source: Production summaries in the DCHC.

TWO

From Indentured Servant to President of General Motors

Charles W. Nash's Michigan Years

> The resignation of Charley Nash left a big hole in the General Motors organization. He had been a vital factor in the success of the corporation and I hated to see him go away. Not only was he a loyal friend and a grand man but I knew him to be one of the country's greatest industrialists.
>
> Walter Chrysler, referring to Charles Nash's resignation of the presidency of General Motors in 1916

The details of the childhood and early adulthood of Charles William Nash (28 January 1864–6 June 1948) are not easily discerned, partly covered by a fog created by faded memories and the lack of written records. No Charles W. Nash collection has survived in any single archive, but scattered materials are found in a half-dozen locations.[1] Some details of Nash's early life may be subject to dispute, but the general topography of his remarkable life is clear. His life story is a genuine tale of rising from poverty and difficult circumstances to great success in the automobile industry. This is not an exaggerated and embellished rags-to-riches tale, as we often see with other automotive giants, including men like Henry Ford and the Dodge brothers. It is remarkable because it is true.

Charles W. Nash was the oldest of three children born to David L. Nash and Anna (Cadwell) Nash on a farm in DeKalb County, Illinois, some sixty miles west of Chicago. The Nash family moved to the extreme northeast corner of Genesee County, Michigan, in 1866, when Charles was only two. The 1870 U.S. Census for Forest Township in Genesee County lists David L. Nash (age 28), his wife, Anna (38), both born in New York state, and children Mazovia (8), Charles (6), and George (4), all born in Illinois. David Nash's occupation was "works in saw mill."[2]

After his parents separated sometime in 1870, Charles Nash became a ward of the court in 1871 at age seven. The court bound him out to Robert Lapworth, a farmer in Flushing in northwestern Genesee County. Under the terms of the contract, Nash would work for Lapworth until age twenty-one. Lapworth would provide Nash with one suit of clothes a year and allow him to attend school four months a year. At age twenty-one, Nash would receive two sets of clothes and $100 in cash. Charles Nash ran away from the Lapworths in 1876 at age twelve. According to Nash, he hid in the woods until the family left for church one Sunday morning, gathered his wretched belongings, and escaped.[3]

Charles Nash walked about fifteen miles to Grand Blanc in the southeastern part of Genesee County, where he went to work on the farm of Lyman J. Hitchcock, identified in the 1870 census as a "produce dealer." In 1888, Hitchcock owned a farm of 209 acres and was a partner in the firm of "Hitchcock, Kline and Company, Wholesale and Retail Dealers in Produce." After a short stay, Nash worked briefly for another farmer, Alexander McFarlan, in Mt. Morris, in the center of Genesee County, some twelve miles north of Grand Blanc. McFarlan appeared in the 1870 census living in Flint, age fifty-eight, and described as a lumberman. An 1873 real estate atlas showed McFarlan owning 220 acres in Mt. Morris. The 1880 census listed him as McFarland and described him as a lumberman and farmer.[4]

Farmwork was seasonal, concentrated mostly on spring planting and fall harvesting. According to W. A. P. John, Nash became an apprentice farm carpenter in the summer of 1877, earning $24 for three months of work. He learned this craft from John Shelben, a Mt. Morris mechanic. Charles Nash then earned $12 for a month's work at harvesting in the fall of 1877. At age thirteen, he saved $25 of the $36 he earned in four months and used his savings to buy ten sheep, which in three years became twenty. Nash told W. A. P. John, "Unless you have worked for nine dollars a month—unless you had to actually count every penny you spent—unless you have had to debate between a warm pair of pants and a dollar in the bank—you can't ever know how hard it was for me to buy those sheep. And you can't ever know the glorious satisfaction I got out of finally buying them." After buying the sheep, Nash "set them to double," a traditional practice of turning over sheep to a farmer who, for the right to keep the wool, would raise the sheep and in three years return twice the number to the owner.[5]

Charles B. Glasscock, who published *The Gasoline Age* in 1937, interviewed Nash at some length and provided details about the sheep investment not available from other sources. This was a carefully conceived decision that would double the original investment in three years, an excellent rate of return by any measure. Nash had worked for a farmer who raised sheep and knew a good deal about them as a

result. When he went to buy sheep from a neighboring farmer, that farmer unsuccessfully tried to "pull the wool over the eyes" of thirteen-year-old Charlie Nash: "He
thought that because I was a little brat he could put something over on me. I wasn't
big enough to lift the sheep out of the pen into the road, and he began to hand out
the poorest ones in the pen. I looked at their teeth and wool and refused to take
them. When he saw I knew what he was doing, he changed his tactics. I picked
out the sheep I wanted and he put 'em in the road. They were a fine little flock of
ewes."[6]

Charles Nash grabbed a smattering of education while working these various
jobs. In an interview he gave a Kenosha, Wisconsin newspaper in October 1936,
Nash explained that he bought books with the profits from his sheep, "and I've
owned sheep and books and worked hard ever since."[7] He told W. A. P. John that
he took jobs working on farms during the winter months so that he could attend
school. Although largely self-taught, Charles Nash learned to read and write suf-
ficiently well to operate successfully in the business world. He had a natural talent
for arithmetic and read enough to gain a broad knowledge of geography, mechanics,
and other subjects.[8]

Nash appears in the 1880 census (age 16) working as a farm laborer for Charles
Elder in Mt. Morris. His entrepreneurial bent was soon evident as well. In 1881 he
and William J. Adams established the partnership of Nash & Adams and became
successful "hay pressers" who served Genesee County farmers. Nash likely sold
his sheep to have the cash for this investment. The 1880 census listed Adams as a
farmer in Burton Township, and his listing in an 1881–82 directory shows him owning 88 acres of farmland. One of the farmers Nash visited in nearby Burton had a
daughter, Jessie Hallock, whom Charles Nash married in April 1884. He returned
to the McFarlan farm, where he earned $300 a year as foreman and where the new-
lyweds also had the use of a cottage. Later in the decade, McFarlan had a farm of
588 acres. After about two years with McFarlan, Nash moved on to manage a farm
owned by Circuit Court Judge William Newton, who in 1888 had a farm of 160
acres.[9]

After his wife developed health problems and required medical care, Charles
Nash moved into Flint in 1889 and worked as a clerk in the hardware/grocery store
of W. C. Pierce, where he earned the standard wage of $1 a day. Modestly listed as
"grocers" in one part of the Flint directory for 1892–93, the advertisement for Pierce
Brothers & Company, 423 Saginaw Street, informed the reader that they offered
"Dry Goods, Carpets, Upholstery Goods, Curtains, Wall paper, Boots and Shoes,
and Groceries."[10]

While working in Flint, Charles Nash met Josiah Dallas Dort, who had partnered with William Crapo ("Billy") Durant to establish the Flint Road Cart Company. In fact, Billy Durant also claimed to have "discovered" Nash in a 1942 letter reminiscing about their early days together.[11] Since Dort ran the factory, it is more plausible that Dort would have hired Nash.[12]

A Career in Carriage Manufacturing

Charles Nash began working at the Flint Road Cart Company in 1891 at age twenty-seven and stayed with the firm, which became the Durant-Dort Carriage Company, for nineteen years. Billy Durant and Josiah Dallas Dort had established the Flint Road Cart Company in late September 1886. Durant convinced Flint's largest carriage maker, William A. Paterson, to make 1,200 two-wheel, two-seat road carts for $12.50 each, which he would sell for at least double that amount. The Flint Road Cart Company produced 4,000 carts in its first year of operation and Durant soon entered the four-wheel carriage trade as well. The firm incorporated under the same name on 9 September 1893, with a capital stock of $150,000. Durant and Dort fashioned a successful business marriage, with Durant handling sales and Dort managing production. On 6 November 1895, the two principal owners changed the firm's name to the Durant-Dort Carriage Company.[13]

According to Frank Rodolf, author of a history of Flint industry, Nash started working at the Flint Road Cart Company in the cushion department at $1 a day and became the foreman in a few months, earning $9 a week. Within a year, he

Cushion Department, Durant-Dort Carriage Company, June 1898. Charles Nash is in the second row, fifth from the left, wearing a vest and tie. *Courtesy Leroy Cole Collection.*

was the cushion department superintendent, earning $12 a week or $600 a year. A photograph of the Durant-Dort Carriage Company cushion department workforce dated 9 June 1898 shows Charles Nash in a coat and tie. The sixty employees in the photograph included thirty-nine boys, roughly twelve to sixteen years old, fourteen women in their late teens or early twenties, and only seven adult men, including Nash. At some point, perhaps before the end of 1898, Durant and Dort made Nash the superintendent of the entire factory as part of management restructuring. Dallas Dort gave up the presidency of the company and moved to Arizona in 1898 to improve his wife's failing health; he was replaced by Alexander Brownell Cullen (A. B. C.) Hardy. Rodolf claims that at some point Nash's salary jumped to $1,200 a year. Becoming the factory superintendent would have justified this raise.[14]

The Durant-Dort Carriage Company grew and prospered in the late 1890s and into the early twentieth century, when automobiles first appeared as serious competition. Durant and Dort created three subsidiary vehicle firms in Flint and another in Jackson, Michigan, and owned an interest in companies manufacturing horse-drawn vehicles in Georgia, Arkansas, Missouri, and Canada. The company reached its peak production in Flint in 1906, making about 56,000 vehicles with about 1,000 men employed. The combined production of all of its operations may have been as high as 150,000 vehicles. In the early twentieth century, Flint enjoyed the title "Vehicle

Durant-Dort Carriage Company Office Building (1895–1906), 316 Water Street, Flint, Michigan. *Photograph by the author.*

City," based on its combined production of more than 100,000 horse-drawn vehicles a year, second only to Cincinnati.[15]

Charles Nash's power and influence in the Durant-Dort Carriage Company also grew tremendously in the first decade of the new century. In October 1900, company stockholders named him a director and vice president, positions he held until September 1913. At some point he also became the general superintendent of all of the Durant-Dort operations. The record is not explicit, but this likely happened in 1901, when A. B. C. Hardy left the management of Durant-Dort to spend a year in Europe recovering from exhaustion. By then, Durant had largely withdrawn from company operations. Dort resumed his presidency, but Nash was clearly in charge of Durant-Dort by 1901, perhaps earlier. According to Rodolf, the directors at some point secretly increased his pay to $5,000 a year, breaking an unwritten understanding that no one at Durant-Dort could earn more than $1,200 a year.[16]

The Durant-Dort records show that Nash took on responsibilities in 1901 that were appropriate for someone who was a general superintendent and not merely the plant manager. The directors instructed him in July to arrange for insurance coverage for the company's inventories. In mid-August 1901, they told him "to take up the matter of labor celebrations on Labor Day," mainly to decide which Durant-Dort vehicles would appear in the festivities. After a young man named Pierce Farrell died in one of Durant-Dort's plants, the directors "suggested that Mr. Nash visit Mrs. Farrell, whose son died at the Axle Works, and endeavor to make such a presentation to her as would satisfy her of the interest and sympathy of the Company." The Factory Benefit Association had paid the basic funeral expenses ($76) and the company had already spent an additional $100.75 to cover "extras" such as the burial plot and flowers.[17]

Charles Nash also had a substantial ownership stake in the company during this period. Durant-Dort encouraged its managers to own stock by awarding shares as bonuses in good years and by allowing employees to buy stock with no cash payment and then "pay" for the shares with the dividends received from the shares. Nash owned stock by September 1900, perhaps earlier. His investment increased from 2,936 shares in September 1901 to 5,000 shares two years later and reached a peak at 10,500 shares in September 1912. Nash apparently starting selling his stake in late 1912 after he became president of General Motors. He was still a director in late May 1913, but by the time of the Durant-Dort stockholders' annual meeting of 10 September 1913, he was not. The stockholders agreed at that meeting to buy Nash's remaining 5,650 shares for $79,100 ($14.00 a share) and Nash accepted their offer.[18]

While working for Durant-Dort, Nash was engaged in other business ventures.

He invested in a farm from August 1903 through August 1912 and the record of expenses and revenues from this venture have survived. Over the first three years that he owned or leased this farm, Nash lost a total of $868, but then starting in the year ending August 1907, he made profits. This was a "mixed" farming operation, with records showing the sale of cows, calves, pigs, sheep, lambs, eggs, butter, wool, potatoes, sugar beets, and straw. The same account book shows that Nash invested in building a house "on Second Street in the 4th Ward" in March–June 1906 and "houses on the corner of Garland and 7th Avenue," but with no year shown. Both properties were in Flint.[19]

In the first fifteen years of the twentieth century, Durant, Dort, and other Flint vehicle manufacturers shifted their resources from horse-drawn vehicles to automobiles, and the Buick Motor Company was the catalyst for this transformation of Flint industry. David Buick developed the first Buick automobile and his name went on millions more, long after he had no connection with the company he founded.[20]

With capital provided by Frank and Benjamin Briscoe, Buick organized the Buick Motor Company in May 1903, with the Briscoes controlling most of the shares. A few months later the Briscoes wanted to liquidate their interest in Buick and convinced James Whiting and the other major stockholders in the Flint Wagon Works to buy Buick Motor Company. They invested $37,500, half the face value of the company's stock issue of $75,000. On 11 September 1903, the *Flint Journal* announced the sale of Buick to the Flint capitalists, who moved the company to Flint and start making cars under the Buick nameplate.[21]

The Buick engineers and mechanics produced the first prototype Buick in July 1904, but by then the company had exhausted the original investment. Whiting then tried to convince Dallas Dort and Billy Durant to take over the management of Buick, but neither man was interested in making automobiles. Durant took a test ride in a Buick over paved streets in Flint on 4 September 1904 and asked Whiting to give him the use of another Buick for testing. According to Arthur Pound, Durant drove the Buick for two months through the worst roads he could find and the Buick's performance changed his mind.

Durant became a Buick director on 1 November 1904 and immediately increased the stock to $300,000 and then to $500,000 in mid-November. The stockholders of the Flint Wagon Works and the Durant-Dort Carriage Company controlled most of the shares. In January 1905, Durant attended the New York Auto Show, where he took orders for more than 1,000 Buicks. Durant built the first Buicks in Jackson, Michigan, but moved production to Flint in 1906 after convincing four Flint banks to buy an additional $100,000 of stock. In September 1905, Buick's capitalization stood at $1.5 million. Dort and Nash, however, still did not share Durant's enthusiasm for the automobile and believed that the carriage industry had a secure future.[22]

Durant, however, had broader ambitions that extended well beyond the Buick Motor Company. He established the General Motors Company on 16 September 1908 with an initial capitalization of $12.5 million ($40 million by 1910). The new holding company immediately bought Buick Motors for $3.75 million and the Olds Motor Works for $3 million. The next year Durant purchased the Cadillac Motor Company for $4.75 million and the Oakland Motor Car Company (later Pontiac), bringing together four of General Motors' five automobile brands. Chevrolet would come later. In his first two years at General Motors, Durant also bought scores of other companies that produced trucks, taxis, and motor vehicle components.[23]

General Motors grew enormously since its foundation in 1908 by purchasing other companies. Durant borrowed much of the money needed for expansion from commercial banks, but by the summer of 1910, the lenders had become skeptical about the future of General Motors. They called in some loans, leaving Durant with little working capital. The bankers met in August 1910 and agreed to keep Durant afloat, but only until they reorganized the automaker. In September a consortium of banks led by the Boston investment banking firm of Lee, Higginson & Company agreed to lend General Motors funds to save it from bankruptcy, but in return demanded control of the company through a five-year voting trust. Durant had no choice but to agree to these conditions. He kept his positions as director and vice president of General Motors, but was no longer in control of the company he founded.[24]

By this time, James Jackson Storrow (1864–1926), the senior partner at Lee, Higginson & Company, became actively involved in the affairs of General Motors. He was the head of the bankers' voting trust, representing the interests of his company. He clashed with Durant and quickly made Charles Nash his protégé.[25]

Charles Nash at Buick and General Motors

By late August 1910, Charles Nash had moved over from the Durant-Dort Carriage Company to run Buick production. According to Pearson, this move came at the request of Nash, who hoped to revive Buick and collect money owed Durant-Dort for bodies it had made for Buick. W. A. P. John claimed that the eastern bankers, including Storrow, agreed to supply Buick with the needed funds to allow it to survive the crisis of August 1910 only if Nash were put in charge of Buick. Nash became president and general manager of Buick on 9 September 1910, the day Durant gave up those positions. Storrow did not regret putting Nash in charge. He wrote to Nash in late May 1912, "You have the right to be proud of the record you have made for the Buick Company during the last 18 months. It has been fine."[26]

At a testimonial dinner given in honor of Charles Nash in Flint in November 1912, Richard Collins, whom Nash appointed Buick's general sales manager in 1910, recalled Nash's struggles to get Buick under control during the first months he was in charge: "Those first few months Nash was in the auto business he was busy dodging creditors and I was busy dodging Nash. We weren't selling any cars. We didn't have any to sell. . . . During those first four months Nash was with the [*sic*] Buick I don't think there was a night or a day when there wasn't some big problem for him to solve and only once do I remember him losing his patience." Collins helped Buick's revival by coining the company's advertising slogan, "When Better Automobiles Are Built, Buick Will Build Them."[27]

After Nash became president and general manager of Buick, James Storrow decided that Nash needed an experienced manager to run the enormous Buick factories in Flint. Fabricating and assembling mostly metal automobiles was a far cry from building wooden carriages. Storrow was a director of the American Locomotive Company (ALCO) and knew Walter P. Chrysler, who brilliantly managed ALCO's Allegheny (Pittsburgh) locomotive erection shops. In spring 1911, Storrow asked

Charles Nash, president of Buick Motor Company,
at his desk, 1911. *Courtesy DCHC.*

Chrysler to meet with Nash in Pittsburgh to discuss the position of works manager for Buick. Chrysler agreed to take the position though he took a pay cut from $12,000 a year to $6,000 because he wanted to work in the automobile industry. Chrysler arrived in Flint in January 1912 and quickly revolutionized the manufacturing methods used at Buick, cutting costs and raising production. Buick built 19,812 cars in 1912, a respectable total, but by 1916, Chrysler had increased production to 124,834 units.[28]

After the bankers' voting trust gained control of General Motors in mid-November 1910 and ousted Durant, James Storrow briefly served as president until early 1911, when he named Thomas Neal to the post. Neal agreed to serve for no longer than two years or until General Motors could operate profitably. When Neal became president of General Motors, he also became president of Buick and Nash became vice president, although Nash still managed Buick.

Storrow remained chairman of the General Motors Finance Committee and closely supervised General Motors' operations. He named Nash a vice president of General Motors in July 1912. Over time, Storrow developed confidence in Nash and on 19 November 1912 appointed him president of General Motors. Neal took the post of chairman of the board, while Storrow continued to chair the finance committee, but he visited Michigan less frequently.[29]

Charles Nash's abilities were recognized nationally. One surviving document is a telegram from W. S. Strong in New York City to Nash, dated 10 July 1912. Strong was chairman of the board of directors at the United States Motor Company.

> Would you consider accepting a prominent position with the United States Motor Co. Would appreciate wire to me at 31 Nashua St. New York stating your attitude and if possible to meet me in New York and when. Please treat matter confidential.

Nash's response that same day was clear—"Impossible for me to consider position mentioned. Am located here for another year."[30] The United States Motor Company was a combination of more than a dozen automobile and truck companies organized in 1910 by Benjamin Briscoe from the Maxwell-Briscoe Company. Most of the companies brought into the combination were unprofitable at the time and the conglomerate went into receivership in September 1912. Nash made the correct career decision to stay with Buick.[31]

The Flint business community gave Charles Nash a testimonial banquet in late November 1912 in recognition of his appointment as president of General Motors. His comments in response to the praise heaped upon him were telling. He recalled driving his first flock of ten sheep down the road while barefoot: "People passed and as they looked over the sheep they admired them and asked me who owned them. I told them they were mine and I was never more proud than at that time." Nash acknowledged his wife for believing in him during some difficult years. He thanked George Hubbard, who had befriended him when he first moved to Flint and signed an $800 banknote for him. Nash also singled out J. Dallas Dort.

> Mr. Dort has been a father to me. I never remember having a father that did me much good, but Dort took the place of one. When I was being helped along by Mr. Dort I would have followed him to the end of the earth and I would now.

Nash went on to note that when Dort was away from Flint for a two-year stretch, "Durant took charge of the carriage company's affairs and then I worked shoulder to shoulder with Durant. Durant had confidence in me—more than any man in the world."[32]

With Nash's promotion to the presidency of General Motors, Chrysler became the president and general manager of Buick. In early 1915, some three years after taking a pay cut to come to Buick, Chrysler was still earning a salary of $6,000 a year. He confronted Nash and demanded $25,000 a year, which shocked the penny-pinching Nash, who told Chrysler he would need to discuss this with Storrow. Shortly after that, when Storrow came to Flint, Chrysler insisted on meeting with him and repeated his demands. According to Chrysler, Storrow told him to calm down because he would receive the pay raise and "did everything but pat me like a

Buick executives, 1912. *Left to right:* purchasing agent Edward Copeland, engineer Walter Marr, works manager Walter P. Chrysler, Charles W. Nash, sales manager Richard H. Collins, and treasurer Floyd A. Allen. *Courtesy SA/KU.*

pet horse." Chrysler announced that he would ask for $50,000 the next year. Storrow was well aware of Nash's tightfisted handling of expenditures. Chrysler reported kidding with Nash: "Charley, please show me the first nickel you ever earned. Mr. Storrow says you've got it hidden somewhere."[33]

In July 1912, Charles Nash held a banquet at the Flint Country Club for Buick branch managers from all over the United States and Canada following their annual meeting in Flint. He urged these men to express their views about the current state of Buick, especially the models. The managers praised the 1912 models and indicated great faith in the 1913 offerings, but they also urged Nash to make a six-cylinder Buick for 1914 in addition to its popular four-cylinder models. The 1916 lineup included a six, but, more important, electric self-starters and left-side drive were now standard in all Buicks. Production increased from 19,812 units in 1912 to 32,889 in 1914, surpassing the 1910 record of 30,525 for the first time. Output in 1915 increased to 43,946 vehicles and then skyrocketed in 1916 to 124,834 units. The Storrow-Nash-Chrysler team revitalized Buick and therefore General Motors just as Billy Durant was regaining control of the company he founded.[34]

James Storrow also worried about Nash's health. In mid-May 1915, he wrote a long letter to Richard Collins, a friend of Charles Nash, expressing his concerns: "I am very much concerned about Nash's health, not because I think he is in necessarily dangerous physical condition, but because I am certain that he is steadily drifting in that direction, without any systematic and intelligent decision to call a halt, get a correct diagnosis and start on the right road." He urged Collins to intervene with Nash's private physician in Flint and asked him to bring in one or more medical specialists from the University of Michigan to diagnose Nash's medical problem. Storrow did not reveal the nature of Nash's symptoms. It is possible that Nash was simply suffering from exhaustion.[35]

Storrow also advised Nash to delegate more responsibility to others within General Motors. In early July 1915, Nash appointed a committee of three executives to study some (unspecified) question, but also wanted to name the man who would carry out the investigation and report to this committee, which would ultimately report to GM's finance committee. Storrow replied to Nash's suggestion with stern words: "I am a little afraid that you are up to your old game of trying to do other peoples' work yourself, and that if you select the man you mention you would be steering the job instead of the committee, and that the man who you are considering will report quite as much, if not more, to you than to the committee, and in my judgement this is not good administration."[36]

While Storrow, Nash, and Chrysler revived General Motors, Billy Durant planned his return to control the company he had founded. A year after losing control to the bankers' voting trust, Durant formed the Chevrolet Motor Company in November 1911 and quickly produced a low-priced car intended to compete with the Model T Ford. Durant used money he earned with Chevrolet and other ventures to buy large blocks of General Motors common stock and convinced other investors to do the same. Historians have told the complete story of his financial maneuvering and manipulations elsewhere, but the result was Durant's ending the bankers' control of General Motors in mid-September 1915. Durant had enlisted the support of Pierre Du Pont, who bought a large stake in General Motors and gave Durant control over the corporation. Durant restructured the board of directors in September 1915, when Du Pont became chairman.[37] James Storrow's mistrust of Durant was evident in a letter he wrote to a friend in late September 1915, after the restructuring of the GM board: "If a good opportunity comes along in the course of the year I shall resign. If things do not seem to be going smoothly or well, Mr. Nash undoubtedly will resign also. I feel obliged to make the fight because it seemed to me [that] we could not permit the Company to be turned over to Mr. Durant to wreck again."[38]

Durant's correspondence with his son-in-law and business confidant, Dr. Edwin R. Campbell, showed Durant's distrust of the Storrow-Nash alliance. Campbell urged Durant to remove Storrow from any position of influence within the company: "He controls Nash absolutely and the only way you can get along with Nash is to take his prop out from under him and then he will play ball with you." As the struggle for control of General Motors continued, Durant declared, "Nash is acting like a baby and Storrow is so disconcerted that he is willing to resort to blackmail to secure even decent representation. It is clearly a matter of conspiracy between the two and an attempt on the part of both to save their faces." Campbell advised his father-in-law that Nash was expendable: "If you get control and can hold Crysler [sic] it would not make any difference about Nash going."[39]

Durant continued to buy additional General Motors stock through the end of 1915 and into the next year by exchanging Chevrolet shares for General Motors shares. By mid-May, Durant had indisputable control of General Motors. Charles Nash made the mistake of supporting the efforts of Storrow and others to reinstitute a voting trust for General Motors and to reverse Durant's apparent victory. Nash allowed the use of his name as a possible trustee in a circular issued to General Motors stockholders on 1 March 1916 calling for a new voting trust. Durant asked Nash and the other parties about the use of Nash's name as a future trustee and concluded that Nash, his longtime lieutenant and protégé, had betrayed him and then had lied about it. Durant confided to his son-in-law in late March, "Nash, according to the reports received, appears to have gotten himself in bad and I am to be a reception committee of one to meet him when he returns from California. I am through with wide-stepping and four-flushing and expect to reach an agreement and have the atmosphere cleared once and for all." Durant confronted Nash and made it clear that Nash was finished at General Motors.[40]

Nash offered his resignation to Pierre Du Pont on 18 April 1916, but asked Du Pont to delay making this public. By mid-May, some automotive industry publications reported his imminent resignation. Charles Nash officially left office on 1 June 1916, ending a twenty-five-year association with William C. Durant, which began when Nash first worked at the Flint Road Cart Company in 1891. With Nash's departure, Durant became the president of General Motors. *Automobile Topics* praised Nash's record at General Motors in announcing his resignation, but erroneously reported that Nash would stay on at the corporation in an advisory capacity for another two months.[41]

Durant understood the necessity of keeping Walter Chrysler at General Motors in the wake of Nash's departure and followed his son-in-law's advice. In early June 1916, Durant offered to make Chrysler president of Buick and to give him a seat on the General Motors board of directors. More important was the stunning salary that Durant offered—$500,000 a year for three years, with $120,000 a year in cash and the balance in cash or General Motors stock. This was ten times Chrysler's salary at the time and he accepted Durant's offer. Walter Chrysler fought almost continuously with Durant while working with him at General Motors, but remained there through October 1919, a little more than three additional years.[42]

Charles Nash House, 307 Mason Street, Flint, Michigan. *Photograph by the author.*

Nash's penny-pinching habits aside, Walter Chrysler greatly admired Charles Nash as an automotive executive: "Charley Nash was precisely the man needed to guide General Motors through the condition in which he found it when he left the Durant-Dort Carriage Company in Flint to become the president of Buick. . . . Nash may have known little about automobiles when he began in 1910, but he did know how to handle men; he knew how to run a factory. Above all, he was loyal; you could not find a man more honest."[43]

Nash and Storrow Purchase the Thomas B. Jeffery Company

Nash was hardly finished as an automaker. Once Durant's complete control of General Motors was imminent, James Storrow tried to buy control of the Packard Motor Car Company and planned to install Nash as president and Walter Chrysler as general manager. Negotiations with the Packard stockholders broke down and Storrow instead bought the Thomas B. Jeffery Company in Kenosha, Wisconsin. Nash became president of Jeffery, which was quickly renamed the Nash Motors Company, and Storrow became chairman of the board. Storrow and Nash were unable to convince Walter Chrysler to leave Flint for Kenosha.[44]

Billy Durant's regaining control of General Motors and the ending of Walter Chrysler's working relationship with James Storrow and Charles Nash involved the breakup of longstanding friendships and was difficult all around. Chrysler, who owed much to Storrow and Nash, did not join them in their new (and risky) automotive venture. Chrysler remained on good terms with both Storrow and Nash, but he remained at General Motors. Buick alone was a much larger operation than the Jeffery company and the salary Durant offered was simply stunning. Storrow had trouble accepting Chrysler's decision and wrote to him in late July 1916 expressing his views.

> The Jeffery Company, of course, is a small affair, and while I think the outlook is mighty attractive from the money-making and business point of view, yet I appreciate that it seemed to you hardly to supply sufficient scope for your time and energy. I cannot help feeling, however, that on the side of profit you would have found it very attractive and, also, would have taken, as the months rolled by, more and more satisfaction to be working for your own company in which you were one of the principal partners and owners.[45]

Storrow and Nash moved ahead without Chrysler and founded Nash Motors Company.

Charles Jeffery (*left*) and Charles Nash (*right*), 1916. *Courtesy DCHC.*

The details of the Nash/Storrow purchase of the Thomas B. Jeffery Company are murky. Charles Nash and Thomas M. Kearny, a Racine, Wisconsin, attorney representing the Jeffery family, reached an agreement in a room in the Blackstone Hotel in Chicago on a hot day in July 1916, and Nash gave Kearny a check for $500,000 to cement the deal. They never announced the precise selling price. Kimes gives a sale price of $9 million, but Rosenbusch claims $10 million.[46]

The Thomas B. Jeffery Company issued a statement on 13 July 1916 announcing its sale to Charles Nash and Lee, Higginson & Company. *Automobile Topics* commented about the sale, "Charles W. Nash, who at the time of his resignation from General Motors, was said to be 'going fishing,' has proved to be a fisherman of uncommon skill." *Automobile Topics* argued that this marriage was an excellent match.

> In respect to geographical location, shipping facilities by land and water, its proximity to Chicago with its great distributive advantages, and the fact that the business is now engaged in the production of both trucks and pleasure cars, the Jeffery is exactly suited to Nash's requirements. In addition, the huge modern plant is one of the few real manufacturing establishments in the industry actually producing as great a percentage

of the parts entering into its products, in all probability, as any other one concern.

The trade journal also noted that the Jeffery company was in excellent financial health and that its products had outstanding reputations.[47]

In early August, Nash, Storrow, and company formed Nash Motors Company under Maryland law, with $5 million in preferred stock and 50,000 shares of common stock with no par value assigned. Charles Nash was the president of the new firm and James J. Storrow the chairman of the board. An article in the *Flint Journal* claimed that the Jeffery company had real estate, plant, and equipment valued at nearly $3 million and total assets of $7.4 million, which probably included inventories of raw materials, parts, and unsold automobiles, and other forms of working capital, including accounts receivable.[48] If "goodwill" and other intangibles were part of the valuation, a purchase price of $9–10 million is conceivable.

The transfer of ownership and control from Charles T. Jeffery to Charles W. Nash appeared smooth and uneventful. In the August 1916 issue of the *Jeffery Circle*, Jeffery introduced Nash to the Jeffery dealers and reassured them that Nash was an outstanding choice to succeed him. According to Jeffery,

> We never entertained the idea of transferring our interests until Mr. Nash's offer came. And we only accepted it because we recognized in him the one man fitted by long years of experience to carry out the Jeffery policies and maintain the Jeffery attitude toward our dealers. Moreover, we realized that his talents were such that we could retire with complete confidence in his ability to make secure the future progress of the Jeffery organization.

Nash then explained his decision to buy the Jeffery company:

> I and my associates chose the Jeffery Company because we believed it had been founded and conducted along sound business lines. Its policies pleased us greatly. We had a number of other opportunities, but we decided against them in favor of this one.

He then offered some more specific attractions—the plant's central location to supplies of materials, its strong line of trucks and commercial vehicles, and the strong dealer body. Nash also announced that Charles Jeffery would stay on as a member of the board of directors, providing continuity.[49]

Charles Nash, at age fifty-two, had finished the first part of a remarkable life that had taken him from indentured servitude at age seven to the presidency of the largest automaker in the world at age forty-eight. He achieved much success by virtue of hard work, thrift, and entrepreneurial spirit well before he came to Flint. He moved to Flint when that city's booming carriage and wagon industry offered Nash and others plenty of opportunities to advance. Working for J. Dallas Dort and William C. Durant at the Durant-Dort Carriage Company and for James Storrow at General Motors opened additional opportunities, which Nash seized. Although some of Nash's success happened because of good fortune, Dort, Durant, and Storrow promoted him based on his performance. Nash's decision to side with Storrow against Durant cost him his position at General Motors. The second part of Charles Nash's life was in many ways equally remarkable because he successfully operated the automobile company bearing his name for another twenty years, finally retiring at age seventy-two. The next chapter will tell that story.

THREE

Nash Motors, 1916–36, and Charles W. Nash in Historical Perspective

Some people may think I am a crank on the subject of quality—and I admit that perhaps I am—but after all to me the greatest pleasure of building anything is the pleasure of building it right. Sometimes I think my disposition toward quality and good workmanship is the result of having worked for many years with tools myself. When a man builds things with his own hands, and prides himself with his work to the point where he can only be satisfied by doing a good job, he is bound to respect quality and scorn cheapness all his days.

Charles W. Nash, December 1934

Charles Nash took control of the Thomas B. Jeffery Company in August 1916 and thoroughly transformed the firm. Combined Jeffery automobile and truck production in 1916 was a mere 6,725 units, less than 1 percent of Ford's output of 734,811 Model T's. Jeffery's production did not place it among the top twenty nameplates. In sharp contrast, Nash Motors could boast production of 138,169 units in 1928, and a number eight ranking among American brands, after Chevrolet, Ford, Willys-Overland, Hudson, Pontiac, Buick, and Chrysler.[1] Nash Motors consistently earned profits until 1933, when it suffered its first loss. Charles Nash spent the last twenty years of his working life at the helm of Nash Motors, as president in 1916–32 and then as chairman in 1932–37. He engineered the merger of Nash Motors with the Kelvinator Corporation in 1937 to form the Nash-Kelvinator Corporation. George W. Mason, the president and chairman of Kelvinator, became the president of Nash-Kelvinator and Charles Nash retired from active involvement in the company he had founded twenty years earlier.

Early Successes and Struggles, 1917–24

Charles Nash began to put his imprint on the Jeffery company shortly after consummating the purchase, but he did so gradually, minimizing disruption to production or personnel. Charles T. Jeffery announced the sale to Nash on 13 July 1916 and Charles Nash and James J. Storrow incorporated the Nash Motors Company in Maryland on 29 July 1916. Charles Nash did not make wholesale changes in the Jeffery mid-management ranks, but he filled key positions with trusted friends and associates, including a few relatives. Storrow became chairman of the board, Charles T. Jeffery agreed to serve as a director, and Nash appointed Thomas M. Kearney, the attorney who negotiated the sale of the Jeffery company, as a director as well.[2]

Nash convinced several key General Motors officials to join him in Kenosha. Walter H. Alford, who had served as comptroller at General Motors under Nash and was considered a financial genius, defected and became vice president and comptroller at Nash Motors. Charles B. Vorhees, who had managed sales for GM's Oakland division, took the same job with Nash Motors. Nash recruited Nils Erik Wahlberg, the chief engineer at Oakland since 1913, to join him in Kenosha. Nash also brought in two of his sons-in-law, James T. Wilson, who had worked as Nash's secretary at Durant-Dort and at Buick, and C. Hascall Bliss, who would work in dealer relations. It is not clear if these men left General Motors for Nash Motors out of dislike for Durant or loyalty to Charles Nash.[3]

For most of the first year of Nash Motors' life, Charles Nash promoted and sold cars with the Jeffery nameplate. In mid-March 1917, Charles Nash personally endorsed the Jeffery line in a series of full-page newspaper advertisements. He explained that after spending the first six months improving the Jeffery factory operations, he finally realized what a fine car the Jeffery Six was. In Nash's words, "It is a great car—a really great car—a wonderful value—and we can prove it anywhere, any time you say. . . . It is so good—so unusually good—that we are proud to back it with our name and our money."[4] Nash Motors was also attempting to bolster its dealer network. An advertisement in *Motor World* promoted the Nash dealership as a very profitable business opportunity: "Nash dealers are making money because they have the complete line of Jeffery pleasure cars and trucks which are made right and priced right."[5]

The 1918 models, introduced in July 1917, bore the Nash nameplate and Charles Nash simultaneously discontinued the Jeffery nameplate. Nash never publicly explained the name change. Jeffery sales had fallen substantially between 1914 (13,513 units) and 1916 (6,725 units), in part because the offerings underwent few improvements. Because the all-new 1918 models bore the strong influence of

Charles Nash and his engineers, changing the nameplate seemed logical, if only to promote sales. Nash's ego probably played a role in the decision as well. One of the rewards of launching a new model automobile was having your name on the radiator.

During the first year of operation at his new company, Charles Nash dramatically increased manufacturing efficiency and production, while exhausting the inventory of Jeffery car parts and ending Jeffery production. Nash and his manufacturing staff restructured the factory before the introduction of the first Nash automobile in July 1917. He held weekly meetings of the factory management, including foremen, every Monday evening starting in September 1916. A photo of the first meeting (6 September 1916) shows Nash and sixty-six others present. The staff discussed production plans and problems, with possible solutions, with everyone encouraged to participate. According to the company newsletter, "Today we find a different spirit in the factory. Any lost motion that might have existed is being gradually eliminated. It is now only a matter of a short time before we will have the production up to big figures."[6]

Charles Nash personally supervised an enormous restructuring of the factory during his first year in control. According to Hascall Bliss, only two pieces of machinery in the entire complex were left in place—Nash scrapped, replaced, rebuilt, or moved

Charles Nash meeting with his managers at
Nash Motors, September 1916.
Courtesy DCHC.

all the rest. The new president spent most of his time on the factory floor, supervising and assisting in the work. In describing Nash's "hands-on" approach, *Automobile Topics* noted, "A dirt smudged company president was a new experience for the factory employees and from that time on they were Nash men heart and soul." The results were impressive. For 1917, Nash nearly doubled Jeffery production over that of 1916, with 12,027 cars and 801 trucks. In addition, the firm produced 6,516 Nash automobiles and 3,000 Nash trucks. Total production came to 22,344 units for 1917 versus only 6,725 units in the previous year.[7]

Nash Motors published a booklet in late 1917 touting its "state-of-the-art" factory—*Full Speed Ahead! The Story of the Nash Idea at Work in the Great Nash Factory*. The twenty-one-page, heavily illustrated booklet started by boasting that the Kenosha factory made 93 percent of the Nash automobile in-house. The factory incorporated Charles Nash's belief in "straight-line production," whereby all of the production processes moved ahead progressively on a straight line from one end of the factory to the opposite end. This booklet showed a factory filled with expensive special-purpose machines of the kind used by Henry Ford at his Highland Park plant in Detroit. Nash's plant had two six-spindle vertical lathes, which progressively machined castings that moved from one spindle to the next via a turntable. The brochure claimed that the Nash factory had two of only four vertical lathes of this size in the world.[8]

Charles Nash's "straight-line production" system closely resembled the moving assembly line Henry Ford installed at his Highland Park plant in 1913–14. It embodied the principles of Frederick Winslow Taylor's scientific management, which highlighted the elimination of wasted motions. Nash had seen Walter Chrysler impose similar production economies at the Buick plant in Flint. Ford's methods were well-known, especially after Arnold and Faurote published a detailed study (1915) of the manufacturing operations of the Ford Highland Park plant.[9]

The 1918 Nash models were the first new cars designed under the Charles Nash regime. Known generically as the Nash 680 series, Nash offered the new models as a five-passenger touring car and a roadster, both priced at $1,295; a seven-passenger touring car ($1,545); a four-door sedan ($1,985); and a two-door coupe ($2,085). They all had what Nash called a "perfected valve-in-head" six-cylinder engine, which was no surprise to the automotive world, given Nash's experience with this type of engine at Buick. Designed by Erik Wahlberg, the new model earned rave reviews in part because of its powerful engine, but also because the car embodied simplicity of design, with important innovations. *The American Chauffeur* observed, "There is not an unnecessary rod or cross bar on the Nash chassis. It is extremely light without

1918 Nash Model 681 (first Nash-designed car). *Courtesy DCHC.*

loss of strength." The 1917 Jeffery Model 671, also a Six, remained in production into 1918 as the Nash Model 671.[10]

Charles Nash left the basic mechanical design of the Nash Six largely unchanged from its introduction as a 1918 model through 1924. To be sure, there were minor styling changes, such as the introduction of a taller radiator and drum headlamps in the 1922 Nash series 690-Six. Charles Nash introduced a Four (series 40) for the 1921 model year. The Nash Four featured the "Nash Perfected Valve-In-Head Motor" and looked similar to the Six, but it had a shortened hood and shorter wheelbase (112 inches versus 121 or 127 inches for the Nash Six). The Nash Four was of course lighter than the Six and in time carried a lower price. Nash also improved the Four in 1922 by introducing rubber engine mounts, the first American automaker to do so.[11] Nash Motors prospered in the first eight years of operations (1916–24) but also faced a serious recession of 1921, as the production figures given in Table 3.1 illustrate.

Following in the tracks of Jeffery, Nash Motors continued production of the four-wheel-drive truck, renaming it the Nash Quad. Jeffery had produced its Quads mostly for the Russian and French governments, but with the U.S. entry into the war, demand increased greatly and the U.S. Army took the entire Nash Quad production. Nash ran double shifts at the Kenosha plant and put out between forty and fifty Nash Quads a day. Nash's production of 11,490 trucks in 1918 made the company the largest truck manufacturer in the world. According to James C. Mays, 9,721 of the total were Quads.[12]

Table 3.1. Nash Motors Production, Calendar Year, and Profits or Losses ( ), Net of Taxes ($ Millions), Year Ending 30 November 1917–36

	Automobiles	**Trucks**	**Total**	**Net Profits ($ Millions)**
1917	18,543	3,801	22,344*	2.0
1918	10,283	11,490	21,733	1.5
1919	27,018	4,090	31,108	5.0
1920	35,084	3,697	38,781	7.0
1921	20,850	103	20,953	2.2
1922	41,652	271	41,923	7.6
1923	56,677	344	57,021	9.8
1924	53,626	203	53,829	9.3
1925	96,121	168	96,289**	16.3
1926	135,520	74	135,594***	23.3
1927	122,606	31	122,637	22.7
1928	138,137	32	138,169	20.8
1929	116,622	11	116,633	18.0
1930	54,605	–	54,605	7.6
1931	38,616	–	38,616	4.8
1932	17,696	–	17,696	1.0
1933	14,973	–	14,973	(1.2)
1934	28,664	–	28,644	(1.6)
1935	44,637	–	44,637****	(0.6)
1936	53,038	–	53,038	1.0

Source: Production summaries, Nash Motors, DCHC. Profits and losses are from Barron's 6 (8 November 1926): 10; Automotive Daily News 9 (3 September 1929): 8; Annual Report of the Nash Motors Company for 1936, 1937, 1938, NAHC.
*Figures include 12,027 Jeffery automobiles, 6,516 Nash automobiles, 801 Jeffery trucks, and 3,000 Nash trucks.
**Includes 10,683 Ajax automobiles.
***Includes 38,662 Ajax and Nash Light Six automobiles.
****Includes Lafayette automobiles.

In mid-April 1918, Nash Motors signed a contract to supply the U.S. Army with 2,904 Quad chassis at a fixed price of $2,871.05 each. Late in April, Nash sold the U.S. government (for $1) a license to subcontract Quad truck manufacturing to other "reputable manufacturers" for the duration of the war, an indication of Charles

Nash Quads, somewhere in France, 1918. *Courtesy DCHC.*

Nash's patriotism. In May and June, the U.S. government issued contracts to the Paige-Detroit Motor Car Company and the Hudson Motor Car Company, both of Detroit, the National Motor and Vehicle Corporation of New York, and the Premier Motor Corporation of Indianapolis, with each company agreeing to manufacture 2,000 Nash Quad trucks.[13]

Charles Nash sacrificed the production of thousands of the popular 1918 Nash cars to produce Quads for the war effort. To manufacture nearly 11,500 trucks in 1918, he cut back car production to a little more than 10,000 units. Nash supported the war effort in other ways as well. He trained army and navy mechanics at the plant and set aside twenty-five acres of company land for "victory gardens." Nash encouraged his men to enlist in the military rather than wait to be drafted, closed the factory to hold a patriotic parade, and ordered a giant American flag to be flown at the plant until the end of the war.[14]

Charles Nash turned down President Wilson's offer of a U.S. Army commission. He preferred to serve his country wearing business clothes and did not need to be in uniform to function effectively. Instead, he accepted the position of assistant director of aircraft engineering and production within the Bureau of Aircraft Production under General John D. Ryan in July 1918. He spent the last six months of the war coordinating airplane design and production at Wright Field in Dayton, Ohio.[15]

Nash was not the only American automaker to contribute to the war effort. Dodge Brothers supplied staff cars and ambulances, and General Motors provided a wide variety of trucks. In many cases, the automobile companies produced unfamiliar and sometimes exotic products. Packard, Ford, and the Lincoln Motor Company manufactured V-12 Liberty aircraft engines, and the Fisher Body Company made de Havilland DH-4 scout bombers. Ford Motor Company assembled Eagle boats (submarine chasers) at what became the Ford Rouge plant in Dearborn, Michigan. Dodge Brothers made recoil mechanisms for two important artillery pieces—the 155-millimeter Falloux general-purpose gun and the 155-millimeter Schneider howitzer.[16]

Through the end of the war, Nash Motors emphasized trucks in its product mix. The April 1917 issue of *Nash News* carried the headline, "Now Is the Time to Concentrate on Trucks," with most of the issue focused on the Nash Quad. An advertisement in the *Saturday Evening Post* in November 1917 and a 1918 Nash truck brochure show models with 1-ton, 1 1/2-ton, 2-ton, and 2 1/2-ton capacity, all rear-drive vehicles.[17]

After World War I, the federal government sold 30,000 surplus trucks and cars at auction. More than 7,000 of the trucks were Quads, sold for a fraction of the cost of a new Quad from the Nash factory. Nash Motors dropped the Quad after the war but introduced new truck models in 1920 and 1921, when the company still had hopes of substantial sales. In 1920, truck production was a respectable 3,697 units, but in the recession year of 1921, output fell disastrously to only 103 units. Nash in essence "froze" the design of its trucks after 1921. Nash Motors built only eleven trucks in 1929, when production stopped entirely, only to return to building them on a modest scale starting in 1947.[18]

Nash Motors' automobile production and sales boomed in the years immediately following World War I, and Charles Nash expanded the company's empire beyond Kenosha. He purchased a half interest in the Seaman Body Corporation of Milwaukee in 1919. Seaman had manufactured chairs, cabinets, sofas, and other household furniture in Milwaukee since 1846. William S. Seaman (1845–1910) invented the soundproof telephone booth, which his company manufactured in large volumes from 1887 until 1919. Starting in November 1913, Seaman made closed car bodies for the Thomas B. Jeffery Company.[19]

The Seaman Company and Nash Motors became closely tied together starting in September 1917, when Nash placed the first of many substantial orders (500 bodies) with Seaman. By the end of 1917, Seaman was operating three plants in Milwaukee and space became a serious problem because of the mounting orders from Nash Motors. Seaman stopped making telephone booths and automobile bodies for companies other than Nash. In the fall of 1919, when Charles Nash bought

W. S. Seaman Company Plant Number Two (1909),
Milwaukee, WI. *Courtesy DCHC.*

a half interest in the company, it already employed 10,000 men in its Milwaukee factories.

From that point on, Seaman worked exclusively for Nash Motors and made all of their closed car bodies, while Nash made open bodies in Kenosha. Seaman's new five-story reinforced concrete factory (1920) doubled in size in 1923 to satisfy growing demand for closed car bodies. On 17 July 1936, Nash Motors purchased the remaining 50 percent of the stock in Seaman Body Corporation for $949,191.50 from Harold H. Seaman, grandson of founder Alonzo D. Seaman.[20]

Perhaps taking a cue from the General Motors strategy of offering a wide range of cars in terms of size and price, Charles Nash and James J. Storrow launched the Lafayette Motors Company in the fall of 1919 to produce a luxury car. Had the effort succeeded, Nash would have had a high-end car to complement the mid-priced Nash Six and the low-priced Nash Four. The initial announcement of the new venture did not mention Nash or Storrow. The new company, based in Mars Hill, Indiana, near Indianapolis, appeared to be the offspring of D. McCall White and Earl C. Howard, respectively the former chief engineer and sales manager from

Cadillac. Lee, Higginson & Company announced that the Lafayette Motors Company, a Delaware corporation, would have capital stock of $6 million (60,000 shares with a par value of $100), but they would issue only 40,000 shares. Charles Nash would serve as president and James J. Storrow as chairman of the board.[21]

The unveiling of the Lafayette came in January 1920, with cars not offered for sale until September. This was a large luxury car, with a V-8 engine producing 90 brake horsepower and luxury prices ranging from $5,000 for a seven-passenger touring car to $6,500 for a four-door sedan. Lafayette also came in roadster, sedan, and limousine models, but all the models were unchanged between 1920 and 1924. This initial introduction received a positive review in *Automobile Topics*, but the Lafayette appeared on the market just as automobile sales went into a deep recession. The company produced only 500 cars in 1920 and 1921 combined, improved to 563 units in 1922, and then fell off to only 156 cars in 1923.

Nash Motors invested heavily in Lafayette, which continued to flounder. Charles Nash moved Lafayette production to Milwaukee in January 1923, into a plant next to the Nash Four factory. Finally, in August 1924, Nash and Storrow advised Lafayette stockholders to accept an offer from Ajax Motors, another Nash subsidiary, to buy their interest in Lafayette for $225,000. According to Kimes, Charles Nash and James Storrow spent $2 million on this failed venture.[22]

Fortunately for Nash Motors, sales rebounded in 1922 and 1923 because of the company's other products. Nash had offered a closed-body sedan since 1918, but for

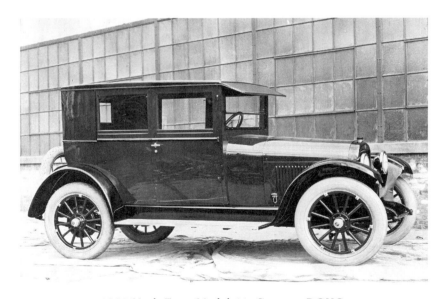

1922 Nash Four, Model 46. *Courtesy DCHC.*

the 1922 model year Nash introduced seven closed-body models, with three versions of Nash Six sedans and four different Nash Four models. Charles Nash introduced the Nash Four Carriole model in May 1922, which sold for a reasonable price (for a closed car) of only $1,350. He had hoped to gain an advantage over the competition, but the Hudson Motor Car Company had already introduced the Essex Coach a few months earlier. By July 1922, the Essex Coach sold for only $1,295. Still, Nash sales nearly tripled between the recession year of 1921 and 1923. Nash Motors profits, a robust $7 million in 1920, fell to $2 million in 1921 but recovered to $7.6 million in 1922 and improved further to $9.3 million the following year. Charles Nash dropped the Nash Four from the offerings after the 1924 model year and began an impressive expansion of Nash Motors that continued through the end of the decade.[23]

Nash Motors in Prosperity and Depression, 1925–36

Nash Motors introduced three entirely new lines of six-cylinder automobiles for the 1925 model year. Their success brought Nash a huge increase in sales, forcing expansion of the company's manufacturing facilities. Production in 1925 nearly doubled from a year earlier and then increased another 40 percent in 1926. Much of the growth came from the inexpensive lightweight Ajax Six, made by a Nash subsidiary in Racine, Wisconsin. Nash's success and prosperity, based on high-quality, durable products, continued through 1929. Nash Motors was very successful in the highly competitive mid-priced automobile market.

The two new Nash lines for the 1925 model year were the Advanced Six series on a wheelbase of 127 inches and the Special Six series on a new 112-inch wheelbase. The Advanced Six series included two touring cars, two sedans, a four-door coupe, and a roadster, while the Special Six was available only as a five-passenger touring car and a five-passenger sedan. All of the new models shared substantial improvements over previous Nashes and were equal or superior to cars offered in the same price range by the rest of the industry.

The 1925 Nashes had four-wheel mechanical brakes (versus rear brakes only), balloon tires, Budd Michelin steel disc wheels, full-pressure lubrication for the engine, counterweighted crankshafts, and an improved steering system. Nash dealers had long wanted four-wheel brakes, but Charles Nash moved forward with the idea in a very deliberate way. The system Nash devised was simpler and used far fewer components than the mechanical braking systems of his competitors, and thus required less lubrication and maintenance and gave greater reliability. Nash modified the 1926 offerings with new Seaman bodies and new engines. Nash redesigned its six-cylinder engine for some 1926 models by enlarging the bore from 3 1/4 to 3 7/16 inches and added a new seven-bearing crankshaft. Nash, which installed this engine on the closed cars in the Special Six line, called it the "Enclosed Car" engine.[24]

The 1925 Nash Sixes were reasonably priced and technically advanced automobiles. The Advanced Six series five-passenger touring car had a base price of $1,375, while the same model in the Special Six series cost $1,095. Along similar lines, the Advanced Six five-passenger sedan listed at $1,695 and its Special Six counterpart carried a price of $1,295. The Nash models were at the higher end of the overcrowded mid-priced market. Looking at six-cylinder five-passenger touring car offerings for 1925, Buick had two models listed at $1,175 and $1,475, while Oldsmobile priced its touring cars at $875 and $1,015. The new Nash models for 1925 were so successful that by November 1924, all of the Nash plants (Kenosha, Milwaukee, and Seaman Body) could not satisfy the demand despite working around the clock six days a week. Charles Nash announced a $1 million plant expansion program at Kenosha.[25]

For Charles Nash, the year 1925 also marked the launch of a new automobile line, the Ajax Six. The Mitchell Motors Company of Racine, Wisconsin, was forced into bankruptcy in April 1923 after manufacturing automobiles at the former Mitchell Wagon factory since 1903. On 31 January 1924, Charles Nash purchased the Mitchell buildings and land at auction, paying $405,000 and outbidding the Hupp Motor Car Corporation of Detroit by a mere $5,000. The Mitchell factory, ten miles north of Kenosha and twenty miles south of Milwaukee, had 500,000 square feet of floor space, in contrast to the Kenosha plant, with its 1,445,500 square feet.[26]

The Ajax Six debuted on 27 May 1925 in Racine, Wisconsin, with a parade, factory tours, a baseball game between teams from Kenosha and Racine, and a raffle with a new Ajax Six as the prize. Racine declared the day an official holiday, and the Racine newspapers printed special "Ajax Editions." Nash offered the Ajax Six as a five-passenger touring car at $865 and a five-passenger four-door sedan at $995. This was a smaller version of the other Nash offerings, with a wheelbase of only 109 inches, but it featured a six-cylinder engine with a seven bearing crankshaft, a feature not found in cars of this size and price.

Sales of the Ajax were only about 27,300 units during the first year, so Charles Nash simply renamed the model the Nash Light Six and sales improved with the more familiar moniker. For 1926, Nash Motors produced 38,622 Ajax and Nash Light Six cars, more than one quarter of total production.[27]

By any measure, Nash Motors was a large corporation by the mid-1920s. With production of 135,520 cars in 1926, the Nash nameplate ranked eighth overall in the U.S. auto industry behind Ford, Chevrolet, Buick, Dodge, Hudson, Willys-Overland,

and Chrysler, and slightly ahead of Pontiac and Durant. The company published a booklet, *What Nash Motors Means to Wisconsin*, in 1926 to emphasize its economic importance to the Dairy State. The total value of Nash production in 1925 was $126 million, which exceeded the production of Wisconsin's dairy industry. Nash Motors was the state's largest taxpayer, adding $880,000 to the state coffers. The company directly employed 13,000, but also purchased materials from hundreds of Wisconsin-based companies and maintained 150 Nash dealers statewide.[28]

An article in *Automotive Industries* in December 1927 found the financial success of Nash Motors since 1916 quite remarkable. The firm had paid out nearly $30 million in dividends, but kept $50 million of its earnings to reinvest in plants and equipment. The net worth of stockholders' equity had jumped from $20.8 million in 1920 to nearly $43.3 million in 1926. An owner of the original stock issue who had invested $100 in 1916 would have held shares in December 1927 worth $4,750 and would have received $500 in dividends and $315 in cash over those years.[29]

Nash Motors did not change the 1927 and 1928 models from 1926, but Nash Motors' sales and profits (Table 3.1) remained robust during those years. The company struggled through 1927 to satisfy the orders pouring into the factory. In September 1927, Charles Nash announced a $1.3 million factory expansion program, which included a $500,000 addition to the Racine factory, which produced the Standard Six; the addition of a new five-story building to the Seaman Body plant in Milwaukee; and a $350,000 addition to the Seaman-Dunning Corporation plant at Pine Bluff, Arkansas, which made wooden parts for the Nash closed bodies. The expenditures paid off. In August 1928, when Nash was starting production of its new "400" series cars for the 1929 model year, the three factories at Kenosha, Racine, and Milwaukee produced 1,020 cars on 23 August, an all-time daily production record for Nash Motors.[30]

The 400 series cars incorporated twin ignition in the overhead valve engines. Each cylinder had two spark plugs, one in the cylinder head and the second in the cylinder wall next to the combustion chamber. The engines also had a higher compression ratio (raised from 4.5 to one to 5.0 to one), resulting in more power. The entire 400 series featured a seven-bearing crankshaft. For 1930, Nash offered two Sixes and its first eight-cylinder engine in its 400 series. The straight eight engine had a displacement of 298.6 cubic inches and developed 100 brake horsepower. The new models, however, did not prevent Nash sales from falling more than 50 percent in 1930 versus 1929, while the company continued to earn profits on lower sales.[31]

The late 1920s brought the departure of three key leaders of Nash Motors. James J. Storrow, longtime sponsor of Charles Nash and chairman of the board of Nash Motors Company since 1916, died on 13 March 1926. Nash said of him,

He was an extraordinary man. I doubt if a man ever lived who had a warmer, bigger heart than Mr. Storrow, and who, on the other hand, was so unable to show it in his daily contact with men. . . . He was the largest man that I have ever met during my thirty-five years in business in a good-size way. If he found he was wrong in his diagnosis of any problem, he did not hesitate to immediately acknowledge he was wrong and place the credit where it belonged—to the man who was right.

Earl H. McCarty, vice president and director of sales, left Nash in February 1929 to enjoy retirement, but returned to the fold in April 1930 as vice president and general manager at Charles Nash's urging. Walter A. ("Judge") Alford was the third key person to leave. Alford, who had served as comptroller, vice president, and a director of Nash Motors since 1916, died in Kenosha in February 1930, with Charles Nash at his side.[32]

Like most of the automobile industry, Nash Motors struggled in the early 1930s and recovered slowly through 1936. Nash introduced a new L-head straight eight engine and a single-ignition six on the 1931 models. Nash Motors cut its prices but still earned profits of nearly $5 million that year. For 1932, Nash introduced synchronizing clutches and oil temperature regulators on all of its models. The 1933 models remained unchanged from 1932, at a time when competitors had changed their styling. Nash sales fell to under 15,000 units in 1933 and the company lost money ($1,188,863) for the first time in its history.[33]

Remarkably, Nash Motors earned profits through 1932, the only automaker other than General Motors to do so. Nash Motors was a very lean operation in terms of inventories of raw materials and finished automobiles. At the end of 1931, Nash's inventories were a mere 3.4 percent of its current assets, in contrast to the five leading companies whose inventories stood at roughly 30 percent of assets. The company built cars only in response to actual orders from its dealers. Dealers received only cars they had ordered, with the particular options and colors they needed.[34]

Nash adopted this ultraconservative policy sometime in the 1920s and was unique within the auto industry. Most automakers established factory production schedules (by quarter) for the entire model year and altered those plans only after severe changes to the anticipated sales volume. They shipped cars to their dealers whether or not the dealers had ordered them. When sales varied greatly from expectations, they would shut down the factory or run on overtime. Alfred P. Sloan introduced improved production controls at General Motors in 1921–24 by requiring dealers to submit ten-day sales reports to GM headquarters. Even with this system, GM continued to produce some cars on speculation and deliver them to the dealers.[35]

Nash redesigned its offerings for 1934, with bodies influenced by the design notions of Russian count Alexis de Sakhnoffsky, who had been hired by Nash Motors to help update the Nash look. The "Speedstream" bodies featured bullet-shaped headlights, ribs running the length of the hood, and a full beavertail rear end. All 1934 Nash engines came with twin-ignition and overhead valves.

Nash Motors introduced several advanced design features in the 1935 models, including hydraulic brakes, an improved suspension system the company called "Synchronized Springing," and all-steel one-piece bodies, which Nash described as "Aeroform Design." Production rebounded to 44,637 units, but Nash still lost $610,277 in 1935. The 1936 Nash 400 series featured intake manifolds incorporated into the cast-iron engine block, an industry first. The rest of the 1936 offerings changed little from the year before, but the company earned profits for the first time in four years.[36]

Nash Motors reintroduced the Lafayette nameplate in 1934, but as a smaller, less expensive version of the "regular" Nash line. Nash changed the nameplate from "Lafayette" to "LaFayette" in the process. This was not the luxury car of the first incarnation of this nameplate. Instead, it was a high-quality smaller car, resting on a 113-inch wheelbase, with a Six, and base prices ranging from $595 to $695. Nash claimed it had many design features, such as a seven-bearing crankshaft, not found on comparably priced competitive cars. Nash dealers wanted a lower-priced car to improve their sales volumes and to allow them to compete in the lower end of the market. Charles Nash gave this new line its own nameplate to dissociate it from the Nash name to promote sales, but also to protect the Nash name against charges that they were cheapening it.

They refined LaFayette for 1936, with streamlined all-steel bodies, hydraulic brakes, and more power. According to a 1935 flier, "Nash-LaFayette Progress," LaFayette contributed greatly to improved Nash sales in 1934 and 1935, but separate production numbers are not available. The second incarnation of the LaFayette nameplate ended in 1940, when the Nash-Kelvinator Corporation dropped the line.[37]

Charles Nash turned over the presidency of Nash Motors to Earl McCarty in January 1932. Nash was sixty-eight years old at the time, but continued to serve as chairman of the board and remained in Kenosha, actively involved in company management.[38] He finally stepped down in fact, if not in name, in 1937 after he orchestrated the merger of Nash Motors Company with the Kelvinator Corporation to form Nash-Kelvinator. In his twenty years as the active head of the company bearing his name, Charles Nash left his imprint through policies he carried out that reflected his philosophies of business management and human relations.

1936 LaFayette. *Courtesy DCHC.*

Business Policies and Practices of
Charles W. Nash at Nash Motors

Charles Nash was a "hands-on" manager who genuinely paid attention to what his customers, dealers, executives, and workers had to say. Nash believed that reducing overhead was the key to success, in both good times and bad. He recalled cutting the monthly electric bill in half in a factory he managed simply by urging the employees to keep lights turned off unless there were needed. In discussing his thrifty habits in a 1934 interview Nash commented, "I never made money by gambling, but by thrift."[39]

Although Charles Nash was a dynamic leader and a strong personality, Nash Motors was not simply a "one-man show." He often deferred to his executives' judgments and tried to explain his decisions when they were unpopular. When Nash bought 50 percent of the stock of Seaman Brothers body business, some of his executives questioned why he did not simply buy all the stock. Nash explained that he wanted to leave the Seaman brothers in charge of production, with continued substantial ownership of the business.[40]

Charles Nash also took great care to reduce inventories of parts and raw materials to a minimum to achieve a rapid rate of turnover at the factory and thus reduce working capital required to operate. The company never ordered more than a ninety-day supply of any part or raw material as a matter of policy. Stockpiling of materials within the factory proper was also kept at a minimum, with materials routed directly from the loading dock or yard storage area to the presses, machine shop, or forge where they needed the materials. Stock within the plant was found only on conveyor belts or on department trucks.[41]

Charles Nash's policies toward Nash Motors dealers were progressive and enlightened. In early 1919, he delivered an address to the Omaha Automobile Dealers' Association in which he showed much understanding of the problems dealers faced. He noted, "You dealers are more essential to the manufacturer than the manufacturer is to you. You are the men and the means by which automobiles are put in the hands of buyers. Neither the manufacturer [n]or the distributor comes into contact with the user except rarely." Nash argued that dealers deserved bank credit from local banks, which often remained skeptical of the "soundness" of the automobile trade.[42]

In an interview with Norman Shidle in 1925, Nash discussed in some detail the ways in which automobile manufacturers could better treat their dealers. First, manufacturers should not overload dealers with cars they do not want. Nash Motors built cars only in response to specific orders from dealers and distributers. Second, auto companies should protect dealers if the factory reduced car prices. Nash Motors always gave dealers rebates to cover losses on cars in stock at the dealership. Third, the car company should standardize parts as much as possible to minimize the inventories dealers would have to maintain. In January 1924, Nash Motors voluntarily increased the dealers' discount on four-cylinder cars by 3 percent, retroactive to 1 July 1923, to improve their profit margin on these cheaper models.[43]

Charles Nash's relationship with his employees was an example of the "benevolent" paternalism of that era. In July 1921, Nash employees formed the Ke-Nash-A Club with the strong support and approval of Charles Nash. The name combined the names of the city and the company. The club was an independent organization promoting social and recreational activities, with voluntary membership. Nash Motors supported the Kenasha Club, but how much influence it exerted is not clear. By the mid-1920s, 90 percent of Nash workers were members. Club dues were fifty cents per month, with twenty cents used for athletic and social programs and the remaining thirty cents went into a fund to support workers who were sick or injured. The club gave members free legal advice and low-interest loans, sponsored a band, and showed movies regularly. The company built and maintained a clubhouse, athletic fields, tennis courts, and a baseball stadium. Charles Nash donated the stadium to his employees in 1923. The facility seated six thousand and was the home of a semi-professional baseball team. The Nash Band, which had twenty-eight members in 1925, gave free concerts at the Nash baseball park every two weeks during the summer months.[44]

Nash Motors sponsored an annual company picnic starting in 1920. The families of workers from the Nash plant in Kenosha attended and, for a short time, the Racine and Milwaukee workers attended as well. The 1926 picnic, held at Forest Park in Kenosha, drew 25,000. The company provided 1,100 gallons of lemonade, 500 gallons of coffee, 1,500 gallons of ice cream with 48,000 cones, and 24,000 packages of Cracker Jacks. They filled the day with various athletic contests between the different plants and departments. Charles Nash delivered a speech praising his workers and enjoyed a picnic lunch with his employees.[45]

For most of Charles Nash's time as the active manager of Nash Motors, his relations with labor were cordial, if paternalistic. In 1922 he began the practice of giving every employee an annual bonus at Christmas. Most employees received a $10 bill, but foremen and higher management received more.

Despite Charles Nash's attempts to portray himself as "one of the boys," he clearly was not and over time became increasingly isolated from the harsh realities of the working conditions in his factories. Typical of owners of his era, he did not understand his workers' complaints, much less have much sympathy for them. In one incident, a worker caught his hand in a machine in the press shop and lost three fingers. Someone shut down the line and Charles Nash came out of his office to investigate. The foreman explained that the accident was upsetting to the men and that the three severed fingers were still sitting on the machine. Nash was furious and ordered the foreman to "brush them off and keep going," and put the assembly line back in motion.[46]

Despite his Christmas bonuses to workers and other acts of benevolence, Nash had to confront organized, disgruntled workers in his plants. He faced serious collective actions by his workers in November 1933, March 1934, and August 1934. The first open conflict between the union and the company was the result of Nash Motors' changing the pay system for its final assembly workers from an hourly rate to piece rates. Workers expected their pay to increase under the new system, but after the first day under the new system, workers claimed the company reduced their pay by 10–15 percent and demanded a return to the old system. When the company refused, the men sat down and on 9 November 1933 Charles Nash closed the plant. The union held its ground and Nash finally agreed to a six-point settlement offered by the union. The key provisions included the company's agreeing to the principle of collective bargaining; its acceptance of the committee elected by the workers to conduct bargaining; and a pledge not to discriminate against strikers who returned to work.[47]

The Nash unions achieved recognition and basic concessions long before workers in Detroit and Flint, Michigan, had similar success. The Communist-led Auto Workers Union launched short-lived, unsuccessful strikes in early 1933 against Hudson, Briggs Body, Murray Body, and Motor Products, all in Detroit. The first solid successes came as the result of the United Automobile Workers' sit-down strike against General Motors in Flint, which extended from December 1936 into March 1937 and a three-week strike in March 1937 against Chrysler in Detroit.[48]

Charles Nash never accepted unions in his factories. He felt betrayed by workers who did not appreciate everything he had given them. At the start of the November 1933 strike, Charles Nash physically struggled with union leader George Nordstrom to control the switch that turned off the assembly line. Nash screamed at Nordstrom, "Is this the kind of pay I get after I gave your dad the money for your education?" Young Nordstrom replied, "What you did for my dad is between you and my dad." Nash refused to recognize the harsh conditions and abuses his workers sometimes faced.[49]

Charles Nash was seventy years old in 1934, increasingly disconnected from the company bearing his name, and looking forward to a complete withdrawal from business. He looked for the right executive to take his place at the helm of Nash Motors and found the man he wanted—George W. Mason, president of the Kelvinator Corporation, a leading manufacturer of household refrigerators and commercial refrigeration equipment. To lure Mason to Nash Motors, Charles Nash had to buy Kelvinator.

Charles Nash (*left*) and George Mason (*right*) in 1937. *Courtesy DCHC*.

The Nash-Kelvinator Merger

According to Beverly Rae Kimes, Charles Nash asked Walter Chrysler for advice in finding a new man to head Nash Motors and Chrysler strongly recommended George W. Mason, president and chairman of the board at the Kelvinator Corporation. Because Mason did not want to give up his position at Kelvinator and did not want to leave Detroit, Nash was forced to orchestrate a merger of the two companies. Both boards of directors approved the merger in principle in late October 1936 and the stockholders concurred in late December.[50]

In analyzing the merger, *Fortune* offered a "pop psychology" explanation: "The logic of the Nash-Kelvinator merger resided in special psychological circumstances. It resided primarily in the need for the seventy-three-year-old Charles W. Nash, maker of the Nash motorcar ever since 1916, for a spiritual son to carry on the management of his chief interest. Mr. Nash has found that son in the practically unknown George Walter Mason, who has made the Kelvinator Corp. great in its field without grabbing so much as an ounce of public glory for himself."[51] According to *Fortune*, this unlikely merger was widely seen as "industrial miscegenation." The merger was in fact a brilliant linking together of two profitable corporations with benefits to both. More important, the merger brought in George W. Mason to run the merged venture.[52]

George Walter Mason (12 March 1891–8 October 1954) was a small-town boy who ended up making refrigerators, but had gasoline in his veins. Born in Valley City, North Dakota, roughly sixty miles west of Fargo, the son of Simon and Annie Mason, he first drove a car in 1906 when he was fifteen. The following year he worked for the local Maxwell dealer during the summer demonstrating cars and teaching new drivers how to operate them. He raced motorcycles on dirt tracks in North Dakota as a teenager and ran a motorcycle distributorship at age sixteen. In 1909 he entered the University of Michigan, where he studied engineering for three years and business administration in his final year. He graduated in 1913 with a bachelor of science degree.[53]

Mason then held a variety of positions that gave him a wide range of experience both in and outside the automobile industry. He first took a position with the Studebaker Corporation in Detroit and he impressed his boss, William Robert Wilson, so much that when Wilson left Studebaker in 1914 to work for Dodge Brothers he took Mason with him. In 1915 Mason became the purchasing agent for the Auto Trimming Company of Detroit and the following year worked for the Wilder Tanning Company in Waukegan, Illinois. At the request of the U.S. Army Ordnance Department, Mason supervised production at the Rock Island (Illinois) Arsenal in

1917 and 1918. After Walter Chrysler put William Wilson in charge of reorganizing the Maxwell Motor Corporation of Detroit, Wilson hired Mason in October 1921 as an assistant to the vice president for manufacturing. A year later, Wilson appointed Mason (age thirty-one) works manager for Maxwell Motor Corporation.[54]

William Wilson became chairman of the board of Copeland Products, a manufacturer of electric refrigerators, in 1926. Wilson asked his protégé to join him there as vice president and general manager and Mason agreed. Named president of Copeland Products in 1927, Mason turned the company around and Copeland soon threatened the position of the larger but poorly run Electric Refrigeration Company, the leading refrigerator manufacturer at the time. In 1928, Electric Refrigeration changed its name to the Kelvinator Corporation to honor Lord Kelvin, the British physicist and inventor. After the giant refrigerator manufacturer lost $2.5 million in 1927 and $1 million in 1928, its board of directors hired Mason as chairman of the board in December 1928 and as president in mid-January 1929. George Mason, not yet thirty-eight years old, quickly made Kelvinator profitable again, even through the early years of the Great Depression, catching Charles Nash's attention.[55]

Under Mason's management, the Kelvinator Corporation earned respectable profits in 1929–36. Sales of Kelvinator refrigerators soared from 39,000 units in 1926 to 306,600 in 1936, second only to Frigidaire's 400,000 units. Mason forced improvements to the design of Kelvinator's refrigerators and spent lavishly on advertising—typically 10 percent of the company's gross income. On the verge of the Nash-Kelvinator merger, George Mason announced that Kelvinator was diversifying its product line to include electric ranges, hot water heaters, oil burners, and washing machines.[56]

General Motors' experiences with its Frigidaire Division bore an eerie resemblance to the record of Nash Motors and Kelvinator. It began when William C. Durant bought the Guardian Frigerator Company of Detroit in June 1918 with his own money for slightly more than $56,000. Durant quickly renamed the company the Frigidaire Corporation and sold it to General Motors a year later for the same price he paid. Frigidaire lost more than $1.5 million through early 1921 and General Motors considered dumping the company. The automaker had also acquired several businesses that Charles Kettering controlled that had knowledge of refrigeration, so General Motors decided to continue with Guardian. They improved the product and turned a profit in 1924. In the late 1920s and 1930s Frigidaire expanded its product lines to include clothes washers and dryers, home freezers, dishwashers, and kitchen ranges.[57]

The details of the Nash and Kelvinator merger reveal the attractions of the merger to both groups of stockholders. The two boards of directors approved the merger on

27 October 1936, the stockholders of both companies, with few dissenting votes, approved the plan on 2 December 1936, and the merger was officially completed on 4 January 1937. A remarkable 70 percent of Nash Motors assets were in the form of cash and marketable securities, while Kelvinator held only 15 percent of its assets in this form. In short, the Kelvinator shareholders got access to Nash cash for future growth. Charles Nash would have argued that Nash stockholders got a vastly superior management team headed by George Mason and with it, the likelihood of much better future earnings and dividends.[58]

Soon after the merger, the Kelvinator side of the business dominated the combined enterprise. The board of directors named in mid-January 1937 included six directors from Kelvinator and eight from Nash. The annual meeting of Nash-Kelvinator stockholders in late February 1937 elected a smaller board of seven directors, with five coming from Kelvinator and only two, including Charles Nash, from Nash Motors. Less than a year later, in January 1938, most department heads of the Nash Motors division of Nash-Kelvinator, except manufacturing executives, moved to the Nash-Kelvinator offices in Detroit. George Mason would run the company from Detroit, as he had intended.[59]

Charles W. Nash served as chairman of the board of the Nash-Kelvinator Corporation until his death on 6 June 1948, but essentially withdrew from company business in early 1937 and retired to his Beverly Hills home. Charles and Jessie Nash had lived in Beverly Hills since 1933, in part to be close to their daughter Mae, who lived in Los Angeles. Starting in the early 1940s, Charles Nash stayed in California. Jessie Hallock Nash, his wife of sixty-three years, died in Beverly Hills in mid-August 1947 at age eighty-three. Charles Nash died ten months later at his home in Beverly Hills, at age eighty-four, from heart disease that had worsened following the death of his wife. His estate went mainly to his two surviving daughters, with Mrs. Ruth N. Bliss of Grosse Pointe, Michigan receiving three-quarters of the estate and Mrs. Mae N. Brenton of Beverly Hills the remaining one-quarter. His third daughter, Mrs. Lena Wilson, had died in 1944 in Kenosha.[60] Putting Charles Nash in historical perspective and understanding his personality and character is difficult because of the lack of surviving personal or family papers.

Charles W. Nash in Historical Perspective

Most of Charles Nash's life was spent in the production of carriages and automobiles. His accomplishments are especially remarkable given his impoverished rural background and lack of formal education. After spending the first twenty-seven years of his life in various occupations in rural Genesee County, Michigan, Nash then worked for nearly two decades (1891–1910) for the Flint Road Cart Company and the Durant-Dort Carriage Company. He entered the automobile industry at a top position at Buick in 1910 at age forty-six. (Henry Ford was forty when he launched the Ford Motor Company in 1903 and John Dodge was fifty when he produced the first Dodge Brothers car.) Nash was forty-eight when he became president of General Motors and was fifty-two when he launched Nash Motors.

Charles Nash managed established companies rather than building his own business from scratch. This is not to diminish his accomplishments, but the Durant-Dort Carriage Company, Buick Motor Company, General Motors, and the Thomas B. Jeffery Company were all well-established concerns when Nash took over their management. Charles Nash was an outstanding manager, especially in manufacturing, rather than an inventive genius. For the most part, the automobiles produced during his twenty years at the helm of Nash Motors were not particularly innovative or path-breaking in terms of engineering or design.

In most respects, Charles Nash's attitudes, beliefs, and lifestyle were all the result of his challenging and impoverished childhood. He worked long hours, took few vacations, and enjoyed modest pleasures like fishing, hunting, and golf. He traveled extensively in Europe in July and August 1910, probably the first substantial vacation in his life. An article in *Automobile Topics* described an Alaskan hunting trip (grizzly bears) extending from mid-August to early October 1924. He also enjoyed shorter vacation trips to fish. In October 1922, while fishing off the coast of Maine, he caught a halibut measuring 6 feet 9 inches long. A July 1930 photograph showed Nash with a 6 1/2-pound walleye pike caught in Minnesota.[61]

His lifestyle was modest for a multimillionaire of that era. He bought Charles Jeffery's large house on Durkee (now Third) in Kenosha, kept a summer home in Minitowish, Wisconsin, and owned a houseboat, *The Summer Girl*, in the Florida Keys. Considering his great wealth, Nash maintained a small staff for his Kenosha mansion—one maid, a cook, a chauffeur, and a handyman. He did not entertain very much and preferred quiet evenings at home with his wife and three daughters. He played golf at the Kenosha Country Club but was not active in the many clubs of the day other than the Elks Club.[62]

Nash generally had little interest in politics, although he was a rock-solid conservative Republican. He left local politics to Walter Alford, who served as president of the Kenosha City Council in the 1920s. Following the death of Alford's son and four other teenagers in a train accident on the grade-level railroad tracks in Kenosha, Nash pushed the Chicago and Northwestern Railroad to elevate its tracks through Kenosha. His position as a director of the railroad gave him enough influence to make this happen.[63]

Nash also suffered from some of the disadvantages of wealth and fame. In December 1925 a blackmailer threatened to kill Nash if he did not pay him $10,000 in cash, to be left in a shoebox at a particular spot. The police arrested the blackmailer when he attempted to retrieve the (empty) box. *Automobile Topics* reported Nash's appendectomy in May 1926 and observed that the doctors in Kenosha "were more successful in getting something out of C. W. Nash . . . than the Wall Street bears had been on the preceding day."[64]

Visitors to Charles Nash's office and factory in Kenosha noticed his lack of pretension. After Norman Shidle visited Nash in 1925, he described Nash's barebones office, with no rug on the floor, a simple oak desk, and a few snapshots of family, friends, and fishing trips adorning the walls. He did, however, have a red light near his desk, connected to the assembly line in the factory. Any stoppage would trigger the light and Nash would go into the plant to investigate. A few years earlier, W. A. P. John noted that Nash ate his lunch at the company's self-serve cafeteria, picking up his tray and food and taking any empty seat available. Once, while Nash's distributors waited for his appearance at a meeting, Charles Nash gave his undivided attention to his granddaughter, who had just returned from Milwaukee and insisted on sharing all the details of her trip with her grandfather. He obliged and kept the distributors waiting until she was finished.[65]

In addition to his "benevolent paternalism" toward his workers, Charles Nash donated generously to charities focusing on youth. He made several large gifts to the Boy Scouts, including a gift of seventy acres of land at Dyer Lake, Wisconsin, in Kenosha County, for a scout camp (Camp Oh-De-Ko-Ta). His largest single charitable contribution was a matching gift of $400,000 to the Kenosha Youth Foundation in 1930 for their building on Library Square, now the Kenosha YMCA. When the foundation faced tough financial straits in 1935, Nash made an additional gift of $35,000. In 1947, toward the end of his life, Nash gave Boys' Town in Nebraska a gift of $200,000 to build a Charles Nash Memorial Trade School.[66]

Charles Nash was generous and considerate on a personal level as well. At Nash's testimonial dinner in Flint in 1912, W. W. Mountain related a story that spoke volumes about Nash's personality. He had gone with Nash and ten others on a hunting trip and Nash did most of the cooking for the entire group. They did a good deal of hiking and when they were finally on the train bound for home, Nash applied liniment he had bought on their sore muscles. Years later, Charles Stewart Mott recalled joining Nash on a bird-hunting trip north of Bay City, Michigan. They had hired a guide, who seemed preoccupied about something, and Nash discovered that the guide's fourteen-year-old daughter had been experiencing pain in her side. Nash thought this might be something serious, drove the guide to his house, and examined the daughter. He arranged for the Pere Marquette Railroad train to make a special stop so that the guide and his daughter could get to Bay City. An ambulance and doctor met them at the train station, all arranged by Nash, and they went immediately to the hospital. Doctors removed the girl's appendix before it burst, thanks to Nash's intervention.[67]

Charles Nash's death brought the expected accolades from friends, acquaintances, and the editorial pages. In examining his life, the *Detroit News* noted, "His course throughout was marked by integrity of character and purpose and solidity of achievement. And, as is usual in the world of doing and making, his own qualities showed up in the things to which he put his hand. His life, which ended Sunday, was an American story which, however typical and familiar, has never palled or lost its power to stimulate and inspire. It will be a sad day for the United States when it does."[68]

FOUR

The Nash-Kelvinator Corporation under George W. Mason, 1936–54

> It will be Nash's answer to the demand from a sizable number of
> motorists for a car that will provide maximum operating economy
> without sacrifice of the essentials of driving comfort which American
> car owners have come to expect in the automobiles they drive.
>
> George W. Mason, announcing the March 1954
> introduction of the Nash Metropolitan
> to the Nash-Kelvinator stockholders

The George W. Mason era began with the merger of Nash and Kelvinator in 1937 and ended shortly after the merger of the Nash-Kelvinator Corporation with the Hudson Motor Car Company in May 1954 to form American Motors. Mason died suddenly in early October 1954 at age sixty-three. His executive vice president, George W. Romney, immediately succeeded him as president. In one sense, we could call this chapter in the life of Nash Motors "the story of the two Georges." More important, it is the story of two mergers, the first forced by Mason as a condition for running Nash Motors and the second engineered by Mason to ensure Nash's survival in an increasingly competitive American automobile industry.

Both mergers were successful over the long run. Kelvinator's superior management team enabled Nash Motors to survive and prosper. The marriage of Nash-Kelvinator with Hudson was a difficult one initially, and one that George Mason was not able to direct because of his death. Instead, George Romney, Mason's handpicked successor, led the new company. In time, American Motors developed market strategies that allowed it to survive and sometimes prosper as an independent automaker until it was bought by the Chrysler Corporation in 1987. The transfer of personnel and practices from American Motors to Chrysler reinvigorated the latter in the 1990s.

End of the Depression Era, 1937–41

Nash-Kelvinator suffered through the national economy's "roller-coaster ride" of the late Depression years along with all the other automakers and electric appliance manufacturers. Table 4.1 illustrates the enormous changes in sales and profits during the five years leading to conversion to wartime production. In 1937, Nash enjoyed the largest production volume (85,887) since 1929 and the largest profits since 1931, but production fell by half in 1938 and losses reached all-time record levels of $7.6 million. Performance rebounded in 1939 and 1940, and then output soared to 89,574 units in 1941, the largest production since 1929. Conversion

Table 4.1. Nash-Kelvinator Automobile Production and Profits or Losses ( ), Net of Taxes ($ Millions), Year Ending 30 September 1937–53

	Production	Net Profits ($ Millions)
1937	85,887	3.6
1938	41,151	(7.6)
1939	60,348	(1.6)
1940	53,718	1.5
1941	89,574	4.6
1942	5,428	3.8
1943	–	4.1
1944	–	3.0
1945	6,148	2.5
1946	72,821	2.6
1947	115,914	18.1
1948	119,862	20.1
1949	139,521	26.2
1950	178,826	28.8
1951	177,613	16.6
1952	137,587	12.6
1953	166,918	14.1

Source: Nash-Kelvinator Corporation Annual Reports, 1937–53, NAHC.

to war production was well underway by late January 1942 and Nash-Kelvinator entered an entirely new era. Nash introduced small and large innovations alike in its car lines before the end of peacetime production. The 1938 models offered a system of "conditioned air" (not air conditioning) by which heated air circulated within the passenger compartment, regulated by a thermostatic control that the company dubbed "the Nash Weather Eye." Filtered outside air filled the passenger compartment, regulated to keep a steady temperature inside. The company's annual report claimed that this was a joint development by the Kelvinator and Nash engineers.[1]

Starting with the 1936 Nash and LaFayette models, customers could get "sleeping car accommodations" as an option, suggesting that owners who camped would find this an attractive feature. The rear seats and trunk area converted into a double bed for sleeping, while passengers could move their luggage into the front seat for overnight storage. An advertisement for the 1940 Nash proclaimed, "Every Nash Sedan Can Be Made into a Sleeper, with Plenty of Room for a Couple of Six-Footers." The conversion kit included screens that fit into the window openings and allowed insect-free fresh air into the sleeping area. They still offered this feature on Nash models through 1957, but starting in 1949 they used a different configuration than earlier versions. The twin beds no longer occupied the trunk area but used the front seat area instead. The front seats could be moved forward and laid flat.[2]

With the growing popularity of the automobile in the early twentieth century, Americans embraced automobile camping as an attractive vacation alternative to the established railroads and hotels, which were expensive and rigid compared to the automobile. Many automobilists modified their cars, predominantly Model T Fords, by attaching tents and tarps to provide sleeping accommodations. Others built homemade "camper" bodies, altered the seats to produce beds, or inserted a bed or cot over the existing seats. Inventors of all descriptions patented various beds for use in automobiles. The timing of Nash's first "car bed" as an accessory in 1936 seems peculiar because auto camping was in decline starting in the late 1920s, replaced by more comfortable tourist cabins and early motels.[3]

Nash-Kelvinator began planning for a low-priced entry into the market right after the merger was consummated in January 1937. The result was the Ambassador 600, introduced in October 1940 as a 1941 model. The company committed $7 million for design and engineering, plant expansion, and tooling for the new model. This was an innovative car, particularly in the low-price field. It featured "unit-body" or "unitized" body/frame construction, much like the Chrysler Airflow models, but in the low-priced field. Four-wheel coil springs provided a comfortable ride and a new L-head six-cylinder engine provided fuel economy ranging from 25 to 30 miles per gallon. The name "600" came from the driving distance (600 miles) the car delivered

1941 Nash 600. *Courtesy DCHC.*

on a single tank of gasoline. Prices ranged from $731 for a three-passenger coupe to $1,215 for a two-door cabriolet. The 600 series jump-started Nash's sales, which reached nearly 90,000 for 1941, the last "normal" year for car production.[4]

The 600 line was competitive price-wise with the other low-priced nameplates. Ford's least expensive offering for 1941 had a price of $600. Plymouth prices ranged from $685 (two-door business coupe) to $1,120 (seven-passenger, four-door limousine), but most Plymouth models sold for less than $850. Chevrolet's offerings ranged in price from $712 (two-door business coupe) to $995 (four-door, eight-passenger station wagon). The addition of the 600 line meant that Nash could compete in the price ranges that represent 93 percent of the automotive market. The company offered two other automobile lines, the Ambassador Eight and the Ambassador Six.[5]

Nash-Kelvinator enjoyed relative labor peace at its Nash plants throughout the tumultuous year of 1937, mainly because the Nash Corporation had signed contracts with its unions in 1933 and 1934. Negotiations for a new contract had begun on 17 November 1937, but stopped in February 1938 over the issue of a minimum work week for Nash workers. Union-management relations remained contentious through 1938 and 1939. The union began another strike on 1 October 1939, demanding a new contract to replace the one that had expired in late 1937. The UAW remained on strike until 24 October, when they agreed to a new contract. Nash faced what the company called "the largest backlog of dealer orders since 1929," giving the company an enormous incentive to settle.[6]

The introduction of the 1940 models brought the usual sales enthusiasm at Nash Motors. The company held the biggest drive-away of new Nash cars in the company's history on 29 August 1939, when dealers picked up and drove away 2,615 cars from the Kenosha factory. The dealers, who had attended a convention in Chicago, boarded special trains that deposited them at the Kenosha factory, where the company treated them to lunch before the dealers drove away their new Nashes. In anticipation of greatly increased sales in 1941 because of the low-priced Nash 600 series, the company announced in June 1940 that it was in the midst of a $6.5 million expansion program at its Kenosha and Milwaukee factories. Production in 1941 exceeded the 1937 performance, which had been the best since 1929. Unfortunately for Nash Motors, the coming of the war ended this promising revival in sales.[7]

Nash-Kelvinator profits for the year ending 30 September 1941 stood at a healthy $4,617,052, the highest since the merger. The company's accounts do not break down profits by division, but outside observers believed that most of the profits came from the Kelvinator side of the business rather than from the Nash side. To be sure, Nash sales had increased about 50 percent between 1939 (60,348 units) and 1941 (89,574 units), but Kelvinator sales quadrupled over the same period. Nash-Kelvinator vice president Harold Perkins told *Fortune* that for the Nash division to equal Kelvinator's profits in 1941, it would have needed to sell about 150,000 automobiles.[8]

Nash-Kelvinator at War, 1941–45

Much like the other American automakers, Nash-Kelvinator began gearing up for war production well before the declaration of war in December 1941 and well before the last Nash passenger car came off the assembly line in Kenosha in late January 1942. The company's record of war production was distinct from that of the other major automakers in that it made very little in war goods even vaguely related to automobile production. Instead, Nash-Kelvinator focused more on aircraft component production than any other automaker. By the end of the war, the company produced more than 158,000 Hamilton Standard hydromatic variable pitch propellers, along with large quantities of spare propeller blades, propeller governors, and propeller feathering accessories. Among the automakers, Nash-Kelvinator had the smallest production of Pratt & Whitney 2,000-horsepower aircraft engines, turning out nearly 17,000. Nash-Kelvinator also manufactured Sikorsky helicopters for the Army Air Force.

In addition, the company made more than 650,000 bomb fuses, 204,000 rocket motors, and other miscellaneous products. Nash-Kelvinator and their subsidiary Ranco supplied more than 200,000 binoculars and binocular cases to the govern-

The last Nash built during World War II (January 1942). *Courtesy DCHC.*

ment. The company manufactured components and parts such as machined carbu-retor castings used by other manufacturers involved in engine manufacturing. They made some components for jeeps and tanks, but this was not a substantial part of their operations. By the end of the war, Nash-Kelvinator had signed cost-plus-fixed-fee contracts to make war products estimated to cost $1,109,455,421, but delivered the war goods to the government for an actual cost of $668,422,304. In contrast, the Chrysler Corporation's defense contracts amounted to $3,518,229,000, more than five times those of Nash-Kelvinator.[9]

Two disparate war products—cargo trailers and flying boats—deserve brief mention. The U.S. Army awarded Nash-Kelvinator its first defense contract on 30 December 1940 for 15,000 one-ton, two-wheel cargo trailers. The company made these at its Racine plant, where production started in mid-March 1941, with the first shipments in April. The army awarded three additional contracts and by the end of production in August 1942, Nash-Kelvinator produced 44,628 trailers at a cost of about $220 each and $456,000 in trailer parts. The total payments under this contract ($10,351,216) were a tiny part of the company's war work.[10]

The navy contract with Nash-Kelvinator to build "flying boats" illustrates the dif-ficulties of wartime production planning. On 3 February 1942, the navy informally placed an order for 112 flying boats with Nash-Kelvinator, with the official contract, worth nearly $68.5 million, signed on 18 August 1942. The aircraft would be 75 feet long, with a wingspan of 124 feet, powered by four 1,250-horsepower engines, and would have a cruising range of 4,000 miles. The navy selected a site on Lake Pontchartrain in New Orleans for final assembly. Nash-Kelvinator would build the wing sections in Grand Rapids and the hull in Milwaukee, and then ship the parts to New Orleans. Delivery of the first flying boats was expected before 1 May 1943. The navy suddenly canceled the contract in late November 1942 after deciding to convert existing flying boats into cargo carriers. The navy reimbursed Nash-Kelvinator for the costs it had incurred ($4.7 million) and shifted the machinery and facilities to other uses.[11]

Nash-Kelvinator's two principal war products—Hamilton Standard propellers and Pratt & Whitney aircraft engines—made substantial contributions to the war effort. In March 1941, the Office of Production Management asked Nash-Kelvinator to build 1,500 Hamilton Standard hydromatic variable pitch propellers per month. The automaker would build these under license from the Hamilton Standard Propeller Division of United Aircraft Corporation using government-supplied equipment. Nash-Kelvinator representatives visited the Hamilton Standard factory in Hartford, Connecticut, in April to see production firsthand.[12]

The federal Office of Production Management announced on 19 May 1941 that Nash-Kelvinator would build the propeller assemblies at the former REO Motor Car Company plant on Cedar Street in Lansing, Michigan. The Army Air Force awarded three contracts to Nash-Kelvinator in 1941 and 1943. As was usually the case with supply contracts, the Army Air Force extended and amended the contracts several times through the end of the war.[13]

Nash-Kelvinator put the first pilot line into operation at the Cedar Street plant in January 1942 and finished the first propeller to be accepted by the government in February. Production then jumped quickly to 135 units in March and 700 in May. The Lansing plant achieved a major milestone in June 1942. It sent two of its propellers, each with more than 1,000 parts, to the Hamilton Standard plant in Hartford to be disassembled, with their parts intermixed with those from two Hartford-produced propellers. There, workers randomly reassembled parts to make four propellers and all the parts fit perfectly.[14]

Nash used a second plant in Lansing, the former REO Motor Car Company truck plant on Mt. Hope Avenue, to make blades and for final assembly, while building the hubs at the Cedar Street plant. In September 1943, the Lansing propeller plants received the Army-Navy "E" production award. Peak monthly production came in October 1943, when Nash-Kelvinator assembled 7,015 complete propellers, making the firm the largest propeller manufacturer in the world for that month, exceeding even Hamilton Standard. The company later agreed in March 1944 to make 8,564 four-blade propellers for the Corsair Navy fighter and the A-26 Invader

Hamilton Standard propeller production, Lansing, Michigan (1944). *Courtesy DCHC.*

fighter-bomber. The firm delivered the first four-blade propellers in September 1944 and completed 4,972 by war's end.[15]

Nash-Kelvinator's propeller manufacturing operations were impressive by any measure. By the end of the war, Nash completed 158,134 propeller assemblies, along with 85,656 spare blades. The automaker was in second place in terms of total output behind only Hamilton Standard (233,021 propellers) and slightly ahead of Curtiss-Wright (144,861). Three additional licensees produced another 159,753 propellers, for a grand total of 695,771 American-made propellers. More than twenty-five types of American and British aircraft used them, including the B-17, B-24, and B-29 bombers.

The second major war project of Nash-Kelvinator was the production of the Pratt & Whitney R-2800 aircraft engine, a radial design with two rows of nine cylinders each, a total cylinder displacement of 2,800 cubic inches, and a two-stage supercharger. The engine developed 2,000 brake horsepower for takeoff. This enormous air-cooled engine was nearly five feet in diameter. Pratt & Whitney, a division of United Aircraft Corporation of Hartford, Connecticut, initially asked Nash-Kelvinator in early 1941 to make components for aircraft engines, but not the complete engine. In March, the automaker sent some of its engineers to Hartford to observe production and by July had leased the REO Motor Car Company truck plant on Mt. Hope Avenue in Lansing, Michigan, to use for producing engine parts.

Pratt & Whitney R-2800
aircraft engine,
Kenosha, Wisconsin.
Courtesy DCHC.

Nash-Kelvinator began production in Lansing later in 1941, but the government inked a new agreement with Nash-Kelvinator on 12 February 1942, making the automaker a prime contractor for Pratt & Whitney engines for the navy. The first contract called for production of 350 engines a month using an enlarged plant in Lansing. The government soon called on Nash-Kelvinator to increase engine production to 700 a month and simultaneously increase propeller output, creating a huge shortage of factory space in Lansing. The solution was to turn over all the Lansing factory space to propellers and to shift the manufacturing of aircraft engines to Kenosha. By early March 1942, Nash-Kelvinator moved machinery from Lansing to Kenosha and began buying additional equipment.[16]

On 9 April 1942, the Defense Plant Corporation agreed to build a new engine factory in Kenosha on a ten-acre parcel that had served as the Nash athletic fields. The factory building of 204,800 square feet included twenty-four production test cells and one dynamometer cell. Work began on the new plant on 1 April 1942 and production started on 1 July. The engine plant cost the government $5.2 million for the buildings and $26.2 million for the machinery and equipment, including engine test equipment, for a total of $31.4 million. The navy reached an agreement with Nash-Kelvinator on 25 May 1942 for the production of 1,500 engines and spare parts, with 870 engines going to the navy and 630 to the British government. Corsair fighter planes used these engines, all Model R-2800-8s. Nash-Kelvinator shipped its first five aircraft engines on 29 December 1942, only nine months after work began on the factory.[17]

In March 1943, the government asked the corporation to increase engine production from 700 units per month to 900 per month. Construction of ten additional engine test cells, one flight test cell, and one dynamometer cell began in September 1943. The buildings were ready in January 1944 and additional equipment in place by 1 March 1944, at a total cost of $2.6 million. Nash-Kelvinator achieved its peak production of aircraft engines in June 1944, turning out 901. Peak employment on aircraft engines reached 11,500, including workers in Kenosha and Milwaukee. Before the war, the Kenosha plant employed only fifteen women, but during the war, average total employment was 9,215, including 2,353 women, more than one quarter of the total.[18]

One of the most demanding parts of aircraft engine production was the inspection process. They inspected nearly every individual part, roughly fifteen million parts every month. The exhaustive inspection process required the use of 70,000 gauges to check the dimensions on all parts at the machines making the parts. The company maintained a staff that in turn checked the dimensions of the close-limit gauges twice a week and the other gauges every two weeks. When production reached 800 engines per month, the inspection department had 1,050 employees—475 male inspectors, 425 female inspectors, 60 foremen and supervisors, and 90 clerks.[19]

Nash-Kelvinator manufactured the B series (Double Wasp) version of the Pratt & Whitney R-2800 series engine. In early 1944, the government planned to move production of the more advanced C series engines from Pratt & Whitney's Hartford plant to Kenosha to free Pratt & Whitney to produce an even more advanced E series engine at Hartford. The government issued letters of intent to Nash-Kelvinator on 2 May and 30 June 1944 for 2,550 of these C-type engines, but then canceled the plans in mid-October. By the end of the war, Nash-Kelvinator produced three versions of the B series engines: the R-2800-8, used in the Vought-Sikorsky Corsair; the R-2800-10, installed in the Grumman Hellcat; and the R-2800-65, used in the twin engine P-61 Black Widow night fighter.

As the company perfected its use of mass production techniques in making the engines, costs fell substantially. The estimated cost per engine in the first contract (May 1942) was $26,600, but by the spring of 1945 the actual cost to the government was only $13,483 per engine. Nash-Kelvinator manufactured 16,987 aircraft engines during the war at a cost to the government of $303,919,125, including the company's fixed fee (profit) of 6 percent. Nash had by far the smallest production of the six manufacturers that built Pratt & Whitney engines in the war. Pratt & Whitney led the pack with 130,117 engines, followed by Buick (74,198), Chevrolet (60,766), Ford (57,178), and Packard (54,714).[20]

Nash-Kelvinator also produced helicopters for the Sikorsky Division of United Aircraft Corporation. In early 1943, Sikorsky was producing two models, the R-4 and the R-5, while starting development of a third model, the R-6. The Army Air Force wanted to place an order for the R-6, but Sikorsky was not able to satisfy the demand and instead suggested Nash-Kelvinator as a contractor.

On 28 May 1943, the Army Air Force authorized Nash-Kelvinator to build 800 Model R-6 helicopters. The government would supply the engines. Because of labor shortages in Kenosha and Milwaukee, the Army Air Force specified that helicopter production take place elsewhere. The company made the fuselage in Grand Rapids, but relied on many subcontractors, including Sikorsky, for most of the drivetrain components including the rotor blades. Nash-Kelvinator would complete final assembly at its Detroit plant on Plymouth Road. The formal contract with Nash-Kelvinator came on 28 August 1943 and called for 900 helicopters.[21]

Production was slow in coming, mainly because Sikorsky made countless changes (some 20,000) to the original design, delaying the delivery of drawings for long periods. As a result, Nash-Kelvinator did not test its first production model until mid-September 1944 and did not receive Army Air Force acceptance of its first helicopter

Sikorsky helicopter inspection, Plymouth Road plant, Detroit, 1943. *Courtesy DCHC.*

until 23 October 1944. When the Army Air Force canceled the helicopter contract on 16 August 1945, Nash-Kelvinator had completed 262 helicopters and had 20 more partially finished. The government paid Nash-Kelvinator more than $17 million for its helicopter work.[22]

Nash-Kelvinator was only one of many automotive companies that contributed substantially to aircraft production during World War II. Most automobile companies made components, including engines, which they delivered to aircraft companies such as Boeing or Curtiss-Wright for final assembly. Ford Motor Company was a major exception. It assembled B-24 bombers at its massive Willow Run bomber plant in Ypsilanti, Michigan, and built complete engineless gliders at its Iron Mountain, Michigan, facility. General Motors built complete Grumman Wildcat fighters and Grumman torpedo bombers, but also provided engines used in a dozen other aircraft. Chrysler built more than half of the engines that powered the B-29 bomber, all at its massive Dodge Chicago plant, but also built fuselage sections for the Martin B-26 bomber and nose sections for the B-29. Packard became the main producer of Rolls-Royce aircraft engines.[23]

Serving as a military contractor brought a host of new problems for all of the automakers, including Nash-Kelvinator. Countless design changes for the war goods meant "on the fly" changes in the midst of production. Drastic, unexpected changes in contracts made planning difficult. In most respects, the war contractors became an extension of the government. To guarantee it would have enough working capital to carry out war production, especially if it faced sudden cancellation of contracts in progress, Nash-Kelvinator arranged a $75 million line of credit in September 1943. Under wartime rules, the government guaranteed to repay the consortium of banks giving the credit 90 percent of the amount used.[24]

The company faced only a handful of strikes during the war. In December 1941, the UAW and other unions had signed a "no-strike pledge" for the duration of the war, but they repeatedly ignored the pledge.[25] Nash-Kelvinator endured a two-day strike at its propeller factories in Lansing in early October 1944. Reductions in the propeller contracts brought the layoff of 500 employees at the Mt. Hope plant. The UAW claimed that the company ignored seniority rights as spelled out in their contract and laid off workers with more seniority that those they kept on the job. The Mt. Hope workers refused to work Monday, 2 October, and the Cedar Street factory workers walked off the job the following day, leaving 6,500 idle. The striking workers agreed to return to work Wednesday, but demanded quick War Labor Board action on the layoffs.[26]

Employment levels at Nash-Kelvinator fluctuated widely during the war, reflecting the disruptions of conversion, reconversion, and drastic changes in government contracts. Average employment in 1940 stood at 11,631 but jumped sharply to 13,511 in 1941, reflecting strong sales of the Nash 600 models. The production disruptions of 1942 dropped the employment level to only 9,956, but the workforce rebounded to 16,209 in 1943. Nash-Kelvinator did not reach the record wartime employment of 1944 (23,529) again until 1949. The average number of employees at Nash-Kelvinator then fell to 18,260 in 1945, reflecting the cancellation of government contracts that took place throughout the year.[27]

All of the American automakers, much like Nash-Kelvinator, converted entirely to war work and ceased automobile production by February 1942, but they all tried to maintain high visibility among their future customers. They all emphasized the important war materials they produced and touted their contribution to the war effort and their patriotism. Nash-Kelvinator was no exception. The firm launched an aggressive advertising campaign in national magazines in the fall of 1942 and compiled the advertisements into a booklet, *Looking Ahead with Nash,* which it distributed to its Nash and Kelvinator dealers. One ad, featuring a navy Corsair fighter plane equipped with a Nash-Kelvinator Pratt & Whitney engine, explained, "Up Where Man Has Never Fought Before, Nash-Built Engines Will Blaze a Road to Victory." Another ad, showing a bomber similarly powered by Nash-built engines dropping bombs, carried the title, "Ice Cubes for Japan." A third showing the Vought-Sikorsky Flying Boat in flight proclaimed, "A Refrigerator and an Automobile Go to War!" The hope was that customers would again buy Kelvinator refrigerators and Nash automobiles in quantity when they were available for purchase.[28]

Reconversion and Postwar Struggles

Nash-Kelvinator began planning reconversion to civilian production well before the end of hostilities, but it could not have planned for the unusual conditions it faced in the years following the end of the war. The company began tinkering with its automobile designs in late 1944 and early 1945 to prepare for postwar production. By 1945, the company had completed new proving grounds near Burlington in Racine County, Wisconsin. In late January 1945, Nash-Kelvinator arranged a long-term low interest loan of $16 million with a group of sixteen banks. The company called this a "peace-preparedness loan," supposedly the first of its kind not connected to military production. Nash-Kelvinator needed additional funds for working capital and plant expansion in the postwar era.[29]

Shortly after the end of hostilities, George Mason revealed Nash-Kelvinator's ambitious postwar plans. Automobile production would increase from the prewar level of 89,000 units to a peak of 250,000 in the postwar era. Similarly, appliance production would jump from the prewar level of 500,000 to 1,100,000 units annually. By the end of the 1945 fiscal year, the company had paid back all the loans it had taken out through its $75 million line of credit and was planning to spend $10 million on new plant and equipment for producing automobiles and appliances. The future looked bright. The company resumed Kelvinator and Leonard appliance production within forty-five days after the end of the war and began shipping appliances in early October 1945. The Kenosha plant resumed shipping automobiles at the end of the month.[30]

Fortune predicted that Nash would produce only about 20,000 cars in the first quarter of 1946, a tiny share of the 690,000 that the War Production Board (WPB) authorized for the entire auto industry. All the independent automakers had generous allotments, because the WPB gave the independents 20 percent of the total. *Fortune* reminded its readers that the Big Three would not easily surrender the 90 percent share of the market that they had enjoyed before the war. Packard Motor Car Company would provide competition only to the mid-priced Nash Ambassador, but the remaining independents would be worthy competitors. The Studebaker Corporation, with its Champion line, would be the most direct threat to Nash, while the Hudson Motor Car Company was also a serious competitor. *Fortune* did not predict smooth, easy sailing for Nash in the postwar era.[31]

Getting production underway in the fall of 1945 was predictably difficult because the company needed to build an inventory of parts before attempting continuous assembly. Strikes at supplier plants hampered the effort to resume mass production, so the output of only 6,148 automobiles in 1945 was not surprising, given the circumstances. As early as October 1945, strikes at Nash's supplier plants already delayed production of the 1946 Nash cars by thirty days. Unfortunately, a series of major strikes in the steel and glass industries crippled Nash-Kelvinator and much of American industry extending from October 1945 through late May 1946.

Labor relations at Nash were peaceful during this period. In early March 1946, the UAW agreed to an 18.5 cents per hour wage increase for 8,000 automotive employees retroactive to 11 February that included a nine-cent raise retroactive from 1 October 1945 to 11 February 1946. The disruption of parts supplies, however, frequently crippled Nash production. In the seven months ending in early June 1946, Nash plants shut down eight times because of parts shortages. Still, the company managed to produce nearly 73,000 cars in 1946, an impressive performance considering the circumstances.[32]

Nash-Kelvinator selectively bought additional factory capacity in the aftermath of the war. In late August 1946, the company offered the War Assets Administration $1,033,000 for the aircraft engine plant in Kenosha, but without any machinery.

The government accepted the bid in late October 1946. The company also bought a former defense plant in El Segundo, California, near Los Angeles for $1,652,000 and an assembly plant in Toronto, Ontario, for $750,000. The three new plants respectively provided 365,000 square feet, 456,750 square feet, and 182,000 square feet of new factory space.[33]

George Mason was the dominant force within Nash-Kelvinator during the eighteen years he directed the firm. For many years, the company revealed almost nothing publicly about Mason's compensation. The Nash-Kelvinator stockholders voted on Mason's compensation at their meeting of 4 February 1953 and the proxy statement revealed the details of Mason's employment contract in place since 30 September 1947. The company paid him a base salary of $125,000 per year and provided for profit sharing, under which he received 2 percent of net earnings above 6 percent of the value of the stock, with a maximum set at $175,000 per year. In the year ending 30 September 1952, Mason earned the maximum in profit sharing. The directors extended his contract for another five years beginning 1 October 1952 with the same base salary, but with profit sharing limited to $125,000 per year. He could carry forward amounts above $125,000, however, into the next year. If Mason ceased serving as the general manager of Nash-Kelvinator, but continued as chairman of the board, the corporation would pay him $100,000 per year.[34]

At Mason's insistence, Nash built trucks in the postwar years although the automaker had not done so since 1929. As the war wound down, Nash's engineers began work on a half-ton pickup truck and both one- and two-ton capacity models. Nash

1949 Nash service truck. *Courtesy DCHC.*

started production in November 1947, but most of the trucks built from then until March 1955 were destined for foreign markets. Dubbed the Nash Haul Thrift line, Nash's postwar trucks kept the same design from 1947 through 1955, when production ended. Nash used at least twenty of the larger models as semi-tractors to haul Nash car bodies from the body plant in Milwaukee to the assembly plant in Kenosha. Some probably saw service at the proving grounds in Burlington, Wisconsin, and in the plant yards, but the vast majority went overseas.[35]

Nash also offered its dealers a tow truck, the Nash Haul Thrift service truck, starting in October 1948. The short wheelbase chassis and cab, assembled at Nash's El Segundo plant, carried a price tag of $1,672, while the wrecker body, boom, and additional equipment came from Ashton and cost an additional $1,127. The company sold a total of 545 Nash Haul Thrift trucks in the United States in 1948 and 1949, with nearly all of them equipped as tow trucks for Nash dealers.[36]

The postwar performance of Nash Motors depended on its automobile lines. The introduction of the all-new Airflyte models for 1949 put Nash back into the thick of auto industry competition. The Airflyte 600 and Ambassador series, both with six-cylinder engines, featured unit-body or "unitized" body frames, a one-piece curved windshield, and fully reclining front seatbacks. The public commonly called them "bathtub Nashes" because they resembled upside-down bathtubs. Airflytes came with coil springs on all wheels and improved carburetion, which enabled the 600 to get more than twenty-five miles per gallon on the highway. Nash was the second American automaker to use unit-body designs exclusively, only a year behind Hud-

1949 Nash Airflyte 600. *Courtesy DCHC.*

son. According to Nash-Kelvinator, "the Airflyte series is designed, engineered and built with the 'touch of tomorrow.'"[37]

Nash-Kelvinator introduced the 1950 models of the 600 and Ambassador series in October 1949 and the compact Nash Rambler in March 1950. The firm renamed the 600 the Statesman and gave it a larger engine and a much larger rear window for improved driver vision. The Ambassador also had a larger rear window, but more important, customers could add a General Motors–built Hydramatic transmission as optional equipment. Nash-Kelvinator in turn sold Weather Eye heaters to General Motors.[38]

The Nash Rambler was the first American compact car of the postwar era. The Rambler had a 100-inch wheelbase and weighed 2,400 pounds, 400 pounds less than the 110-inch wheelbase Statesman and 900 pounds less than the Ambassador, which sported a wheelbase of 121 inches. In a significant engineering departure from other Nash models, the Rambler used semi-elliptic leaf springs in the rear (versus coil springs) and Hotchkiss drive. On the convertible version, the sliding top moved along a pair of side rails mounted along the top of the side windows. The Rambler came equipped with the same 82 brake horsepower, six-cylinder engine used in the 1949 600, but its lighter weight brought improved mileage. A stock Nash Rambler completed the American Automobile Association–sponsored Mobilgas Economy Run of 840 miles on 6–7 March 1951 and achieved 31.05 miles per gallon.

1950 Nash Rambler. *Courtesy DCHC.*

Nash built 26,000 Ramblers during the first model year, offering only two versions, a convertible and a station wagon. Customer interest was high and Nash added the Rambler Country Club two-door hardtop coupe for the 1951 model year. The least expensive Rambler for 1951 carried a price tag of $1,673, compared with the Statesman two-door sedan ($1,790) and the Ambassador two-door sedan ($2,137). For the 1951 model year, Nash produced about 80,000 Ramblers and 125,000 standard-size models. Calendar year production for all models in 1951 was 177,613, down about 1,200 units from the previous year.[39]

Nash held its own in terms of ranking among American nameplates in the post-war years. In 1949, for example, Nash produced 142,592 units, tenth among U.S. nameplates, behind Chevrolet, Ford, Plymouth, Buick, Pontiac, Dodge, Oldsmobile, Studebaker (228,402), and Mercury (203,339), but barely ahead of Hudson (142,462). Packard held the fourteenth position, with 104,597 units, while upstart Kaiser-Frazer stood at number sixteen with production of 57,995 units. Over the five years of 1949–53, Nash was in either tenth or eleventh place among American automakers in terms of production.[40]

Nash-Kelvinator struggled in the early 1950s because of the impact of the Korean War on the American economy—materials shortages and the imposition of government control over critical raw materials and prices. The firm generally enjoyed labor peace. Nash-Kelvinator agreed in mid-March 1950 to give its employees pensions, averting a strike. A strike at Borg-Warner, a major supplier to Nash, disrupted automobile production for parts in November and December 1951. Workers at the Nash body plant in Milwaukee walked out briefly in November 1953, a rare exception to the labor peace the company enjoyed.[41]

Rising labor costs squeezed the company and materials costs soared at a time when the government restricted critical raw materials and limited price increases for automobiles. The company claimed that the policies adopted by the federal Office of Price Stabilization (OPS) forced manufacturers to absorb most of their increased costs. Nash-Kelvinator had difficulty getting the supplies of steel, copper, aluminum, and other materials it required for appliances and automobiles, but paid much more for these materials than before. In late December 1950, the company announced a 25 percent reduction in production in January 1951 due to raw materials shortages. Wages increased more than 20 cents per hour over the previous year and the employee pension plan, first implemented in 1951, cost Nash-Kelvinator almost $5.6 million. Profits fell from $28.8 million in 1950 to $16.6 million in 1951 (Table 4.1), although production was virtually unchanged.[42]

Nash's innovative automobile designs did not end with the 1950 Rambler. Nash introduced the Nash-Healey, a two-passenger convertible roadster with a price tag of $4,063, at the Chicago Auto Show in February 1951. The car supposedly was the result of a chance meeting in late 1949 between George Mason and Donald Healey, British sports car manufacturer, on the *Queen Elizabeth* sailing from Europe to the United States. Mason wanted to boost Nash's stodgy image among car buyers and Healey was looking for engines for his sports cars. They agreed to build a hybrid sports car using Nash engines and other mechanical components. They developed a prototype that appeared in European auto shows in 1950 and then began building the car in December 1950 at Donald Healey's factory in Warwick, England.[43]

Healey assembled the first 104 Nash-Healey sports cars at his factory between December 1950 and March 1951. Nash supplied a modified Ambassador six-cylinder engine that developed 125 brake horsepower, the transmission, drivetrain, and the front and rear axles. Healey provided the suspension system and the aluminum body. Italian automobile designer Pinin Farina restyled the Nash-Healey roadster for 1952, making the hand-built bodies at his plant in Turin, Italy, and completing the final assembly there. The new model had a more powerful engine that developed 140 brake horsepower, used a steel body, and had a price tag of $5,868. Farina built 150 Nash-Healey sports cars in 1952, all sold by Nash dealers in the United States. For the 1953 and 1954 model years, a hardtop coupe ($6,399) joined the convertible roadster ($5,909) in the lineup. Production of only 106 units in 1953 and 90 in 1954 reflected the limited appeal of this expensive sports car. Nash-Kelvinator discontinued the Nash-Healey in August 1954 after producing only 506 units.[44]

The Nash-Healey was the first of dozens of joint ventures involving American and

1953 Nash-Healey hardtop coupe.

European automakers that were popular from the 1950s on. These efforts typically used American engines in European sports car bodies and resulted in low-volume, expensive sports cars. Examples include the Ford GT40, the Pantera, and the Sunbeam Tiger, to name a few. They were often the result of egocentric auto executives trying to improve the public image of an otherwise stodgy lineup of cars. Lee Iacocca's ill-fated "Chrysler TC by Maserati" was an effort to boost his company's image by placing a Maserati body on a Chrysler chassis. Chrysler invested nearly $500 million to produce an exotic vehicle with sales of only 7,300 units in 1989–91. These efforts were not at all like the mostly successful joint ventures of recent years to build mainstream popular cars.[45]

Nash left the Rambler unchanged in 1952 but completely overhauled the Statesman and Ambassador series. To celebrate Nash's fiftieth anniversary of automobile production, dating from the first Rambler of 1902, they renamed the two lines "Nash Golden Airflytes." Mason called on Pinin Farina to create the styling for these cars and Nash-Kelvinator used his name in its advertising. The wheelbase of the Statesman increased from 112 inches to 114 1/4 inches and both car lines had new engines with more horsepower. The new models did not generate increased sales, and Nash production fell to 137,587 for 1952 from 177,613 in the prior year.[46]

Pinin Farina's work on the 1952 models is worth recalling. After George Mason viewed several Farina-designed bodies at the Paris Auto Show in October 1949, he asked his executive assistant, George Romney, to visit Farina in Turin and convince the Italian designer to submit designs for the 1952 Nash cars and for the 1952 Nash-Healey. Farina agreed and in February 1950 he and his son-in-law, Renzo Carli, brought preliminary drawings to Detroit. Mason also hired Edmund E. Anderson as Nash's new design director. Anderson, who had served as the studio chief for both Oldsmobile and Chevrolet, arrived at Nash in February 1950, the day Farina left Detroit for Italy. Anderson and his small staff simultaneously developed a second design proposal for the 1952 Nash, but Nash management, including Mason and Romney, did not like either proposal. The top management ordered Anderson and his staff to "fix" the Farina design. The resulting 1952 Nash Golden Airflyte models, although promoted as a Farina design, were really the work of Ed Anderson. As a loyal corporate citizen, Anderson approved the advertising campaign.[47]

The 1952 Golden Airflyte models remained essentially unchanged for the 1953 and 1954 model years. The Nash Rambler was completely restyled for 1953, with a lowered hood, enclosed rear and front fenders, and a reworked grille. The Rambler did not change in any significant way in 1954, except that Nash added a four-door sedan and a four-door station wagon on a 108-inch wheelbase. The other Rambler offerings had the original wheelbase of 100 inches from the time of its introduction.[48]

The newly minted American Motors Corporation, an amalgam of Nash-Kelvinator and the Hudson Motor Car Company, introduced the Metropolitan, the first American economy subcompact car, in March 1954. The sales history of the Metropolitan will be considered in a later chapter of this book, but the conception and design of this innovative model occurred under George Mason's direction at Nash-Kelvinator.

At the end of World War II, Mason pushed for the development of a very small economy car in addition to the Rambler. This was a market segment Nash could develop without fear of competition from the Big Three. Mason guessed that postwar suburbanization would create the two-car family with a more economical compact or subcompact model becoming the second car. In 1948, he hired independent industrial designer William Flajole to submit proposals for a two-seater. The following year, Mason had George Romney conduct customer surveys on small cars based on a preview of the experimental car. Romney held these "sur-views" in dozens of cities. When asked if they preferred an 18-horsepower engine versus a 36-horsepower version, the public voiced an overwhelming preference for the larger engine. The first Metropolitan came with a 42-horsepower engine. Using the frame and engine of a Fiat Topolino as the foundation, Nash built a prototype that eventually became the Metropolitan. Dubbed the "NXI" (Nash Experimental International), Mason displayed the little car at the Waldorf-Astoria Hotel in New York in the winter of 1950. The general reaction of the public seemed favorable and Nash distributed 250,000 questionnaires asking for comments and suggestions about the design.[49]

After Mason presented a prototype of this tiny car, renamed the NK-I (for Nash-Kelvinator-I), to his board of directors in early November 1951, the board authorized him to proceed with the program to bring the car to market, but he soon realized that they could not build this small car economically in the United States. He considered Fiat and Austin as possible European partners and, by late 1953, had settled on the British automaker. The Austin Motor Company would assemble the Metropolitan at its plant in Longbridge, England, using the Austin A40 overhead-valve four-cylinder engine, which developed 42 brake horsepower. Fisher & Ludlow of Birmingham, England, would build the unit bodies and ship them to Longbridge for assembly. Immediately prior to the new car's introduction, Nash-Kelvinator gave it the Metropolitan name, reflecting its appeal to both city and suburban drivers.[50] In his letter to the stockholders in December 1953, George Mason announced the introduction of the Metropolitan in March 1954. He claimed that it would "feature a basically new and American concept of small car design." Mason added, "It will be Nash's answer to the demand from a sizable number of motorists for a car that will provide maximum operating economy without sacrifice of the essentials of driving comfort which American car owners have come to expect in the automobiles they drive."[51]

1954 Nash Metropolitan.

The Nash-Kelvinator Merger with Hudson: The Birth of the American Motors Corporation

In mid-May 1952, the *Detroit News* reported that the Packard Motor Car Company was actively seeking a merger with another automaker and that Packard president James J. Nance had identified Nash-Kelvinator as the desired merger partner. In October 1953, rumors of merger talks between Nash-Kelvinator and the Hudson Motor Car Company started to appear in the newspapers. The two companies officially announced their "consolidation" in mid-January 1954, pending stockholders' approval. They named the combined business the American Motors Corporation.[52]

George Mason had proposed a merger with Packard in 1946 and pursued several merger opportunities in the years that followed. His pursuit of mergers seemed unwarranted, given Nash-Kelvinator's apparent growth and profitability in the postwar years. The company's performance in 1947–53 was good, although not remarkable, but the long-term trends were not encouraging. In the years 1947–50 net profits (on sales) fluctuated between 6.6 percent and 7.2 percent (Table 4.1). This measure of performance fell to 4 percent in 1951 and slipped further to 3 percent in 1953. Nash-Kelvinator announced record sales for 1953 of $478,697,891, but net profits, some $14.1 million, were only half of the 1950 profits.[53]

Pessimistic projections for the near future encouraged George Mason to seek an automotive merger partner and he found one with the Hudson Motor Car Company. The Hudson-Nash merger was part of a larger pattern of automobile industry consolidation and concentration that began in the 1910s. The emergence of the giant Ford Motor Company in the 1910s, the subsequent success of General Motors in the mid-1920s, and the emergence of Chrysler in the late 1920s put the smaller companies at a severe cost disadvantage in competing with the Big Three. By the mid-1930s, General Motors, Ford, and Chrysler captured nearly 90 percent of the American car market. Many independent automobile companies that barely survived the 1930s, such as the Hupp Motor Car Company, chose to leave the industry at the end of World War II.

The major independent car companies (Nash, Hudson, Studebaker, and Packard) performed well during the years following the end of World War II, at least through 1952. In 1941, they held 9 percent of the domestic market, based on new car registrations. Their share jumped to 13.9 percent for 1946, 10.6 percent for 1947, and 12.5 percent in 1948. For 1949, their market share stood at 11.8 percent and then remained above 10 percent between 1950 and 1952. They increased their market share in part because they were more agile in ramping up production after the war. Before the first of the Big Three offered its first all-new postwar model, the 1949 Ford (introduced in late 1948), the leading independent automakers had already done so. They also enjoyed the fruits of the enormous pent-up demand for cars that resulted from the four-year drought of new cars during the war. The independents also benefited from labor peace in the postwar years. In contrast, General Motors suffered a five-month strike beginning in November 1945; Ford had a major strike in 1949; and Chrysler shut its operations for one hundred days in the early part of 1950 because of a strike.[54]

The independent automakers experienced a drastic loss in market share starting in 1953, when the share of new car registrations for the major independents fell to 7.6 percent and then dropped further to 4.4 percent in 1954. Their total sales, which had peaked at 651,000 units in 1950, fell off to 445,000 units in 1952 and then to only 246,000 units in 1954. Combined Nash and Hudson production fell from 228,499 units in 1952 to 95,198 in 1954, while Studebaker and Packard production experienced a slightly less severe decline from 225,518 units in 1952 to 112,855 in 1954.

Several developments combined to produce this "perfect storm" that forced the independent companies to the brink of bankruptcy. In early 1953, the federal government removed the production and price controls it imposed during the Korean War and the Big Three were finally able to use their production capacity. Chevrolet and Ford began a price war in 1953 to increase their share of the market and to achieve the top sales position and continued this price competition in 1954. All the independents suffered. In contrast, combined Ford and Chevrolet output leaped from 1,655,478 cars in 1952 to 2,809,114 units in 1954. Already too small to be efficient compared to the Big Three, the independents became even less competitive with smaller volumes.[55]

All of the independents faced serious cost disadvantages because of their small size. Engineering and design costs, along with tooling costs, had to spread over a smaller volume of production. Lawrence White has argued that sheet steel stamping plants became efficient at a volume of about 400,000 units, well above the production of any of the independents in the early 1950s. Their relatively high production costs were reflected in relatively high prices for their base models. In 1952–54, the lowest price four-door sedan from Ford cost between $1,678 and $1,701, while the list price for a similar Chevrolet ran between $1,670 and $1,680. In contrast, Nash list prices ranged from $2,158 to $2,178 and Hudson was even more expensive, priced between $2,256 and $2,311. With lower volumes, advertising was more expensive per car sold. In 1950, Ford and Plymouth spent $8 in advertising for each car sold and Chevrolet spent $6. Nash spent $19.50 and Hudson spent $24.50 per car sold. Big Three dealerships also sold larger volumes of cars and made more profits than those of the independents. In 1950, the average number of cars sold per dealer, by brand, was the following: Chevrolet (198), Ford (175), Nash (149), and Hudson (75). Finally, the increasingly negative news about the condition of the independent companies starting in 1953 severely hurt sales. Customers worried about being stuck with an "orphan car" whose manufacturer was no longer in business.[56]

The independents all faced similar dilemmas that were largely the result of their small size and lack of capital. They were too small to attempt to sell a full range of products along the lines of General Motors. Packard specialized in luxury cars, but the rest (Studebaker, Hudson, Nash, and Kaiser-Frazer) appealed to the broad, mid-priced market, the most competitive market segment. Kaiser-Frazer failed to raise capital through a 1948 stock sale and could not introduce new models for 1949, which seriously damaged its reputation. Hudson's effort to introduce a compact car, the 1953 Hudson Jet, was a dismal failure.

Except for the 1947 Studebaker and the 1948 Hudson models, none of the independents achieved significant styling breakthroughs either. Because these smaller companies could not afford expensive new features such as V-8 engines and automatic transmissions, they bought them from General Motors. Only Studebaker had its own V-8 by 1953 and Packard followed in 1955. Packard introduced its Ultramatic transmission in 1951, but Nash, Hudson, and Kaiser-Frazer bought Hydramatics from General Motors into the mid-1950s. The automobiles coming from the independent car companies simply became less appealing over time.[57]

Before successfully orchestrating the merger with Hudson, George Mason had proposed several other mergers starting right after World War II. Unlike most of his contemporaries at the helms of the other independent automakers, Mason foresaw the difficulties the independents would encounter merely to survive in the postwar automotive industry. A December 1954 article in *Fortune*, "Last Stand of the Auto Independents?" painted Mason as the lone visionary: "[He] appears to be the only executive among the independents who foresaw clearly what could happen to them in a fully competitive market. He realized that they had been favored by government under the postwar material-controls plans, and that their large percentage of the market was unrealistic. . . . Mason saw the time was coming when 150,000 to 200,000 units would be required to provide the cozy profits obtainable from half that number."[58] The independents belatedly "merged to survive" rather than merging when they were still profitable. The consolidations began in April 1953, when the chronically unprofitable Kaiser-Frazer Corporation bought out the consistently profitable Willys-Overland Company, maker of Jeeps and passenger cars. The merger of Nash and Hudson and the combination of Studebaker and Packard came in 1954, reducing the number of independents from six to three.[59]

Tom Mahoney, George Romney's biographer, has suggested that Mason was more inclined to consider mergers because of his experience with the Nash-Kelvinator marriage. He first approached Hudson and Packard in 1946 and made a more serious detailed proposal to both companies two years later. Mason predicted that the independents would face difficulties once the postwar "sellers' market" was satisfied. The long and often bitter history of competition between the independents and the enormous egos of their executives delayed significant mergers until 1954, too late to help several of them survive long-term.[60]

In summer 1947, George Mason began discussions with James Alvin Macauley, the chairman of the board at Packard and a friend of Mason's since the 1920s. Mason and Macauley offered a merger proposal to the Packard board of directors on 3 February 1948. This would be a takeover, in which they would exchange six shares of Packard stock for a single share of Nash-Kelvinator stock. Macauley would retire and Mason would become the president and chairman of the board of the merged company. Packard's current president, George Christopher, would be out of a job. The Packard directors rejected the proposed merger.[61]

Macauley then tried another strategy to strengthen Packard. He offered George Romney, who was the general manager of the Automobile Manufacturers Association, a position at Packard. He would serve as executive vice president with a salary of $50,000, a seat on the board of directors, and a promise of the presidency within two years. George Mason offered George Romney a position as his special assistant at a lower salary and Romney took a month to decide to work for Nash-Kelvinator. Romney admired Macauley and Mason, but he knew that Macauley would soon leave Packard, which had a deeply divided board of directors. Romney was especially impressed with Mason's serious analysis of the postwar automobile market and Nash's future. Romney seemed content to learn the Nash-Kelvinator operations while serving as Mason's apprentice without the pressures of being in charge.[62]

The prospect of a Nash-Packard merger arose again in May 1952 with the arrival of James J. Nance as Packard's new president and general manager. Nance understood that part of his job was to find a suitable merger partner for Packard. Nance had just left the position of president of Hotpoint, General Electric's home appliance manufacturer, so he had spent years as a competitor of Kelvinator's George Mason. Shortly after Nance's arrival, Packard proposed building V-8 engines for Nash, with Nash providing one-quarter of the capital costs of a new engine plant. Packard also suggested that Nash purchase Packard's Ultramatic transmission. C. Wayne Brownell, a Packard vice president, suggested that Nash and Packard dealers could carry each other's models. The two automakers negotiated unsuccessfully in mid-November 1952 about sharing components. Mason had hoped that Nash would buy V-8 engines from Packard, which in turn would buy rear axles, six-cylinder engines, and perhaps bodies from Nash.[63]

Packard and Studebaker both suffered operating losses in 1953, in contrast to Nash-Kelvinator's profits of $14.1 million. In March 1954, the investment firm of Smith, Barney & Company proposed a merger of all the remaining independents. Nance seriously considered Hudson as a partner for Packard, but his need to be the dominant figure in any new company ruled out Nash-Kelvinator. In February 1954, as the Nash-Hudson merger was consummated, Mason and Romney met with Nance and Packard executives at the Book-Cadillac Hotel in Detroit. They laid out the advantages to Packard of joining the Nash-Hudson combination, but Nance rejected their advances. Packard's choice as a merger partner was Studebaker and by mid-August 1954, the stockholders of both companies approved the merger.[64]

The Nash-Hudson merger happened suddenly and secretly in late 1953 and early 1954 after a long gestation. George Mason had broached the subject of a merger with A. Edward Barit, president of the Hudson Motor Car Company, first in 1946 and again in 1948, but Barit was not interested. Hudson's performance after 1950 deteriorated faster than the other independents. It shipped 143,586 automobiles in 1950, but then saw its shipments fall to 92,859 in 1951 and even further in 1952 to 79,117 units.[65]

At Barit's request, Mason met with him on 16 June 1953 at the Book-Cadillac Hotel in Detroit for a two-hour lunch. They left with an agreement on the essential elements of a merger. Hudson and Nash would become divisions, along with Kelvinator, in a new entity called American Motors. The Hudson and Nash nameplates would both survive the merger. Because the two companies had different accounting systems and different fiscal years, their accountants struggled for six months to decide the value of their assets. Mason and Barit had other details to negotiate as well.[66]

Reports of a possible Nash-Hudson merger appeared in several newspapers in early October 1953, but neither company would comment on the rumors. Barit stated, however, that if such a merger ever happened, the new company would keep the Hudson nameplate. Mason agreed, but then suggested that the two companies could cooperate to the advantage of both, but without a merger. Barit confirmed in early November that the two firms were discussing a merger while Mason rejected as "ridiculous" the claims of some automotive analysts that the independents could not survive unless they merged with other automakers. With rumors of a merger in the air, Mason issued a lengthy statement to the Nash dealers late in 1953 assuring them that Nash-Kelvinator had done very well in the fiscal year ending September 1953 and that any merger that might take place would serve their best interests.[67]

The egos of the top managers were not an issue in the merger because A. Edward Barit, then sixty-four, did not want any active role in the new company and several other top Hudson officials were ready to retire. George Mason would be the chairman of the board and president of American Motors, and Barit would receive a four-year consulting contract. Shares of Nash-Kelvinator stock would be exchanged one-for-one for shares of American Motors, while three shares of Hudson stock were exchanged for two shares of American Motors stock. Ratification of the agreement took place at special meetings of stockholders of both companies held on 24 March 1954. A few Hudson shareholders sued to block the merger, claiming that the directors did not provide vital information about the merger and that the exchange of shares was unfair. The lawsuits went nowhere, and in late April the directors of both companies approved the merger, to take effect 30 April 1954. They offered Hudson shareholders who did not want American Motors stock $9.80 per share. An additional lawsuit challenged that valuation, but eventually court-appointed appraisers set the value at $9.81 a share. The holders of 7 percent of the Hudson shares opted for the cash payments.[68]

George Mason did not live to see the merger fully consummated. He died suddenly on Friday, 8 October 1954, at the age of sixty-three. Mason had returned from a fishing trip in Wyoming the previous Sunday, became ill, and went to Harper Hos-

pital in Detroit. There, he died of a combination of pneumonia and pancreatic failure. His funeral at Christ Church Cranbrook in Bloomfield Hills, Michigan, drew a
throng of seven hundred. Notable automotive leaders present included Henry Ford
II, K. T. Keller, chairman of the board at Chrysler, and James J. Nance, president
of Studebaker-Packard. George W. Romney, executive vice president of American
Motors, delivered the eulogy. Romney said of his mentor: "He gave encouragement
and assurance to all he met, and sought out their best elements. A talk with him
always made people feel better. He never mentioned another person's weaknesses.
He sought not the most out of life, but rather the good and the truth." Romney spoke
of Mason's "common touch" with people of all walks of life. He was always thoughtful and considerate of others, showing genuine concern about their well-being and
for the well-being of their families. Mason was a generous philanthropist, loved
nature, and was a deeply religious Christian. The *Detroit News* added in its editorial,
"Among the giants in the field, Mr. Mason was an archetype of all that is connoted
by 'dynamic.' The last weeks of his life, spent hunting in the West while keeping a
close hand on large and complex affairs, were typical of the strenuous pace he set for
himself." Praise for Mason's energy, kindness, and generosity seemed to flow from all
corners of the automotive industry and from Detroit society.[69]

George Mason was to speak at the annual dinner meeting of the Detroit Round
Table of the National Conference of Christians and Jews in mid-November 1954.
The topic was "Cooperation in American Life." George Romney spoke in place of
Mason and the meeting served as a commemoration of Mason's life and his "contri-
butions to the brotherhood of man."[70]

Among his many interests, George Mason was an avid and expert fly fisherman
who wrote into his will a bequest of 1,450 acres of land to establish a fourteen-mile-
long trout fishing preserve to be left in its natural state. The land, said to be worth
at least $1 million, bordered the South Branch of the Au Sable River in Crawford
County in the northern part of Michigan's Lower Peninsula. He granted the lands
to the State Conservation Department, along with $25,000 to stock the stream with
trout for twenty-five years and another $25,000 to build a rustic chapel on the river.
The state accepted Mason's gift on 1 November 1955 and agreed to keep it permanently as a fish and game preserve.[71]

George Mason also maintained a close, long-term relationship with the University
of Michigan. In June 1950, the University awarded Mason (Class of 1913) an honorary Doctor of Laws degree. His citation read, "In times of national emergency his talents have been directed in important ways toward the production of means to secure
us from foreign aggression; in peaceful days, he has been a builder of that economic
strength which is the foundation of our country's prosperity and security."[72]

Despite George Mason's weight of 250 pounds and his unlimited appetite for cigars, he was an active outdoorsman who loved to hunt and fish. An expert duck hunter, Mason was a founder of Ducks Unlimited, which promoted the preservation of wild ducks. Mason played golf and scored in the 90s. He was also active in Boy Scouts of America's Great Lakes region. His other charitable interests included the Leader Dogs for the Blind, Junior Achievement, and the Detroit United Foundation Torch Drive. Mason was an expert amateur photographer. As a teenager growing up in North Dakota, his first love was motorcycles. He owned dozens and raced them at county fairs and at the dirt tracks in North Dakota. A newspaper reporter who interviewed Mason two months before he died claimed that Mason still rode a motorcycle around the American Motors headquarters in Detroit.[73]

George Mason was a pivotal leader within the independent sector of the mature auto industry from the mid-1930s through the mid-1950s. Today he is unknown outside a few historians of Kelvinator, Nash, or American Motors. No car bore his name. He not only engineered the creation of American Motors but had planned its future as well as anyone could. George Romney quickly succeeded Mason as chairman of the board, president, and general manager of American Motors and continued the consolidation of Nash-Kelvinator and Hudson.

Nash-Kelvinator's merger partner, the Hudson Motor Car Company (1909–54), developed and grew into a formidable independent car company at roughly the same time as Nash Motors and Nash-Kelvinator. The histories of the two firms were parallel only in terms of chronology. They each had distinct leaders, products, and corporate styles. The next two chapters consider the storied history of the Hudson Motor Car Company, and chapters 7–9 will treat the American Motors Corporation (1954–89).

FIVE

The Founding of the Hudson Motor Car Company and the Roy D. Chapin Era, 1909–36

There have been many low priced cars, but never one so big, strong, speedy and good looking as this one. In the Hudson "Twenty" you get the best automobile value ever offered for less than $1000. In this car, you find that something called *class*—that something which other cars at or near this price have lacked.

Advertisement, *Saturday Evening Post*, 19 June 1909

The Hudson Motor Car Company, the automaker that joined with Nash Motors in 1954 to form the American Motors Corporation, had a long and distinct history in Detroit. On 28 October 1908, Detroit department store magnate Joseph L. Hudson (1846–1912) entered a partnership with four young men who wanted to start a new automobile company in what was still a very young automobile industry. The sixty-two-year-old Hudson had operated a clothing store in Detroit since 1881 and he owned the largest and most profitable department store in the city. Hudson invested in this fledgling auto company largely at the urging of Roscoe B. Jackson (1879–1929), who was married to Hudson's niece, Louise Webber. She argued in a letter to the editor of the *Detroit News* a half-century later that Hudson joined this automotive venture simply because he loved her and her husband.[1]

J. L. Hudson was not a novice in the Detroit automobile industry when he invested in the Hudson Motor Car Company. In the summer of 1904 he had invested in the Detroit Auto Vehicle Company and held the post of company vice president. The firm produced a touring car and delivery vehicle starting in the middle of 1905. The Detroit Auto Vehicle Company went bankrupt in October 1907, perhaps leaving Joseph L. Hudson a bit skeptical about this fledgling industry.[2]

Roscoe Jackson had worked at the Olds Motor Works since 1904. There he met four men who would be pivotal players in the foundation of the Hudson Motor Car Company: Roy D. Chapin, Howard E. Coffin, Frederick O. Bezner, and James J. Brady. They were sometimes known as "The Four Horsemen." Except for Coffin, they were all in their twenties when they started the Hudson Motor Car Company. Despite their youth, the four had more automotive industry experience than most others, having worked at the Olds Motor Works since 1901, 1902, 1903, and 1898, respectively. Two additional passive investors were part of this partnership as well—Hugh Chalmers and Lee Counselman.

The Road to Hudson

Three of the young men who founded the Hudson Motor Car Company—Chapin, Coffin, and Jackson—first met as students at the University of Michigan. Howard Coffin's widowed mother ran a boardinghouse serving university students, including Roy D. Chapin and Roscoe Jackson. According to George May, Horace Loomis, an engineer at the Olds Motor Works, took Chapin on a test run in an Oldsmobile on Grand Boulevard in Detroit in April 1901, reaching speeds upward of eighteen miles per hour. Chapin reportedly blurted out, "This is the stuff for me. I'm going to quit school and join up." James J. Brady had already worked for Olds since 1898 and within two years after Chapin's arrival, Howard Coffin, Roscoe Jackson, and Frederick Bezner also landed positions at the Olds Motor Works. The five men remained partners and associates through the start of the Hudson Motor Car Company and beyond.[3]

These ambitious young men came from very different backgrounds. Roy Dikeman Chapin (23 February 1880–16 February 1936) was one of three Chapin children born to Edward Cornelius Chapin and Ella King Chapin. He grew up in Lansing, Michigan, the location of the state capitol and Ransom E. Olds's first automobile company. Edward Chapin was a prominent lawyer who gave his family a comfortable middle-class lifestyle. The future automotive industry leader had contracted pneumonia several times as a child, so his parents prohibited him from playing sports.

He instead developed entrepreneurial abilities as a teenager. Chapin turned an early interest in amateur photography into a profitable business, producing photographs of people and buildings, which he then sold. Chapin sold magazines, established a newspaper for his high school, and became business manager of his high school yearbook. He took on many odd jobs, including working for the U.S. Weather Bureau's Lansing office. He reported early morning temperatures by flying a kite equipped with a thermometer to an elevation of 1,000 feet. Most of his earnings went into buying photographic equipment and supplies.

Roy D. Chapin graduated from high school in June 1897, but waited more than a year before enrolling at the University of Michigan. Meanwhile, he worked full-time for the Weather Bureau. He sought admission to Michigan in the fall of 1898 and in February 1899 finally enrolled as a student. Chapin became a member of the Phi Delta Theta fraternity and in the fall of 1899 took the position of steward (business manager) for the fraternity house. He quickly made the near-bankrupt fraternity solvent again.[4]

Howard Earle Coffin (6 September 1873–21 November 1937) was born in West Milton, Ohio, the son of Julius Coffin and Sarah Jones Coffin, who had emigrated from England. His widowed mother moved the family to Ann Arbor, Michigan, where she managed a boardinghouse. Coffin graduated from public high school and studied engineering at the University of Michigan from 1893 to 1896. Lack of money forced him to leave the university and take a part-time job at the U.S. Postal Service in Ann Arbor. Before returning to the university, Coffin built his first gasoline-powered automobile in 1897 and a steam-powered car the following year. Howard Coffin returned to the University of Michigan in 1900 and earned a degree in mechanical engineering in 1902. He became chief experimental engineer for the Olds Motor Works in 1902 and served as chief engineer from May 1905 to April 1906, when he left Olds along with the others.[5]

James J. Brady (3 May 1878–15 June 1925) easily had the most impoverished background of any of the Hudson founders. He was one of seven children born to Francis J. Brady (a botanist and horticulturalist) and Isabelle Dunn Brady, who died when James was young. Francis Brady married Mary Ann Dunn, the younger sister of his first wife and had six additional children with her. James Brady was forced to quit school at age seven and earned a meager living selling newspapers. He also worked as a telegraph operator and in a printing shop before taking a job with Ransom Olds in 1898. Ransom Olds had not selected a name for his new automobile and offered a $5 prize for the winning name. In late 1900, James Brady coined the name "Oldsmobile" and won the prize. Brady was working as a timekeeper at the Olds Motor Works in Detroit when a disastrous fire destroyed the entire factory complex on 9 March 1901. He saved one Oldsmobile prototype from the burning buildings—the famous Oldsmobile runabout. Around 1902, Brady became traffic manager at the Olds Motor Works, in charge of coordinating the movement of materials to the factory.[6]

Frederick O. Bezner (3 September 1879–18 October 1951) was born in Jerseyville, Illinois, the son of Frederick K. Bezner and Anna Marie Prediger Bezner. He graduated from Jerseyville High School and earned a degree from the Chicago Business College. Bezner first worked as a stenographer for the Goodrich Transportation

Company of Chicago in 1898–1900; as a "city buyer" for the National Cash Register Company in Dayton, Ohio (1900–1902); and as the assistant purchasing agent for the Detroit Copper and Brass Rolling Mills (1902–3). The Olds Motor Works hired Bezner in 1903 as its assistant purchasing agent. He served in that post until 1905 and then as purchasing agent until 1906, when he left the company.[7]

Roscoe B. Jackson (30 January 1879–19 March 1929) was born in Ionia, Michigan, the son of Andrew J. and Francis Bradbury Jackson. Educated in the Ionia public schools, Jackson earned a degree in mechanical engineering from the University of Michigan in 1902. He joined the Olds Motor Works in 1904 as the assistant plant manager, became the assistant general manager in 1905, and in 1906–7 served as the plant manager. Jackson then held the position of general manager for the E. R. Thomas Company in Buffalo, New York, in 1908. In September 1908 Jackson married Louise A. Webber, the niece of Joseph L. Hudson, and returned to Detroit in search of a new position.[8]

All five men who came to work together at the Olds Motor Works in Detroit— Roy Chapin, Howard Coffin, James Brady, Frederick Bezner, and Roscoe Jackson— played significant roles in the events that eventually led to the formation of the Hudson Motor Car Company in October 1908. From the beginning, however, Roy Chapin was the charismatic leader of the group.

An article that appeared in *Forbes* in 1924 provided details of Chapin's early days at the Olds Motor Works not found elsewhere. According to author O. D. Foster, Roy Chapin appeared at Ransom Olds's office shortly after riding in the curved-dash Olds, desperately wanting a job, and Olds reluctantly agreed to hire him as a "demonstrator" (test driver) at $35 a month. Roy Chapin was one of the dozens of new employees Ransom Olds hired while trying to launch his 1901 models in the wake of the disastrous fire of March 1901. Chapin's photographic skills may have helped him land this job. He took photographs of factory operations, car parts, and finished cars, and many of his photographs appeared in the earliest catalogs and advertisements. During a month-long strike that commenced on 20 May 1901, Roy Chapin learned to operate much of the machinery in the Detroit factory. He achieved notoriety by driving a curved-dash Olds from Detroit to New York City via Canada starting on 27 October and arriving in New York on 5 November. The company intended the trip to serve as a promotional stunt to show the reliability of the Oldsmobile. Chapin reached New York in the middle of the New York Automobile Show and sent the following telegram back to Detroit: "Arrived here at eleven in good order total distance eight hundred twenty miles time seven one half days average 14 miles per hour used 30 gallons gasoline 80 gallons water." This durability run helped generate a flood of orders for Oldsmobile.[9]

Roy D. Chapin at the wheel of an Oldsmobile during the trip from
Detroit to New York City, November 1901. *Courtesy NAHC.*

Olds gave Roy Chapin responsibility for the "repairs department" (service department) sometime in 1902. He then worked increasingly on sales and officially became
sales manager at Olds in 1904. Frederic Smith, who took charge of the Detroit plant
in 1902, gave Chapin increasing control over sales operations. Chapin established
regional franchises for Oldsmobile and was personally involved in interviewing dealer
prospects all around the country. Roy's mother wrote to Frederic Smith expressing
concern that he was giving Roy too many responsibilities and too much work for
too little pay, possibly threatening his health. Smith assured Mrs. Chapin that he
viewed Roy as the brightest and most promising of all the young managers at Olds
and admitted that Roy's pay did not reflect his value to the Olds Motor Works.[10]

By 1903, Ransom E. Olds lost most of his power in the company he had founded
to the Smiths and in the summer of 1904 resigned from the board of directors and
sold his stock in the Olds Motor Works. Olds had given up majority control of his firm
in May 1899, when Samuel L. Smith, a Michigan copper baron, became the majority
stockholder in the Olds Engine Works by investing $200,000 in the venture. Smith
moved the company headquarters to Detroit and built the first automobile plant in
the city. He wanted his sons Frederic and Angus to gain executive experience in a
manufacturing enterprise. Olds clashed with the Smith sons over the product line,
with Olds favoring the inexpensive Olds runabout, while the Smiths preferred larger

luxury models for the rich man's market. The changing product line of the company also distressed Roy Chapin and his partners at the Olds Motor Works, prompting them to leave the firm less than two years after the departure of Ransom Olds.[11]

For these ambitious young men at the Olds Motor Works, the departure of Ransom Olds severely limited their opportunities for future advancement within the company. The Smiths began shifting operations to Lansing following the 1901 fire and forced the executive staff, including Chapin, to move there in 1905, limiting their chances of finding employment elsewhere in the Detroit auto industry.[12]

The Olds Motor Works sold the world-famous Oldsmobile runabout, also known as the curved-dash Olds, from 1901 through 1907 at the base price of $650. Starting in 1904, the firm also offered a touring runabout ($750) and a light tonneau ($950), but in 1905 added a heavy touring car priced at $2,000. When Oldsmobile phased out the runabout and tonneau in 1906, the Palace touring car ($2,250) accounted for most Oldsmobile production.[13]

Under the Smiths, the profitable company of Ransom Olds lost money, primarily because the lines of large cars failed to attract buyers. The Olds Motor Works lost $340,000 in 1905 and earned only modest profits of $45,000 the following year. Chapin entertained a job offer from a New York auto company, but his insistence that he bring Coffin and two other colleagues with him killed his chances. By mid-1905 Howard Coffin had designed a new mid-priced Oldsmobile and the Smiths agreed to produce it, authorizing Bezner to line up the needed suppliers of parts and components. To the dismay of Chapin, Coffin, and friends, the Smiths canceled the new car in late October 1905, ten weeks before the New York Auto Show.[14]

Chapin and the others wanted to leave the Olds Motor Works and produce Coffin's car, but lacked the necessary capital to do so. Chapin resigned from his position at the Olds Motor Works effective on 1 March 1906. Chapin, Coffin, Bezner, and Brady had just signed a formal contract on 28 February 1906 establishing a partnership for manufacturing automobiles. The venture began with a mere $6,000 in capital, but at least a formal agreement was in place.[15]

After leaving Olds, Roy Chapin and his sister Daisy went to San Francisco for a six-week vacation. One of Chapin's friends, E. P. Brinegar, arranged a meeting between Chapin and Edwin Ross Thomas, the founder of the E. R. Thomas Motor Company (1902–12) based in Buffalo, New York. The Thomas Flyer was a large, expensive automobile that had won many endurance races and enjoyed a good deal of popularity. Chapin proposed to create a new firm, the E. R. Thomas-Detroit Company, to build the car Coffin designed. In its first year of production, the Detroit-based company would deliver its entire production of 500 cars to Thomas, who would sell them through his existing dealerships.

The new company would have capital stock of $300,000, but the founders would pay only half in. Chapin proposed that Thomas contribute $100,000 in cash and that he and his three partners would add the remaining $50,000. Thomas, who wanted to diversify his offerings to give his dealers additional product, agreed to the proposal. Luckily, Roy Chapin, his sister Daisy, and Thomas left San Francisco by train only a few hours before the disastrous earthquake of 18 April 1906 devastated that city. The Articles of Association of the E. R. Thomas-Detroit Company were dated 2 May 1906 and notarized by Edward C. Chapin, Roy's father.[16]

The four Detroit men needed to find $10,000 immediately and then an additional $40,000 to keep their share of the stock. They came up with the $10,000, and by May 1906 they had $20,000 from Thomas, giving them $30,000 to start the enterprise. They briefly had the use of free office space in the Majestic Building in Detroit and rented a 20,000-square-foot building to serve as their factory. Bezner arranged contracts with suppliers of the parts and components they needed, but with a twist—suppliers had to guarantee the performance of their products or face financial penalties. The partners started production in the fall of 1906 and were quickly producing fifty cars a month. E. R. Thomas paid in the promised $100,000, but it was not until mid-June 1907 that Roy Chapin arranged a loan from the Old Detroit National Bank for the $40,000 balance still owed by the four Detroit partners.[17]

By the end of June 1907, the conclusion of the fiscal year, Chapin and his partners had fulfilled their contract to supply Thomas with 500 cars. The new venture paid its stockholders dividends amounting to 80 percent of the original investment. The E. R. Thomas-Detroit Company sold the Thomas-Detroit cars manufactured in 1907 and 1908 as the Thomas-Forty model, referring to the horsepower of its engine, but with no mention of its Detroit origins. Thomas advertised the model as "a fit companion to the superb 60 H. P. Thomas Flyer." The Thomas-Forty came in two versions, a touring car and a runabout, both selling for $2,750, hardly low-priced models.[18]

Roy Chapin generated some outstanding free publicity when the police arrested him in July 1907 for speeding in a Thomas-Detroit in Mishawaka, Indiana, while competing in the 1907 Glidden Tour. They charged him with exceeding the speed limit of 25 miles per hour, he had to pay a fine of $11.50, and the incident generated priceless national publicity for the Thomas-Detroit car. Nearly a year later, Thomas-Detroit cars placed first in two important durability races—a 262-mile reliability run in Minneapolis and a 320-mile Rocky Mountain endurance race that started and ended in Denver.[19]

The Thomas-Detroit Company continued to prosper, assembling 750 cars in its second year of operation ending in spring 1908. In fall 1907, construction began on

1907 Thomas-Detroit Forty. *Courtesy NAHC.*

a new factory on Jefferson Avenue in Detroit, with Albert Kahn, already the leading Detroit designer of automobile factories, as the architect. The young capitalists
running the Detroit operation were not satisfied with their utter dependence on E.
R. Thomas to sell their cars. With two-thirds of the stock, Thomas could change
policies at his whim or sell the company to new owners. Coffin had developed an
improved and lower-priced model, which further spurred Chapin and his partners
to seek a new corporate structure that would allow for an independent dealership
system. The partners did not have the financial means to buy out Thomas but hoped
to find another capitalist to buy Thomas's stock and take over as president.[20]

Bezner happened to read a newspaper report in late 1907 about the resignation of Hugh Chalmers from the vice presidency of the National Cash Register
(NCR) Company in Dayton, Ohio. Chalmers was a super-salesman who was earning $72,000 a year when he left National Cash Register at age thirty-five. The part-
ners in Thomas-Detroit decided to approach Chalmers, with the blessing of E. R.
Thomas. Chalmers agreed to buy half of Thomas's stock and to serve as president
of the company at a salary of $50,000. He would also create independent sales and
dealer organizations. The arrangement became official at a board of directors' meeting on 3 December 1907, when E. R. Thomas resigned as president and the board
elected Hugh Chalmers to replace him. In mid-June 1908, the stockholders voted to
rename the firm the Chalmers-Detroit Motor Company. At that point, Thomas and
Chalmers each controlled one-third of the stock in the new venture, while Chapin,
Coffin, Bezner, and Brady owned the remaining third.[21]

Hugh Chalmers (3 October 1873–2 June 1932) already had a remarkable career before coming to Detroit. Born in Dayton, Ohio, the son of Thomas Chalmers and Jeanette Bell Chalmers, he attended the Dayton public schools before quitting at age fourteen to work as an office boy for the National Cash Register Company. He became vice president and general manager at National Cash Register in 1900 at age twenty-seven. Chalmers advanced so quickly because he was a sales wizard. Once he came to E. R. Thomas-Detroit, Chalmers would have complete control over all matters relating to selling and advertising automobiles.[22]

Hugh Chalmers produced a detailed description of the managerial organization of his company, *Pyramid Plan of Organization, Chalmers-Detroit Motor Co., Detroit, Michigan*, published in 1908. The stockholders made up the top of the pyramid, with the board of directors below them, followed by Hugh Chalmers, president, and Roy D. Chapin, treasurer and general manager. Each of these layers of the pyramid reported to the layer above. Eight pyramids below Chapin made up the functional divisions of the firm and all reported to Chapin, except for the selling pyramid, whose manager reported directly to Chalmers.[23]

A new Coffin-designed car, known as the Chalmers-Detroit 30, debuted in late June 1908. This five-passenger touring car, powered by a four-cylinder engine producing 30 brake horsepower, retailed for $1,500, a much lower price than the Thomas-Detroit car. Their advertising touted "This Astounding Car for $1,500," suggest-

Directors of the Chalmers-Detroit Motor Company, 1908.
Left to right: Roy D. Chapin, Hugh Chalmers, E. R. Thomas, Howard Coffin, Frederick O. Bezner, and James J. Brady. *Courtesy DCHC.*

1909 Chalmers-Detroit 30. *Courtesy NAHC.*

ing that it was the equal to cars selling for $2,500 or more. This model was a great success. For the fiscal year ending 30 June 1909, the company sold 2,476 Chalmers 30s and 611 of the more costly Chalmers 40 models, for a total of 3,087 cars. They earned profits of more than $1 million on sales of $4.75 million, or 21.4 percent, and paid stockholders a dividend of $300,000, or a 100 percent return on investment. Chalmers-Detroit sold more than 6,000 cars in the following fiscal year.[24]

Despite this success, Roy Chapin and his partners were not satisfied with controlling only one-third of the stock in Chalmers-Detroit. At some point in fall 1908, Roscoe Jackson and George W. Dunham, both Olds Motor Works alumni, came to Chapin and his partners looking for jobs. Dunham had designed a car they thought Chalmers-Detroit might offer. Chapin and Coffin hired Jackson and Dunham to work on a new Model 20, which Coffin had designed as a low-priced model to sell for less than $1,000. The hiring of Jackson and Dunham marked the launch of the Hudson automobile.[25]

Hudson's Beginnings and Early Success

On 28 October 1908, the following men entered into an agreement that became the foundation for the Hudson Motor Car Company: Joseph L. Hudson, Roscoe Jackson, Hugh Chalmers, Howard Coffin, Frederick Bezner, Roy Chapin, James Brady, and Lee Counselman. They formed a partnership "for the purpose of build-

Joseph L. Hudson.
Courtesy DCHC.

ing models of certain proposed low priced automobiles; and, if considered advisable, a Company was to be formed, under the laws of the State of Michigan, to manufacture and sell automobiles patterned after the said models." On 20 February 1909 the partners formally filed the *Articles of Association of the Hudson Motor Car Company.* The capital stock consisted of 10,000 shares, par value of $10, for a total capitalization of $100,000. They subscribed only $90,000 of stock and paid in a mere $15,000 as cash. When the directors held their first meeting on 6 March 1909, they held the 9,000 shares as follows: Joseph L. Hudson, 1,584 shares; Hugh Chalmers, 1,334; Jackson, Coffin, Chapin, Brady, and Bezner each held 1,083 shares; Lee Counselman had 666 shares; and George Dunham owned a single share.[26]

Roy Chapin and his partners launched the production of Hudson automobiles soon after the formal incorporation of the Hudson Motor Car Company. The company bought the Selden patent license held by the defunct Northern Motor Car Company, which allowed them to manufacture cars without fear of lawsuits. George Selden patented the automobile in 1895 and the automakers producing cars under the patent formed the Association of Licensed Automobile Manufacturers in 1903 and successfully defended the patent until 1911. The Hudson company bought an 80,000-square-foot factory at the corner of Mack and Beaufait avenues in Detroit, which had been used to build the Aerocar in 1905–8.

First Hudson plant (1909), Mack and Beaufait avenues,
Detroit. *Courtesy NAHC.*

By late May 1909, the company had 1,452 orders for the Hudson Twenty roadster
in hand. The first national advertisement, which appeared in the *Saturday Evening
Post* on 19 June 1909, described the Hudson Twenty, priced at $900, as "Strong-
Speedy-Roomy-Stylish." This advertisement resulted in approximately 1,500 additional inquiries from potential customers and dealers about the new model. By the
time the car was in production, the company had nearly 4,000 down payments of
$25 on the new model. Hudson assembled its first car on 8 July 1909. With about
five hundred men employed at their factory, Hudson built 1,100 cars by the end of
the year and had orders for thousands more.[27]

The Hudson triangle emblem overlaid the text in the *Saturday Evening Post* advertisement of mid-June 1909, although it was not visible on the car proper. The meaning of the triangle is disputed. In his biography of Roy Chapin, J. C. Long argues that
it stood for the three partners—Chapin, Coffin, and Bezner—but there no corrobo-
rating evidence to support this view. Similarly, Don Butler claims that the triangle
represented three key features of Hudson automobiles—performance, service, and
value. The Hudson Motor Car Company published a twenty-two-page booklet, *Finishing the Triangle*, in late 1909 or early 1910, promoting the Hudson automobile. It
explained the meaning of the triangle: the first (left) side stood for the work of the
designer who engineered the car and the workers who built it; the second (right) side
represented the dealers who enthusiastically embraced the Hudson without seeing
the finished product; and the top of the triangle stood for the satisfied owners of
Hudson automobiles. The triangle stood for the successful Hudson automobile.[28]

1910 Hudson Model 20 touring car, with Hudson pioneers (*left to right*)
Roscoe B. Jackson, O. H. McCormack, Howard E. Coffin, and Roy D. Chapin.
Courtesy DCHC.

Roy Chapin spent most of the summer of 1909 touring the plants and facilities
of the major automobile makers of Europe, who were in most respects still leading the world in automotive engineering, styling, and production methods. Chapin
was especially interested in European methods for developing advanced designs
and maintaining high-quality products. He sent dozens of lengthy reports about his
observations to Hugh Chalmers and the rest of the Chalmers-Detroit management
team. He believed that Chalmers-Detroit could benefit from the lessons he had
learned from the failures and successes of the European companies.[29]

When Roy Chapin returned from Europe, he found that Hugh Chalmers was
uninterested in most aspects of the Chalmers-Detroit operations other than sales
promotions. Chalmers also wanted to emphasize the more expensive models in their
offerings. In late October 1909, the E. R. Thomas Motor Company offered to sell its
stock in Chalmers-Detroit to General Motors, reminding Chapin and his partners that
Hugh Chalmers could easily do the same and leave them without any real power.

Shortly thereafter, Chapin, Coffin, and Bezner offered to sell their shares in
Chalmers-Detroit to Hugh Chalmers and in return they would buy his shares in
Hudson. Chalmers was receptive and they came to an agreement on 6 December
1909, which would take effect on 20 December. Chalmers paid the three men a
total of $788,000 for their shares of Chalmers-Detroit. The three partners had made
a tidy profit since they had invested only $80,000 in Chalmers-Detroit in June 1907.

They in turn paid Chalmers $80,040 for his stock in Hudson. James Brady chose to remain a stockholder in Chalmers-Detroit and sold his Hudson shares to the trio of Chapin-Coffin-Bezner for $54,000, giving Brady a nice profit.[30]

In early January 1910, Chapin, Coffin, Bezner, and Brady resigned their positions at Chalmers-Detroit. After the buyout of Chalmers and Brady, Joseph Hudson served as chairman of Hudson and Roy Chapin became president. Howard Coffin became chief engineer and vice president, Roscoe Jackson held the positions of treasurer and general manager, and Frederick Bezner took the post of secretary. The *Detroit News* reported the breakup as a pure business decision completed in a friendly way.[31]

Although Roy Chapin and Hugh Chalmers had several disagreements over the years, each held the other in high regard. Roy Chapin was one of eighteen directors of the Detroit Athletic Club (DAC) who held a dinner on 21 December 1916 to honor Hugh Chalmers for his four years of service as the first president of the DAC (1913–16). Chapin delivered the speech honoring Chalmers and spoke at great length about working with Chalmers in the fledgling Detroit automobile industry. In mid-January 1917, Chalmers sent Chapin a long letter of thanks for his comments at the dinner. Commenting on their business association and friendship, Chalmers noted,

> I do appreciate my coming in contact with you in 1904 and value your friendship very highly. I think that both of us, as we grow older, will look back upon our meeting and business associations with a great deal of satisfaction and pleasure.

Chapin responded graciously,

> It was the first opportunity I have had to tell the public of the trials and tribulations we went through together, and to give you credit for having the foresight, nerve and everything else to go into the automobile business at the time you did.[32]

A cynic might dismiss these testimonials as self-serving or disingenuous, but neither man had any motive to falsely praise the other. Their business relationship had ended seven years earlier. Besides, Chapin had organized the testimonial dinner for Chalmers.

The Hudson Motor Car Company was an immediate success. Faced with a flood of orders for the popular Hudson automobile, Chapin and his partners decided that they needed a large new factory. The *Detroit News* reported in late January 1910 that Hudson had bought one hundred acres of land on East Jefferson Avenue near Grosse Pointe in an area formerly known as Fairview Village. The land bordered on what Detroit then called "Connor's Avenue," now Conner Street, and was situated near a new line of the Detroit Terminal Railway, a connector railroad running through the industrial sections of Detroit.[33]

Construction of the new manufacturing complex began with ground breaking on 7 May 1910. The second issue of *The Hudson Triangle*, Hudson's in-house magazine, claimed that the factory would cost $500,000. Designed by Albert Kahn, the plant consisted of two-story reinforced concrete buildings that could be expanded to four stories. The factory opened in late October 1910 and provided 223,500 square feet of space, nearly three times the space available at the Mack Avenue factory. According to the *Detroit News*, electric elevators and electric traveling cranes eased the movement of parts, components, and cars within the factory. The plant could produce sixty cars per day. The facility had many amenities for the employees, including drinking fountains, lockers, showers, a hospital, dining rooms, restrooms, smoking rooms for the men, and recreation grounds.[34]

Even with the new factory, Hudson struggled to satisfy the enormous demand for the Hudson Twenty. Two early reviews of the car, in the *Horseless Age* (June 1909) and in *The Automobile* (July 1909) offered gushing praise. Hudson was the first car at this price ($900) to offer a slide-type selective transmission, with three forward gears and one reverse. Up-to-date features included a pressed steel frame, cone clutch, and double-acting rear brakes. With a wheelbase of 100 inches and 32-inch wheels, this was a much roomier car than most other models selling for less than

Hudson Motor Car Company plant, Detroit (1915). *Courtesy DCHC.*

Chief officers, Hudson Motor Car Company, 1916. *Courtesy DCHC.*

Roy D. Chapin, 1921.
Courtesy DCHC.

$1,000. The Model T Ford, incidentally, sold for only $50 less than the Hudson Twenty. Hudson turned out 4,556 cars in calendar year 1910, putting the fledgling company in eleventh place among U.S. automakers.[35]

Roy Chapin, Howard Coffin, and Frederick Bezner had informally agreed that they would retire after becoming millionaires, preferably by age thirty. Chapin and Bezner were millionaires by 1910, as was Coffin, who was in his late thirties. The three founders had increased Hudson's capital stock from $100,000 to $1 million by capitalizing the surplus. They owned 62,316 shares of the total stock issue of 100,000 shares and tried, without success, to sell most of their shares to the other Hudson executives so they could withdraw from active management. Over time, Coffin and Bezner reduced their direct involvement in Hudson and left Chapin and Jackson with the burden of running the company. Howard Coffin bought real estate in Georgia and Bezner moved to Europe and withdrew from any significant role in Hudson affairs. Roscoe Jackson managed Hudson on a day-to-day basis, but Chapin made the strategic decisions regarding product, sales, production, and finance.[36]

Growing Pains, War, and Prosperity, 1910–25

Hudson experienced substantial growth during its first decade and a half of operation, with the usual growing pains that face a new company in a volatile and competitive market. Table 5.1 illustrates Hudson's substantial growth. Between 1910 and 1919, the Hudson Motor Car Company ranked between ninth and eleventh in production among American car companies. (In 1911, however, it held seventh place.) Production and sales growth usually came from successful new models, including a mid-priced Six in 1914, the Super-Six introduced in January 1916, and the Essex, which debuted in 1919 and quickly moved Hudson the following year into seventh place among the U.S. automakers. The introduction of a reasonably priced closed car, the Essex Coach, brought extremely rapid growth in sales. In 1925, Hudson-Essex sales of 269,474 vehicles ranked third in the U.S. auto industry, behind only Ford and Chevrolet.[37]

Hudson quickly moved "upmarket" from its original Hudson Twenty priced at $900. The company introduced the Hudson 33 in 1911, with a 33 brake horsepower engine and a price of $1,250 for the least expensive touring car. Designed by Coffin, it featured a "monobloc" engine, whereby the engine and transmission were encased as a single unit. In the middle of the 1912 model year, the Hudson 33 came with a self-starter made by the Disco Company of Grand Rapids, Michigan, as standard equipment. Hudson was an industry leader in introducing the self-starter. In 1912 only 1.7 percent of American cars came with the self-starter as standard equipment.[38]

Table 5.1. Hudson Motor Car Company Shipments, by Calendar Year and Profits, Net of Taxes ($ Millions), Year Ending 30 June 1910–13, 31 May 1914–15, 5 December 1916, and 30 November 1917–25

	Hudson	**Essex**	**Total**	**Net Profits ($ Millions)**
1909	1,100	–	1,100	NA
1910	4,556	–	4,556	0.6
1911	6,486	–	6,486	0.5
1912	5,708	–	5,708	0.8
1913	6,401	–	6,401	0.8
1914	10,261	–	10,261	1.2
1915	12,864	–	12,864	1.4
1916	25,772	–	25,772	2.7
1917	20,976	–	20,976	1.5
1918	12,526	92	12,618	1.2
1919	18,175	21,879	40,054	2.3
1920	22,268	23,669	45,937	1.2
1921	13,721	13,422	27,143	0.9
1922	28,242	36,222	64,464	7.2
1923	46,337	42,577	88,914	8.0
1924	59,427	74,523	133,950	8.1
1925	109,840	159,634	269,474	21.4

Source: "Hudson Shipments, Calendar Years 1909–1957," DCHC; "Hudson, Net Profits, 1910–1952," NAHC.

Hudson discontinued the Model 20 in 1912 and in the following model year introduced its first six-cylinder car, the Model 54, and the last of its four-cylinder cars, the Model 37. The new Six had an engine producing 54 brake horsepower, weighed more than 3,500 pounds (versus 1,800 pounds for the Hudson Twenty), and sold for $2,450 and more. For the 1914 model year, Hudson dropped four-cylinder car production and introduced a lightweight and less expensive Six, the Model 40, which sold at $1,750 and above. Except for the four-door seven-passenger phaeton, which weighed 3,939 pounds, the remaining Model 40 offerings for 1914 weighed less than 3,000 pounds, making them the lightest six-cylinder cars in America.[39]

Early Hudsons through 1915 were wholly "assembled automobiles," with Hud-

1911 Hudson Model 33 Torpedo. *Courtesy NAHC.*

son manufacturing none of the components. For the first three years of production, Hudson bought engines from the Atlas Engine Works of Indianapolis, Indiana, and from the Buda Company of Harvey, Illinois. In 1911, Hudson convinced the Continental Motor Manufacturing Company of Muskegon, Michigan, to build an engine plant in Detroit and awarded Continental a contract for 10,000 engines in late 1911. Hudson sold the engine maker a thirty-acre parcel next to Hudson's Detroit plant and Continental began producing engines for Hudson in April 1912. Three more years passed before Hudson made any of its own engines.[40]

Hudson produced a two-page advertisement that appeared in the *Saturday Evening Post* in late September 1912 titled, "The 48 Engineers Who Designed the Hudson." The ad claimed that forty-eight engineers were involved in designing the Hudson 37 and the Hudson 54 models. Hudson described these engineers as "staff" and included small images of all forty-eight men. The ad named Howard E. Coffin as "the foremost engineer in the industry." This and other Hudson advertisements touched off an intense exchange of letters starting in mid-December 1912 between James Couzens, the secretary-treasurer of the Ford Motor Company, and Roy Chapin over the claims made by the Hudson Motor Car Company. Couzens argued that Henry Ford, not Coffin, was the auto industry's most important engineer. The exchange between Couzens and Chapin involved more than a dozen letters and continued into mid-January 1913, with neither party conceding anything.[41]

1913 Hudson Model 54 Phaeton. *Courtesy NAHC.*

The Hudson Motor Car Company was among the leaders in the auto industry in abandoning four-cylinder engines and moving exclusively to sixes. Howard Coffin wrote a fifty-five-page booklet, *Critical Analysis of Motor Cars of 1914*, published by Hudson, which proclaimed "The Conquest of the Six" and showed its many advantages over the Four. He dismissed the arguments made against the Six by sellers of Fours and argued that the Six offered smoother engine performance with less wear-and-tear on engine components. The booklet included a table showing the rapid adoption of the Six between 1908 and 1914. Of forty-two manufacturers listed, thirty-seven offered a Six by 1914, including the newly introduced Jeffery Six. The table was deceptive because it excluded the Ford Motor Company and Willys-Overland, the number one and number two producers of automobiles in 1914. Dodge Brothers, which started large-scale production in 1915, produced four-cylinder cars exclusively for ten years.[42]

Still, there was definitely a trend toward six-cylinder cars in the 1910s and 1920s. In the very early days of the industry, through 1905, most cars had only one or two cylinders. Six-cylinder cars accounted for 10 to 14 percent of the total in 1907–9, but only 8 percent in 1912. With the introduction of several Sixes by Hudson and others, six-cylinder cars accounted for 24 percent of the market in 1916 and then the share fluctuated between 17 and 26 percent in 1917–24 before leaping to 37 percent in 1926. Throughout this era, the enormous production of four-cylinder Model T Fords distorted the figures. If we exclude Fords from the calculations, Sixes accounted for 42 percent of the market in 1916 and 55 percent in 1926. Hudson, particularly with the development of the Super-Six motor, first offered in its 1917 models, clearly placed itself in the middle of the automobile market in terms of the weight, power, and price of its offerings.[43]

Although Hudson's early models sold well, Roy Chapin and his partners fretted in the mid-1910s over the company's future direction and potential financial perils. In 1915 alone, they took significant steps to produce more of their own components, which they assumed would bolster profits. In a note to his fellow stockholders, Chapin noted that while sales jumped a healthy 21 percent for the year ending 31 May 1915 versus the year before, net profits (after taxes) for both years stood at 10 percent of sales, which he deemed disappointing. Accounting practices varied a great deal from company to company, but Dodge Brothers earned average profits on sales of 16 percent per year for the two years ending in June 1917, an impressive performance for a newcomer to the industry.[44]

Starting in 1915, Chapin explored several merger opportunities. In late November 1915, he approached Henry B. Joy, president of Packard Motor Car Company, about a possible merger of the two companies. Following a private meeting at Chapin's home, Joy viewed the prospects favorably. Both firms were strong, profitable operations with excellent staffs. Joy remarked, "your company is the cleanest, most cohesive organization." He wanted to pursue the merger idea further and volunteered to make Packard's financial information available to the Hudson people. This would have been an intriguing combination of the premier producer of luxury cars in America with a highly successful manufacturer of mid-priced and low-priced offerings. The merger never happened, for reasons the records do not reveal.[45]

Rumors of a blockbuster merger involving Hudson were afloat in early June 1916. Newspapers speculated on a merger directed by John North Willys, the owner of Willys-Overland, the second largest automobile producer in the United States. The combine would include Willys-Overland, the Hudson Motor Car Company, the Chalmers Motor Company, United Motors, the Autolite Company (starting and lighting equipment), and several other parts manufacturers. Willys would bring several truck makers and a tire company into the combine later. He would organize the resulting enterprise as a holding company, much like General Motors. The long-term plan was for this combine eventually to merge with General Motors and form a dominant automobile conglomerate. John North Willys confirmed the rumors and revealed that the enterprise would issue $200 million in stock.[46]

There was substance behind the newspaper reports. Chapin received more than a dozen offers to invest in the "New Motors" conglomerate, including a pledge of $10,000 from George Tiedeman, Chapin's father-in-law. Chapin convened special meetings of the Hudson directors on 12 June and the stockholders on 16 June to consider selling all the assets of Hudson to the new entity, Central Motors Corporation. There is no clear indication of the decisions made by the stockholders, but Chapin noted the failure of the proposal in a letter of 17 June 1916: "As you probably have noticed, I was mixed up in what started out to be a fairly big merger proposition. However, we finally gave the whole proposition up as it got too complicated to please anybody connected with it." Chapin also made an announcement to the Hudson dealers in *The Hudson Triangle* that Hudson's management had decided not to pursue the consolidation plan then under consideration. This was not the only scheme floated to bring more financial stability to Hudson.[47]

Merger proposals continued to crop up, largely because Chapin and his original partners wanted to turn their Hudson stock into cash, walk away from management worries, and simply enjoy their wealth. At the end of World War I, Chapin and Roscoe Jackson proposed a merger of Hudson, Dodge Brothers, Timken (roller bearings), and Continental Motors, with Dodge Brothers controlling the new corporation. Chapin and Jackson insisted on receiving cash for their shares of Hudson, which probably killed the deal.[48]

Hudson achieved a series of breakthroughs starting in 1916 that established the company's long-term viability. The first was the Super-Six engine, which defined the identity of the Hudson Motor Car Company for several decades. Hudson was fully committed to six-cylinder engines by 1914, but the Super-Six made Hudson the industry's leader. The Super-Six engine, like most successes, had many fathers. Howard Coffin, as chief engineer, had broad oversight over the project. Charles H. Vincent left the Packard Motor Car Company, where he worked with his brother Jessie G. Vincent, to head the Super-Six engine project. Hudson engineer Stephen I. Fekete developed and patented the first fully balanced crankshaft in the industry, which allowed the engine to operate at higher speeds with little vibration. Fitted with the improved crankshaft, the output produced by the otherwise identical Hudson Six engine increased from 42 to 76 brake horsepower. This was also the first engine that Hudson produced in-house.[49]

Hudson introduced its new line of six-cylinder models with the new engine at the New York Auto Show in January 1916. Dubbed the "Super-Six," the new line replaced the other Sixes, the Model 40 and Model 54. The lowest-price Super-Six models, the two-door roadster and the four-door phaeton, sold for $1,375. Production of Super-Sixes in 1916 was double the output of the previous models the year before (25,772 versus 12,864) and four times that of 1913, the last year the Hudson offered four-cylinder engines. As a result, the company continuously expanded its Detroit factory, which by 1913 enclosed 380,818 square feet, more than double the

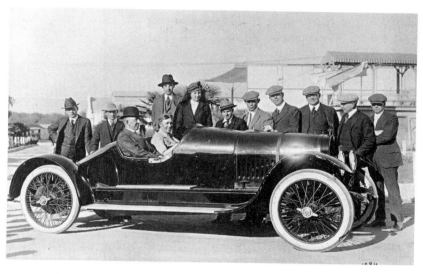

1916 Hudson Super-Six, December 1916. Race car driver Ralph Mulford is
behind the wheel, with Richard Kinderdell at his side. Edsel B. Ford and
Eleanor Clay Ford are standing on the running board. *Courtesy DCHC*.

original space of 172,282 square feet. With the success of the Sixes, the factory
more than doubled in size by 1915, when it incorporated 813,883 square feet of
floor space.[50]

Hudson's Super-Six *was* superior to its competitors' Sixes. To help promote the
1917 Super-Sixes, Hudson produced a large-size eighteen-page brochure, *Hudson
Super-Six: It Solved Motordom's Knottiest Problem: Holds All Worth-While Records*.
Inside the brochure the company proudly proclaimed, "Hudson Super-Six Saved
Other Sixes: It Stopped the Trend to Eights and Twelves." The new engine provided
not only more power and greater speed (60 miles per hour and higher) but also faster
acceleration than other sixes or eights. Drivers had no trouble seeing the difference
between the Super-Six and other six-cylinder cars.

Much of the brochure focused on the Super-Six's success in a wide range of
speed races and endurance contests. Roy Chapin decided that racing was an effective way to increase sales. Hudson driver Ralph Mulford established more than a
dozen speed, acceleration, and endurance records with the Super-Six in 1916 alone.
The Hudson Motor Car Company ended its sponsorship of racing in August 1917
because of the war. Hudson would have faced public criticism had it continued
racing "as usual" under wartime conditions, so the company simply stopped the
program.[51]

1916 Hudson Super-Six seven-passenger touring car (October 1916) at
Columbus Circle in New York City, after finishing a transcontinental round trip,
New York to San Francisco. *Courtesy DCHC.*

World War I affected the Hudson Motor Car Company on several levels. Roy
Chapin and Howard Coffin spent much of the war serving the War Department in
Washington. In April 1917, Howard Coffin began a leave of absence from Hudson
to serve as the chairman of the United States Board of Aeronautics, later the Aircraft
Production Board, which spearheaded the development of the Liberty aircraft engine.
In early November 1917, Secretary of War Newton Baker named Roy Chapin chairman of the Highways Transport Committee of the Council on National Defense.
This was a civilian committee charged with advising the War Department on the use
of trucks and the highway system to speed the movement of materials bound for ship-
ment to Europe from the East Coast. The government paid Chapin $1 a year for his
service, which extended through the end of the war. Chapin moved to Washington for
this period and left the management of Hudson to Roscoe Jackson.[52]

The precise scope and scale of Hudson's involvement in World War I are difficult
to determine because of the lack of documentary evidence. Surviving photographs
from 1917 show that Hudson built three styles of field ambulances and an "overseas
limousine," a command car designed to transport seven officers, all based on the
Super-Six chassis. For 1918, Hudson also built a personnel car, designed to carry

1917 Hudson ambulance built for the U.S. Army. *Courtesy NAHC.*

fourteen to thirty-five men. There is solid evidence that Hudson assembled Nash Quad trucks through a license issued by Nash and the U.S. Army. By 1 November 1918, Hudson had contracts to build 3,000 Quads but delivered only 219 by the end of the war.[53]

Don Butler has claimed that Hudson designed a six-ton tank using a Super-Six engine and had a contract to produce 1,000 of them for the U.S. Army. There is no surviving evidence that Hudson built a single tank. Butler has also claimed that Hudson received another contract to build 2,500 artillery shells a day, but this was canceled at the conclusion of the war. Michael J. Kollins has credited Hudson with building Curtiss O-X-5 aircraft engines during the war, but there is not a shred of evidence that this happened.[54]

The sharp decline in Hudson car production in 1917 and 1918 is perhaps evidence of a shift of resources into war production, but it is also an indication of materials shortages and transportation problems. Getting new cars delivered to the dealerships became a substantial problem as railroad cars became scarce throughout 1918 and the government restricted their use. By March 1918, the government allowed Hudson to use about 250 railroad cars per month, one-quarter their usual number. As a result, Hudson had to rely on large "drive-aways" to deliver their new cars to dealerships as distant as Atlanta, Baltimore, and Boston.[55]

By mid-November 1918, with the war over, the government canceled several contracts that Hudson had just received, including a contract to make tank engines and transmissions and a separate contract to make shells. Roscoe Jackson viewed the cancellations as positive and sought to have all remaining contracts for war goods eliminated as quickly as possible because they were disrupting automobile production. He and Chapin shared the same skeptical view of the war contracts: "I agree with you in every particular with reference to the war contracts, and we are not spending a nickel on these contracts that we can avoid and have held up everything as much as we could—machinery, equipment, etc." In a two-page spread in *The Hudson Triangle* in February 1919, the only war products shown were the various wheeled vehicles mentioned earlier and a single tank transmission, which the company perhaps produced for a brief time.[56]

Well before extricating themselves from war production, Chapin and the other Hudson leaders wanted to make a smaller, lower-priced four-cylinder car to complement the successful Super-Six. In late September 1917, they announced the formation of Essex Motors, a company supposedly independent from Hudson, to make the new car. Launched with $500,000 of paid-in capital, the leaders of the new firm were all Hudson officers. William J. McAneeny, the factory superintendent for Hudson, became president of Essex; Roscoe B. Jackson became the Essex vice president; and A.(Abraham) E.(Edward) Barit, who served as Hudson's treasurer, took the same post with Essex. The board of directors at Essex included Roy Chapin, Frederick Bezner, and Orville H. McCornack, Hudson's sales manager. Howard Coffin was notably missing.[57]

Hudson officials chose "Essex" after considering the names of several English counties. They had planned to introduce the new models in 1918, but shortages of factory space, materials, and labor delayed the introduction by a year. In early March 1918, Roscoe Jackson calculated that Hudson would need to sell the Essex at $1,360 just to break even, but their intent was to offer it for $1,250 or less. Jackson warned that Hudson needed to get bigger if it had hopes of competing with Ford, General Motors, and Dodge Brothers. He pointedly asked Chapin, "Are we going to put ourselves with the winners or the losers?"[58]

Hudson's managers initially planned to build the Essex in a Detroit plant on Franklin Street that they would lease from the Studebaker Corporation, but Studebaker needed the space for war production, rendering Hudson's plans moot. Hudson instead built two small factories adjacent to the existing Hudson plant. By the end of 1919, the Hudson-Essex factory complex incorporated 1,300,000 square feet of factory space, up sharply from the 814,000 square feet in use at the end of 1915. The expansion program cost $2,250,000, with $1,250,000 for land acquisition and buildings, and the rest for machinery.[59]

The new Essex model first appeared for public viewing on 11 January 1919 at the Los Angeles Auto Show, held in three enormous tents. The first offering was a

1919 Essex four-door sedan. *Courtesy DCHC.*

five-passenger touring car, followed in March with a five-passenger four-door sedan and a roadster in June. Although the Essex and Hudson models were not precisely comparable, contrasting them is nevertheless instructive. The 1919 Hudson four-door, four-passenger phaeton sold for $2,075 and weighed 3,320 pounds, while the Essex four-door, five-passenger touring car carried a price of $1,395 and weighed 2,450 pounds. For the same model year Hudson offered a four-door, seven-passenger sedan that sold for $2,775 and weighed in at 3,775 pounds, while the Essex four-door, five-passenger sedan had a price of $2,250 and weighed 2,955 pounds. The Essex was so successful that for the 1919 fiscal year, its sales (21,879) were greater than the sales of the Hudson Six models (18,175).[60]

The men who designed the Essex included the Swiss engineer Emile Huber; Stephen Fekete, also credited with the Super-Six engine; and Stuart Baits, who later became chief engineer at Hudson. The engine was a four-cylinder F-head inline design, with overhead intake valves and exhaust valves in the engine block. The engine had a counterbalanced crankshaft and automatic spark advance, both unprecedented features in a modestly priced car. The engine, with 179 cubic inch displacement (CID), developed a remarkable 55 brake horsepower, nearly three times the output of a Model T Ford. The Essex was a high-performance, but moderately priced car, which the Hudson company and its dealers emphasized when promoting it.[61]

Hudson also proved the reliability of Essex by putting it through several endurance contests. In mid-December 1919, Essex completed a series of tests at the Cincinnati Speedway in which an Essex stock chassis covered 3,037 miles in 50 hours at an average speed of 60.7 miles per hour in one run and a grand total of 5,870 miles in 94 hours 22 minutes. The race that brought Essex enormous notoriety was a transcontinental endurance contest in which Essex cars carried U.S. Mail between New York and San Francisco. This was the first time an automobile delivered U.S. Mail coast to coast. The contest began on 6 August 1920 with two Essex touring cars starting in New York and ending in San Francisco, while two additional Essex touring cars traced the same route but started in San Francisco. Essex set a New York–San Francisco record of 4 days, 19 hours, 17 minutes and a San Francisco–New York record of 4 days, 21 hours, 56 minutes.[62]

Roy Chapin and the Hudson Motor Car Company revolutionized the automobile market by introducing a moderately priced Essex closed-body car, the Essex Coach, in late 1921 as a 1922 model. Closed-body cars (sedans) usually carried a price 40 to 50 percent higher than an open-body car, such as a touring car, on a similar chassis. The two-door, five-passenger Essex Coach used a special Fisher body mounted on an Essex chassis. Chapin initially offered the Essex Coach at $1,495 in late 1921, but in early 1922 he dropped the price to $1,295, only $200 more than the touring car. The price differential fell to only $100 for 1923 and then to only $45 the following year. The 1924 Essex Coach, powered by a new six-cylinder engine, which initially sold for $975, carried a price of $945 in June 1924. At the start of the 1925 model year, Chapin dropped the price of the Essex Coach to $895, $5 *lower* than the price of the touring car on the same chassis.[63]

1923 Essex Coach, with Roy D. Chapin behind the wheel. *Courtesy NAHC.*

The 1924 Essex Six, introduced in mid-December 1923 with great fanfare, replaced the four-cylinder Essex. In reviewing the new model, *Automobile Topics* argued that it was not only more attractive than the Essex Four it replaced, but was a remarkable value at a mere $975. In Detroit, sixteen "associate dealers" displayed the car Saturday evening and all day Sunday until midnight. Potential buyers, some 12,000 in total, flooded the displays, bought all the available cars, and placed hundreds of advance orders.[64]

The 1924 Essex Six Coach was two inches longer than the 1923 model, but nearly 300 pounds lighter. The six-cylinder engine had a smaller displacement (130 cubic inches versus 180) and delivered less brake horsepower (an estimated 34 versus 55) than the four-cylinder engine on the 1923 models. This six-cylinder engine did not provide enough power and Hudson brought out a replacement engine in June 1924 which had a displacement of 145 cubic inches and developed 40 brake horsepower. Sales took off after Hudson improved the engine.[65]

The inexpensive Essex Coach brought a tremendous increase in sales and profits for Hudson and revolutionized the American automobile market. Although the Coach had an austere, boxy appearance, dubbed a "packing crate" by its critics, customers accepted the design because it offered a reasonably priced closed car. Combined Hudson and Essex sales for 1925 (see Table 5.1) had tripled since 1923 and net profits nearly tripled. Hudson's total sales of 269,474 vehicles in 1925 ranked third in the industry behind only Ford (1,643,295) and Chevrolet (444,671), but well ahead of fourth-place Willys-Overland (215,000).[66]

In his autobiography, Alfred Sloan described Chapin's introduction of an inexpensive closed car as a development "which was profoundly to influence the fortunes of the Pontiac, the Chevrolet, and the Model T." In recalling Chapin's price cuts for the 1925 models, Sloan noted, "Nothing like this had ever been seen in the automobile industry, and the Essex Coach had a considerable vogue. This suggested that closed cars, priced on a volume basis, could in the future dominate even the low-price field." Sloan grudgingly admitted that Chapin's success with the Essex Coach forced General Motors to accelerate its plans to produce more closed automobiles.[67]

The introduction of the Essex Coach did not by itself cause the move away from open cars toward closed cars. Closed cars accounted for only 4 percent of passenger car production in the United States in 1917, but steadily climbed to 22 percent in 1921. The Essex Coach accelerated this trend by closing the price gap between closed and open cars. In 1922, closed cars on average cost 44 percent more than open cars, but by 1926 the differential was only 5 percent. The share of closed cars in automobile sales jumped sharply from 22 percent in 1922 to 72 percent in 1926. Automotive historian Ralph Epstein credits Hudson with initiating the change.[68]

The Hudson Motor Car Company underwent additional changes in the early 1920s. The owners of Hudson and Essex stock received stock in a newly capitalized company whose shares the company now offered on the New York Stock Exchange. The deal, made final in April 1922, converted the 200,000 shares of the old company into 1,200,000 shares in the new company. The original partners (Chapin, Coffin, Bezner, and Jackson) received 720,000 shares of the new stock valued at approximately $14 million, retaining a controlling interest in Hudson, and $7 million in cash. The public offering of Hudson stock on 28 April 1922 sold before noon.[69]

There were also significant changes in the Hudson management structure. Roy Chapin resigned as president on 20 January 1923, replaced by Roscoe B. Jackson, and took the post of chairman of the board. Chapin remained involved in long-term strategic decisions and was the public spokesman for Hudson, but withdrew from day-to-day operations. By the end of the 1923 fiscal year, Frederick Bezner was no longer a vice president and a year later, he was no longer a director.[70]

By most measures, the Hudson Motor Car Company enjoyed tremendous success in its first decade and a half of operations. The Hudson and Essex automobiles were well-designed, innovative, and popular. The Hudson Super-Six and the Essex Coach were path-breaking cars that had enormous impact on the American automobile industry. Hudson-Essex became one of the top-selling brands in the United States and the firm earned respectable profits in each year from 1909 onward. Roy Chapin's successful efforts in promoting and selling Hudson and Essex automobiles emphasized speed and durability runs. Much like the rest of the American automakers, Hudson enjoyed additional success in the late 1920s before facing the challenges of the Great Depression.

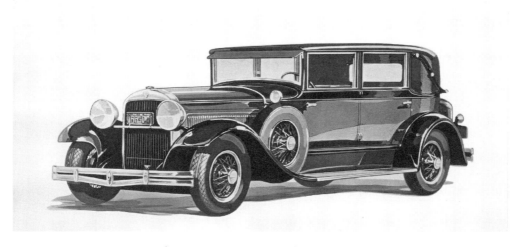

1929 Hudson Super-Six sport sedan. *Courtesy NAHC.*

Prosperity, Depression, and the End of the Roy Chapin Era, 1925–36

The Hudson Motor Car Company had great success in the late 1920s, with healthy sales and profits through 1929 (see Table 5.2). In 1929 Hudson shipped more than 300,000 cars and ranked third in the industry behind only Ford and Chevrolet. The Essex nameplate grew at the expense of the Hudson brand; by 1929 Essex accounted for two-thirds of the company's sales. The firm adopted new strategies in selling its cars and continued the process of vertical integration begun earlier by producing a substantial part of its body requirements. The late 1920s also brought significant changes in the vehicles Hudson sold, including styling refinements and equipment upgrades.

As part of an ongoing move toward vertical integration and self-sufficiency, Hudson began making its own bodies in mid-1926 at a large plant at Conner and Gratiot avenues, roughly three miles northwest of the main Hudson plant. During the

Table 5.2. Hudson Motor Car Company Shipments, by Calendar Year and Profits, Net of Taxes ($ Millions), Year Ending 30 November 1925 and 31 December 1926–36

	Hudson	Essex	Terra-plane	Commercial Vehicles	Total	Net Profits ($ Millions)
1925	109,840	159,634	–	–	269,474	21.4
1926	70,261	157,247	–	–	227,508	5.4
1927	66,034	210,380	–	–	276,414	14.4
1928	52,316	229,887	–	–	282,203	13.5
1929	71,179	227,653	–	2,130	300,962	11.6
1930	36,674	76,158	–	1,066	113,898	0.3
1931	17,487	49,338	–	720	58,585	(8.5)
1932	7,777	17,425	16,581	412	42,195	(8.5)
1933	2,401	1	38,150	430	40,982	(4.4)
1934	27,130	–	56,804	1,901	85,835	(3.2)
1935	29,476	–	70,323	1,282	101,080	0.6
1936	25,409	–	93,309	4,548	123,266	3.3

Source: "Hudson Shipments, Calendar Years 1909–1957," DCHC; "Hudson, Net Profits, 1910–1952," NAHC.

previous decade, two of the largest Detroit-based independent body manufacturers, Fisher Body Company and Briggs Manufacturing Company, provided most of the Hudson and Essex bodies. The Edward Budd Company, based in Philadelphia, supplied some steel bodies in 1925. The new Hudson body plant, which cost $10 million, was to turn out 1,500 steel closed bodies daily for the Essex. Briggs remained a significant supplier for a decade, but Hudson expanded its own body-making capacity to the point where it supplied all of its needs for its high-volume lines. In the second half of 1926, for example, Hudson produced all of the bodies for the Hudson and Essex Coaches and the Essex sedan, Briggs provided bodies for the Essex touring car, and a Massachusetts firm, Biddle & Smart, supplied bodies for the Hudson touring car, brougham, and sedan models.[71]

Biddle & Smart began manufacturing carriage bodies in Amesbury, Massachusetts, near the New Hampshire border, in 1880. The firm announced its entrance into the automobile body business in 1905 and soon provided custom bodies to automakers such as Peerless, Lincoln, Chalmers, and White, among others. Biddle & Smart first supplied Hudson with bodies for its 1923 seven-passenger and five-passenger sedan models, and Hudson became Biddle & Smart's most important customer through 1931, when the Amesbury firm stopped making automobile bodies. Their peak shipments came in 1926, when they delivered 41,000 bodies to Hudson. All of the Biddle & Smart bodies were aluminum, as the firm could not stamp steel bodies.[72]

The Hudson and Essex lines underwent hundreds of changes in equipment, size, and styling between 1925 and 1936, which will not be detailed here. The offerings involved a bewildering set of choices of body styles, made more complex by the policy of changing model designations and sometimes styling in midyear. Hudson, Essex, and Terraplane (starting in 1934) offered one series of models in January through June and then a second series from July through December. For 1931, for example, a customer had a choice of seventeen distinct Hudson models and eleven Essex models. In 1934, the Hudson automobile was available in thirty different versions and the Terraplane in twenty-six.[73]

The single most notable trend in the Hudson-Essex-Terraplane lines was the move toward larger and more powerful engines. For 1927, Hudson replaced its L-head inline Six (289 CID and 76 brake horsepower) with a new F-head inline Six, also with 289 CID, but generating 92 brake horsepower. The new engine could produce a cruising speed of 70 miles per hour and a top speed of 80. To stop this faster Hudson, the company introduced four-wheel mechanical brakes by Bendix as standard equipment in 1927. Previously, brakes on the rear wheels only had been the standard. In 1930, Hudson replaced its six-cylinder offering with the Hudson

Great Eight, equipped with an L-head eight-cylinder engine with 214 CID and an output of 80 brake horsepower. The 1930 models were much lighter than the previous year's (by 600 to 1,000 pounds), so this engine produced adequate power.

The 1931 models, named the Hudson Greater Eight, had larger engines and lower prices than the 1930 models, but did nothing to stop the sales skid. By 1932, the eight-cylinder engine had grown to 254 CID and produced 101 brake horsepower. Hudson reintroduced a Super-Six model in 1933, but dropped it after only one year.[74]

As the 1920s ended, the Hudson and Essex models remained enormously popular. As sales approached 300,000 units a year, the firm struggled to keep up production. By 1927, the factory typically turned out 1,500 cars a day, but on 13 July 1927, Hudson set an all-time production record of 1,831 cars. In July 1928 the company opened a $1 million plant addition that allowed it to apply color lacquer to fenders, hoods, and other body parts in large quantities. In early 1929, the factory turned out an average of 1,900 cars a day or more than 200 an hour using only a single shift. Hudson factory managers had perfected "straight line production," which required flawless coordination of the movement of all the parts and components to final assembly.[75]

The late 1920s marked significant changes at Hudson before the onset of the Great Depression. In July 1929, Hudson entered the commercial vehicle business

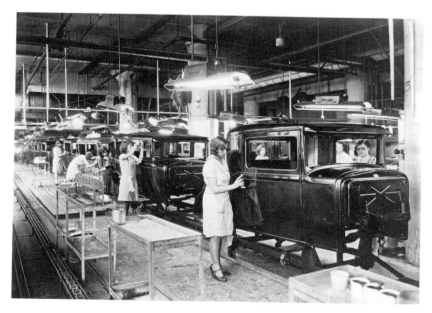

Hudson factory, striping line, 1930. *Courtesy DCHC.*

1929 Hudson Dover truck. *Courtesy DCHC.*

with the "Dover" line built on the Essex Super-Six chassis, with bodies supplied by Hercules Products of Evansville, Indiana. Hudson introduced the Dover line to capture a share of the booming commercial vehicle market of the late 1920s. Dover commercial vehicles were based on the Essex chassis, featured the Essex Super-Six motor, and had 3/4-ton capacity. Dover was available in Open Express (pickup), Screenside, Canopy Express, and Panel Delivery bodies. The Dover name lasted only a year, replaced by Essex and, starting in 1933, by Terraplane. Hudson was one of the latecomers to commercial vehicles and the production figures (Table 5.2) were never substantial.[76]

On 8 July 1929, the Hudson Motor Car Company quietly celebrated its twentieth anniversary. Earlier in the year (in March) Roscoe B. Jackson, Hudson's president and general manager, died suddenly at age fifty. William J. McAneeny, who had been with Hudson since 1909 and was a substantial stockholder, succeeded Jackson. A. E. Barit, who had served as secretary since 1923, was elected vice president and treasurer in 1929. Except for Roy Chapin, who remained involved with Hudson mostly in an advisory capacity, the original founders were practically gone. Bezner had left in the early 1920s to pursue his aviation interests in Europe and Coffin would retire in 1930, but remain as a consultant.[77]

The Hudson Motor Car Company annual report for 1928 was the first annual report to provide details regarding the company's operations. According to the report, the company produced the vast majority of its components in-house. Hudson used a Teletype system that issued printed orders to coordinate production, particularly assembly. This was the only system of this type used in the automobile industry. Throughout production, the Central Inspection Department of roughly 750 men inspected all raw materials, parts, and components and every manufacturing and assembly operation. They also embedded individual inspectors in the various production groups throughout the plant.[78]

The 1928 annual report also included details about the Hudson workforce and its organization. Most of the 25,000 employees, except the office force, worked in groups or "gangs" in which the collective production of the group, measured in terms of quantity and quality, largely determined pay, a "group piece-rate" system. The report stated, "We are very proud of our freedom from labor disturbance." The Central Employment Department received credit for this outcome. It settled all employee grievances according to a policy of "fair play." The Safety Department worked to reduce work-related accidents and Hudson maintained a first-aid room in each plant.[79]

The same annual report offers a rare glimpse into Hudson's sales operations, particularly its overseas sales. The company claimed 5,000 distributors and dealers in the United States and Canada, with an additional 2,000 worldwide. Hudson shipped nearly 18 percent of its cars to Canada and overseas to foreign distributors and operated assembly plants in England, Germany, and Holland. The report claimed that more than half of all American passenger cars sold in England were Hudson and Essex models.[80]

In September 1929, the Guardian Detroit Company, a banking house, issued a detailed analysis of Hudson's current condition and an optimistic forecast of its near-term future. The analysis focused on Hudson's success in selling cars abroad during the 1920s. Overseas sales in 1922 amounted to nearly 7,700 cars, or 8.4 percent of the company's shipments. For 1928, Hudson shipped a remarkable 50,587 vehicles overseas, or 17.9 percent of the total. The company sold its first Hudson in Britain in 1911 and the first Essex there in 1919. At the time of the Guardian report, Hudson had assembly plants in England and Germany, with another ready to begin operating in Brussels and projected to assemble 15,000 cars a year. Hudson distributors also assembled cars in Australia, New Zealand, Japan, Argentina, and Brazil.[81]

Sales of Hudson and Essex cars combined fell 62 percent in 1930 from the year before and another 49 percent from 1930 to 1931. The bottom came in 1933, when Hudson-Essex sales fell to 40,982 units, in contrast to 300,962 in 1929. Both the Hudson and Essex nameplates suffered losses of approximately 90 percent of their 1929 sales by 1932 (see Table 5.2). The sales declines brought enormous hardship to Hudson's workers, whom they laid off in droves. In November and December

Hudson
Administration
Building, 1930.
*Courtesy
DCHC.*

Hudson secretaries, ca.
1930. *Courtesy JMC.*

Display Room,
Hudson plant in
Detroit, February
1931.
Courtesy JMC.

1930, when Hudson was "ramping up" production of the 1931 models, the company recalled 5,700 employees back to work, bringing the total employed in mid-December to only 9,244, or roughly one-third of the 1929 levels. After earning a tiny profit in 1930, Hudson posted substantial losses in each year from 1931 through 1934 (Table 5.2). The automaker's surplus funds on hand fell from $38.7 million at the end of 1929 to a dangerously low level of only $4 million at the end of 1934, before recovering the following year.[82]

On 21 July 1932, the Hudson Motor Car Company officially unveiled a new model that was as important to the automaker's success as the Hudson Super-Six and Essex Coach had been in earlier days. The new model, the Essex Terraplane, was a much smaller and lighter car than the standard Essex. Stuart G. Baits, Hudson's chief engineer, designed a lightweight but strong frame that saved weight. Body panels bore some of the structural torsion loads, so this unique body design represented a move toward unit-body design. The shorter wheelbase (106 inches versus 113 inches in 1931) combined with a narrower chassis produced weight savings of 400–500 pounds.

A new and improved engine produced 70 brake horsepower, which gave the Terraplane outstanding performance. The engine still used "splash lubrication" rather than a pressurized system but was advanced in other respects. A water pump replaced the old thermosyphon system of circulating water in the engine. Terraplane had a very small but durable transmission, and the power train was secured to the chassis with rubber mounts, reducing vibration. Frank Spring, who had joined Hudson the year before as its first stylist, designed the Terraplane body. Selling at $425 to $610, Terraplane was Hudson's first entry into the low-priced field and would compete directly with Ford, Chevrolet, and Plymouth.[83]

The introduction and early promotion of the Terraplane was simply brilliant. The choice of *Terraplane* was a conscious effort to link the car with speed, excitement, and modernity of flight. Hudson explained: "Two brothers named Wright flew a power-kite off the bleak sands of Kitty Hawk—and gave *airplane* to the world. Genius and daring, in quest of new thrills, Added hulls and keels to winged motors—and gave us *hydroplane*. Today, the earthbound automobile takes on phantom wings—and you have the TERRAPLANE." Hudson replaced the vocabulary of driving with the vocabulary of flight—"riding" became *gliding*, "hill climbing" was *soaring*, "curving" was *banking*, and "accelerating" became *taking off*.[84]

Americans were enraptured with airplanes, flight, and pilots during the 1920s and 1930 and Hudson rode this wave of enthusiasm with the Terraplane. Charles Lindbergh's New York to Paris solo flight of 1927 electrified the nation and turned him into a national cult hero. "Barnstormers" visited county fairs, performed aerial stunts, and sold rides. The airplane and flight came to represent speed and excitement and freedom, but also the progress brought by science and technology.[85]

Connecting the Terraplane to flying included endorsements. Amelia Earhart, the world-famous aviatrix who had completed a solo flight across the Atlantic in May 1932, christened the Terraplane at its unveiling at the Hudson plant on 21 July 1932. She smashed a bottle of aviation fuel over the radiator of the Terraplane. Hudson's engineers had weakened the bottle by etching lines in it with acid, so it broke easily without damaging the car. Roy Chapin presented Orville Wright with the first Terraplane off the assembly line. A crowd estimated at 25,000 attended the festivities. The company presented 2,000 dealers from forty states with special bronze-colored "demonstrator" Terraplanes, which they drove home after parading them through downtown Detroit.[86] The ceremonies overwhelmed Ethel Denham, who wrote in *Automotive Industries,* "The Hudson Motor Car Company really deserves an editorial break on their introduction yesterday of the Terraplane, here. With the temperatures well up in the nineties, ceremonies were short and to the point, run off like clock work, impressive and enthusiasm-promoting."[87]

The Terraplane *was* fast, although the claim that it "could amble at 80 mph all day and still do 20–25 mpg" was a bit exaggerated. It was not likely that the Terraplane could maintain 80 miles per hour all day and certainly would not get 20–25 miles per gallon at that speed. In January 1933, Hudson added an eight-cylinder engine that delivered 94 brake horsepower and made Terraplane even faster. Kit Foster has

Amelia Earhart christening the first Essex Terraplane,
Detroit, July 1932. *Courtesy DCHC.*

Amelia Earhart with her 1932 Essex Terraplane. *Courtesy DCHC.*

argued that the Terraplane Eight outperformed the Ford V-8 in tests of acceleration. By 1934, "Essex" disappeared and the line became simply "Terraplane."[88]

Hudson entered Terraplanes in dozens of speed, acceleration, endurance, hill-climbing, and economy contests in 1931–35 and the new car won consistently. Brothers Chet and Al Miller drove most of the Terraplanes to victory. Terraplanes won contests in Canada, Britain, South Africa, and the Midwest, and at Daytona Beach, at Pike's Peak, in the Alps, and at the Bonneville Salt Flats in Utah.[89]

Terraplane did not bring instant recovery or prosperity to Hudson, whose sales continued to skid through 1933 (Table 5.2), but the new model slowed the downward spiral. The company sold only 7,777 cars carrying the Hudson nameplate in 1932 and a mere 2,401 in 1933, the fewest Hudsons sold since 1909, the company's founding year. When Hudson returned to profitability in 1935 and 1936, Terraplane accounted for three-quarters of the total sales.

Hudson continued to refine and improve its Hudson and Terraplane models from 1934 through 1936, the year Roy Chapin died. Over the years 1934–36, Hudson cars were exclusively Eights and they sold Terraplanes as Sixes only. The 1935 models came equipped with the Bendix "Electric Hand," a system that used a finger-controlled two-inch lever attached to the right side of the steering column to shift gears through electrically activated vacuum units. The driver still used the clutch in the customary way.[90]

The company developed the styling of the Depression-era Hudsons and Terraplanes under the direction of Hudson's first stylist, Frank S. Spring (1893–1959). Spring first worked in the automobile industry in the early 1920s as an engineer and not as a body stylist. He joined the custom coach builders, the Walter M. Murphy Company of Pasadena, California, in 1923 as an engineer. Hudson's president William J. McAneeny met Spring and decided to hire him as Hudson's first style engineer in September 1931. Spring was responsible for the 1933 Terraplane Eight and subsequent models during the rest of the decade. He hired Arthur H. Kibinger in 1934 to work as his assistant and the two men and their small staff created the Hudson-Terraplane cars of the mid- and late 1930s. In the fall of 1938, the entire Hudson styling staff consisted of eight men.[91]

Hudson's top management underwent a gradual but thorough transformation in the 1930s culminating with the death of Roy D. Chapin in February 1936. The process began with the death of Roscoe Jackson in March 1929 and the retirement of Howard Coffin in 1930. Following the death of Jackson, William J. McAneeny became president and general manager, positions he held until May 1933. Roy Chapin reluctantly served as secretary of commerce in the Hoover administration from July 1932 until the Roosevelt administration assumed power in March 1933. With the Hudson Motor Car Company struggling with poor sales and losses, Roy Chapin assumed Hudson's presidency on 20 May 1933, a decade after he had vacated that position in favor of Jackson. In June 1934, Chapin named A. Edward Barit general manager and Stuart G. Baits, Hudson's chief engineer, to the additional post of assistant general manager, presumably to help ease Barit's workload.[92]

During Roy Chapin's brief return as Hudson's president, he returned the company to a reasonably sound financial footing. By early 1934, Hudson faced creditors, including suppliers and banks, pressing the automaker to pay its outstanding bills and loans. Chapin put together a package of $6 million in loans to Hudson from a combination of six private banks, four investment houses, and the Federal Reserve Bank of New York. The agreements were finally in place in April 1935, after nearly a year of negotiations.[93]

Chapin's efforts to revive sales, improve the products, and further reduce costs paid off. Sales of 85,835 vehicles in 1934, while not impressive by the standards of the late 1920s, did represent a doubling from the 1933 results. Shipments jumped to 101,080 units in 1935 when Hudson produced modest profits of nearly $600,000, the first since 1930. Still, Hudson fared poorly in 1929–36 compared with the other auto companies. The company's rank in terms of production fell from third to eighth place. Hudson's decline in output over those years (59 percent) was worse than Ford's (48 percent) and far worse than Pontiac (15 percent), Buick (8 percent), and Studebaker (6 percent). Competitors such as Oldsmobile and Dodge had production increases of 85 percent and 120 percent, respectively. Chapin had begun to turn Hudson around, but unfortunately did not live to see any additional recovery.[94]

Roy Chapin became ill with influenza on Sunday, 9 February 1936, while at home in Detroit. When his condition worsened, he went to Henry Ford Hospital in Detroit on Wednesday, contracted pneumonia, and died on Sunday, 16 February 1936, a week before he would have turned fifty-six. As expected, A. Edward Barit succeeded Chapin as president of the Hudson Motor Car Company. This succession was confirmed at the Hudson board of directors' meeting on 25 February 1936. Barit kept the post of general manager, Stuart G. Baits remained assistant general manager, and H. Murray Northrup, then the chief engineer, became a director. The management transition following Chapin's death was seamless.[95]

Roy Dikeman Chapin: A Retrospective

Roy Chapin's funeral took place at his spacious home on Lake Shore Drive in Grosse Pointe, Michigan, in mid-afternoon on 19 February 1936. Hundreds of friends and close business associates paid their last respects to Chapin. The Reverend Francis C. Creamer of Christ Church Chapel, Grosse Pointe, recited the Episcopal ritual. They laid the body to rest temporarily in the mausoleum at Woodlawn Cemetery in Detroit, awaiting future burial in the Chapin family cemetery plot. The only automotive notable among the pallbearers was A. Edward Barit from Hudson.[96]

Editorials and comments from several of Chapin's fellow automakers are an indication of their great respect for him. The *Detroit News* noted, "Roy Dikeman Chapin was one of the few pioneers in the automobile industry who entered it not as an engineer, but as a salesman. It was quite as important to put the new product on the market, and to make it popular, as it was to design and manufacture it. Mr. Chapin was a young man with energy, enthusiasm and ideas. The industry needed such men, and he made good." Former president Herbert Hoover said of Chapin, "He not only contributed greatly to the building up of the motor industry, but all his life he has given a large measure of constructive public service. His death is a real national loss." Edsel Ford, a longtime close friend of Chapin, observed, "Mr. Chapin's death is a serious loss to Detroit. Men like Chapin are greatly needed in times such as these. He was a constructive force in the development of the life of Detroit and in the motor industry. He was noted for meeting difficulties with incomparable calm and resourcefulness. On the personal side, he was a man of deep friendliness and unusual ability."[97]

Roy D. Chapin was one of a half-dozen important early leaders in the emerging Detroit automobile industry who had a lasting impact on its development during the first quarter of the twentieth century. He was an important contributor to the early success of the Olds Motor Works. Roy Chapin was the leading force in the foundation and business success of the Thomas-Detroit and Chalmers-Detroit companies, and then led the formation of the Hudson Motor Car Company, all before 1910 and all before he turned thirty. Other contemporary automotive pioneers of this era, including Henry Ford, E. R. Thomas, Hugh Chalmers, Charles Nash, the Dodge brothers, and Walter Chrysler, were in their forties or beyond when they got started. Chapin and Chalmers were among a handful of industry pioneers who were not machinists, mechanics, or engineers.

To be sure, Chapin could succeed in the industry relying mainly on his skills in sales and promotion because he had Howard Coffin as his partner. He succeeded in large part because much like Ransom Olds, Henry Ford, the Dodge brothers, Walter Chrysler, and others, Roy Chapin was a visionary. Once Hudson was operating with some success, he recognized the need to offer unique and upgraded products like the Hudson Super-Six, the Essex Coach, and the Terraplane to expand the company's position in the automobile market. These new products all involved considerable risk, but they reaped handsome rewards because they worked. Roy Chapin deserves to be mentioned in the same breath as the more well-known automotive leaders of this era.

Putting the life and career of Roy D. Chapin in perspective is a challenge because much of his important work took place outside the automobile industry proper. He and a handful of other visionary automobile leaders, particularly Henry B. Joy of the Packard Motor Car Company, worked tirelessly to promote better roads both in Michigan and nationally. He was a leader in the Michigan Good Roads Association in the 1910s and 1920s, and advanced the study of roads and highways at the University of Michigan. Starting in 1919, he funded a fellowship for the study of hard-surfaced roads and promoted annual conferences on highway engineering held by Michigan's engineering college. Along with Carl Fisher, the father of the Indianapolis 500 Speedway, Chapin and Henry Joy launched the Lincoln Highway Association in 1913 to construct a coast-to-coast paved highway from New York City to San Francisco. Following Chapin's death, *Automotive Industries* published a retrospective on him titled "Roy D. Chapin—A Man of Service to His Country and His Industry," which nicely summarized his work beyond the Hudson Motor Car Company.[98]

Roy Chapin was also widely recognized internationally as an automotive industry leader. He worked to establish the Pan American Highway Commission, which met in Washington in June 1924. He spoke at meetings of the International Chamber of Commerce held at Brussels in 1925 and at Stockholm in 1927 and served as a delegate to the 1929 meeting in Amsterdam. He served as an official representative of the United States at the Permanent International Commission of Road Congresses and helped organize their Sixth International Road Congress in Washington in 1930. The next year, the French government honored Chapin with its Order of Officier of the Legion of Honor for his leadership in promoting highways worldwide.[99]

As a leading figure in the automobile industry and a staunch Republican, Chapin had access to presidents Harding, Coolidge, and Hoover. In the late 1920s, he led several delegations of top automobile executives to meet with congressional leaders and presidents to discuss taxes and other matters of interest to the automobile industry. Although Ford Motor Company rarely participated, leaders from General Motors, Chrysler, Packard, Nash, and Willys normally joined Chapin for these political excursions.[100]

Roy Chapin reached the pinnacle of public service when he agreed to President Hoover's request that he join the Hoover administration as secretary of commerce. President Hoover phoned Roy Chapin in late July 1932 to ask him to join his cabinet, but only a long meeting with Hoover on 3 August convinced him to take the post. With no end in sight for the economic depression, Hoover hoped that Chapin might help revive the economy and his reelection prospects. Although Chapin was sworn in on 8 August 1932, the Senate did not officially confirm his appointment until 14 December 1932. He spent most of his term making optimistic speeches about the economic future of the country and on 22 August 1932 made the first of several radio addresses to the nation on the NBC network. Following Hoover's crushing defeat at the polls on 8 November, Roy Chapin and the rest of the administration became lame ducks who remained in office until 4 March 1933. Chapin's short term as secretary of commerce did not reflect in any way his leadership or political skill.[101]

Roy Dikeman Chapin's life and career, both in the automobile industry and outside it, were remarkable and exemplary in many respects. It is one of the cruel twists of fortune that he is barely known outside a small circle of automotive historians. Unlike Ransom Olds, the Dodge Brothers, Henry Ford, Charles Nash, and Walter Chrysler, Roy Chapin's name did not become an automotive nameplate. To this researcher's knowledge, there are no schools, parks, or roads named after Roy Chapin. In April 1946, work was underway on the Crosstown Highway, an expressway extending west to east through Detroit, now designated as Interstate 94. The State Highway Department was considering names for this highway and there were two finalists—Roy D. Chapin and Edsel B. Ford. The American Automobile Manufacturers Association preferred Chapin and the Detroit Board of Commerce passed a resolution endorsing the choice of Chapin. The Detroit City Council apparently had the final say and the Ford family specified that they would agree to the use of Edsel's name only if the City Council came to a unanimous decision. They chose Ford over Chapin, perhaps because Ford's death (1943) was a more recent memory than Chapin's.[102]

SIX

Hudson under A. E. Barit, 1936–54

He was one of the most cautious men I've ever seen. He was very taciturn. But I had great respect for him. Several people sat up there on the roof and told him what they thought he wanted to hear. I made up my mind that I would always tell him what I thought. I don't know of anyone who could tell you what Mr. Barit thought.

Joseph W. Eskridge, head of the Hudson Experimenta
Body Division and vice president
in charge of manufacturing,
Hudson Motor Car Company, 1951–54

A. E. Barit led the Hudson Motor Car Company through very difficult times—the coming of organized labor and collective bargaining in 1937, the return of severe depression conditions in 1938, the end of civilian production during World War II, severe postwar conversion challenges, and then a crippling sales crisis in the early 1950s. Barit was at the helm during Hudson's long-term decline, which had begun with the Great Depression. In an act of desperation, Hudson merged with Nash Motors in 1954 to form the American Motors Corporation. Hudson was in such poor shape by 1954 that it would not have survived as an independent automaker, but in most respects, it did not survive even with the merger. After 1957, the Hudson and Nash nameplates both disappeared and they became "orphan cars."

Following as he did on the heels of Roy D. Chapin made Barit's job difficult and invited comparisons that are unkind to Barit. Chapin and Barit were very different men. Abraham Edward Barit (30 August 1890–14 July 1974) was born to poor parents in Jersey City, New Jersey. He had spent almost his entire adult life working for the Hudson Motor Car Company in a wide range of positions. Shortly before Roy Chapin died, he said of Barit, "He has a more thorough knowledge of every angle

A. Edward Barit, 1940.
Courtesy DCHC.

of the automobile business than any man I ever knew." Barit had briefly worked as a secretary for the purchasing agent at the Chalmers-Detroit Motor Company but joined Hudson in the same position sometime in 1909. Appointed assistant purchasing agent in 1911, he then served as purchasing agent from 1915 until 1929. Named a director of the company in 1921, Barit also held the position of company secretary from 1923 to 1929. He became the treasurer and a vice president of Hudson in 1929, the company's twentieth year in business. Barit served as president and general manager of Hudson's Canadian operations starting in 1932, and Chapin named him Hudson general manager in 1934. He seemed the logical choice to replace Roy Chapin.[1]

The Struggles of the Late 1930s

The Hudson Motor Car Company's record in the late 1930s was in many respects a continuation of the pattern of the early 1930s—absolute declines in sales and profits from the late 1920s (see Table 6.1)—but, perhaps as important, relative decline compared with the rest of the industry. The manner in which Hudson operated changed substantially with the arrival of organized labor and labor contracts starting in 1937. Hudson's management had also changed in personality and style. The company's products were not particularly innovative or stylish and failed to capture the

Table 6.1. Hudson Motor Car Company Shipments, by Calendar Year and Profits, Net of Taxes ($ Millions), Year Ending 31 December 1936–45

	Hudson	Terraplane	Commercial Vehicles	Total	Net Profits ($ Millions)
1936	25,409	93,309	4,548	123,266	3.3
1937	19,848	83,436	8,048	111,342	0.7
1938	43,682	6,599	808	51,078	(4.7)
1939	81,521	–	640	82,161	(1.4)
1940	86,865	–	1,035	87,900	(1.5)
1941	78,717	–	812	79,529	3.8
1942	5,396	–	67	5,463	2.1
1943	69	–	–	69	1.6
1944	–	–	–	–	1.7
1945	4,735	–	270	5,005	0.7

Source: "Hudson Shipments, Calendar Years 1909–1957," DCHC; "Hudson, Net Profits, 1910–1952," NAHC.

interest of potential customers. To some extent, the early Hudson-Essex-Terraplane models reflected the sense of style of a salesman, Roy D. Chapin, while the later Hudsons mirrored the sensibilities of an accountant, A. E. Barit.

The Hudson Motor Car Company ran its manufacturing operations in Detroit into the early 1930s in an environment in which labor unions were simply absent. The first substantial labor unrest at Hudson reported in the local newspapers came on 7 February 1933, when striking workers shut down the Hudson body plant, demanding substantial pay increases. Max F. Wollering, Hudson's vice president in charge of manufacturing agreed to meet with a committee of workers to discuss their demands on the condition that the workers be Hudson employees and not be associated with Communists. Robert M. Pilkington from the U.S. Department of Labor blamed the strike on "the Communist element." Picketers effectively shut down the body plant on Conner Avenue, and the main assembly plant was forced to go to half-day operations. The body plant reopened Monday, 13 February 1933, when most of the workers reported to work. The pickets entirely disappeared the next day and the workers gained nothing from the strike.[2]

Labor unrest reappeared a little more than a year later. When the Automobile Workers of America, American Federation of Labor, began to organize, the company established the Hudson Industrial Association (HIA), a company-backed union in late spring of 1933. Hudson then negotiated with HIA and granted its workers pay raises in July and August 1933 and in February 1934. There is no indication that the Hudson workers took any further action.[3]

Labor disputes at Hudson later in 1934 were about which union would represent the Hudson workers in future negotiations with the company. In late August, the company ran an election of representatives to HIA against the protests of the independent Associated Automobile Workers of America (AAWA). On 15 February 1935, the Automobile Labor Board supervised an election to decide which labor organization would represent Hudson workers. The result was a draw, with each group winning exactly half the seats.[4]

Hudson's workers joined the wave of sit-down strikes led by the United Automobile Workers (CIO) against the automakers starting in 1936. There were scores of strikes against auto companies and supplier companies beginning with the sit-down strike against General Motors in Flint, which began on 30 December 1936 and ended forty-four days later on 11 February 1937 when General Motors agreed to negotiate a collective bargaining agreement with the UAW. Chrysler workers sat down inside the Chrysler plants on 8 March 1937 and remained until 25 March, when Chrysler agreed not to reopen the plant until it had negotiated a contract with the union.[5]

The Hudson sit-down strike also began on 8 March 1937 and lasted an entire month before the two sides reached an agreement. The UAW made a series of demands regarding wages, hours, working conditions, and seniority, but the main stumbling block that stymied negotiations was the union's insistence that the company recognize it as the sole bargaining agent for all of Hudson's employees. Michigan's Democratic governor Frank Murphy initiated negotiations between the parties at his office in Lansing in early April and they reached an agreement on 8 April 1937. The Hudson workers ratified the contract on Saturday, 9 April 1937, and Hudson resumed production Monday. The agreement included seniority provision governing layoffs, a general grievance mechanism, and a system for resolving disputes over "speed-ups." The company recognized the UAW as the exclusive bargaining agent *for its members*, but not for all Hudson workers. The company, however, agreed that it would not support or bargain with any rival labor organization in its plants.[6]

When the first contract expired on 8 April 1938, Hudson demanded concessions, which the union would not agree to. In late November 1938, the two sides reached an agreement, which the Hudson workers ratified. The contract, which extended until 1 December 1939, did not provide for any pay increases, but officially recognized the UAW as the exclusive bargaining agent for all the hourly workers. The

UAW and Hudson fashioned additional contracts in December 1939 and December 1940, all without strikes. In the 1940 contract, Hudson in essence agreed to a union shop—that is, joining the UAW and remaining in good standing was a requirement for employment. Claude E. Bland, the president of the Hudson Local 154, claimed that nearly 100 percent of Hudson workers were union members.[7]

Labor peace at Hudson lasted only until May 1941, when the union demanded a 15-cents-an-hour blanket pay raise for all employees, in response to sharp increases in the cost of living. Five days after a strike began at Hudson, federal labor conciliator James F. Dewey entered the negotiations on 20 May 1941 and helped craft a settlement one day later. The workers approved the agreement and were back at work on 22 May 1941. The settlement included an 8-cent raise, with a promise of 2 cents more if the government allowed Hudson to increase automobile production. The General Motors workers received a 10-cent increase, but that company was in far better financial shape than Hudson.[8]

The Hudson Motor Car Company, along with the rest of the auto industry, suffered in the late 1930s, as the recovery of 1935–37 (Table 6.1) turned into the recession of 1938 and sales plummeted. Hudson's sales fell 54 percent in 1938 versus 1937, while the industry as a whole had a sales decline of 48 percent. Sales in 1938 nearly fell back to the dismal levels of 1932–33 and put Hudson in eighth place among American nameplates. Hudson and the rest of the industry recovered in 1939 and 1940 before beginning to convert to war production in 1941. However, Hudson recovered more slowly than the rest of the industry and saw its sales ranking in 1941 slip to thirteenth.[9]

The company restyled the 1936 Hudson-Terraplane models from 1935 and added two significant mechanical improvements. Hudson replaced the linear styling of 1935 with a style relying on curves and contours, making the 1936 models appear more bulbous. The 1936 models came with hydraulic brakes, a first for Hudson, but with a twist. If the driver depressed the brake pedal beyond three-quarters of its maximum distance, presumably because of hydraulic failure, the car's mechanical brakes for the rear wheels engaged, stopping the car. The 1936 Hudsons also came equipped with a new front suspension system dubbed Radial Safety Control.[10]

The 1937 models also changed considerably from the 1936 offerings, growing wider and longer. In 1938 Hudson downgraded the Terraplane from a distinct brand to one of the Hudson car lines. The name disappeared altogether in 1939. The company introduced the Hudson 112 for 1938, so-named because of its 112-inch wheelbase. The new Hudson model was six inches shorter and about 250 pounds lighter than Terraplane, but more important, the company priced it to compete with Ford, Chevrolet, and Plymouth. The least expensive 1938 Terraplane, a two-door, three-passenger coupe, sold for $789, but the identical model Hudson 112 carried a price of $694. The Terraplane had a more powerful engine (101 horsepower versus 83 horsepower for the Hudson 112) and better performance but carried a higher price tag. Hudson produced only 6,559 Terraplanes in 1938 and let the marque disappear.[11]

The 1939 Hudsons featured significant styling changes from the 1938 models, including new grilles and headlights. Hudson also introduced its exclusive Auto-Poise Control suspension system, which consisted of a torsion bar anchored to the frame and the front wheel spindles. The system was supposed to keep the wheels in a straight-ahead position, which would help the driver coming out of curves. Hudson moved the gearshift lever from the floor to the steering column on all models and introduced Airfoam seat cushions for added riding comfort.[12]

The entire Hudson line went through a substantial restyling for 1940. The front suspension system was fully independent for the first time and used coil springs with telescopic shock absorbers placed within the springs. A Hudson Eight set an AAA Class C record for a mile at Bonneville in August 1939, and Hudson Eights won virtually every race they entered in 1940, all under AAA supervision.[13]

The company entirely restyled the 1941 Hudson from the cowl back, while keeping the hood and fenders from 1940. They also lengthened the wheelbases by three inches over the 1940 models. Hudson called the new clean look "symphonic styling," meaning that all the elements, including interior and exterior color schemes, meshed into a coherent style. The company also updated the 1942 models with new

Last 1942 Hudson built during World War II, February 1942. *Courtesy DCHC.*

fenders and other refinements, but production ended on 9 February 1942, as the automobile industry moved quickly into war production. Hudson's combined vehicle production of 5,463 units for 1942 reflects the unique circumstances the company faced. The transition to military production, however, was already well underway more than a year before the United States officially began hostilities against the Axis.[14]

Hudson at War

Much like the other American automakers, Hudson resisted converting from civilian car production to defense work until the declaration of war in December 1941. The company's performance over the long course of the war was at best mixed. Under the auspices of the U.S. Navy, Hudson produced the 20-millimeter Oerlikon automatic anti-aircraft cannon at a plant in Center Line, Michigan, just north of Detroit, starting in July 1941. The navy abruptly canceled this contract with Hudson in October 1943 and transferred it to the Westinghouse Corporation. Hudson focused on aircraft component production throughout the war and made almost no auto-related products such as trucks and tanks. The company successfully manufactured rear fuselage sections for the Martin B-26 Marauder medium bomber from early 1941 through March 1944. The company also assembled wings for the Curtiss-Wright SB 2C Helldiver dive-bomber and the Lockheed P-38 fighter. Late in the war, starting in July 1944, Hudson built armored cabins for the Bell P-63 King Cobra fighter. The company's last major contract was for fuselage sections and wings for the Boeing B-29 heavy bomber. Hudson started production in mid-1944, but struggled with the B-29 work through the end of the war.[15]

Hudson's first substantial war contract was for the manufacture of the Oerlikon 20-millimeter automatic cannon, the primary anti-aircraft gun used by the U.S. Navy. In mid-January 1941, Hudson announced it had signed a contract with the navy to manufacture "parts for guns and torpedoes" at a 400,000-square-foot factory complex costing $13 million to be built on a 113-acre site just north of Detroit. It would employ 4,000. In late April 1941, with construction underway, the projected plant had grown to a million square feet, the site was 135 acres, and the projected cost was $20–30 million. Naval anti-aircraft guns would be the major product manufactured there. In late July 1941, the U.S. Navy announced it was awarding a $14,038,500 contract to Hudson to manufacture these guns.[16]

Work at the Naval Ordnance Plant got underway in stages. The first machines began operating on 21 July 1941, but the navy did not require Hudson to deliver the first three "sample guns" until December. By mid-September, the navy increased the

Hudson-built Oerlikon anti-aircraft guns, 1942. *Courtesy DCHC.*

contract to 8,000 guns. Hudson managed to produce only thirty-four guns in Janu-ary 1942, but then output climbed quickly to 1,053 guns in April, making Hudson the largest manufacturer of Oerlikon guns in the country. The navy, pleased with the performance, awarded Hudson contracts for an additional 10,000 guns. Hudson increased production nearly every month in 1942 and over the last four months of the year turned out more than 1,500 a month. Output peaked at 2,330 guns in September 1943 and when Hudson lost this contract at the end of October, it had produced a grand total of 33,201 Oerlikon guns for the navy.[17]

Most of Hudson's war work involved the production of aircraft parts or sections that airplane manufacturers assembled elsewhere. Hudson established an Aircraft Division in February 1941 and produced aerilons for an (unnamed) eastern airplane manufacturer. The company named George Goin, the former aircraft production supervisor for the Ford Motor Company, as the head of its aircraft operations. Hud-son also appointed Tom Towle, who had worked for twenty years in the aircraft industry, as the head of aeronautical engineering at its Aircraft Division. It is pos-sible that Hudson took these actions mainly to establish its credentials to qualify for military aircraft contracts.[18]

Inspecting Hudson-built aluminum aircraft pistons, 1943. *Courtesy DCHC.*

In mid-September 1941, Hudson reported that production of pistons and rocker arms for Wright Aeronautical Corporation's radial aircraft engines had fallen far behind the contract production schedule, which called for 350 complete sets by 1 September 1941. At mid-month, Hudson had delivered only twenty-five sets. The fault lay with Wright, which had failed to deliver the required plans and specifications on time. Many automakers had similar problems when working with aircraft manufacturers. Production then climbed quickly, with 1,092 pistons delivered in October; 6,900 in January 1941; and 13,152 in April 1942. Through the end of the contract in January 1945, the overall achievement was impressive—1,030,000 pistons and 1,460,000 rocker arms.[19]

Another major Hudson contract in the early years of the war was for the production of fuselage tail sections for the Glenn Martin B-26-B Marauder bomber. On 21 July 1941 the Hudson directors approved a contract that called for 1,200 fuselage tail sections, with Hudson delivering the first ones in March 1942 and the last 100 in August 1943. The estimated contract cost was $11,327,610, with Hudson collecting a fixed fee (fixed profit) of $566,358, which was 5 percent of the contract price. After producing two fuselage sections in March 1942 as required, output reached fifty in July, well above the quota of sixteen. By September 1942, when production (and the quota) reached sixty-five tail sections, Glenn Martin asked Hudson to increase

Hudson-built Martin B-26-B fuselages, 1942. *Courtesy DCHC.*

production to 200 units a month. In March 1943, Hudson turned out 115 fuselages and then maintained production of 120–130 units per month in July–October 1943. Hudson's overall performance was impressive. It delivered 1,891 of these fuselage sections to Glenn Martin.[20]

Hudson's second major aircraft contract involved the manufacture of outer wings for the Curtiss-Wright SB2C Helldiver dive-bomber for the navy. In February 1942, the company agreed to build 4,000 pairs of wings at $8,000 per pair, for a contract of approximately $32 million. A Curtiss-Wright inspector observed at the end of December 1942, "The Hudson Company rates highly in the spirit they show, the efficiency and industrious attitude of their personnel, their tooling, and the results shown." The first delivery (three sets) came in January 1943 and production climbed quickly to 133 wing sets in October 1943. Monthly production in 1944 varied from 146 to 300 sets of wings. By the end of the war, Hudson turned out 4,250 sets of wings for this deadly airplane.[21]

Hudson began work on three additional aircraft contracts in 1944 and these contracts continued until the end of the war. The first was the manufacture of armored cabins (cockpits) for the Bell Aircraft Company P-63A fighter plane, the King Cobra. The company received a letter of intent from Bell in September 1943 that called for the production of 6,000 cabins, but in March 1944, Hudson agreed to a contract for 2,830 cabins. By war's end, the company had completed 3,041 cabins.[22]

Bulkhead section of B-29, Hudson plant, July 1944. *Courtesy DCHC.*

The second of the new aircraft contracts involved the manufacture of fuselage tail sections and outer wings for the Boeing B-29 heavy bomber. The contract was with the Glenn L. Martin Company, one of several aircraft companies making the B-29. They intended this work to replace the work Hudson was doing on the B-26 fuselage sections. The original contract of July 1944 called for 300 tail sections and 300 sets of wings. In December 1944, the automaker completed 141 tail sections. By the end of May 1945, when the surviving records stop, Hudson had produced 802 fuselage sections for the B-29. The contract extended to the end of the war, so the total was probably several hundred higher.

The third aircraft contract Hudson had in the last years of the war was for the production of wings for the Lockheed P-38 fighter. Hudson signed a contract with Lockheed in July 1944 to make 2,600 sets of wings, but had already begun work based on an earlier letter of intent from Lockheed issued in December 1943. Hudson completed the first set of wings in July 1944 but as late as November 1944 managed to turn out only five sets of wings. Production then jumped to thirty-one in January 1945, but Hudson delivered a total of 791 sets of wings through May. Production figures for June, July, and August have not survived, but Hudson's total production was probably between 1,000 and 1,200 sets of wings, less than half the number their contract specified.[23]

Hudson took on contracts for war products unrelated to aircraft to allow for full

use of all of its production facilities. In February and April 1942, the Hudson directors approved letters of intent to manufacture 37-millimeter armor-piercing shells
for the army and a variety of other products. Hudson landed an initial contract for
120,000 37-millimeter shells, quickly supplemented with an order for an additional
675,000, for a contract worth $1,114,000. The company turned out 68,000 shells
in June 1942 and then 104,600 in July, well above the required deliveries of 93,000
shells. The last specific mention of shell production covered September 1942
(69,278 shells) and marked the end of that contract. Total production amounted to
310,551 shells.[24]

In late November 1942, Hudson's directors approved a contract with the navy
to manufacture 2,000 Hall-Scott 265 brake horsepower gasoline engines to power
landing craft. Built under license from the Hall-Scott Motor Company of San Francisco, the straight-six engine displaced 998 cubic inches. Making this engine, known
as the Hudson Invader, permitted the company to use its engine plant. Production
began in December 1942 (10 units), and in January 1943, the navy increased the
contract to 3,000 engines. Output jumped to 250 engines in March 1943 and then
varied between 180 and 312 engines per month through October 1943. The contract ended in September 1944, when the company made only 41 engines. Hudson
manufactured a total of 4,004 Invader engines.[25]

The disruption of civilian production and drastic changes in the labor market
brought by the war affected all the automobile manufacturers. Hudson's workforce
engaged in defense work leaped from 1,683 in August 1941 to 6,000 by January
1942, when Hudson's total employment was roughly 10,000–12,000 workers. Once
war production was fully underway, employment jumped from roughly 11,000 in
April 1942 to 20,512 by mid-December. In July 1943, when Hudson had 22,625
employees, they were split nearly equally between the Naval Ordnance Plant in
Center Line and the main plant in Detroit. By mid-November 1943, the totals fell to
12,000, reflecting Hudson's loss of the Naval Ordnance Plant in October, which will
be discussed later in this chapter. There is considerable evidence of Hudson hiring
many women and African Americans during the war, but few firm numbers. In mid-
May 1945, the hourly workforce was 38 percent female and 62 percent male.[26]

Changing social conditions during the war disrupted workers' "normal" work
life. Simply getting to work at isolated factories such as the Hudson Naval Arsenal
became challenging, with wartime rationing of tires and gasoline. In June 1942,
Hudson workers at that plant joined in a Detroit citywide ride-sharing program.
Increased night work required adjustments as well. Hudson issued stickers to its
night workers pleading for potential door-knockers and door bell-ringers to "Please
let this night worker get his sleep."[27]

Although Hudson hired women to work in most production and inspection positions throughout its factories, its female plant guards took on celebrity status. The company announced in August 1942 that its successful experiment with female plant guards at its main plant in Detroit prompted the company to hire and train twenty-nine women to guard its Naval Ordnance Plant. In November 1942, Hudson announced that it was training another sixty female guards for the Naval Ordnance Plant. Hudson recognized the need to provide child care for women workers with young children. In December 1943, a day care center opened near the Detroit Hudson plant to care for children ages two to five. Hudson donated the services of its doctors and nurses, St. Rose Catholic Church donated its social hall, and the Detroit Board of Education provided funds made available through the federal Lanham Act.[28]

The war did not by any means eliminate labor-management conflict at Hudson and elsewhere. Ten days after Pearl Harbor labor leaders and industrialists made a "no-strike, no-lockout" pledge for the duration of the war. The UAW repeated this pledge in April 1941, but strikes nevertheless took place, although they were unauthorized "wildcat" strikes. The appearance of African American workers on jobs and in departments where they were previously absent sometimes touched off protest strikes commonly known as "hate strikes." The first of these came in January 1942, when Hudson transferred two African Americans to the milling machine department at the naval arsenal and two hundred white workers briefly stopped work. The management withdrew the workers after white union members insisted the workforce remain segregated.[29]

Hudson also faced a short-lived "hate strike" at its naval arsenal in June 1942, but the company, the UAW, and the government combined to end it quickly. On 18 June, workers in several departments at the Hudson Naval Arsenal walked off their jobs when Hudson placed African American workers in production work. Secretary of the Navy Frank Knox informed the UAW local that the navy would fire striking workers and prevent them from finding work in other war plants. Hudson fired four ringleaders with the blessing of the national UAW leadership, including president R. J. Thomas. UAW regional director Richard Frankensteen blamed the Ku Klux Klan for the troubles. This was apparently the last incident of this type at the naval arsenal.[30]

The War Labor Board (WLB), which controlled wages and salaries, sometimes undermined labor peace at companies like Hudson. In early January 1943, the WLB denied Hudson's request to raise the wages of about 800 employees in fifty-three rate classifications, but approved an increase in vacation pay from $30 to $45. Hudson argued that the workers in those classifications had not received the 15 percent pay increase allowed by the WLB in January 1941. The WLB ruled in February 1944 that Hudson could increase the pay workers would receive instead of vacations from $45 to $54 per week.[31]

Hudson was mostly strike-free during the war but suffered more work stoppages in 1944 and 1945 than in previous years. A devastating strike began on 1 May 1944 when foremen at Hudson and the Briggs Manufacturing Company walked off their jobs. The strikers were members of the Foremen's Association of America and demanded recognition for bargaining purposes. They defied the WLB demand that they return to work and threatened to remain out until the WLB agreed to take jurisdiction over their dispute with management. The strike finally ended on 18 May 1944, and the next day the WLB announced a series of conferences to settle the disputes between foremen and management at a half-dozen Detroit defense plants.[32]

Hudson suffered a crippling three-day strike starting on 29 March 1945 that stopped production of aircraft components. To protest the firing of an assistant union steward two weeks earlier, allegedly for telling the men not to work too fast, 110 inspectors failed to come to work and Hudson management shut down the plant. When workers at the machine shops and the engine plant joined the strike, 13,000 additional Hudson workers lost their jobs. The company and the union agreed to negotiate the fate of the fired assistant steward, thus ending the walkout. In late June 1945, 100 engineering employees walked out in a dispute over work assignments, touching off a brief two-day strike that involved 11,400 employees working on all of Hudson's aircraft contracts.[33]

Hudson fulfilled its military contracts on time and within budget early in the war. In January 1943, the Army Air Force awarded Hudson the coveted Army-Navy Production Excellence Award, more commonly known as the "E" Award, for its record in producing the Martin B-26 bomber fuselage sections. Fewer than one-third of military contractors received this award. Colonel Alonzo M. Drake, representing the Army Air Force, cited Hudson's record of completing more than the required fuselages in the early months of the contract, its excellent safety record, and the absence of work stoppages. In November 1943, Hudson's Aviation Division received a second E award, which took the form of a white star to be added to the E flag.[34]

On 5 October 1943, Rear Admiral W. H. P. Blandy sent a telegram to the employees of the Hudson Naval Ordnance Plant announcing that the navy was ending Hudson's management of the plant and turning over the facility to the Westinghouse Electric and Manufacturing Company. We will never know the precise reason why the navy made this decision. Their "official" reason was the desire to consolidate the operation of the Hudson plant with their two ordnance plants in Canton, Ohio, and Louisville, Kentucky, both run by Westinghouse. Publicly, the navy offered no detailed explanation for the change. The loss of this management contract was a major blow to Hudson's prestige if not to its profits.[35]

Several observers suggested that the navy was pleased with the production and the cost of the Oerlikon guns but displeased with the other work performed at the naval arsenal. The navy expected Hudson to produce specialized products, such as catapults for launching airplanes, in quantities as small as a dozen. They also expected Hudson to repair damaged ordnance at the plant, in effect serving as a specialized machine shop. Hudson was most comfortable with mass production of standardized products, while the navy often required "one-of" production. Perhaps Westinghouse, with its experience in producing customized, "one-of" electrical equipment, was a better "fit" for the navy.[36]

The naval arsenal was not the only part of Hudson war production that was problematic. Documents generated in May–October 1951, when Hudson was pursuing work as a subcontractor (with Lockheed) for the new Boeing B-47 jet bomber, offer glimpses of the earlier problems. In September 1951 two Hudson officials, J. J. Murphy and Paul W. West, attended a meeting with air force officials to discuss Hudson's possible role in B-47 production. One of these was Brigadier General A. H. Johnson, a high-ranking officer in the air force's Procurement and Planning Division. Johnson, who was familiar with Hudson's work during World War II, claimed that Hudson had "a record of being slow in getting into production" during the last war.[37]

Johnson's comments struck a sensitive nerve among Hudson officials who had managed the wartime aircraft contracts, including Barit. In early October, H. M. Northrup sent a five-page confidential memo to Barit recalling the history of World War II aircraft contracts at Hudson. Northrup was Hudson's vice president in charge of operations and a director during the war and held the same positions in 1951. He argued that Hudson satisfactorily fulfilled contracts for the B-26 and the B-29 fuselage sections and that Hudson never held up B-29 assembly because of delivery delays on its part.

Northrup argued that Hudson's problems in delivering Curtiss-Wright Helldiver wings were not entirely of their own making. They had to endure many delays in getting information and blueprints from Curtiss-Wright. He also blamed Lockheed for most of Hudson's struggles to produce wings for the Lockheed P-38. The drawings provided by Lockheed were full of major errors and inconsistencies, forcing Hudson and Lockheed to redesign the wings. The riveting required to assemble the wings was difficult and Hudson had to use inexperienced workers for this work. The combination of poor design and poor workmanship produced a large rejection rate and for a seven-week period in October and November 1944, Lockheed inspectors stopped production at Hudson. Lockheed initially rejected forty wings, but eventually accepted all but three.[38]

Putting Hudson's performance in perspective is difficult, given the lack of a comprehensive study of the automobile manufacturers' involvement in World War II production. Most of the automakers with aircraft contracts struggled with airplane manufacturers who were not prepared to engage in mass production of their products. They all confronted inconsistent blueprints and specifications and they all struggled with constant changes in design. None of them started with workers experienced in airplane assembly and most relied heavily on women to perform this work. These problems were not unique to Hudson, which seemed to have more trouble overcoming these difficulties than others. To be sure, Hudson did not have the engineering resources that companies like General Motors, Ford, and Chrysler had at their command to take on these challenges.

Hudson also did not perform particularly well during the war in terms of profits. None of the automakers in fact earned the contractual 5 or 6 percent "fixed fee" on the value of their war contracts. The government seldom altered the contracts if costs, especially labor costs, proved higher than anticipated. Although Hudson and the other car companies produced some civilian cars in early 1942 and late in 1945, the overall sales and profit figures for 1942–45 how small profits were. Hudson had sales of $421.9 million over those years and earned profits of only $6.1 million, or 1.5 percent of sales. Nash Motors, with larger sales of $724.5 million, earned $13.5 million, or 1.9 percent on sales. The Chrysler Corporation, which dwarfed both Hudson and Nash, had wartime sales of $3.6 billion and profits of $100.2 million, or 2.8 percent of sales.[39]

Hudson's poor performance caught the attention of one company director who severely criticized Barit's leadership. Carsten Tiedeman, the brother of Inez Chapin, Roy Chapin's widow, took detailed minutes of the Hudson directors' meetings from June 1941 through June 1945 while he served as a director. He prepared the minutes for the benefit of his nephew, Roy Chapin Jr., and Inez Chapin. Tiedeman included scathing criticisms of Barit's performance and his management style as part of his reports. The Hudson board of directors consisted of nine company officers and only two outsiders. At the start of his service as a director, Tiedeman suggested that the board replace several company officers with outsiders. When Barit argued that they might offend directors whom they would ask to leave, Tiedeman suggested that they all resign. Having the board packed with Barit's handpicked officers gave him absolute control over decision-making.[40]

Tiedeman served as a gadfly to Barit for the duration of the war. In April 1942 he insisted that Barit give the directors monthly statements of the status of each war contract. At their meeting of 20 July 1942, Barit objected to Tiedeman's taking detailed notes of the meetings, which Tiedeman argued would not be necessary if Barit would give the board written reports about company operations. At a January 1944 meeting, Tiedeman pointed out that the loss of the naval arsenal contract was far more serious for Hudson than Barit had estimated. He sarcastically noted that Hudson had no serious renegotiation problems with the government because its profits were pathetically low and cited Willys-Overland's 1943 profits of $22 million versus Hudson's profits of only $1.6 million.[41]

While holding on to his control of Hudson, Barit rejected two promising offers from notable industrialists to buy substantial stakes in Hudson—the first by Henry J. Kaiser in November 1943 and a second by the Fisher brothers, highly successful automobile body builders, in May 1945. George Mason, president of Nash-Kelvinator, approached Barit in 1946 with a proposal to merge the two companies, but Barit was not interested. In all three instances, Barit prevented the infusion of new capital into Hudson and, more important, the involvement of experienced and innovative businessmen. Perhaps he feared that the Chapin family interests would combine with either Kaiser or the Fishers to wrest control of Hudson from him. Barit maintained control, with tragic results for Hudson in the end.

In late November 1943, Barit revealed that Hudson was involved in discussions with Kaiser, the noted West Coast builder of Liberty ships, about building a new Kaiser-designed Jeep that the army was testing. Hudson would build the Jeep and pay Kaiser royalties on his design. Kaiser, however, was also interested in receiving options to buy Hudson stock. Tiedeman suggested that Hudson sell him the large block of shares the company had issued but never sold (20 percent of the total stock) and do so at the market price, which was lower than the book value. Barit objected to this strategy but Tiedeman observed that with Kaiser financially and otherwise involved with Hudson, the stock values would climb. It was clear at the next directors' meeting that Barit was only interested in a deal to manufacture Kaiser's Jeeps and did not want to sell Kaiser a stake in Hudson. By February 1944, any possible deal with Kaiser was moot because the government had decided to delay indefinitely the production of the Kaiser Jeep.[42]

The most significant effort by outsiders to buy a stake in Hudson came in mid-May 1945 when the five Fisher brothers, founders of the Fisher Body Corporation, offered to buy the unissued Hudson stock, some 400,000 shares, which would give them a 20 percent interest in the company. This offer did not come directly from the Fishers. B. A. Tomkins, vice president of the New York Bankers Trust Company and a financial advisor to the Roy Chapin family, made the offer on their behalf. On their part, the Fishers were coy, saying that their interest in Hudson was like a flirtation a young man might have with a pretty girl until he met another one more to his liking.[43]

The Chapin family interests, represented by Carsten Tiedeman, likely initiated the Fisher brothers' "flirtation." Their intention was to create an alliance of stockholders who could wrest control of Hudson from Barit and presumably replace him as president. When the annual Hudson stockholders' meeting began on the morning of 21 May 1945, Barit announced that 76 percent of the outstanding shares were represented in person or by proxy. Tiedeman then asked that the Hudson directors adjourn the meeting, but Barit refused. Tiedeman tried other tactics, but Barit and the corporation counsel stymied Tiedeman's efforts. Tiedeman threatened to take the matter to court. Finally, Barit addressed the "real" issue underlying this dispute: "I was told before this meeting that an attempt would be made to interfere with the meeting and delay sought until a board could be elected that was friendly to the Fisher Brothers." He then stated that he did not believe the offer from the Fishers was a fair one and that it needed "further study" before he would bring it to the stockholders.[44]

The power struggle continued in the directors' meeting that directly followed the stockholders' meeting. Barit proposed a change to the company's bylaws so that instead of two directors having the right to call a special stockholders' meeting, a majority would be needed. Tiedeman moved for a thirty-day delay in the vote, to allow more time for careful consideration of the issues. His motion lost 7–4 and the original motion then passed 7–4 as well. Barit and his allies had clearly turned back this effort to change Hudson's management. Less than a year later, the Hudson directors offered the remaining unsubscribed stock to the current stockholders, whereby a stockholder could buy one new share for every seven he already held. This move raised much-needed working capital, but also made it unlikely that any new player would get a large block of Hudson stock in the future.[45]

A. Edward Barit could not ignore another potential future rival waiting in the wings—Roy D. Chapin Jr., the first child born to Roy and Inez Chapin. Roy D. Chapin Jr. (21 September 1915–5 August 2001) attended Grosse Pointe Country Day School through the eighth grade and then spent three years (1929–32) at the Los Alamos Ranch School in New Mexico. The U.S. government commandeered the New Mexico school in 1942 and converted it into the Manhattan Project's Los Alamos Laboratory. Roy Chapin Jr. then spent an academic year (1932–33) at the Hotchkiss School in Lakeville, Connecticut, finishing two years' work in one year. He attended Yale University from 1933 to 1937, where he earned a degree in business administration. While at Yale, he worked as a salesman at the local Hudson dealership in New Haven.

Upon graduating from Yale, Chapin married Ruth Mary Ruxton and worked in an investment office before going to work for Hudson in 1938. He initially worked for about a year in the Engineering Department as a mechanic and test driver, imitating the career path of his father at the Olds Motor Works thirty-five years earlier. Chapin held a variety of jobs in automobile sales and distribution, accounting, and production planning, including managing aircraft contracts. In mid-June 1945, Vice President Northrup asked the local draft board to extend Roy Chapin Jr.'s occupational deferment, which was about to expire, because of the critical work he was doing in aircraft production. At age thirty, the son of Hudson's founder had accumulated considerable management experience but remained at the lower rungs on Hudson's middle management.[46]

Hudson in the Postwar Years, 1945–54:
Success and Struggle

Much like the rest of the auto industry, Hudson struggled to convert from war production to making cars for the civilian market. The company faced shortages of critical materials, particularly steel, but labor unrest also contributed to the slow return to normalcy. Demand for new cars in the postwar period was robust and supplying the demand was the main challenge. Much like the rest of the auto industry, Hudson sold slightly updated versions of its 1942 models as the 1946 and 1947 offerings. The all-new 1948 models sold well, as the figures in Table 6.2 show, and the new design gave Hudson solid sales and profits for 1948–50. The Korean War brought materials shortages and Hudson suffered from a great deal of labor unrest, but the company's weak products of the early 1950s brought the company's end. Hudson and Nash Motors merged in early 1954 to become the American Motors Corporation, marking the end of independence for both. Hudson's fate was a direct result of its failure to offer automobiles that consumers wanted to buy.

Hudson was one of the first U.S. auto companies to resume civilian production, with the first car coming off the line at the end of August 1945. Dealers had cars available for sale on 1 October 1945. Hudson operated only one automobile assembly line until February 1946, when government work finally ended and the company started a second line. Hudson produced only six-cylinder cars until June 1946, when they began making eights. The 1946 models were virtually identical to the 1942 models, except for a restyled front grille featuring a recessed center section, also known as the "tunnel grille." The 1947 models were virtually identical to those sold as 1946 models.[47]

Table 6.2. Hudson Motor Car Company Shipments, by Calendar Year and Profits, Net of Taxes ($ Millions), Year Ending 31 December 1945–57

	Cars	Commercial Vehicles	Total	Net Profits ($ Millions)
1945	4,735	270	5,005	0.7
1946	90,766	3,104	93,870	2.4
1947	100,393	2,917	103,310	5.8
1948	142,454	–	142,454	13.2
1949	144,685	–	144,685	10.1
1950	143,586	–	143,586	12.0
1951	92,859	–	92,859	(1.1)
1952	79,117	–	79,117	8.3
1953	78,183	–	78,183	(10.4)
1954	32,293*	–	32,293	(6.2)**
1955	52,688*	–	52,688	–
1956	22,588*	–	22,588	–
1957	1,345*	–	1,345	–

Source: "Hudson Shipments, Calendar Years 1909–1957," and "Statistical Summary since 1917, Hudson Motor Car Company," both in DCHC.
*Includes Hudson Rambler models.
**Loss through 30 April 1954 only.

A strike of five hundred foremen and their sympathizers crippled Hudson's production for all of September 1945. The foremen, members of the independent Foremen's Association of America, struck on 1 September, protesting pay cuts. The strike ended on 8 October, when an agreement crafted by the Federal Conciliation Service received the approval of the foremen. The company and the union began negotiating a new general contract at the end of January 1946 and reached an agreement granting increases of 18.5 cents per hour to most hourly workers. The union members and the federal Regional Wage Stabilization Board approved the agreement. In May 1946, the Hudson foremen voted to have the Foremen's Association of America represent them, and at the end of July 1946 the National Labor Relations Board (NLRB) certified the results.[48]

Shortages of parts and steel plagued Hudson's conversion to civilian car production. In late July 1946, Hudson shut down because of a shortage of door hardware and glass that resulted from a strike at the Dura Company in Toledo. Steel shortages were an ongoing headache for the company, which shut down for a week in late

1946 Hudson Super-Six convertible. *Courtesy NAHC.*

September 1946, for three days in late November 1946, and for a week at the end of December. Because Hudson started to build civilian cars a bit earlier than other automakers, its production through the first quarter of 1947 was nearly 4 percent of U.S. passenger car output, double the company's 2 percent share before the war. In September 1947, the company assembled the three millionth vehicle since its 1909 birth.[49]

The Hudson Motor Car Company introduced its first new postwar models on 7 December 1947. The 1948 models, better-known as the "Step-down" Hudsons, incorporated radically new engineering and styling and brought Hudson enormous success in the postwar automobile market. Hudson's production of 142,454 cars in 1948 was the largest since 1929, and its profits of $13.2 million were the largest since 1928. Under the general direction of stylist Frank Spring, Hudson's designers quietly built step-down prototypes in 1943 and 1944 despite the government's prohibition of such work as nonessential for the war effort. This was a team effort, with vice president Stuart G. Baits, chief engineer Millard Toncray, body engineer Carl W. Cenzer, and chassis engineer Dana Badertscher making major contributions. Bob Andrews, a young stylist who joined Hudson in 1945, was responsible for most of the design details.[50]

The basic design of the 1948 Hudsons was innovative if not revolutionary. They welded the body and steel box-section frame together and the floor dropped between the outer frame members, making it the lowest part of the structure. This was a unit-

Advertisement for the 1948 Hudson. *Courtesy DCHC.*

body design, much like the 1934 Chrysler Airflow and the 1935 Lincoln Zephyr. Hudson dubbed it a "monobilt" body. Passengers had to step over the side rails of the frame and then down onto the floor, thus the "step-down" label. The overall result was a very low-slung car, only 60 inches tall, with a low center of gravity. Passengers also had more headroom than in traditional designs. Because the frame was placed outside the rear wheels, the step-down model was 78 inches wide, with rear seats 64 inches wide. It looked sleek and "modern" and generated large crowds when Hudson displayed it.[51]

The U.S. Patent Office awarded two patents, one for the "Motor Vehicle Body Frame," and the other for the "monobilt" design. Millard H. Toncray, Walter I. Nyquist, and Carl W. Cenzer applied for one patent on 26 June 1948. Toncray and Frank S. Spring applied for a second patent on 22 July 1948. The Patent Office granted both patents on 3 February 1953. The applicants, all employees of the Hudson Motor Car Company, assigned the patents to the company. Although most automobile companies eventually used the unibody design, Hudson did not license other manufacturers under these patents.[52]

The step-down was really a "semi-unitized" design, with the unitized body back of the firewall built as one piece and the front of the car containing the engine, transmission, and front suspension built as a subframe. They welded and bolted the two sections together late in the assembly process. According to Michael Lamm and Dave Holls, the semi-unitized design also had drawbacks. Major changes in body panels were more expensive to make than with traditional body-on-frame designs.

Hudson stayed with the same basic design from 1948 through 1954, when American Motors eliminated separate Hudson models.[53]

According to Bob Hall's article in *Automobile Quarterly*, the company invested $16 million to rebuild the assembly line from scratch for step-down production. Assembly of the step-down required much more space than earlier models. Unfortunately, the size of the plant, especially the limited painting capacity at the Gratiot body plant, restricted production. The plant manager at the time, Joe Eskridge, claimed they could paint only 40 bodies an hour. If the body shop could paint 40 bodies an hour for sixteen hours a day, 300 days a year, it would have a theoretical annual capacity of 192,000 bodies. Hudson built roughly 140,000 step-down Hudsons per year in 1948, 1949, and 1950, but could have sold many more. The same plant that produced 300,000 cars in 1929 turned out less than half that volume of step-down Hudsons.[54]

Two Hudson historians dispute the claims that the unit-body design and limited plant capacity explain the much lower production levels for step-down Hudsons than for earlier models. Bob Elton argues that unit-body designs are no more expensive to alter than body-on-frame designs. Changes require new dies for new stampings regardless of the car's architecture. Hudson's real disadvantage came from using too many distinct parts, which complicated assembly. While General Motors used only two styles of door handles on forty-eight cars, Hudson used six different door handles on the same body. Hudson typically required twice as many fasteners as General Motors and painted many body parts with two colors.[55]

Ed Ostrowski also disputes the claim that limited production capacity, especially in the paint shop, restricted sales of the step-down Hudsons. Using maximum monthly production figures for the years 1948–51, he projected an average production capacity of 187,000 units per year. Taking the January 1951 peak production of 19,785 units as the standard implies an annual capacity of more than 230,000 cars. Hudson's *Annual Report* for 1948 announced that the company operated "at near capacity levels" in the fourth quarter and produced 51,660 cars. Even with summer shutdowns, vacation shutdowns, and other "normal" disruptions, including occasional strikes, the plant's capacity was probably close to 200,000 units, well above the actual production of 140,000 units. The often-repeated claim that factory capacity limited Hudson sales of the step-down models is at odds with the facts.[56]

The 1948 Hudsons came in two broad car lines—the Super and the Commodore, with either a six or an eight available in each line. The straight eight, with 254 CID producing 128 brake horsepower, remained unchanged from earlier models. Hudson did, however, produce an entirely new Super-Six engine for the step-down models. The new engine had a displacement of 262 cubic inches and produced

1948 Hudson convertible brougham. *Courtesy DCHC.*

121 brake horsepower, nearly as much as the eight. The company added a two-door convertible brougham model to both lines in August 1948. The original step-down models were mid-priced cars.

The 1949 Hudsons offered no changes in their exterior appearance from 1948. The Commodore name changed to Commodore Custom and most interiors saw refinements. There were some minor mechanical alterations to gear ratios and lubrication systems but few significant changes. The company held prices for the new models at the same level as the end-of-the-model-year prices for the 1948 Hudsons, a remarkable accomplishment in those inflationary times.[57]

On 18 November 1949, Hudson introduced a new line, the 1950 Pacemaker, which had a shorter wheelbase than the other Hudson offerings (119 7/8 inches versus 124 inches), weighed at least 100 pounds less, and came with a less powerful six. Pacemaker had its own engine, a "destroked" version of the Super-Six, with displacement reduced from 262 to 232 cubic inches and brake horsepower reduced from 123 to 112. The least expensive Pacemaker, the two-door, three-passenger coupe, sold for $1,807; the cheapest Super-Six carried a price of $2,102; and the least expensive Custom Commodore cost $2,257. Hudson assembled nearly 63,000 Pacemakers in 1950, or 44 percent of its total production. The company introduced the rest of its 1950 lineup in mid-February 1950, with prices cut between $88 and $167 compared with the previous model year. The rest of the 1950 offerings included a Custom Commodore convertible model that Hudson debuted in mid-April.[58]

1951 Hudson Hornet. *Courtesy DCHC.*

Hudson followed up with a new car line for 1951, the "Fabulous Hudson Hornet." This was simply a Hudson Commodore (wheelbase of 124 inches) with a high-performance engine and distinct badges and details. Hudson's engineers reworked the Super-Six engine to create a power plant with a displacement of 308 cubic inches that developed 145 brake horsepower, more than any six in the industry. The company also introduced the stylish Hollywood model available in four series—the Super Custom Six, the Custom Commodore Six, the Custom Commodore Eight, and the Hornet Six. The Hollywood was a two-door pillarless hardtop with available solid color or two-tone paint scheme and a lot of exterior chrome.[59]

The tinkering continued in 1952 with the introduction of the Wasp, which replaced the Super Custom Six series. The company built the Wasp on the Hudson 119 7/8-inch-wheelbase and gave it a 127 brake horsepower six engine with a displacement of 262 cubic inches. Hudson intended the model to serve as a lower-priced running mate to the Hornet. The shorter wheelbase and smaller engine allowed Hudson to price the Wasp $265 less than the Hornet. In June 1952, Hudson offered a dual carburetor system dubbed the Twin H Power package for the Hornet and Wasp. For 1953, the company introduced a Wasp with a smaller engine (232 CID producing 112 brake horsepower), which replaced the Pacemaker. They renamed the Wasp with the larger engine (262 CID) the Super Wasp. General Motors' Hydramatic transmission, which was an option on some 1951 models, could be ordered for all of the 1952 Hudsons.[60]

Engineer V. W. Piggins led Hudson's involvement in racing Hornets in NASCAR, AAA, and other stock car circuits. Hudson finished third on the NASCAR circuit in 1951 behind Plymouth and Oldsmobile. The following year, Hudson won twenty-seven of thirty-four NASCAR Grand Nationals and easily captured first place overall.

1952 Hudson Wasp. *Courtesy NAHC.*

1954 "Fabulous Hudson Hornet" race car, with driver Marshall Teague. *Courtesy DCHC.*

Olds and Plymouth tied for second place with three wins each. Hudson had twenty-two NASCAR victories in 1953 and seventeen in 1954, but captured first place overall in both years. Hudson had similar success with the Hornet in AAA stock car races during the same time frame. The company's stable of drivers included Marshall Teague, Herb Thomas, Frank Mundy, and Tim Flock. Then as now, the precise relationship between racing success and sales was unclear.[61]

Hudson's sales, which had averaged roughly 143,000 units per year in 1948–50 with the success of the step-down Hudsons, fell to 92,859 cars in 1951 and to less than 80,000 units for 1952 and 1953. Some decline in production was the result of materials shortages during the Korean War and severe labor disruptions starting in 1951. The greatest drag on Hudson in the marketplace was likely its failure to develop a V-8 engine and sticking with the step-down style too long. The last great investment that Barit and Hudson made in new product—the compact-size Hudson Jet—proved fatal.

A. Edward Barit announced in May 1952 that Hudson would build a small, light-weight car to compete with similar offerings from Ford, Chevrolet, and Plymouth. He believed that Hudson could duplicate the success that Nash had three years earlier with its Rambler and that Kaiser-Frazer enjoyed with its Henry J model. The resulting 1953 Hudson Jet featured a step-down unit-body frame, a scaled-down Hornet engine that produced 104 brake horsepower, a wheelbase of 105 inches, and a weight of about 2,800 pounds. The Murray Corporation produced the body and reportedly spent $5 million preparing their plant for this model. Hudson spent about $16 million developing the Jet.[62]

Unfortunately for Hudson, the Jet was the wrong car at the wrong time in terms of what customers wanted. Hudson designer Frank Spring originally produced a design

First 1953 Hudson Jet off the line. *Courtesy JMC.*

that closely followed the Fiat 1400, but he was overruled by Barit, who insisted on a more "boxy" design. Chicago dealer Jim Moran, who alone sold 5 percent of Hudson's production, also had a great influence. He liked wraparound rear windows, so they redesigned the Jet to incorporate his views. Spring developed three styling proposals, including one extremely ungainly design that incorporated the styling "suggestions" from Barit and Moran, along with two more attractive prototypes. To Spring's horror, Barit chose the ugly version.[63]

The resulting Jet weighed between 150 and 300 pounds more than the Rambler and the Henry J, and carried a list price ($1,858) between $78 and $188 *higher* than the list prices of low-end Fords, Chevrolets, and Plymouths. Competitive prices from the Big Three were even lower than list prices because dealers offered customers deep discounts for most of 1953. Sales were a disaster—21,143 Jets in 1953 and 14,442 in 1954, for total of just over 35,500. The last Jet came off the assembly line on 23 August 1954 after less than two years in production. Hudson spent more than $450 in development costs for every Jet it sold. The company's 1953 losses of $10.4 million, higher than during the worst years of the Great Depression, sealed Hudson's fate.[64]

Hudson produced a custom-built "dream car" in very small numbers in Italy that sold in the United States in the summer of 1954. Hudson officials approved the idea of this two-passenger closed coupe, dubbed the Italia, in early 1953 to improve Hudson's image and rekindle interest in its products. Stuart Baits, Hudson vice pres-

1954 Hudson Italia. *Courtesy DCHC.*

ident, and stylist Frank Spring commissioned the coach maker Carrozzeria Touring of Turin to design and build the first Italia body, to be mounted on a Jet chassis. The Italian coach maker agreed to produce the first twenty-five Italias for $2,300 each. Hudson would deliver these cars to their dealers for a net price of $4,800 and the dealers in turn would sell them to customers for roughly $6,000. Touring delivered the initial (and only) order to the United States (twenty-five units) in fall 1954, after the formation of American Motors. This "dream car" arrived much too late to help Hudson.[65]

Hudson briefly returned to defense production during the Korean War, but little evidence has survived to document the automaker's military work. They received an order in May 1951 to manufacture components for the Wright R-3350 aircraft engine. In late August 1951, the Glenn Martin Company gave Hudson a contract to build rear fuselages and tail sections for the B-57 Canberra Night Intruder, a British-designed bomber. Glenn Martin renewed this contract in February 1954, with production to extend well into 1955. In late September and late October 1951, the Boeing Airplane Company and the Douglas Aircraft Company, respectively, awarded Hudson contracts to build forward fuselage sections for the RB-47 and the B-47 medium bombers.[66]

Unpopular automotive products and production bottlenecks do not fully account for Hudson's postwar struggles. Labor unrest in the form of "wildcat" protest strikes plagued the company's operations, especially in 1951. In the years 1947–50, Detroit's newspapers reported six to eight strikes each year at Hudson, with most lasting only a day or two. Virtually none involved contract negotiations; they usually resulted from company disciplinary actions against shop stewards or workers, disputes over work standards, or efforts by a group of workers to gain recognition. They often involved "grieving by strike" rather than using the contractual grievance procedure.

The year 1947 was typical of the pattern of disputes. In late January, the chief steward ordered a male worker to defy a foreman's instruction to provide relief to a female worker. Hudson suspended the steward for two days and 14,000 workers walked off their jobs in protest. The contract clearly stated that only women provide relief for women. A similar two-day strike of 14,000 Hudson workers occurred in early April when the company suspended a steward for two days. Fifty-one men who drove cars off the assembly line struck in mid-April to protest disciplinary action taken against some of them, and Hudson was forced to close the plant. In mid-June a strike of five hundred office workers and 100 engineers closed the entire plant for two days. On 1 August 1947, 39 workers in Hudson's body plant went on strike over wage demands and 9,000 walked out, closing the body plant for four days. In early December, 21 arc welders went on strike, demanding higher wages for new work they did on the new models. Hudson shut down the plant and sent 12,000 workers home.[67]

The same pattern recurred in 1948, 1949, and 1950, but with different issues and individuals involved. Labor relations at Hudson reached an all-time low in 1951. The worst battle began on 11 June 1951, when Hudson sent 10,000 workers home because paint and assembly line workers failed to do their work. The dispute, which extended with few interruptions until 14 August, involved production standards. Beginning on 24 July, Hudson workers simply stayed away from work. In early August, the union urged President Truman to seize the Hudson plants to use for war production.

Hudson and the UAW reached an agreement settling these disputes on 14 August, with 8,000 workers returning to their jobs. The two parties would negotiate all time standards for disputed jobs. This was hardly the end of the dispute, however. In September and October 1951, the UAW and Hudson sued each other for "breach of contract." There is no evidence that either lawsuit went to trial, suggesting that both sides dropped their claims. By any measure, this was the low point of labor-management relations at Hudson. There was only a handful of short-lived strikes in 1952 and 1953, with none recorded in 1954, the year of the merger with Nash-Kelvinator.[68]

A. Edward Barit in Retrospect

Assessing A. E. Barit's tenure as president and general manager of the Hudson Motor Car Company is difficult because he inherited a less-than-healthy company, even by Depression standards, when he succeeded Roy Chapin in 1936. Conditions in the automobile industry were never truly "normal" for most of his time in office. Still, there are few positive achievements associated with his leadership and many negative developments. Carsten Tiedeman's observations of Barit's management style and judgment paint him as a rigid and unimaginative leader mainly concerned with protecting his position as the head of Hudson. When the company clearly could have used an influx of capital and new leadership, he dismissed out of hand the proposals made by Henry J. Kaiser and the Fishers, as well as the initial approaches by George Mason.

Edward Barit was an ineffective manager with no creative vision for Hudson. Under his direction, Hudson mishandled its military contracts during World War II. Barit approved the step-down Hudson design for the postwar years, but the company failed to capitalize on its success. The Hudson Jet, Barit's pet project, brought Hudson to the edge of bankruptcy and forced the merger with Nash. An unnamed

Hudson engineer noted the obvious—that the company failed to produce enough cars that customers found appealing. The step-down Hudson was popular, but the Hudson plant could satisfy only a small part of demand. Customers went elsewhere, never to return. As sales volumes fell, Hudson raised prices on its full-sized cars, making them as expensive as Buicks. The compact Jet retailed for $1,858 at a time when customers could buy a Ford, Chevrolet, or Plymouth for $1,500. Hudson had no future under those circumstances.[69]

In sharp contrast to George Mason, who hired a young George Romney as his heir-apparent, Barit brought no new managerial blood into Hudson. He gave Roy Chapin Jr. only minor positions in sales during the early postwar years and most of these jobs involved working away from Detroit. In the fall of 1945, he exiled Chapin to the Chicago zone offices of the Hudson Sales Corporation, and a year later Chapin became the regional sales manager for the Toledo Zone, which covered most of Ohio and parts of Michigan. Barit appointed Chapin a director in May 1946 to replace Carsten Tiedeman and to represent the Chapin family interests. Chapin became the assistant zone manager for the Hudson Sales Corporation in January 1948 and then a special sales representative in August 1948. He established the Boston and Philadelphia sales zones and managed those and other zones at various times. Chapin's first promotion to a position with substantial responsibility came in January 1952, when Barit named him assistant sales manager for Hudson. In contrast, Robert Barit, his son, became vice president in charge of purchasing in 1951. The appearance of nepotism is unmistakable.[70]

Chapter 4 laid out the basic chronology of the merger of Hudson and Nash-Kelvinator, which we will not repeat here. For A. E. Barit, the merger was a last-minute desperate effort to avoid bankruptcy for Hudson. A year after the merger, Barit revealed to the *Wall Street Journal* the details of his fateful lunch meeting with George Mason on 16 June 1953 at the Book-Cadillac Hotel in Detroit, where they worked out the basic framework of the Nash-Hudson merger. The two men began discussing their common problems in getting an adequate supply of steel and the problems their dealers had in getting credit in the tight money market. Both faced the loss of dealerships, which further reduced sales at a time when tooling costs kept increasing. Both automakers needed to manufacture and sell more cars, and they concluded that a merger was the only way to increase their sales volume. Hudson was the more desperate of the partners. In 1953, Hudson produced 76,348 cars (1.76 percent of the industry total) and lost $10.4 million, while Nash-Kelvinator produced 152,141 units (3.51 percent of the industry total) and earned profits of $14.1 million.[71]

In the proxy statement issued to Hudson stockholders before the meeting of 24

March 1954 to approve the merger, Barit explained the advantages of the merger to Hudson and Nash-Kelvinator. He cited a variety of "economies of large scale" that American Motors would enjoy, including savings in design and engineering; lower prices of raw materials and components; reduced administrative costs; savings in tool and die costs, which they could spread over a large volume; and a greater public acceptance because the new company would offer a wider variety of models. Hudson stockholders would enjoy a greater diversification in their investment because of the appliance production from Kelvinator. A *Wall Street Journal* article about the merger emphasized the creation of a larger dealer body by combining the 2,000 Hudson dealers with the 1,600 Nash dealers, though the combined total of 3,600 dealers still compared unfavorably with third-place Chrysler's 10,500 dealers.[72]

The merger brought an end to the independent operation of the Hudson Motor Car Company and Nash Motors. Both long-lived companies had enjoyed great success for most of their histories and had introduced path-breaking cars with engineering and design innovations. Within a few years of the merger, the Hudson and Nash nameplates and identities disappeared as well. The way in which the merger finally worked out will be considered in the next chapter, but it was in no sense a merger of equals. In the first three years of the merger, Hudson's identity literally disappeared—the Hudson nameplate, the Detroit factories, and the vast majority of Hudson employees. Barit was at the helm during Hudson's end and was responsible for the disaster.

SEVEN

George W. Romney and American Motors, 1954–62

Among the advantages of the move are pooling of executive abilities, research and engineering resources, and purchasing power; opportunities for new manufacturing economies and improved methods; reduction of individual overhead and administrative charges; [and] a diversification of products and a spreading of tooling costs over more units with less costs per unit.

A. E. Barit, describing the benefits of the merger of Nash-Kelvinator and Hudson, 14 January 1954

Merging Nash Motors and the Hudson Motor Car Company in the spring of 1954 was easier to achieve on paper than in reality. The sudden death of George Mason in early October 1954 made a smooth merger of the two automakers even more difficult. The combined production of Nash and Hudson cars in 1954 (99,774 units) was less than half the two companies' total the year before. After a robust recovery to 194,175 cars in 1955, output skidded to a mere 104,189 units in 1957. The merger brought the closing and sale or demolition of the Detroit Hudson plants, with most automotive operations concentrated in Kenosha and Milwaukee. Most of the Hudson management and factory workers lost their jobs when the merger was completed. By the end of 1957, the Nash and Hudson nameplates had also disappeared, replaced by Rambler. With George Romney's vision and leadership, American Motors specialized in making smaller cars, achieved sales success, earned profits, and survived through his presidency, which ended in 1962 when Romney ran for governor of Michigan.

George W. Romney's Life, Career, and Rapid Rise to the Leadership of American Motors

More than five months after the Nash-Kelvinator merger with Hudson was officially consummated on 30 April 1954, George Mason died suddenly on 8 October 1954. Four days later and only one day after Mason's funeral, the American Motors Corporation (AMC) board of directors named forty-seven-year-old George W. Romney as the company's president, general manager, and chairman of the board, replacing George Mason in all three posts. In mid-November 1954, the AMC directors set Romney's salary at $125,000 per year starting on 1 October. Four years later, they raised his base salary to $150,000 per year, but with bonuses he earned $200,700. While Romney did not expect to become the leader of AMC in the early months of the merger, Romney was prepared for the challenge. Since joining Nash-Kelvinator as a special assistant to George Mason in April 1948, Romney quickly climbed the executive ladder. Mason appointed him vice president in 1950, and executive vice president and director in 1953. Mason groomed Romney to succeed him, and Romney succeeded in leading American Motors.[1]

George Wilcken Romney (8 July 1907–26 July 1995) was a fascinating man of the twentieth century. He was a member of the Church of Jesus Christ of Latter-

George Romney, 1951.
Courtesy DCHC.

day Saints (Mormon Church) who moved back and forth between politics, business, and public service throughout his adult life. He worked for the Aluminum Company of America (ALCOA), for the Automobile Manufacturers Association (AMA), and in various posts for Nash-Kelvinator and the American Motors Corporation. He also served as governor of Michigan, ran unsuccessfully for president, and held a cabinet post in President Richard Nixon's administration.[2]

George W. Romney was the fourth son born to Gaskell and Anna Amelia Pratt Romney at a Mormon colony in Colonia Dublan, Chihuahua, Mexico. George Romney's grandfather, Miles Park Romney, had moved to Mexico with his four wives after the United States outlawed polygamy in 1885. Gaskell Romney was a successful carpenter and house builder who operated a planing mill in Mexico. He had only one wife. Most of the Mormon colonists in Mexico left that country under duress during the Mexican Revolution of 1912. Revolutionary forces led by Pancho Villa looted their settlements, forcing the Romneys and their fellow Mormons to flee to El Paso, Texas, in late July 1912, leaving all of their property behind. Between 1912 and 1922, the Romneys lived in California, Idaho, Utah, Idaho again, and Salt Lake City for a second time.[3]

With all these family moves, George Romney's education was a patchwork. In Salt Lake City, he attended Roosevelt Junior High School and then the Latter-day Saints University high school and junior college. In an effort to uphold the Romney family tradition of athletic prowess in sports, George valiantly tried out for the high school football, basketball, and baseball teams. Using sheer determination to overcome his small size, Romney had modest success in all three sports.[4]

Romney attended junior college in Salt Lake City rather than enroll in an eastern university so that he could pursue his budding romance with Lenore LaFount. He met her in 1924, when she was fifteen years old. Ironically, they were part of a larger group of boys and girls who ventured out together in an old beat-up Nash owned by one of Romney's friends. They would later marry in July 1931. In the Mormon Church, young men who reached the age of twenty and had reached the rank of elder normally went on a mission to spread their faith at their own expense. Romney served as a missionary in Great Britain for two years starting in October 1926. He solicited door-to-door, but also honed his speaking skills by addressing groups in public parks and in meeting halls.[5]

Romney returned to Salt Lake City in January 1929. He worked in the construction industry and took night classes at the University of Utah, but spent the rest of his time dating Lenore LaFount. When the LaFount family moved to Washington, D.C., George followed suit in September 1929. He landed a job as a stenographer working for Senator David I. Walsh, a Democrat from Massachusetts. His dictation skills were not good enough to continue at that job, but Senator Walsh gave him a new position as a legislative clerk. Romney conducted research and gathered information for Walsh regarding major tariff legislation coming before Congress (the Hawley-Smoot Act). He gained valuable insight into politics and the inner workings of Congress. Romney also made valuable contacts with officials from ALCOA when he supplied them with tariff information regarding their industry. This earnest young man so impressed them that they offered him a job and Romney worked nine years for the aluminum giant.[6]

Romney accepted an apprenticeship with ALCOA and started work on 10 June 1930. He learned about manufacturing aluminum and worked in sales at the end of his training. ALCOA then assigned him to their Washington office in fall 1931 to work as a lobbyist. ALCOA had a monopoly on aluminum production in the United States and the company's owners were concerned about possible antitrust action. The U.S. attorney general brought an antitrust case against ALCOA in April 1937. By the time a final decree came down in 1945, Reynolds Metals and Kaiser Aluminum had created real competition, so the Justice Department did not dissolve ALCOA.[7]

George Romney attended night school at George Washington University for much of the time he worked in Washington, but he did not earn a degree there. He also became the Washington representative of the Aluminum Wares Association, a trade group of manufacturers of cooking utensils. While serving in that position, he became good friends with Pyke Johnson, a representative of the AMA. This trade organization had roots extending back to the Association of Licensed Automobile Manufacturers (ALAM), established in 1903 to defend the Selden patent on the automobile against infringement. Adopting a new name in 1934, the AMA, was headed by Alvin Reeves and had its headquarters in New York City. Its main function was the cross-licensing of automotive patents. In 1939, Reeves retired and the AMA decided to move its main office to Detroit.

Pyke Johnson, who was the AMA's Washington representative and executive vice president, needed to hire a manger for the Detroit office. At Johnson's invitation, George Romney visited Detroit and met with the principal officers of the AMA, who offered Romney the job. At age thirty-two, Romney earned a substantial salary of $10,000 at ALCOA. The AMA offered a salary of $12,000, which ALCOA promised to match, but Romney accepted the Detroit position on 28 September 1939 and began his career in the automobile industry. The AMA opened offices in Detroit's New Center Building in January 1940 and remained there until 1998, when the organization ceased to exist.[8]

As the United States began to drift toward war, the AMA became increasingly involved in war production. In May 1940, President Roosevelt named William S. Knudsen, the president of General Motors, as director of the National Defense Advisory Commission to oversee industrial production of war goods. At Knudsen's suggestion, the AMA developed plans to coordinate the production and assembly of aircraft parts by the automobile industry. The AMA organized the Automotive Committee for Air Defense, gave it $100,000 for expenses, and put Romney in charge. Following Pearl Harbor, the AMA reconstituted itself as the Automotive Council for War Production (ACWP) and named Romney its managing director. In March 1942, Pyke Johnson resigned from the AMA to become the head of the Automotive Safety Foundation in Washington and Romney became the AMA's general manager.[9]

Romney became the spokesperson for the automobile industry and was an unabashed defender of management's prerogatives against incursions by government and organized labor alike. In March 1945, the Senate War Investigating Committee headed by Senator James M. Mead held hearings in Detroit to examine charges that labor hoarding by auto industry management contributed to substantial losses in war production. Romney denied that there was significant labor hoarding and blamed government interference in factory operations and government controls over labor for the inefficiencies that did occur. Romney blamed union practices of restricting output for the loss of production. The ACWP disbanded on 1 October 1945, but Romney's battles with government and organized labor continued for decades.[10]

George Romney was the key figure in organizing a very successful celebration, the Automotive Golden Jubilee, which commemorated the fiftieth anniversary of the appearance of the first cars in Detroit—Charles B. King's car of 6 March 1896 and Henry Ford's Quadricycle on 4 June 1896. The jubilee kicked off on 31 May with a dinner honoring fourteen automotive pioneers. The celebration continued with a four-hour parade on Saturday, 1 June, witnessed by a million people, followed by a concluding rally at Briggs Stadium on 9 June. Romney organized the entire celebration in only ten weeks.[11]

Executives in the auto industry who knew Romney's work at the AMA recognized his managerial competence. In late April 1948, James Alvin Macauley, the chairman of the board of the Packard Motor Car Company, offered Romney the position of executive vice president at a salary of $50,000 and a seat on the Packard board of directors. In two years he would replace George Christopher, the president of Packard. George Mason soon offered Romney the position of executive assistant with a salary of $30,000 and a vague promise that he would give Romney an executive job within a year or two. Mason gave Romney a month to come to a decision. Romney accepted the less lucrative offer from Mason in part because he believed that Nash-Kelvinator was a much sounder company than Packard. The opportunity to learn the

Nash-Kelvinator operations before taking on any major responsibility also appealed to him.[12]

George Romney spent his first two years at Nash-Kelvinator as Mason's executive assistant with vaguely defined responsibilities. He began by spending several months learning how the company built and repaired Nash cars and Kelvinator appliances. Romney visited all the various plants and other facilities operated by Nash-Kelvinator, learned how the organization functioned, and talked with hundreds of factory workers, foremen, and mid-level executives about their complaints and suggestions for improvements. Mason gradually gave Romney more important assignments and greater responsibility.[13]

On 8 February 1949, ten months after coming to Nash-Kelvinator, Romney presented Mason with a series of seven reports outlining areas within the company that needed improvement: executive communications; employee attitudes; Kelvinator quality; Nash engineering; Nash-Kelvinator public acceptance; future executive personnel; and "some observations on merger." The reports ranged from two to eight pages in length.

In his report on merger possibilities, Romney examined potential merger partners for Nash including Hudson, Packard, Studebaker, and Willys. He argued that full-fledged mergers among the independents were unlikely because they were still in strong financial shape in 1949. He viewed a cooperative arrangement with Packard far short of a merger as the best opportunity for Nash. Packard could supply Nash with V-8 engines and Nash could build Packard's bodies. The two firms could develop common designs for parts and stampings and then buy from each other. They could also jointly buy common parts from outside suppliers and realize additional savings. One of Romney's more radical ideas was that the two firms could share decentralized assembly plants. Mason agreed with Romney's recommendations and implemented most of them several years later.[14]

Mason initially gave Romney some small assignments. Romney was in Europe in fall 1949 as an industry delegate at a conference of firms engaged in the metal trades. Mason admired some European cars designed by the Italian stylist Pinin Farina and asked Romney to sign Farina to a consulting contract with Nash. Farina, who was primarily designing bodies for Fiat, agreed to a contract after Romney visited him in Turin. Mason named Romney a vice president in February 1950, nearly two years after Romney came to Nash-Kelvinator. More important, Mason gave Romney responsibility for the publicity surrounding the introduction of the new 1950 Rambler line. Romney was one of only a handful of Nash executives who shared Mason's enthusiasm for the small car.[15]

Nash-Kelvinator suffered from an appalling failure of internal organization and communication between its senior and mid-level managers. Typically, the administration did not communicate news of changes in personnel or policy effectively within the company. Managers, much less workers, had little knowledge of company operations. Romney established a series on monthly "town hall" dinner meetings for the salaried employees, whereby each meeting was devoted to explaining how one department within Nash-Kelvinator worked. Romney created the position of director of communications in 1954 to improve internal communications.[16]

Many failures of communication derived from George Mason's personality. Nash-Kelvinator was clearly a one-man show, with Mason making all decisions of any consequence. According to George Romney, Mason was not very articulate, but he also did not understand the need to communicate his ideas clearly to others in his organization. Nor was he comfortable aggressively promoting Nash-Kelvinator products against its competitors. He was reluctant to hurt people, even if they unjustly attacked him. Mason generally avoided disputes and confrontations at all costs.[17]

In January 1953, Mason appointed Romney executive vice president at Nash-Kelvinator, elevating him to the number two position within the company. When Romney became the president, manager, and chairman of the board at American Motors in October 1954, he was already an experienced executive. His work with Senator Walsh, ALCOA, and the AMA gave him a broad background and he learned the inner operations of Nash-Kelvinator during the six years he worked there before the merger. The initial, monumental challenge that he and Mason faced was the consolidation of Nash and Hudson into a single, more cost-efficient automobile company. The death of Mason and the disastrous sales of Hudson and Nash cars in 1954 made the task even more daunting.

Consolidation of Nash and Hudson

Although American Motors struggled to survive in the mid-1950s, it was more successful in the longer run than the other independent automakers. By 1954 only Hudson, Nash-Kelvinator, Studebaker, Packard, and Kaiser-Willys had survived. Kaiser-Frazer had merged with Willys-Overland in April 1953 to form Kaiser-Willys Corporation, which stopped making automobiles in 1955 and focused on Jeeps. Studebaker and Packard merged in 1954 to form Studebaker-Packard and moved Packard production from Detroit to South Bend, Indiana, in 1956. The company ended its operations at South Bend in 1963, but continued building cars in Hamilton, Ontario, until 1966, when Studebaker ended automobile production. Starting with horse-drawn wagons for the Union Army, Studebaker had manufactured over-the-road vehicles for more than a century.

The newborn American Motors Corporation faced multiple challenges during its first four to five years of operations. They combined the Nash and Hudson lines of cars into an integrated production process in Kenosha and Milwaukee, Wisconsin. Both brands disappeared after the 1957 model year, replaced by Rambler. American Motors also struggled with a one-sided supply contract with Studebaker-Packard for two years. AMC tried without great success to obtain military contracts to keep its Detroit Special Products Division afloat. They carried out various cost-cutting measures, including efforts to negotiate a contract with the UAW that would differ from the union's national contracts with the Big Three automakers. However, the most fundamental problem American Motors faced through 1957 was its inability to sell its cars.

The grim realities of the market forced changes in the original merger plans envisioned by George Mason. Romney merged what were supposed to be independent Hudson and Nash divisions into a single automotive division. The sales operations and the dealerships of the two brands remained separate, but only for a few years. Only two of the nine directors at Hudson, A. E. Barit and Roy D. Chapin Jr., became directors at American Motors. They were a distinct minority on the AMC board, which had nine members in 1954 and eleven in 1955. Hudson employed 8,900

A. E. Barit (*left*), George Mason (*center*), and
George Romney (*right*), May 1954. *Courtesy DCHC.*

workers at the time of the merger, but a year later, 5,454 of them were unemployed and only 204 Hudson workers had taken jobs in Kenosha.[18]

Within a month of the consummation of the Nash-Hudson merger, American Motors announced that it would redesign the 1955 Hudson models and assemble them in Kenosha, Wisconsin. Engines would come from Detroit, but they would build the bodies in Milwaukee and most of the remaining parts in Kenosha. The decline of Hudson sales in 1954 made the continued operation of the Detroit Hudson plant uneconomical. With a break-even production level of roughly 65,000 units a year, but an output of only 13,373 cars in the first five months of 1954, the plant was doomed. For most of 1954, a two- or three-day workweek was the norm at the Detroit plant. The complex jig and fixture arrangement used to make the step-down Hudson made retooling the old Hudson plant prohibitively expensive, so AMC simply scrapped the equipment and closed the plant. A letter of 27 May 1954 from Stuart Baits to the Detroit Hudson employees announced the decision and AMC officials informed Walter Reuther, president of the UAW, the same day. On 31 October 1954, the last Detroit-built Hudson came off the assembly line.[19]

The impact on the Detroit Hudson workers was devastating. The initial agreement between AMC and the UAW, announced in late January 1955, did not give Hudson workers much incentive to take jobs in Wisconsin. The agreement gave laid-off Hudson workers preference over brand-new hires at Kenosha, but once hired, the Hudson worker lost his Hudson seniority rights. Only 480 Hudson workers expressed enough interest in this offer to have a physical exam, and only 204 made the move to Wisconsin. AMC probably required a physical to discourage Hudson workers from transferring. Perhaps the union assumed that most Hudson workers would find jobs in Detroit. More important, when the Detroit Hudson plant closed in fall 1954, several thousand AMC employees in Wisconsin remained laid off, some for as long as twenty months. Allowing former Hudson workers to "bump" former Nash workers with less seniority would have been a political nightmare for the union. The company and the union came to a new agreement on 1 April 1955 granting only about 700 Hudson workers full seniority rights, but few of them took jobs in Wisconsin.[20]

The shift of Hudson production to Wisconsin and the closing of the Detroit Hudson plant marked the end of an era. Part of the plant, perhaps one-fifth, remained in use briefly for the manufacture of engines and for some defense work. American Motors sold its Detroit body plant in December 1955 and later demolished the Hudson factory complex. The 1954 Hudsons, the last assembled in Detroit, were also the last real Hudsons built, although Nash cars that carried the Hudson badge continued through 1957. Both Hudson and Nash disappeared the following year, replaced by the Rambler nameplate.[21]

The reactions to the transfer of Hudson production to Wisconsin were predictable. Hudson dealers believed that the production economies realized from the consolidation would result in lower prices on Hudson cars. The wife of a laid-off Hudson worker sent Stuart Baits a bitter letter after receiving a flyer from American Motors urging its Detroit workers to consider buying American Motors cars or Kelvinator appliances.

> What a colossal nerve you have. After laying off your employees, you have the audacity to mail your old employees a leaflet, to come & view your appliances & cars. May I be so bold as to ask, what would they use for money? These men have been out of work four months. Still, their mortgages, utilities, taxes, & etc, go on just the same. I really cannot say just what I am thinking of you, but your shell-like ears would burn to a crisp, if I ever met you in person.

She signed the letter, "The wife of one of your unfortunates."[22]

The reaction was understandably different in Wisconsin. The first Kenosha-built Hudson rolled off the assembly line on 6 January 1955. American Motors held a "Wisconsin Welcomes Hudson" rally at the plant later that afternoon. On the evening of 6 January, *Kenosha Evening News* publisher Ralph S. Kingsley hosted a chicken dinner in downtown Kenosha to welcome Hudson. The guest of honor was Alan Ameche, the University of Wisconsin's All-American football player, who received the first Wisconsin-built Hudson as a gift.[23]

Complicating the first eighteen months of AMC's existence were the often unpleasant relations with James Nance, president of Packard since March 1952 and president of the newly formed Studebaker-Packard Corporation beginning 1 October 1954. George Mason and James Nance had agreed on the need to merge all four independents (Nash, Hudson, Packard, and Studebaker) into one company. Each viewed the Nash-Hudson merger and the Studebaker-Packard merger as the first step toward an eventual merger into a single firm. Because both men envisioned themselves as the top man of any combination, the likelihood of that happening was nil. In the interim, they discussed selling parts, including engines and stampings, to each other to save costs. Packard and AMC signed a contract in August 1954 that seemed to signal the start of cooperation between the two firms. The relationship quickly unraveled, however, with the death of George Mason in October 1954. Two years later, cooperation between the two companies had entirely ended.[24]

The failure of cooperation between the companies reflected the competing personalities and egos of James Nance and George Romney. American Motors, which desperately needed a V-8 engine for its full-sized models, signed an agreement with Packard to buy a new V-8 engine Packard had developed and an equal number of Packard's ultramatic (automatic) transmissions. Over the first three years of the contract, AMC would pay 30 percent of Packard's tooling costs. There was a "reciprocal purchases" clause in the contract, which stipulated that Packard would try to purchase an equal amount of parts and components from AMC, but "The failure of Packard to make purchases from AMC in such amounts, or in any amount, shall not, however, be deemed a breach of this agreement, or excuse any failure of performance by AMC. Packard will be the sole judge of whether or not products offered to it by AMC can be purchased by Packard on a competitive and advantageous basis." Packard had no legal obligation to buy any parts from AMC and did not.[25]

George Romney believed that AMC and Packard had an unwritten understanding that AMC would supply Packard with bodies from its unused Hudson body plant in Detroit. James Nance did not. In late October, Packard took an option to buy the Murray Body Corporation plant in Detroit, which outraged Romney. He ordered Meade Moore, AMC's vice president for automotive research and development, to move forward to develop a V-8 engine. In early September 1955, Nance offered to sell the smaller Studebaker V-8s to AMC in return for AMC's six-cylinder engine. Romney refused the offer because AMC needed all of its six-cylinder production for its popular Rambler models. In late September, Romney gave Vance the required one-year notice that AMC would no longer buy V-8 engines from Packard. American Motors spent $10 million on its own V-8 engine, which it could produce at a savings of $200 per engine over the Packard engine.[26]

Mason and Romney had hoped to keep part of the Detroit Hudson plant operating with defense contracts. In late November 1954, Romney formed the Hudson Special Products Division to handle orders for military equipment. He named Stuart G. Baits general manager, Joseph W. Eskridge vice president in charge of manufacturing, and J. F. Jones vice president in charge of sales. Romney announced in mid-November 1954 that Hudson would build the Mighty Mite vehicle for the Marines. AMC had bought the rights to manufacture and sell this vehicle, which was a light-weight version of the World War II–era Jeep. It would weigh 1,159 pounds less than the Jeep and would come with an air-cooled aluminum die-cast engine. AMC announced nearly two years later that it had developed a four-cylinder aluminum V-4 engine that weighed only 200 pounds and developed 62 horsepower. The *Wall Street Journal* reported that Hudson delivered a prototype to the Marine Corps on 8 April 1955. As of mid-April 1955, AMC's Special Products Division was making Hudson engines, Douglas B-47 nose cones, Martin B-57 fuselages, Curtiss-Wright engine components, and 30-caliber machine gun mounts. This work, however, occupied only one-quarter of the former Hudson factory space.[27]

In early February 1958, Romney warned that AMC would likely close its Special Products operations by May because of lack of work. Employment had dropped from about 3,000 in early 1956 to a mere 300 working in Hudson's former parts plant on Vernor Highway near Conner Avenue. This plant remained in operation through 1963, primarily producing the Mighty Mite. Between March 1958 and March 1961, Hudson received government contracts worth a total of $16.6 million to make 2,250 Mighty Mites. To put this in perspective, these orders provided jobs for only 250 workers in the Special Products Division in Detroit. The last contract came in mid-January 1962 for an additional 1,000 Mighty Mites.[28]

One substantial economy that AMC realized after the merger was the consolidation of production in Wisconsin. Starting with the 1955 models, the distinct, separate Hudson step-down models disappeared. Instead, Hudson cars with different grilles, trim, and nameplates came off the same assembly lines as Nashes. Don Butler has claimed that AMC spent only $11 million for the design work and tooling for the combined models, versus spending about $24 million had the models remained distinct. Nash dealers sold the Ambassador, Statesman, and Rambler models, while Hudson dealers sold the Hornet, Wasp, and Rambler cars. The Hudson Jet disappeared.[29]

For the 1955 model year, the new company developed a traveling display, "The All American Motor Show," which stockholders viewed in Detroit in early December 1954. The display, which went to twenty-six cities, included Hudson and Nash cars, along with Kelvinator and Leonard appliances. When the automotive trade journals reviewed the 1955 Hudson and Nashes, there was no effort made to hide the fact that they were mechanically similar. Hudson kept its old six-cylinder flathead engine to use up its inventory of engines made in Detroit, while the Nash version had an overhead valve six. Some wags called the new Hudsons "Hashes" and they did not fool customers.

There were, however, some real changes from 1954. George Mason had insisted that the 1955 models have "wrap-around" windshields, which delayed the official kickoff of the new models until 23 February 1955, two months after the motor show. The Packard V-8 engine (320 CID, 208 horsepower) was available to buyers of the Nash Ambassador and Hudson Hornet and Wasp. American Motors recognized the inefficiency of selling identical lines of cars through two separate dealer networks and by the end of 1955 merged the two groups of dealers. By then, the number of dealers had fallen to about 1,900. The separate nameplates would last only through the 1957 model year.[30]

The 1956 models had distinctive new styling that set them apart from the 1955 models. The grilles and rear styling were notably new and the grille featured prominent "Vs," so they called the look of the 1956 models "V-line styling." Two- and three-toned paint schemes were available for the first time. The extensive use of chrome, particularly in the grilles, and the introduction of two- and three-tone paint schemes were important elements in automotive styling in the mid-1950s. Chrysler's Forward Look models of 1955–58, designed by Virgil Exner, featured elaborate color combinations for the exteriors. The 1957 AMC models offered dual headlights for the first time, but the styling otherwise did not change much from 1956. To replace the Packard-built V-8s, American Motors equipped its 1957 cars with its own new, more powerful V-8 engine, which generated 255 horsepower from a displacement of 327 cubic inches.[31]

For the 1955 and 1956 model years, American Motors built Hudsons, Nashes, and Ramblers on the same assembly line in Kenosha. Starting with the 1957 models, Ramblers had their own separate assembly line in a revamped manufacturing operation in which Nashes and Hudsons shared a second assembly line. The same year, Nash and Hudson dealers continued to sell Ramblers, as did a few dealers who sold Ramblers exclusively, but the Nash Rambler and Hudson Rambler names

Assembly line, Kenosha, Wisconsin, showing Nash, Hudson, and Rambler Cars assembled on the same line, 1955. *Courtesy DCHC.*

disappeared. They were all Ramblers. This change was a precursor to dropping the Hudson and Nash brands for the 1958 model year.[32]

After the merger, American Motors dealers offered their customers the unique Nash Metropolitan. Introduced in March 1954, this was the smallest car American Motors ever produced. Although Hudson dealers sold a few Metropolitans, Nash dealers sold the overwhelming majority. The Metropolitan's 85-inch wheelbase and weight of 1,785 pounds were substantially less than the Nash Rambler's 100 inches and 2,435 pounds. Its Austin A-40 engine had a displacement of 1,200 cubic inches and developed 42 horsepower. The Metropolitan carried a retail price of $1,445 for the hardtop and $1,469 for the convertible, when a Nash Rambler four-door sedan sold for $1,945. Although the Metropolitan was clearly a niche car, it made an initial splash. By the end of 1954, the Austin Motor Car Company shipped a total of 13,905 from England, with 11,769 coming to the United States and the rest to Canada and other foreign destinations.[33]

The design remained the same for 1955, but shipments fell off to only 4,383 units. For 1956, AMC made some minor face-lifts to the Metropolitan and introduced a larger engine, which had a displacement of 1,500 cubic inches and developed 52 horsepower. Shipments rebounded to 9,068 in 1956, jumped to 15,317 for 1957, and peaked at 22,209 in 1959. Shipments then tumbled to 13,874 units in 1960, when the other AMC models, the Rambler and Ambassador, were selling extremely well. In mid-1960, American Motors informed Austin that they were ending the Metropolitan program to concentrate on the Rambler American. Rambler dealers continued to sell surplus Metropolitans through 1961 and 1962. Over the model's life span, AMC sold 83,442 Metropolitans in the United States and an additional 11,544 in Canada and overseas, for a grand total of just under 95,000 units.[34]

Once George Romney was firmly in control of American Motors, he made changes in the administration to prepare the company for more efficient operations. On George Mason's recommendation, Romney hired Roy Abernethy in October 1954 to replace Henry Clay Doss as vice president for sales at the Nash Division. In mid-December 1955, Romney elevated Abernethy to the new position of vice president for automotive distribution and marketing. He eventually served as president and chief executive officer of American Motors in 1962–66.

Roy Abernethy (29 September 1906–28 February 1977) spent his entire adult life in the automobile industry. Born in West Monterey, Pennsylvania, near Pittsburgh, Abernethy worked as an apprentice auto mechanic in Pittsburgh starting in 1925 and attended the Carnegie Institute of Technology at night, studying civil engineering and automotive engineering. Starting in the early 1930s, Abernethy held a series of sales positions with Packard, each with greater responsibility. In 1948, Packard

Jayne Mansfield with Ralph Abernethy and
a 1956 Rambler Cross Country. *Courtesy DCHC.*

named him its eastern regional sales manager, based in New York. He became the assistant general sales manager for Packard in 1951 and held that post until leaving in 1953 to become vice president and general sales manager at Willys Motors.[35]

Over time, the remaining holdovers from Hudson left AMC. In December 1956, right after the American Motors directors decided to stop making Hudson cars, A. Edward Barit resigned in protest from the AMC board of directors and from his consulting position. Barit was not a sympathetic character. AMC paid him $12,500 a month ($150,000 per year) over the first fifteen months of his four-year consulting contract and was going to pay him $50,000 a year for the rest of the contract. When George Romney became president and general manager of AMC, he earned $125,000 a year. Shortly after Barit's resignation, Stuart G. Baits, an AMC vice president who had served with Hudson for more than twenty-five years, retired. His replacement, Joseph W. Eskridge, served as vice president and general manager, special products, from 1957 through 1963. Other than Roy D. Chapin Jr., Eskridge was the last significant holdover from the Hudson Motor Car Company.[36]

Romney recognized the abilities of Roy D. Chapin Jr. and quickly moved him into higher management posts. Romney appointed him assistant treasurer of AMC in November 1954, promoted him to treasurer in late April 1955, and then named him vice president and treasurer. By the end of 1956, Romney promoted Chapin to the post of executive vice president and general manager of the automotive division.[37]

The consolidation of the former Hudson and Nash operations stretched out more than three years. The closing and disposal of excess plant capacity was one critical requirement for the integration of production at Kenosha and Milwaukee. In December 1955, AMC sold the Detroit body plant at Gratiot Avenue to Philip Moskowitz of Cincinnati for $2,175,000. The Cadillac Division of General Motors then purchased the plant in August 1956 and made body panels there for another twenty-five years.[38]

Demolition of the main Hudson plant in Detroit began in December 1957 but dragged on for nearly five years. American Motors sold the property to a group of local investors who planned to demolish the plant and build a $1 million shopping center in its place. Louis M. Sarko, the head of the investment group, owned Arrow Wrecking Company, which immediately began demolition. In September 1960, the City of Detroit sued American Motors, the Jefferson-Conner Shopping Center, and the Arrow Wrecking Company to force them to complete the demolition, which had stopped in February 1960. The city argued that the partially dismantled buildings had become a public nuisance, injuring pedestrians and motorists and serving as a breeding ground for rats.[39] George Romney announced in early November 1960 that American Motors would spend $300,000 to complete the demolition "as a matter of civic responsibility." Demolition work resumed in mid-December 1960 and took a year to complete. Ironically, today this vacant factory site is a storage lot for new vehicles from a nearby Chrysler plant.[40]

American Motors attempted to fashion labor contracts with the UAW that did not precisely imitate the "pattern agreements" the union had signed with the Big Three automakers. The day American Motors began, George Mason hired Edward L. Cushman as AMC's director of industrial relations. Cushman was an economist who became a very successful industrial arbitrator before coming to American Motors. On the eve of AMC's first anniversary, the company announced that it could not follow the "pattern settlements" of the rest of the industry because its circumstances were different from those of the Big Three. Cushman claimed that the contract AMC had with the UAW actually provided higher pay scales than those at the Big Three. In 1955, for example, American Motors paid its assembly line welders seven to fifteen cents more per hour than their counterparts at the Big Three.

Cushman and UAW vice president Leonard Woodcock negotiated the entire summer of 1955 and reached an agreement on 2 September 1955, two weeks after the old agreement expired. Instead of the annual pay raises of 21 cents, 27 cents, and 33 cents per hour they won at the Big Three, the UAW accepted more modest increases of 14 cents, 20 cents, and 26 cents for its American Motors workers. This brought AMC's labor costs more in line with those of the Big Three. All the UAW locals approved the agreement in early October, except for the UAW local at AMC's body plant in Milwaukee. The Milwaukee local fell into line in late November after a second vote.[41]

George Romney faced a critical decision that would affect AMC's future—what new models would the company develop? Romney envisioned a rapidly increasing market for small cars, which AMC could capture. He moved the new Ramblers, scheduled for the 1957 model year, up a full year. The 108-inch wheelbase Ramblers for 1956 replaced the earlier 100-inch wheelbase Nash Ramblers the company had offered since 1951. The 1956 Ramblers were a disaster, with a drop in sales from 1955, largely due to production problems and poor quality. Operating losses for 1956 were a staggering $19.7 million *after* a tax credit of $1.4 million and $10.6 million realized from the sales of assets.[42]

Romney remained the perennial optimist, however, and inspired many at American Motors with his vision of the future. When he introduced the 1956 models in October 1955, he described AMC's underdog position: "We are the David. We have a round pebble called the Rambler. We are going to flank the 'Big Three'—not meet them head-on." Romney held a press conference at Detroit's Statler Hotel on 24 April 1956 to celebrate AMC's second anniversary. He predicted that they would introduce AMC's 1957 models on time for the first time since the merger.[43]

In George Romney, American Motors had an inspirational leader who served as a cheerleader during these difficult days. He was optimistic and cheerful to the point of sometimes annoying colleagues and coworkers. He inspired others to believe in his vision of the company's future. Without George Romney at the helm, American Motors probably would not have survived the first four years of its existence. Romney routinely gave "pep talks" to AMC's managers, dealers, and factory workers. He once advised his dealers, "If you have some men who lack enthusiasm, fire them with enthusiasm or fire them." Romney told assembly line workers, "The differences between success and failure or mediocrity are small."[44]

George Romney introduced wide-ranging economies in 1956 to reduce expenses and to lower AMC's break-even point. The top twenty-five executives took pay cuts ranging up to 35 percent. AMC cleaned its offices less frequently and sheet toilet paper replaced rolls. These economies and others reduced the break-even point in automobile production to 150,000 units, but production in 1956 was still well below that figure, at 104,189 units.[45]

George Romney and the AMC directors discovered in March 1957 that corporate "raider" Louis E. Wolfson had bought more than 350,000 shares of American

Motors stock at a time when AMC had 5,670,000 shares outstanding. The stock market grossly undervalued AMC's stock, which sold at $6 a share when the company's assets were roughly $20 a share. Wolfson was also interested in merging AMC with a profitable company to take full advantage of the automaker's tax-loss carryover of more than $3 million, which would expire in 1957. His precise plans were not fully formed, except that he intended to make money. He suggested several mergers of AMC with other firms, including the Chrysler Corporation. Selling Kelvinator, which was profitable, was another possibility. He publicly expressed confidence in George Romney and denied any intent to change AMC's management.[46]

Wolfson presented Romney and the AMC directors with a wide range of possible merger partners. Romney met with Wolfson more than a dozen times, was consistently cordial and cooperative, but resisted Wolfson's proposals. In late June 1958, newspapers reported that Wolfson was selling 100,000 shares of AMC stock and planned to sell his remaining shares. A few days later, the Securities and Exchange Commission (SEC) charged Wolfson with using deceit to manipulate the price of AMC stock and had a U.S. District Count enjoin him from any further dealings in AMC stock.[47]

American Motors was a struggling automaker in the mid-1950s and the 1958 models were critical to its survival. The figures in Table 7.1 clearly show the strug-

Table 7.1. American Motors Production by Calendar Year, Sales ($ Millions) and Profits, Net of Taxes ($ Millions), Year Ending 30 September 1954–62

	Production	**Sales ($ Millions)**	**Net Profits ($ Millions)**	**Profit as Share of Sales (%)**
1954*	99,774	400.3	(11.1)	–
1955	194,175	441.1	(7.0)	–
1956	104,189	408.4	(19.7)	–
1957	114,084	362.2	(11.8)	–
1958	217,338	470.3	26.1	5.5
1959	401,446	869.8	60.3	6.9
1960	485,745	1,057.7	48.2	4.6
1961	372,485	875.7	23.6	2.7
1962	454,784	1,056.4	34.2	3.7

Source: "Calendar Year Production, American Motors and Its Predecessors," American Motors Corporate History file, NAHC; American Motors Corporation, Annual Reports, 1954–62, NAHC.
*Includes Nash and Hudson production before the merger.

gles AMC endured in 1954–57, when sales and production were too small to generate profits, even in the peak year of 1955. Companies that consistently lost money needed to resort to loans to keep operating and American Motors was no exception. The company had outstanding loans of $69,350,000 in 1954 and in August 1956 arranged long-term loans and revolving credit from a consortium of banks for $67,570,000. AMC's outstanding debt fell to $33,750,000 in 1957 and the company emerged debt-free by mid-1958. Romney expressed absolute confidence that the automaker would earn profits based on its 1958 automobile offerings.[48]

The Move to Smaller Cars and a Return to Prosperity, 1958–62

George Romney took a calculated gamble when he pushed American Motors into emphasizing the compact Rambler in its product plans starting with the 1956 models. Two years passed before this strategy yielded major dividends. In 1958, when the American automobile industry suffered a major decline in sales, American Motors nearly doubled its production from 1957 and increased its market share from 1.76 percent to 4 percent. AMC's market share jumped again in 1959 to 6 percent.[49]

George Romney's success in turning around American Motors by focusing on small cars brought him national exposure and fame. He gained additional notoriety from his very public iconoclastic views of the automotive industry's products and economic structure. Romney's fame began with his attacks on the large cars made by the Big Three automakers. He delivered a speech to the Motor City Traffic Club of Detroit on 27 January 1955 in which he called the large American car "The Dinosaur in the Driveway." He noted that "cars 19 feet long, weighing two tons, are used to run a 118-pound housewife three blocks to the drugstore for a two-ounce package of bobby pins and lipstick." The dinosaurs were gas-guzzlers, saddling their owners with huge costs each year. They were large, costly to operate, and had poor handling and performance.[50]

According to one industry analyst, Romney single-handedly changed the preferences of American car buyers: "George Romney brought off one of the marketing coups of the mid-20th century United States. Against prevailing practice and inbred belief, he changed the product and sales pattern of a dominant industry. He sold the Rambler and the concept of the compact car. At the same time, he sold one more entity, George Romney." Romney was hardly "a voice in the wilderness." His attacks on big cars resonated with millions of Americans who were unhappy not only with the big cars but with the lack of choice offered by the Big Three. In its 1958 automotive issue, *Consumer Reports* gave the Rambler high marks, rare kudos from a highly critical magazine. John Keats's *The Insolent Chariots* (1958) was a nasty frontal attack on big cars. George Romney was perhaps the most visible voice of this movement, but he was not alone.[51]

Romney shocked his fellow automotive executives when he testified before the Senate Subcommittee on Antitrust and Monopoly of the Judiciary Committee on 7 February 1958. He called for a reform in the antitrust laws to encourage more competition in American industries, including the automobile industry. The two giants of the Big Three, General Motors and Ford, should each be split into several independent companies to create a minimum of six to eight automotive competitors. Romney also railed against the monopoly power of the large industrial unions, including the UAW. He attacked the "pattern bargaining" strategy of the UAW as inherently unfair to Studebaker-Packard, American Motors, and Chrysler.[52]

Romney's fame, however, did not bring about AMC's revival. The change in company fortunes was the result of its new model offerings for 1958, combined with the serious national economic recession that year. The symbolic step of eliminating the Nash and Hudson nameplates was an important part of the revival. Neither name created positive images in the minds of consumers. Hudson was known for stock car racing, but little else. Nash had become a stodgy, unattractive car. One advertisement showed a dog chasing a Nash, with the caption, "He'll only chase a Nash," to which wags replied, "because that is the only car he can catch."

Combining overlapping, competing dealerships eliminated waste and focused on the Rambler brand. Before making the final decision, Romney and Roy Abernethy met with Midwest AMC dealers in late September 1957 to get their advice. The dealers believed that the Nash and Hudson names made selling the cars more difficult and they applauded the change. A *Detroit News* editorial, "A Tear in Parting," bemoaned the loss of the Hudson marque.[53]

American Motors introduced a new 100-inch wheelbase Rambler American for 1958, returning to the smaller Rambler the company had offered for the 1951–55 model years. AMC revealed its plans publicly in August 1957 and officially introduced the new Rambler American in early January 1958 at the Chicago Auto Show. The Rambler American was about three feet shorter overall than the average American automobile. A new Ambassador, with a 117-inch wheelbase and a 327 CID V-8 engine producing 270 horsepower, replaced the large Nash and Hudson models. American Motors also offered two models on a 108-inch wheelbase—the Rambler Six and the Rambler Rebel V-8—along with the Metropolitan, with a wheelbase of 85 inches. All of the 1958 models also offered improved protection against rust.

The company, however, was still far from becoming exclusively a small car specialist. Of the 1958 model year sales of 162,182 units, the Rambler Six was by far

1958 Rambler American. *Courtesy NAHC.*

the best-seller, with 106,640 units, followed by the Rambler American (30,640), the Ambassador (14,570), and the Rambler Rebel V-8 (10,056). For the 1960 model year, when sales were 458,949 units, the two V-8 models, the Rambler Rebel and the Ambassador, accounted for only 9 percent of total sales.[54]

Fuel economy was a strong selling point for the Rambler, and American Motors entered the car in scores of economy runs. A stock six-passenger Rambler station wagon completed an economy run from Los Angeles to New York in June 1956 at an average speed of 40.35 miles per hour and achieved the remarkable fuel economy of 32.09 miles per gallon. American Motors also received endorsements from drivers who used Ramblers in their daily business. John Timber, Detroit's first cab driver to use a Rambler, reported fuel usage in city traffic of 18 miles per gallon, versus 13 miles per gallon for his other cabs.[55]

The Rambler also became a symbol of the "upstart" challenging of the establishment, that is, the large cars of the Big Three. On 9 July 1958, the musical group the Playmates released the novelty song "Beep Beep (The Little Nash Rambler)," which quickly rose to number four on the pop music chart. The first and last stanzas (out of a total of five) transmit the feel of this tune.

While riding in my Cadillac, what to my surprise,
A little Nash Rambler was following me, about one-third my size.
The guy must have wanted to pass me out

As he kept on tooting his horn (beep beep)
I'll show him that a Cadillac is not a car to scorn.

Chorus: Beep beep (beep beep)
Beep beep (beep beep)
His horn went beep beep beep (beep beep)

Now we're doing a hundred and twenty, as fast as I could go.
The Rambler pulled alongside of me, as if we were going slow.
The fellow rolled his window down and yelled for me to hear:
"Hey, buddy, how can I get this car out of second gear?"

An article in *Business Week* in January 1958 had noted that Romney had little choice but to gamble on small cars, given AMC's near insolvency in October 1956. Romney had noted the sharp increase in the sales of small foreign cars, especially Volkswagens, starting in 1955. Even with AMC's extraordinary sales successes of 1958, industry analysts remained skeptical about the company's future. A *Fortune* article published in January 1959 carried the title "Will Success Spoil American Motors?" The article argued that the success of American Motors and European automakers like Volkswagen in selling compact cars had encouraged the Big Three to introduce competing compacts. To be sure, October 1959 brought the introduction of the Chevrolet Corvair, the Ford Falcon, and the Plymouth Valiant models for 1960.

Fortune speculated that American Motors should enjoy and make the most of 1959 as a year of grace before the onslaught of the Big Three's compact cars. AMC was well situated at the start of 1959. The company had paid off all of its bank loans in July 1958 and launched a $10 million expansion program to increase capacity to 450,000 cars by the end of 1959. Economies had reduced AMC's break-even point to 125,000 cars, so the company would survive even if it lost a good part of its sales to the new compacts. *Fortune* also speculated that AMC's 1960 sales would probably be no greater than 300,000 units and might be as little as 200,000. The actual production in 1960 (485,745 units) shows how badly these observers underestimated AMC's strengths.[56]

Romney had AMC well positioned to increase production of its compact cars as demand for them increased. Following the sales surge of 1958, American Motors began an ambitious program to increase its capacity. In mid-June 1959, AMC's board of directors agreed to a long-term plan to increase yearly capacity from 450,000 cars to 660,000. They immediately committed the company to spend $17.5 million on

1959 Ambassador custom four-door hardtop. *Courtesy DCHC.*

the first stage of expansion, which would increase capacity to 552,000 units. A new engine line ($10.7 million) and rear axle line ($4.9 million) were the major expenses. At the end of November 1959, the directors agreed to a second round of investment of $23.4 million. Converting the Simmons bed factory in Kenosha into a new body plant ($14.2 million) and providing a third assembly line ($7 million) were the major expenses in the second capital program.[57]

While riding a wave of sales successes starting with the 1958 model year, American Motors had to respond to the new compact cars introduced as 1960 models by the Big Three. George Romney pushed Edmund E. Anderson, AMC director of styling, to "reskin" the entire 1961 lineup while keeping the 1960 chassis. The 1961 Rambler American had an entirely new look, but was more compact than the model it replaced. While using the same 100-inch wheelbase, the new American was five inches shorter and four inches narrower. Anderson gave the Ambassador a "euro" front-end design, which hurt sales. The following year, AMC built the Ambassador on the 108-inch wheelbase of the Rambler Classic. Anderson generated a line of cars for 1961 that looked new and fresh, but were in fact inexpensive reskinned models. Sales in 1961 fell by more than 100,000 units from the previous year, but American Motors persevered in a depressed year for autos. Sales rebounded in 1962 and American Motors survived the competition of the Big Three's compact cars.[58]

Starting in 1959, American Motors faced increasing competition from the Big

Three's compact cars and from the growing popularity of the Volkswagen Beetle. On the heels of the 1960 Ford Falcon, Chevrolet Corvair, and Plymouth Valiant, General Motors introduced the Chevy II in 1961 and Chrysler brought out the Dodge Dart in 1962. Sales of compacts from the Big Three jumped from a paltry 200,000 in 1959 to nearly one million in 1960, which represented 16 percent of all U.S. sales by the domestic automakers. After dipping to sales of only 762,000 units in 1961, the Big Three then sold over one million compacts in 1962 and again in 1963, or roughly 15 percent of all sales by the domestic automakers. The popularity of AMC's compact cars fell sharply in the mid-1960s and sales dropped to 425,000 units in 1967, in part a reflection of the success of the "pony cars" such as the Ford Mustang and the Plymouth Barracuda. The Volkswagen Beetle remained the most persistent competitor for Rambler throughout the 1960s. U.S. registrations of new Volkswagens had already reached 120,000 in 1959 and then grew steadily to 383,000 units in 1965 and 420,000 units the following year. In both 1965 and 1966, Volkswagens accounted for two-thirds of all imports sold in the United States. Model year sales peaked at 390,079 units in 1968, remained well above 300,000 units through 1973, but then fell off dramatically in 1975 to only 78,412 units.[59]

American Motors did well in the period 1958–62 because it was well positioned to benefit from the wave of interest in smaller cars that developed in that era. Sales of imported cars nearly doubled between 1957 (207,000 units) and 1958 (379,000 units), when they captured 8.1 percent of the American market. Ramblers and imports combined captured over 12 percent of the market. Studebaker-Packard introduced its compact Lark in 1959 and it was immediately successful. For the 1959 calendar year, imports (609,000), Rambler (363,000), and Lark (133,000) together captured 18.4 percent of the U.S. market. It was in this context that the Big Three moved swiftly to bring out their own compact models. Starting in 1960, sales of imports fell off each year through 1962, but American Motors continued to thrive and keep its costs under control.[60]

The company continued to insist that its economic circumstances were such that it could not afford to give its workers the same contract provisions the UAW won at the Big Three. When contract negotiations began in April 1958 to reach a new agreement before 17 October, the expiration date of the old one, Edward Cushman called for a two-year wage freeze at AMC. The talks stalled until 8 October 1958, when negotiations resumed against the background of the 17 October deadline. Marathon sessions brought a last-minute settlement, a three-year contract that followed the pattern of earlier agreements with the Big Three.

The next national contract negotiations between AMC and the UAW, which began in July 1961, started off with both sides calling for a reconsideration of all phases of their relationship. In late July, AMC dropped a bombshell by proposing a profit-sharing plan for all of its workers. Edward Cushman's proposal, which he called "progress sharing," involved workers getting 10 percent of net profits after taxes and after the company had set aside an amount worth 10 percent of the stockholders' equity. A joint management-union committee would determine how they would allocate the profit-sharing "pot." Initially, two-thirds of the total would pay for improved pensions and insurance benefits for the workers and one-third would be used to buy AMC stock for the employees. By the end of August, the union and the company reached a tentative agreement that granted a general pay raise and provided improved retirement benefits.[61]

Ratification of the agreement was not a simple matter. The Kenosha local, the largest at AMC, narrowly rejected the agreement in early October. The UAW's executive board ordered another vote at Kenosha, citing the poor turnout for the first vote. In a second tally, Kenosha UAW Local 72 approved the contract by a 2–1 margin, with more than ten thousand casting votes.[62]

George Romney continued to fine-tune his top executive corps. In December 1960 he named Roy Abernethy, vice president for automotive marketing and sales, to the posts of executive vice president and director. Abernethy joined Roy D. Chapin Jr., executive vice president and general manager (automotive division), and Bernard A. Chapman, executive vice president and general manager (appliance division), on the AMC board of directors. Romney also gave Chapin responsibility for international sales. In November 1961, Romney named Abernethy AMC's general manager and appointed Chapin president of American Motors Export Corporation, a wholly owned subsidiary.[63]

While Romney successfully led American Motors through a dangerous period of its existence, he also became involved in public affairs. In December 1956, the president of the Detroit Board of Education, William D. Merrifield, and Dr. Samuel Miller Brownell, Detroit's superintendent of schools, asked Romney to head the Citizens Advisory Committee on School Needs, and Romney agreed to serve. Romney and the committee worked tirelessly for eighteen months and produced a set of 182 recommendations for improving the Detroit school system. More important, in the spring of 1959, Detroit voters approved $60 million in new bonds and $30 million per year in new property taxes to improve the schools.[64]

Michigan's state government was stalemated in the late 1950s, with a Republican legislature at loggerheads with the liberal Democratic governor, G. Mennen Williams. In June 1959, Romney announced the formation of Citizens for Michigan, a nonpartisan group that would propose needed reforms, mainly a new Michigan constitution. While Romney was a vice chairman of the Constitutional Convention that met in 1961 and 1962, he considered seeking the Republican nomination for governor of Michigan.[65]

After praying for "guidance," George Romney announced on 10 February 1962 that he would seek the Republican nomination for governor. He initially promised to finish his work on the Constitutional Convention, but that proved impossible, given the obvious conflict of interest. The AMC directors met on 12 February and granted Romney a temporary leave of absence to run for governor. He would resign as president and chairman of the board and became vice chairman instead. The board named Richard E. Cross chairman and CEO, with an annual salary of $90,000, and Roy Abernethy became president and chief operating officer, with a salary of $125,000.[66]

The George Romney Era in Perspective

Romney never returned to an active role in American Motors. Elected Michigan's governor in November 1962 and reelected in 1964 and 1966, he unsuccessfully ran for the presidency in 1968. George Romney's accomplishments at American Motors cannot be overstated. He inherited a newly formed company made from defective Nash and Hudson pieces. He made difficult decisions, including killing off the Nash and Hudson marques, decisions that George Mason would likely not have made. He was a relentless leader who molded the American Motors executives into a team that he inspired to believe in his vision of a successful company focused on compact cars. He worked tirelessly to make his vision of an automobile market that offered consumers more choices into a reality. Romney seemed in most respects to be a "fish out of water" as a leader of an American car company in the 1950s. He was a sober, sincere, earnest crusader and an iconoclast who was not bashful about promoting his ideas. Imagining American Motors surviving the difficult years from 1956 to 1962 without George W. Romney at the helm is difficult. At the same time, Romney did not run the company as a one-man show and left behind a seasoned, competent group of managers well equipped to continue his successes. Right after Romney's departure, at least one business writer predicted that AMC would continue to be profitable without him.[67]

EIGHT

American Motors in Sickness and in Health, 1962–78

We are not going to attempt to be all things to all people. We are going to concentrate on those areas of consumer needs we can meet better than anyone else.

Roy D. Chapin Jr. to the American Motors
stockholders upon being named chairman and
chief executive officer, 10 January 1967

American Motors continued to endure several crises and recoveries during the middle years of its existence. During the five years (1962–66) following the departure of George Romney from active management, the company's fortunes slipped under the leadership of Roy Abernethy. During the chairmanship of Roy D. Chapin Jr. (1967–78), American Motors survived, recovered, and even prospered. The company introduced innovative, unique automobiles—Javelin, Hornet, Gremlin, Pacer, and others—which allowed AMC to survive the competition of the Big Three automakers. Roy Chapin transformed American Motors, which sold its Kelvinator Appliance Division to White Consolidated Industries in July 1968 and then purchased the Kaiser Jeep Corporation in February 1970. AMC created a separate division, AM General, to manufacture trucks for the military, vehicles for the U.S. Postal Service, and urban transit buses.

The Struggles of the Roy Abernethy Presidency, 1962–66

Following George Romney's resignation as board chairman and CEO of American Motors on 12 February 1962, the management team of Roy Abernethy and Richard

Roy Abernethy (*left*), Richard E. Cross (*middle*), and
Edward L. Cushman (*right*), ca. 1963. *Courtesy DCHC.*

E. Cross took the reins. Initially, Abernethy served as president and chief operating officer, while Cross was board chairman and chief executive officer. By mid-
November 1962, Abernethy also became the CEO and Cross limited his duties to
that of chairman. Romney had remained an AMC director following his resignation
as president and chairman, but resigned his director's post on 15 November 1962
after winning the race for governor of Michigan. Edward L. Cushman, an AMC vice
president, replaced Romney as a director.[1]

American Motors enjoyed improved sales in 1962 and 1963 over the disastrous
year of 1961, and production in 1963 nearly equaled the record figure of 485,745 in
1960. As Table 8.1 shows, sales and profits then experienced a major decline from
1964 through 1967. Abernethy had abandoned the formula Romney had used to
bring prosperity to the company. Romney did not try to compete across the board
with the offerings of the Big Three automakers but instead focused on niche markets,
particularly the market for compact cars, where the Big Three were weak. Romney
kept tooling costs to a minimum by making frequent cosmetic face-lifts to AMC's
offerings, but seldom did a complete makeover. Abernethy, however, attempted to
make the AMC products more competitive with those of the Big Three in terms of
style, which required frequent costly redesigns. AMC's share of the U.S. car market,
which stood at 6.09 percent for 1962, fell steadily during the Abernethy years to a
low in 1967 of only 2.79 percent.[2]

Table 8.1. American Motors Production by Calendar Year, Sales ($ Millions) and Profits, Net of Taxes ($ Millions), Year Ending 30 September 1961–67

	Production	Sales ($ Millions)	Net Profits ($ Millions)	Profit as Share of Sales (%)
1961	372,485	875.7	23.6	2.7
1962	454,784	1,106.2	34.2	3.1
1963	480,365	1,204.8	37.8	3.1
1964	393,863	1,095.4	26.2	2.4
1965	346,367	990.6	5.2	0.5
1966	279,225	870.4	(12.6)	–
1967	229,058	778.0	(75.8)	–

Source: "Calendar Year Production, American Motors and Its Predecessors," American Motors Corporate History file, NAHC; American Motors Corporation, Annual Reports, 1961–67, NAHC.

The American Motors offerings in the early 1960s consisted of three car lines—the Rambler American Six, the Rambler Classic Six, and the Ambassador (V-8). The 1962 lineup was essentially the same as in 1961, but the 1963 models were noticeably different. The Classic and Ambassador models had longer wheelbases than they had in 1962 (112 inches versus 108 inches), were three inches lower, and featured curved glass door windows and entirely new styling. The American did not change substantially, but AMC added a two-door hardtop model to the line. In mid-February 1963, the company announced that it was offering a V-8 engine as an option to its Rambler Classic line.[3]

Then a remarkable thing happened: *Motor Trend* named the 1963 Rambler Classic and Ambassador "Car of the Year." The magazine admitted that it road-tested the American Motors models more extensively than normal: "While the award is based on pure progress in design, we like to make sure the car is also worthy of the title in critical areas of performance, dependability, value, and potential buyer satisfaction." Jim Wright, *Motor Trend's* technical editor, admired the innovative unit-body design, which reduced the number of components, saved 150 pounds, and resulted in a body that had cleaner lines and greater strength than competitive models. He also cited excellent fuel economy, good handling, adequate performance, interior room and comfort, and overall manufacturing quality. In line with the rest of the auto industry, American Motors doubled its standard warranty on the 1963 models to twenty-four months or 24,000 miles.[4]

The 1964 model offerings were a preview of AMC's changing model mix. The

Rambler Classic Six and the Ambassador received new grilles but few other changes. The Rambler American, however, underwent complete restyling, with the wheelbase lengthened from 100 to 106 inches. This was the first AMC model entirely designed by Richard Teague. In February, American Motors introduced an "idea car" (concept car) dubbed the Tarpon to its stockholders at their annual meeting. This was a sporty two-door "fastback" or "glassback" intended to appeal to young drivers.[5]

American Motors left the Rambler American largely unchanged for 1965 but gave the Rambler Classic and the Rambler Ambassador brand-new front-end styling and a 232 CID six-cylinder engine, which also served as the Marlin's base engine. Ambassador had a longer wheelbase (116 versus 112 inches) and was a foot longer than the 1964 version. In May 1964, Roy Abernethy promised that American Motors would reverse its 1964 sales slump by introducing sporty cars as part of the 1965 offerings. In March 1965 AMC introduced its Marlin, a two-door, hardtop fastback that resembled the Tarpon but was stretched to use the larger Rambler Classic wheelbase (112 inches) at Abernethy's insistence. AMC stylists labeled the Marlin, which weighed 3,234 pounds and carried a sticker price of $3,100, the "Carp." It was not competitive with the Ford Mustang and the Plymouth Barracuda, "pony cars" introduced a year earlier.[6]

The Marlin was an enormous blunder from a design and marketing point of view. In the fall of 1965, Malcolm Brooks wrote a scathing review of the Marlin in *Automobile Quarterly*. In discussing Detroit's recent fastback designs, Brooks declared

1965 Marlin. *Courtesy NAHC.*

that the Marlin "is by far the ugliest of the lot." The buying public seemed to agree. After making 10,327 Marlins in the 1965 model year, production dropped by more than half in 1966 and to a mere 2,545 units in 1967, the final year of production, for a grand total of 17,419. In contrast, the Mustang and the Barracuda sold 1,167,019 units and 126,068 units, respectively, during their first two and a half years of production.[7]

American Motors tweaked its Rambler American, Rambler Classic, and Rambler Ambassador models for 1966 with redesigned front ends, grilles, and, for the Ambassador, a new roof. Abernethy announced in August 1965 that American Motors would emphasize larger, more luxurious models in 1966 to compete more effectively with the Big Three. They put more emphasis on "sporty" styling, with three new hardtops: the Ambassador DPL, the Classic Rebel, and the American Rogue. Sales fell off precipitously in 1966 and the company endured losses for the first time since 1957. Unfortunately for Abernethy and American Motors, this strategy of going upscale failed.[8]

Abernethy and Cross tried several approaches to revive AMC's sinking sales: they hired a new advertising agency; the company upgraded its warranties on its new cars; and they cautiously reentered competitive racing. In mid-February 1965, the company announced that it would seek proposals from advertising agencies to handle its accounts. Its advertising agency at the time, the New York firm of Geyer, Morley, Ballard, Inc., resigned its AMC automotive account but kept the Kelvinator business. They had served AMC and Nash for a total of twenty-eight years. AMC announced in early April that the New York advertising agency Benton & Bowles, Inc., would handle its 1966 Rambler advertising.[9]

In early September 1966, American Motors announced that it was matching the extended warranties on new 1967 model cars announced by Ford and General Motors. They all extended the warranty on the power train (engines, transmissions, rear axles) from 24 months/24,000 miles to 5 years/50,000 miles. Given market competition, AMC had little choice but to match its competitors.[10]

The company also reentered competitive racing in 1966 after publicly criticizing other auto companies that raced and emphasized speed in their advertising. Members of the Automobile Manufacturers Association had pledged in 1957 not to use speed or power in advertising. Chrysler and Ford returned to factory-sponsored racing in the early 1960s. In early 1963, Roy Abernethy publicly blasted the other car companies for emphasizing speed and blamed them indirectly for the high national accident rate. By May 1966, AMC had reversed its position on racing. The company entered Ramblers in performance trials at Daytona Beach and promoted their successes in Rambler advertisements.[11]

American Motors faced a sales slump and losses in 1966 and was prepared to take desperate measures to recover. In his letter to Roy Chapin Jr. announcing his plans to retire as chairman, Richard Cross delineated an aggressive program to find a merger partner for AMC. They had already had discussions with the U.S. Justice Department about the possible antitrust implications of a merger with a variety of partners, including Chrysler, Kaiser-Jeep, International Harvester, White Motor Corporation, Borg Warner, General Electric, and Sears, Roebuck. Within a few years, AMC completed deals with Kaiser Jeep and with White Consolidated Industries.[12]

American Motors had remarkable success in selling Ramblers in Canada and overseas during the 1960s. Overseas sales amounted to roughly 44,000 units in 1962 and then climbed to 72,348 in 1964 and remained at roughly 74,000 in 1965 and 1966. Renault assembled Ramblers in Belgium for the Common Market, and the rest of the foreign sales consisted of Ramblers manufactured in Kenosha and shipped overseas CKD (complete knock down) for assembly in foreign factories. They did not achieve the peak figures for 1965 and 1966 again until fiscal year 1974, when they sold 95,794 cars and Jeeps in Canada and overseas.[13]

In addition to the challenges American Motors faced in selling its cars, Abernethy also occasionally had to deal with less-than-harmonious labor relations during his term as president and CEO. They began the innovative "progress-sharing" program with the three-year contract signed on 15 September 1961, and similar programs also went into effect for salaried workers and executives. The company-union joint committee decided that two-thirds of the money would be used to pay for the improvements in pension and insurance benefits negotiated in the contract and the remaining one-third to buy shares of AMC stock, which the company held in the individual employee's name. The payout under the first year of the plan was nearly $9.8 million, with one-third, or roughly $3.4 million, spent to purchase stock for the workers. Each worker on average received roughly $128 in stock.[14]

By the third and final year of the agreement, some workers expressed discontent with parts of the profit-sharing program. They preferred to receive cash or AMC stock that they could sell anytime. As negotiations for the next contract loomed, the UAW sent mixed signals about its desire to continue profit sharing.[15]

Negotiations for the 1964 contract began in July 1964, with a three-year agreement reached on 18 October. The contract brought AMC workers the same economic benefits as workers at the Big Three and continued profit sharing, with workers paid in cash and not in stock. UAW Local 75 at the Milwaukee body plant narrowly rejected the agreement in early December, with fewer than one-third of the members voting. In a second vote on 7 December 1964, the members approved the national contract by more than 1,000 votes, with more than two-thirds voting.[16]

A national labor contract did not guarantee labor peace at the local plant level. Disputes over local work rules, disciplinary actions, and grievances brought a strike at the Kenosha assembly plant in early June 1965. The UAW struck AMC on 23 August 1965 over hundreds of unresolved grievances on work standards, disciplining of shop stewards, and the scheduling of short work weeks. The strike dragged on for twenty-one days, idled 17,000, and held up the production of the 1966 models. After voting, the UAW uncovered irregularities in the Local 72 (Kenosha) ratification vote and the International UAW ordered a second vote on 24 September, with the agreement approved by a 2–1 margin.[17]

The failure of Abernethy's sales strategy brought American Motors to the brink of disaster and precipitated his ouster in January 1967. AMC's U.S. market share, which stood at 6.42 percent for calendar year 1960, fell to 4.70 percent in 1964 and reached 2.79 percent in 1967. In early June 1965, two small stockholders formed the AMC Shareholder Communications Committee to inform the financial community of AMC's problems in the hopes of finding solutions before the company went bankrupt. By the summer of 1965, the financial world saw a gloomy future for American Motors, and Bernard Thomas, the executive director of the dissident shareholders group, called on Roy Abernethy to step down. The company had to borrow $50 million from a consortium of banks in late summer 1965. The conditions of the loan limited the payment of dividends and AMC did not pay any dividend to shareholders in December 1965. In mid-March 1966, AMC negotiated a $75 million line of credit from a group of New York banks, another indication of financial weakness.[18]

A new force appeared within American Motors in late January 1966, a few days before the AMC shareholders' meeting. Detroit industrialist Robert B. Evans, a sixty-year-old millionaire, had quietly purchased about 280,000 shares of AMC stock, making him the largest stockholder. At the time, about nineteen million shares were outstanding. He appeared at the annual meeting on 2 February, but was vague about his intentions regarding AMC. He publicly supported the current leadership of Richard Cross and Roy Abernethy. In early March 1966, Evans replaced a retiring AMC director and a month later, when the directors appointed a new five-member executive committee of the AMC board, he became a member.[19]

AMC's top management changed in 1966. Edward Cushman, who had been in charge of labor relations at AMC since 1954, announced in late March that he was leaving AMC to become a vice president at Wayne State University in Detroit. Cushman retained his position on the AMC board. George Gullen Jr., who had been vice president for industrial relations at AMC under Cushman, also took a position at Wayne State University in August. American Motors quickly named Frank G.

Armstrong, a labor relations specialist and former vice president at the Burroughs Corporation in Detroit, to replace Cushman. Armstrong received the title of vice president in charge of administration but did not become a director.[20]

A second major change in the management team that had replace Romney in 1962 came at the AMC directors' meeting of 6 June 1966, when Richard Cross resigned as chairman and the board named Robert B. Evans to replace him. More changes were to come. In mid-September, AMC named Roy D. Chapin Jr. to the position of executive vice president and automotive general manager. William V. Luneburg became vice president of automotive manufacturing and would report to Chapin. Industry observers believed that Chapin's promotion made him the heir-apparent to Abernethy.[21]

At the directors meeting of 9 January 1967, only three weeks before the shareholders' meeting, Robert Evans resigned as chairman and Roy Abernethy retired as president and CEO. Roy D. Chapin Jr. became AMC's chairman and CEO, and Luneburg became president and chief operating officer. The resignation of Evans, who had only been with American Motors for about a year, came as a surprise to industry observers. Evans, who remained a major stockholder, apparently viewed his service as chairman as temporary and held it only until the board was prepared to name Chapin to the position.[22]

Roy D. Chapin Jr. celebrating his thirtieth anniversary
with the company, May 1968. *Courtesy DCHC.*

Despite Abernethy's claim that he had simply decided to retire early at age sixty once he was eligible to do so, there was a widely held belief at the time that the AMC board of directors fired him. Chapin's first statement about AMC product plans was a repudiation of Abernethy's failed strategy of trying to compete head to head with the Big Three: "We are not going to attempt to be all things to all people. We are going to concentrate on those areas of consumer needs we can meet better than anyone else." At a shareholders' meeting five years later, Evans, who still served as a director, explained the housecleaning of January 1967: "We put Chapin and Luneburg in to undo the terrible things that the previous administration had done," meaning the regime of Richard Cross and Roy Abernethy.[23]

The Roy D. Chapin Jr.–William V. Luneburg Regime, 1967–78

The Chapin/Luneburg tandem directed American Motors for a decade. Chapin had spent his entire adult working life with Hudson and American Motors, while Luneburg was a relative newcomer to AMC but not to the automobile industry. Luneburg joined the Ford Motor Company as a financial analyst in 1949, became the budget manager at the Ford Division, and managed the giant Ford Rouge plant in 1956–59. Luneburg accepted the position of executive vice president at the Mather Spring Company in Toledo, Ohio, in 1959 and remained there until accepting the position of vice president for finance at AMC in March 1963. Fortunately for AMC, Luneburg found the spring business boring and wanted to return to the automobile industry.[24]

Chapin and Luneburg achieved some impressive, if brief, successes, as Table 8.2 shows. Production and sales expanded in most years, but profits were disappointing overall. Much of the sales increases reflect the addition of Jeep sales following AMC's purchase of Kaiser Jeep in 1970. Still, American Motors would not have survived this period without the revival of its automobile lines under the direction of Chapin and Luneburg.

In the long term, American Motors faced an additional challenge that began in the mid-1960s and grew increasingly problematic in the 1970s and 1980s—satisfying federal regulations regarding tailpipe emissions and safety. Because AMC specialized in small cars, it generally had no trouble meeting federal Corporate Average Fuel Economy (CAFÉ) standards. California led the way in imposing emissions standards starting with the 1963 model cars. Congress passed the Motor Vehicle Air Pollution and Control Act of 1965, imposing California's standards on the nation for the 1968 model year, with additional reductions for 1970. Senator

Table 8.2. American Motors Production by Calendar Year, Sales ($ Millions) and Profits, Net of Taxes ($ Millions), Year Ending 30 September 1967–78

	Production	**Sales*** **($ Millions)**	**Net Profits*** **($ Millions)**	**Profit as Share** **of Sales (%)**
1967	229,058	651.2	(66.7)	–
1968	268,439	761.1	4.8	0.6
1969	242,898	737.4	4.9	0.7
1970	321,915**	1,089.8	(56.2)	–
1971	288,720	1,232.6	10.2	0.8
1972	350,336	1,403.8	30.2	2.2
1973	449,890	1,739.0	86.0	4.9
1974	448,135	2,000.2	27.5	1.4
1975	429,537	2,282.2	(27.5)	–
1976	387,803	2,315.5	(46.3)	–
1977	343,717	2,236.9	8.2	0.4
1978	368,022	2,585.4	36.7	1.4

Source: "Calendar Year Production, American Motors and Its Predecessors," American Motors Corporate History file, NAHC; American Motors Corporation, Annual Reports, 1967–78, NAHC.
*Sales and profit (loss) figures starting in 1967 are stated in terms of automotive operations only, reflecting the discontinuance of appliance operations in 1968.
**Starting in 1970, production figures include Jeeps but exclude AM General products.

Edmund Muskie's Clean Air Act of 1970 mandated 90 percent reductions from the 1970 standards for hydrocarbons and carbon monoxide by 1975 and for oxides of nitrogen for 1976. These requirements were so unrealistic that the Environmental Protection Agency (EPA) granted the automakers a two-year extension to meet the standards. Congress also enacted the National Traffic and Motor Vehicle Safety Act of 1966 and charged a new agency, the National Highway Traffic Safety Administration (NHTSA), with setting safety standards. NHTSA mandated seventeen safety standards for the 1968 models and twenty-eight additional standards for the 1969 models.[25]

Meeting the new government mandates was costly for all the automakers, but they created particular hardships for American Motors and Chrysler, the two smallest producers. Chrysler's engineers had developed a "Chrysler Clean Air Package" of engine modifications that greatly reduced emissions, and Chrysler installed this system on all of its 1968 models. Unfortunately for Chrysler, the 1970 Clean Air

Act specified that the devices used to reduce pollution on the 1977 models had to work flawlessly for five years or 50,000 miles and Chrysler's system required periodic engine tune-ups. Only GM's catalytic converter could meet the standard, so Chrysler and American Motors had to buy catalytic converters from GM, which developed the device first and was pleased to have American Motors and Chrysler share the costs of its pioneer work. According to James Flink, the tailpipe emission system on the 1977 models cost General Motors $200 per vehicle, but twice that amount for Chrysler.[26]

American Motors inked an agreement with General Motors for its AC Spark Plug Division to supply AMC with catalytic converters from 1 July 1974 through 30 June 1977. The contract called for maximum purchases of 226,000 catalytic converters in the first year, 244,000 in the second year, and an astonishing 800,000 in the third year. The unit price was approximately $67. There were likely subsequent contracts between AMC and GM for catalytic converters, but no records survive to confirm this.[27]

Starting in November 1969, General Motors agreed to give American Motors engineering consulting services to help AMC develop air pollution emission control devices for its vehicles. The first agreement went into effect on 7 November 1969 and extended until 31 December 1971. General Motors would give AMC the services of some of its engineers working on emission controls and, perhaps as important, make its engineering laboratories and other testing facilities available to American Motors. Subsequent similar agreements, usually extending for one or two years, carried this relationship forward until at least October 1980. These agreements were always subject to U.S. Department of Justice review and approval, which always came, if sometimes grudgingly.

The surviving records include dozens of letters from Forrest A. Hainline Jr., AMC's general counsel, to the attorneys in the Department of Justice's Antitrust Division. In December 1975, the EPA asked for the right to attend these GM-AMC meetings, but AMC strongly rejected the request. The meetings narrowly focused on specific engineering problems. Much of the meeting held on 14 October 1980, for example, involved the analysis of the problem of volatile silicone gasket materials fouling oxygen sensors. The AMC-GM relationship had a classic win-win-win outcome. American Motors was able to reduce the costs of complying with federal pollution standards; General Motors helped AMC survive, resulting in less potential antitrust scrutiny from the Justice Department; and the Justice Department promoted competition in the automobile industry by helping keep American Motors alive.[28]

In the shorter term, Chapin and Luneburg first had to grapple with a serious financial crisis in the early part of 1967, a cash flow problem created by operating losses in fiscal years 1966 and 1967. In the opening weeks of 1967, Chapin and Luneburg, the newly anointed AMC leaders, met with the company's bankers to arrange additional loans. Five pages of Chapin's notes have survived that lay out the "pitch" he made to the bankers. Chapin noted, "Many of you know me from the dark days of ten years ago when I was Treasurer of the young disorganized groping company that was AMC in its youth, a company selling about 120,000 cars a year with a net worth of $127,000,000, long-term debt of $14,000,000, plus its bank debt." Chapin went on to outline AMC's product plans, its cost-cutting program, and its commitment to making the company profitable. By early February, American Motors had $95 million in short-term bank loans in place, achieved by pledging everything the company owned, including inventories, as collateral. In early May 1967, the twenty-four banks holding the loans agreed to extend the due date from 31 May 1967 until the end of the year.[29]

AMC wanted to sell its Kelvinator Division to raise cash and reduce its debts. In June 1968, AMC announced the sale of Kelvinator to White Consolidated Industries of Cleveland for $32.5 million. American Motors used the proceeds from the sale to further reduce its short-term bank loans from $52.5 million to $20 million. AMC also received an additional $12.5 million by selling Kelvinator's accounts receivable and by the end of 1968, American Motors eliminated its short-term debt, which had stood at $95 million in February 1967. Selling Kelvinator allowed AMC to focus all of its attention and resources on its core automobile business.[30]

The new management team returned to the company's earlier emphasis on smaller economy cars, while appealing to younger buyers with innovative, if sometimes quirky, new models. The shift began with two new models introduced for the 1968 model year—the AMX and the Javelin. Abernethy had approved plans for the two, after strong lobbying by Roy Chapin Jr. and Richard Teague. Both had evolved from a show car, the AMX (American Motors Experimental), which had been exhibited at a meeting of the Society of Automotive Engineers in Detroit in January 1966. This was a two-passenger fastback design with a fiberglass body, with roughly the same dimensions as the Corvette. The first model exhibited was simply a body, with no operational mechanical components. In April 1966 at the New York Auto Show, AMC introduced a fully operational AMX with a steel body hand-crafted by Vignale of Italy. The AMX prototype toured the country as part of AMC's Project IV show along with three other idea cars (the Vixen, Cavalier, and AMX II). Although the Javelin and the AMX had vastly different dimensions, they shared dozens of stampings and mechanical components. Richard Teague presented the company's top management with a clay model of Javelin later in 1966 and they accepted Teague's design with only minor changes.[31]

Richard A. Teague (1923–91) was a remarkable automobile designer who served as the styling director at American Motors in 1961–64 and vice president for design in 1964–83, a substantial part of AMC's existence. The *Wall Street Journal* recognized him as a specialist in "styling on a shoestring," referring to AMC's chronically impoverished condition. Born in Los Angeles on 26 December 1923, Teague worked as a child actor but became a hotrod enthusiast as a teenager, owning several souped-up Fords. Several tragedies jolted his life—three different automobile accidents killed his father, turned his mother into an invalid, and cost him an eye. He took a job at age nineteen working as a stylist for Northrop Aircraft while attending the Los Angeles Art Center School.[32]

Teague made preliminary drawings of aircraft and missiles after the war but got his first "real" job in automotive styling in March 1948 with General Motors. He left GM in early 1951 after working mainly on Cadillac designs. Teague joined the Packard Motor Car Company in early 1952 as Packard's chief stylist. As Packard was going out of business, Teague went over to Chrysler in 1956 along with several Packard designers and became the chief of the Chrysler Division's studio. A victim of internal power struggles within Chrysler, Teague took a job with American Motors in September 1959, working for Ed Anderson, Teague's former boss at GM. According to Teague, when he came to American Motors, the styling department had a staff of only eighteen. When Anderson left AMC in late 1961, Teague became the styling director and then in February 1964 became AMC's vice president for design.[33]

The Javelin, introduced as a 1968 model, was the sporty compact car that Dick Teague and Roy Chapin Jr. originally wanted produced in 1965. Beverly Rae Kimes described Javelin in *Automobile Quarterly* as "nattily handsome, sprightly, tidy, alto-

1968 Javelin sports hardtop. *Courtesy NAHC.*

1968 AMX. *Courtesy NAHC.*

gether appealing—and for that, hearty congratulations to Dick Teague are certainly due." Javelin was the last of the "pony cars," appearing more than three years after the Ford Mustang and the Plymouth Barracuda. American Motors assembled 55,124 Javelins for the 1968 model year and 40,675 for 1969, an enormous success when contrasted with the Marlin. One can only speculate on Javelin's success had AMC introduced it at the beginning of the "pony car" era rather than toward the end.[34]

The AMX was a two-seater with bucket seats and no options. It used a lot of Rambler American mechanical components and a lot of Javelin stampings. The AMX was simply a cut-down Javelin. Three V-8 engines were available for AMX—a 290 CID, 343 CID, and a new AMX390 engine with 390 CID producing 315 horsepower. American Motors was careful to refrain from calling the AMX a "sports car" and to avoid any comparisons with the Chevrolet Corvette. They instead called it a "personal sporty-type car." In 1968, AMC sold 6,725 AMXs, which carried a price of $3,245. More important than the sales numbers was the fact that Javelin and AMX together generated great interest in American Motors cars among younger customers and brought an increase in dealer traffic.[35]

With its Javelin and AMX models, American Motors was a significant player in the brief period in the 1960s when "muscle cars" enjoyed great popularity among young drivers. Muscle cars evolved in part from the pony cars of the mid-1960s, starting with the 1965 Ford Mustang, Plymouth Barracuda, and AMC Marlin. Within two years of the Mustang's initial introduction, Ford made the car bigger and heavier but, more important, added high-performance engines as an option. In 1965, Pontiac's chief engineer, John DeLorean, dropped a large V-8 engine into a Pontiac Tempest, added improved suspension and better brakes and dubbed it the GTO. Chrysler became the muscle car specialist among the Big Three, with the Dodge Charger (1966 model), the Plymouth Road Runner (1968), Plymouth Duster (1970), and Dodge Challenger (1970). Muscle cars never accounted for more than 10 percent of American auto sales and quickly lost their popularity in the early 1970s because the increased costs of gasoline and auto insurance made them prohibitively expensive to drive.[36]

Chapin and company made several additional moves to give American Motors a new image. They hired an innovative advertising agency and returned to competitive racing. In mid-June 1967, Chapin announced that the New York advertising agency Wells, Rich, Greene would replace Benton & Bowles for 1968. Mary Wells, Richard Rich, and Stewart Greene, all in their thirties, had left the Jack Tinker & Partners agency only fourteen months earlier. While at Jack Tinker, they created the famous Alka-Seltzer campaign. Mary Wells, the agency's head, known as "the Cinderella of Madison Avenue," was also a rare commodity—a woman at the head of an ad agency. Chapin wanted AMC to attract the highly individualistic, "non-average buyer," and the new agency reflected the shift in sales philosophy.[37]

AMC also reentered competitive racing under Chapin's leadership. In May 1967 the company entered three Rambler Americans in the four-thousand-mile trans-Canada Shell Centennial Rally. This was the first competitive race American Motors officially entered other than economy runs. In early 1967, Chapin hired Victor G. Raviolo as vice president in charge of auto engineering, research, styling, and product planning. He formed a temporary committee at AMC to decide how the firm should approach competitive racing. By August 1967, AMC was officially sponsoring a Rambler Rebel SST "Funny Car" to run on drag strips. A month later, the company created the new position of manager of performance activities and named Carl Chakmakian to fill it.[38]

American Motors competed in several types of racing in the late 1960s, with mixed results. In February 1968, two AMXs fitted with special 304 CID and 397 CID engines by Craig Breedlove of Torrance, California, set ninety new Class C records and sixteen new Class B records at the Goodyear track at San Angelo, Texas. Breedlove and his wife set all the records. AMC also teamed with Breedlove later in 1968 for an attempt at a new land speed record for wheeled vehicles with an American Motors–powered car called the American Spirit.

The company established the Javelin Racing Team that competed in the Trans-Am road races in 1968 and 1969; the team finished respectively in most races but did not win any. Javelin typically finished second behind the Chevrolet Camaro. In late 1969, American Motors signed a three-year agreement with Roger Penske Racing Enterprises to manage the Javelin Trans-Am program. With Mark Donahue at the wheel, Penske managed three wins for American Motors for the 1970 season, when Mustang won six times. When the other companies withdrew their factory support for their cars for the 1971 Trans-Am season, Javelin was left with no real competition.[39]

AMC's offerings for the 1969 model year included few changes from the 1968 models. Only the Ambassador, the last of Abernethy's design legacy, underwent major restyling. Its 122-inch wheelbase was four inches longer than the 1968 Ambassador, making it the largest model American Motors ever manufactured and clearly a "full-size" offering. One indication that AMC was changing its product mix was the introduction of the limited production SC ("Super Car") Rambler, a Rambler Rogue hardtop powered by the same 390 CID, 315 horsepower engine found in the AMX. This version sold for $2,998, nearly $1,000 more than the base Rambler. Hurst Performance Research designed the performance package including a Hurst shift linkage with a T-handle. AMC intended to produce only 500 of these "Scramblers," as customers dubbed them, but demand was so great that the company assembled 1,512 units.[40]

For American Motors, the seven-month period beginning on 25 September 1969 and ending on 1 April 1970 witnessed a series of pivotal developments. In late September 1969, AMC introduced its Hornet line of compact cars, replacing the Rambler American; AMC bought Kaiser Jeep Corporation in late November; and in April 1970 the automaker introduced its Gremlin, the first American-built subcompact car. All three developments bore the imprint of Roy D. Chapin Jr. and they helped bring a four-year stretch of prosperity for American Motors. The Hornet and Gremlin models also bore the imprint of stylist Dick Teague.

Teague initially struggled with his superiors at AMC who did not share his notions of automotive design. With the success of Javelin and AMX, Teague's prestige increased greatly and, more important, Roy Chapin gave Teague freedom to control his designs. The Hornet, Gremlin, and later the Pacer were all successful models. In 1969, Teague's styling staff, which averaged thirty-five years old, had only sixty-five members at a time when General Motors had 1,000 employees and Ford had 800 in their respective styling departments.[41]

The company unveiled its new compact car, the Hornet, to the automotive press on 13 August 1969 at Lake Geneva, Wisconsin. The Hornet, a famous Hudson model in the early 1950s, replaced the Rambler as AMC's compact offering. Roy Chapin Jr. told the audience that the company dropped the Rambler name because

1970 Hornet sedan. *Courtesy DCHC.*

"it was associated almost completely with economy and price at the expense of performance and design." AMC wanted it known that "it was doing much more to meet consumer needs than just building plain, economy cars." The Hornet was two inches shorter than the Rambler it replaced, despite having a wheelbase that was two inches longer. It came in two-door and four-door sedan models, with a 199 CID six-cylinder engine (128 horsepower) standard and an optional 232 CID six (145 horsepower). American Motors believed the Hornet would compete with the imports and the Ford Maverick. American Motors priced the base Hornet at $1,994, or $1 below the base price for the Maverick, which made Hornet the lowest-priced domestic car.[42]

AMC's subcompact Gremlin, officially introduced at dealerships on 1 April 1970, was the subject of much speculation starting in January 1970. Longtime *Detroit News* automotive writer Robert Irvin called the Gremlin the "anti-(VW) Beetle machine" based on reports from AMC that it would compete with the Beetle in size and price. American Motors showed off the new model on 12 February in Palm Springs, California. Roy Chapin described it as "a personal car—big enough to be comfortable for the driver and with good handling characteristics." Nevertheless, Gremlin was not really comparable to the Beetle. Its wheelbase and overall length were two inches longer than the Beetle, but it was nearly ten inches wider, and, more important, it weighed a lot more (2,633 pounds versus 1,871 pounds). The basic six-cylinder

1970 Gremlin. *Courtesy DCHC.*

engine (the same as the Hornet's) delivered 128 horsepower versus 57 horsepower from Volkswagen's four-cylinder engine. Gremlin came in two-passenger and four-passenger versions for the first two years, but the two-person version was never popular. The four-passenger model carried a sticker price of $1,959, or $120 more than the Beetle. Remarkably, AMC priced the four-passenger Gremlin only $35 less than the cheapest Hornet.[43]

None of the Big Three's "import fighters" of this era competed with the Beetle based on price or fuel economy. The subcompacts they introduced, starting with the Ford Maverick in April 1969, typically weighed 600–700 pounds more than the Beetle, cost $200 more, and delivered 22 miles per gallon versus the Beetle's 27. To be sure, Gremlin beat the Chevrolet Vega and the Ford Pinto, both 1971 models, to market by a full six months. The Vega cost $2,100 and weighed 2,400 pounds, so it was also not competitive with the Beetle. Chrysler did not offer its first subcompact, the Dodge Omni/Plymouth Horizon, until the 1978 model year. The Big Three seemed unconvinced that customers really wanted automobiles the size of the Beetle, but more important, they did not believe that they could make such cars profitably.[44]

American Motors had to face the competition from the Big Three's "import fighters" in the early 1970s, but more important, Japanese cars became an even greater threat in the years following the Arab oil boycott of 1973–74. Toyota and Nissan each sold more cars in the United States by 1975 than Volkswagen, which Honda later surpassed in 1978. The Japanese automakers accounted for 70 percent of all imported cars sold in the United States in 1974 and 1975. Upstart Honda, with its subcompact Civic, posed still another direct threat to American Motors. Honda sales in the United States, a mere 43,000 cars in 1974, skyrocketed to 375,000 in 1980 and reached 641,000 units in 1988. Typically, the Japanese automakers offered American customers cars that were more fuel efficient and reliable than their American counterparts. The impact on AMC's automobile production after 1974 (see Table 8.3) was catastrophic.[45]

American Motors tried to survive by introducing unique models such as the Gremlin and Pacer, while cutting design and tooling costs to the bare minimum. For example, the company saved expensive tooling costs by making the Gremlin a derivative of the Hornet. The result was another example of the genius of Dick Teague, who also developed the whimsical name Gremlin for the new model. The Gremlin was simply a Hornet with a wheelbase reduced by twelve inches and with an overall length cut by eighteen inches. The Gremlin shared the Hornet's body shell and most of its mechanical components, including the drivetrain. Because the new model shared so much with the Hornet, the tooling costs for Gremlin were an almost negligible $5 million.[46]

Despite being eighteen inches shorter than Hornet, the Gremlin weighed only 37 pounds less. The resulting fuel economy was 23 miles per gallon versus VW's claim of 27 miles per gallon for the Beetle. AMC offset this disadvantage by giving

Table 8.3. American Motors Production by Calendar Year,
Passenger Cars and Jeeps, 1970–78

	Passenger Cars	**Jeeps**	**Jeeps as Share of Total (%)**
1970	276,110	45,805	14.2
1971	235,669	53,051	18.4
1972	279,132	71,204	20.0
1973	355,855	94,035	20.9
1974	351,490	96,645	21.6
1975	323,704	105,833	24.6
1976	292,087	95,718	24.7
1977	226,640	117,077	34.1
1978	214,537	153,485	41.7

Source: "Calendar Year Production, American Motors and Its Predecessors," American Motors Corporate History File, NAHC.

the Gremlin a 21-gallon fuel tank. The fact that the Gremlin did not compete head to head with the Beetle did not hurt sales. Teague commented on Gremlin's appeal: "The Volkswagen, for example, is regarded by many as 'smart-ugly,' and the very limited number of people who have seen the Gremlin seem to regard it as 'smart-pretty.'" Early reviewers of Gremlin, including Robert Irvin, commented on the car's "cute" appearance and its "peppy performance," which made it "fun to drive."[47]

American Motors launched a new advertising campaign touting its 1971 models, with the ads asking the question, "If you had to compete with GM, Ford, and Chrysler, what would you do?" Each line of AMC cars provided a different answer—for example, "You'd bring out the first American subcompact, the Gremlin, six months before GM and Ford" and "You'd bring out the Hornet Sportabout, the only compact wagon on the market."[48]

The signature development of Roy D. Chapin Jr.'s term as chairman of American Motors was the purchase of the Kaiser Jeep Corporation from Kaiser Industries Corporation, a deal completed in February 1970. Kaiser Jeep manufactured several models of four-wheel-drive Jeeps for civilian use, right-hand-drive trucks for the U.S. Post Office, and trucks for the U.S. Army. Jeep's well-documented history will not be repeated here.[49]

At the end of World War II, Willys produced the CJ2A (Civilian Jeep), also known as the Jeep Universal, and introduced a Jeep station wagon in 1946 to broaden its offerings. The company added two-wheel-drive and four-wheel-drive pickup trucks in 1947 and a two-wheel-drive automobile, the "Jeepster," in 1948. After the outbreak of the Korean War, Willys produced a newly designed military Jeep, the M-38. The company also introduced a compact car, the Aero-Willys, but it sold poorly.[50]

Kaiser Motors Corporation (formerly the Kaiser-Frazer Corporation) bought Willys-Overland Motors in 1953 for $60 million and renamed it Willys Motors, Inc., which in 1965 became the Kaiser Jeep Corporation. A new Universal Jeep, the CJ-5, appeared as a 1954 model and remained in production through 1983. It was wider and longer than the CJ-3 it replaced and offered more interior space and more comfort while remaining a rugged Jeep. Although Kaiser Jeep earned profits in the late 1960s, principal owner Edgar Kaiser wanted to leave the motor vehicle industry at a time when American Motors wanted to broaden its product line.[51]

Roy Chapin's staff reported on the possible acquisition of Kaiser Jeep to the American Motors board of directors meeting on 5 May 1969. The report described Kaiser Jeep's product lines, sales records, and profits since 1960. The purchase would give American Motors new products for its dealers to sell, including sport utility vehicles and trucks, and would add approximately 1,600 dealers, 200 of which were already selling AMC cars. Gerald Meyers, AMC's group vice president for product development, opposed the purchase because of Kaiser Jeep's weak position in retail markets. *Dun's Review* called the purchase "Chapin's Folly," but the deal was made because there were two willing partners.[52]

The AMC board authorized the company's officers to negotiate a purchase. In late October 1969, AMC announced the broad outlines of the purchase agreement, which involved a price of $82.5 million, mostly in stock. American Motors would pay $10 million in cash, $10 million in five-year notes issued by AMC, and the rest as 5.5 million shares of stock (worth about $62.5 million). Kaiser would own 20 percent of AMC stock and become the largest shareholder. The agreement still required the formal approval of the stockholders of both companies (AMC's stockholders agreed on 4 February 1970), but also had to pass a review by the Justice Department's antitrust division. The Justice Department did not object to this deal, probably because it made the auto industry more competitive.[53]

One notable change to American Motors' image was a new corporate logo introduced in September 1969 to accompany the 1970 car lines. With the Rambler nameplate disappearing, replaced by the Hornet, AMC had to change all the Rambler signs that adorned their dealerships and product literature. They hired Lippencott & Margulies, a New York–based marketing consultant, to develop the new logo. Lippencott & Margulies had developed the successful Chrysler Pentastar in 1962. For AMC, they came up with a modern-looking symbol composed of white and red triangles and a blue rectangle, supposedly representing "AM." This was part of AMC's broader corporate identity program developed after AMC discontinued the Rambler name.[54]

American Motors enjoyed unexpected profits in the third quarter of the fiscal year ending on 30 September 1971 and ended the fiscal year with a $10.2 million profit. The results surprised automobile analysts because AMC's passenger car sales declined from 276,110 in 1970 to 235,669 in 1971. They remained skeptical about AMC's chances to survive, especially after Gremlin sales suffered with the introduction of two high-volume subcompacts in the fall of 1970—the Chevrolet Vega and the Ford Pinto. AMC earned profits despite the sales slump because the company substantially reduced its manufacturing costs while simultaneously improving product quality.[55]

AMC increased the share of parts made in-house and moved production to more efficient plants. The company made its own electrical wiring, soft trim, exhaust pipes, underbodies, and some seats, all of which they had previously purchased from outside venders. They closed an inefficient Jeep engine plant in Toledo and concentrated all engine production at Kenosha. Among other changes, AMC closed its Kenosha Lake Front plant and greatly enlarged and modernized its main body plant in Milwaukee. The result of these changes was a reduction of AMC's break-even point for car production from 300,000 to roughly 240,000 cars per year. American Motors simultaneously strengthened its "quality assurance" systems both in manufacturing and in purchasing.[56]

Offering potential AMC buyers an extended warranty on the 1972 models also helped boost sales. American Motors introduced its Buyer Protection Plan, which covered all repairs, including parts, for the entire car except for the tires, which the tire manufacturers covered. The warranty covered parts like spark plugs, filters, brake linings, wiper blades, and the like for the first year or 12,000 miles. If a dealer needed to keep the car overnight, the owner received a free loaner car from the dealer. This plan represented a noticeable improvement over the warranties offered by the Big Three, which were generally limited to parts that broke. It helped improve sales—AMC executives claimed an increase in market share from 2.8 percent for the 1971 models to 3.2 percent the following year.[57]

Spurred by this success, AMC offered an extended warranty on its 1973 models. Buyers could extend their new-car warranty to cover 24 months/24,000 miles for an additional $149. American Motors would provide four oil changes and a tune-up at 15,000 miles at no additional charge. Company officials estimated the value of the maintenance work at $100, so the extended warranty cost only $49 net. Company managers were surprised that customers did not embrace the extended warranty program. By mid-October 1972, fewer than 10 percent had purchased it.[58]

AMC Diversifies, 1970–78

The addition of Kaiser Jeep in early 1970 muddies any discussion of AMC's products because Jeeps, postal vehicles, military trucks, and transit buses became part of the American Motors product mix. The next section of this chapter will first trace AMC's automotive products through the 1978 model year, when Roy D. Chapin Jr. retired, then examine the Jeep product line, and, finally, look at the various vehicles produced by the AM General Division of American Motors.

For 1971, AMC made almost no changes to the Gremlin or Ambassador models and introduced a Hornet four-door Sportabout station wagon, which had sales of 73,471 units for the 1971 model year. The remodeled Rebel became the Matador, while the restyled Javelin offered an AMX version with a V-8 engine and four seats, which replaced the previous two-seat AMX. For 1972, there were few changes except that V-8 engines were available as an option for the Matador, Javelin, and Gremlin, while the Ambassador received a new grille. The only major change for the 1973 model year was the introduction of a two-door hatchback model for the

Hornet. The Matador and Ambassador received major restyling for 1974, while the Hornet, Gremlin, and Javelin lines all had minor face-lifts. This was the final year for Javelin, introduced in 1968, and for Ambassador, a model offered by Nash since 1932. Both models suffered poor sales.[59]

AMC's cars of the early 1970s typically received good reviews based largely on their affordable prices and low operating costs. Christopher Willcox reviewed the 1974 Hornet Hatchback and Sportabout for the *Detroit News* and was generally positive about both models. His summary statements included, "At $2,749, the Hornet Hatchback is an all-purpose bargain" and "The Sportabout won't win any prizes for styling, rise or performance, but its economy makes it a practical car for the fuel conscious." Vincent Courtenay reviewed the 1974 Matador station wagon and praised its performance, handling, and good fuel economy, considering its size and 360 CID engine: "Here's a real sleeper on the market. Its performance ranks it in the first line of cars, yet it's reasonably priced."[60]

AMC officially introduced its 1975 Pacer models at its dealerships on 28 February 1975 after months of hype. The design history of the Pacer is worth noting. In June 1971, Dick Teague attended a meeting where various company executives tossed out new-car design ideas. Gerald Meyers, who was group vice president for product, did not like any of the proposals and Teague broke the stalemate with a radical design proposal—a wide, small car with lots of glass. Teague quickly sketched what he later called a "grubby doodle"—a four-wheeled football covered in glass with a roll bar in the middle.

American Motors introduced the Pacer to automotive writers in early January 1975 at Palm Springs, California, thereby getting a great deal of free publicity two months before the car was for sale. The Pacer was a wide, small car, only one inch longer than the Gremlin, but nine inches wider. Glass covered more than 37 percent of the Pacer's total surface area, versus 20–25 percent on most cars. The new model had other innovative features. The curbside door was four inches longer than the driver's door. American Motors spent $60 million to bring it to market, or five times what the company spent on the Gremlin. Robert Irvin, automobile columnist for the *Detroit News,* tested a Pacer in California in January and reported on the new model in glowing terms. The interior roominess was the most impressive feature: "Inside it is a big car in about every sense of the word. There is ample room in front for the driver and passenger to stretch out, and even put a child between them if need be."[61]

Pacer sales seemed to take even the most optimistic American Motors officials by surprise, but only for a short time. To be sure, they expected their advertising blitz that began in mid-February 1975 to grab the attention of potential car buyers. AMC

1975 Pacer X. *Courtesy DCHC.*

planned to spend half its 1975 advertising budget on the Pacer. By mid-March, the company was increasing Pacer production from 530 units a day to 700, as dealer orders flooded in. The new model was generating 44 percent of AMC's sales in mid-March. After months of continued robust sales of the Pacer at a time when overall car sales were flat, AMC was clearly well ahead of the other car companies in serving consumers' needs.

By early August, AMC increased production of the (unchanged) 1976 model Pacers to 800 units a day. The only negative aspect of Pacer's success was that it severely cut into the sales of the Hornet and Gremlin models. Production of Hornets fell from 186,275 for the 1974 model to 85,961 units for 1975, while Gremlin production fell from 171,128 units to 56,011 units. Pacer production for the 1975 calendar year was 145,528 units, a remarkable figure for a ten-month year. In February 1976, *Automotive Industries* named Richard A. Teague "Man of the Year" based on his design of the Pacer. He was the first stylist to receive this honor in the twelve-year history of the award.[62]

In the model years 1976–78, American Motors made modest changes to its offerings until it introduced the new Concord luxury car in 1978. For 1976, a larger six-cylinder engine (258 CID) was available as an option for the Pacer, but the Hornet, Gremlin, and Matador were largely unchanged. In the 1977 model year, the last for Hornet, AMC offered a limited edition AMX hatchback package for the Hornet. Gremlin received a new grille, new bumpers, and an enlarged rear window. More important, starting in February 1977, Gremlin buyers could have an optional four-cylinder 121 CID (80 horsepower) engine made by Volkswagen. The 1978 model year was the last for Gremlin and Matador. AMC also introduced the Concord V-8 luxury car as a replacement for the Hornet.[63]

Some eighteen months after the initial introduction of the Pacer, Roy Chapin Jr. revealed that its sales had declined after an encouraging start. Many saw the design as too radical, "a greenhouse on wheels," and some customers feared that the use of so much glass weakened the car. The company hoped that the new Pacer station wagon available in 1977 would help reverse that trend, but it did not. After a promising start with sales of 145,528 units in 1975, Pacer sales dipped to 117,244 units the following year, to 58,264 units in 1977, and to a dismal 21,231 units in 1978. Chapin admitted that Pacer's poor sales were his biggest single disappointment. He had expected AMC to sell 150,000 Pacers a year.[64]

American Motors introduced one new model for 1978, the Concord. Some observers claimed that the Concord was simply a Hornet with a luxury face-lift, a claim denied by AMC officials. Concord shared the same 108-inch wheelbase as the Hornet but had refined front and rear suspension systems designed to reduce vibration and noise. It received mixed reviews during its initial months on the market. Observers found the European styling attractive, but found Concord too expensive for a small car. A local reviewer gave Concord high marks for ride and handling on the highway and in the city, but complained about the performance from the 258

1978 Concord two-door sedan. *Courtesy DCHC.*

CID six-cylinder engine. Concord was successful, at least for the 1978 model year, when sales reached 121,292 units, well above Hornet's production of 77,843 in the last year of its life.[65]

When American Motors formally took control of Kaiser Jeep in early 1970, Jeeps were practical vehicles designed for work or off-road use, but they certainly were not stylish. There were two civilian descendants of the World War II Jeep—the CJ-5, with a wheelbase of 84 inches, and the CJ-6, with a wheelbase of 104 inches. The Jeep Wagoneer station wagon had the closest resemblance to station wagons offered by the mainstream American automakers, except that it was a four-wheel-drive vehicle. The Jeepster Commando line included a half-ton pickup truck and a boxy station wagon, roadster, and convertible. Finally, Jeep sold a line of half-ton and three-quarter-ton pickup trucks, nearly all four-wheel drive, under the Gladiator marque.[66]

American Motors began to leave its mark on Jeep beginning with the 1971 model year. AMC cut back Jeep's offerings from thirty-eight to twenty-two models and replaced the ancient four-cylinder engines with its own overhead valve inline sixes and V-8s. The first offering under AMC's regime was the Jeepster Commando SC-1 station wagon, a special edition Commando with special trim and an optional V-6 engine delivering 160 horsepower. For 1973, Jeep introduced its Quadra-Trac four-wheel-drive system, initially available only in Wagoneers with automatic transmissions and in select pickup trucks. The system used a third differential that directed

1971 Jeepster Commando SC-1. *Courtesy NAHC.*

1974 Jeep Cherokee. *Courtesy NAHC.*

power to the wheels with the best traction and eliminated excess tire wear and drive line stresses, which were problems when using four-wheel drive on smooth surfaces. The Quadra-Trac system allowed Jeeps to operate all the time in the four-wheel-drive mode.[67]

The first entirely new model was the 1974 Jeep Cherokee S, a two-door sport utility vehicle intended to compete with the Ford Bronco and Chevrolet Blazer. The Cherokee replaced the Commando. Standard equipment included a six-cylinder engine, but a V-8 was available, along with an automatic transmission. A *Detroit News* test of Cherokee gave it high marks for ride, handling, and roominess. American Motors continued paring down the Jeep offerings, a process begun in 1971. For the 1974 model year, there were two versions each of the C-J, Cherokee, and Wagoneer, plus three Townside pickup trucks, for a total of nine models.[68]

American Motors took a major step in further popularizing the Jeep when it introduced the CJ-7 for 1976. Its 94-inch wheelbase was midway between the CJ-5 (84 inches) and the CJ-6 (104 inches), which the CJ-7 replaced. The new model featured a new frame and suspension system, a removable hardtop and an optional soft top, and the first automatic transmission offered in a CJ model. Reviewers gave the CJ-7 rave reviews for its ride, comfort, and handling, both on-road and off-road. The company introduced a new four-door version of the Jeep Cherokee for 1977, further widening Jeep's customer appeal. At the end of 1978, American Motors had 1,999 dealers who carried Jeeps, 1,846 who carried passenger cars, and 1,517 who carried both lines.[69]

1976 Jeep CJ-7. *Courtesy NAHC.*

Jeep operations were an unqualified success over the first ten years AMC was in control. American Motors simplified the lines of models offered by Jeep and made the models more appealing to the average consumer. Calendar year production, a respectable 45,805 units in 1970, more than doubled to 105,833 in 1975. Calendar year sales, a different measure of success, reached 161,912 units in 1978, not far below AMC's passenger car sales of 214,537. American Motors did not distinguish between the profits from its Jeep operations and those from the rest of its operations, but AMC's healthy profits in 1978 came from Jeep and not from its declining passenger car business.[70]

When American Motors bought Kaiser Jeep in late 1969, it got more than just the Jeep business. Willys Motors produced a half-ton right-drive delivery van for the U.S. Postal Service starting in 1960. Willys also won a contract in 1962 to build the M151 quarter-ton truck, which resembled a military Jeep and was better-known as the "Mutt." Large contracts followed in 1964 for 5-ton 6 x 6 trucks (M39 series) and 2 1/2-ton 6 x 6 trucks (M44A2 series), and in January 1967, Kaiser Jeep produced a 1 1/4-ton truck (M715 series), all for the army.[71]

Following the American Motors takeover of Kaiser Jeep, AMC renamed the Defense and Government Products Division the General Products Division of the Jeep Corporation and moved its offices to Wayne, Michigan. In April 1971, AMC reorganized the General Products Division into a wholly owned subsidiary, AM General Corporation, to manage the automaker's government contracts.[72]

AM General continued to specialize in U.S. Postal Service vehicles and "tactical

1974 DJ-5 Dispatcher postal delivery vehicle. *Courtesy NAHC.*

wheeled vehicles," another name for military trucks. The company manufactured the Jeep DJ-5 Dispatcher quarter-ton delivery vehicle for the U.S. Postal Service from 1970 through 1982 and the DJ-5M in 1983–84. AM General offered these in right-hand- and left-hand-drive versions and built more than 136,000 of this model between 1970 and 1984, primarily for the Postal Service. They also built the FJ-8 half-ton Fleetvan from 1970 into the early 1980s and the FJ-9, a one-ton delivery van for the Postal Service.[73]

The Postal Service and AM General experimented with an electric-powered Postal Jeep in the mid-1970s, but it ultimately proved impractical. The Postal Service awarded a $2 million contract to AM General in 1974 for 352 electric vehicles and the company delivered the first fourteen in late May 1975. Dubbed the Electruck and designated as the Jeep DJ-5E, the vehicle weighed 3,618 pounds, had an announced cruising speed of 33 miles per hour, and a range of 29 miles with 80 percent of the battery discharged. The 27-cell battery, which delivered 54 volts, weighed 1,305 pounds. By January 1976, 117 were operating in Los Angeles, Evansville, and Washington, D.C., three cities with serious pollution problems. Despite Postal Service claims that these vehicles were a great success, no additional contracts for electric trucks followed.[74]

Through the 1970s, AM General continued to produce military trucks it had developed in the 1960s, plus additional new models. In September 1977, the com-

1972 AM General Flyer electric transit bus. *Courtesy NAHC.*

pany won its largest contract from the U.S. Army, for 5,507 M915 series 14-ton heavy-duty trucks, with the army having the option of buying an additional 5,507. This order was worth $252 million to AM General, which claimed to have a backlog of $671 million in orders.[75]

AMC also entered the urban transit bus business in 1971, but withdrew seven years later after mixed success. In early October 1971, Cruse W. Moss, president of AM General Corporation, announced an agreement with Flyer Industries of Winnipeg, Canada, to acquire rights to the Flyer diesel and electric city transit buses for sale outside Canada. AMC would manufacture the buses at its plant in Mishawaka, Indiana, near South Bend. Two American companies, General Motors and Flxible, dominated the sales of diesel transit buses, which amounted to 2,000–3,000 units a year. AMC believed that new federal spending to improve urban mass transit, with roughly $900 million already budgeted, would increase the annual sales of buses to 4,000–6,000 units, perhaps as many as 8,000. The Mishawaka plant had a capacity of roughly 1,000 buses a year.[76]

AM General had a good deal of early success in the transit bus business. In 1973 it received a contract worth $24.3 million to build 620 of its 53-passenger buses for the Washington, D.C., Metropolitan Transit Authority. Orders for 108 buses for New Orleans and 60 buses for Nashville came in short order, followed by orders for 240 buses for St. Louis, 100 for Kansas City, and smaller orders for a half-dozen other cities. They delivered the first buses to Washington, D.C., in January 1974 and completed the order by the end of the year. This was a promising start, and AM General appeared to have a bright future in the bus business given additional federal funding to upgrade urban mass transit systems.[77]

In June 1972 the federal Urban Mass Transportation Administration (UMTA) awarded the three urban bus manufacturers—General Motors, Flxible, and AM General—$6.2 million contracts each to produce prototypes of the "transit bus of the future." In 1974, roughly halfway through the UMTA Transbus program, General Motors announced that it would spend $30 million to develop a new bus known as the RTS-2. In January 1975, UMTA announced that its standards required a floor height of no more than 22 inches and that the contractor must provide a ramp or lift for wheelchair accessibility. Unfortunately for American Motors, only the GM RTS-2 bus met the requirements. AMC argued that the changes in effect awarded General Motors a noncompetitive contract for future bus orders. At UMTA's urging, a consortium of large transit systems (including Houston, Dallas, San Antonio, Oakland, and Long Beach) required the "Interim Bus" specifications in requesting bids for new buses in June 1976. Two years later, AM General stopped making urban transit buses.[78]

AM General also produced articulated buses for a short time. This design, which bent in the middle for ease of operation in tight city streets, was based on a bus produced by Machinenfabrik Augsburg-Nurnberg (MAN). AM General initially won an order for 150 of these buses from the Seattle Transit Authority and a second order in 1977 for 234 articulated buses from a consortium of ten transit authorities. MAN in Germany built the buses, which AM General assembled at a plant in Marshall, Texas. Considering that AM General was a brand-new entrant into the bus business, its overall record was impressive. From 1974 through 1978, AM General made a total of 5,800 buses, including 220 electric trolley coaches and 398 articulated buses.[79]

After leaving the bus business, AM General refocused on its military truck business and in 1980 produced a prototype of a new tactical wheeled vehicle they nicknamed "Hummer." They delivered eleven prototypes of this new vehicle to the U.S. Army in 1982 for testing, and in March 1983 the army awarded AM General a contract for 55,000 Hummers. Later that year, American Motors sold AM General to LTV Aerospace and Defense Company for $170 million, making additional funds available for automotive operations. AMC had no choice but to sell AM General because the French automaker Renault gained a controlling interest in American Motors. American law prohibited awarding military contracts to foreign-owned companies.[80]

The middle years (1971–75) of the Chapin-Luneburg management team were the most prosperous ones American Motors had enjoyed since 1958–64 under George Romney and Roy Abernethy. Total sales reached a plateau of about 450,000 units 1973–74 (see Table 8.2) and profits reached a record level of $86 million in 1973.

The AMC directors paid a dividend to the stockholders in late March 1973, the first dividend since August 1965. Roy Chapin optimistically predicted that AMC would sell 400,000 cars in calendar year 1973. Auto industry observers were also gushing over AMC's success. *Detroit News* automotive writer Robert Irvin wrote articles with titles such as "American Motors Back in Big League" and "AMC Returns to 'Big Four' Status."[81]

The sales increases and profits masked the company's long-term competitive weakness in automobiles because much of the sales increases and a good deal of the profits came from Jeep, not from passenger cars. Table 8.3 shows the growing contribution of Jeep to the sales totals. To be sure, AMC's share of the American market in passenger cars improved from 3.1 percent in 1970 to between 3.5 and 3.8 percent in 1973–75, but by 1978 this number fell to only 1.5 percent. The decline reflected the increased share of the American market captured by foreign, mainly Japanese, automakers in this decade, but it was not as serious as it might appear because the calculations exclude Jeep.[82]

American Motors had to modify its production plans to take into account the surge in Jeep sales in the late 1970s. The company converted its Brampton, Ontario, plant to Jeep production for the 1979 model year and began plans for an expansion to the main Jeep assembly plant in Toledo. In mid-October 1978, AMC president Gerald C. Meyers announced the need for a new $27.5 million paint plant in Toledo to increase production capacity from 660 to 1,000 Jeeps per day. In February 1979, AMC announced that it would convert part of the Kenosha plant to produce Jeeps; three plants would be making Jeeps. The company planned to spend $30 million for the production of the Wagoneer and Cherokee models in Kenosha. For the first three months of 1979, North American Jeep production was up 44 percent compared to the previous year.[83]

American Motors could take advantage of the success of its products in the marketplace because, with few exceptions, labor disputes between 1967 and 1978 did not interrupt production. AMC's workers finally ratified new local and national agreements on 5 November 1969, ending a twenty-day strike that disrupted the introduction of the 1970 models, including the Hornet. The AMC national contract in essence gave AMC workers the same benefits that UAW workers in the Big Three received under their new contracts.[84]

The next contract negotiations, which began in August 1970, did not produce an agreement until mid-April 1971 but did not involve a strike. Negotiations between the UAW and AMC were intermittent at best and did not become serious or intense until March 1971. The two sides finally reached agreement on 13 April 1971 on a contract that would run for three years and five months, expiring 16 September

1974, the expiration date for the Big Three agreements.[85]

Intense negotiations began in late July 1974 for the next contract and the lack of a settlement touched off a three-week strike starting on 16 September 1974. The two sides reached a tentative agreement on 1 October and the UAW workers at AMC ratified a one-year deal three days later. Both sides extended the contract that expired in mid-September 1976 and little work was done until January 1977, when AMC asked the union to extend the expired contract until the end of the year, citing its precarious financial condition. In late September 1978, the AMC workers approved a two-year contract with the company.[86]

The transformation of American Motors under Roy D. Chapin Jr. and William V. Luneburg included the introduction of a series of innovative automobile models, leaving the appliance business, and buying Kaiser Jeep. In the final years of Chapin and Luneburg's administration, AMC began a relationship with the French automaker Renault that later led to Renault gaining control over AMC, a topic for the next chapter. Another defining transformation was the building of an ultramodern corporate headquarters outside Detroit. This building, dubbed the American Center, symbolized AMC's prosperity and permanence.

In late May 1973, AMC announced the purchase of a twenty-five-acre parcel in

American Center building.
Photograph by the author.

suburban Southfield, Michigan, northwest of Detroit. Roy Chapin met with Detroit mayor Roman Gribbs and denied that AMC was abandoning its headquarters on Plymouth Road in Detroit. Instead, the company would spend $4.5 million to upgrade the older office building to create more engineering and technical office space. He promised that employment at Plymouth Road would remain at 1,700 workers. When AMC made an official announcement in early July, it revealed that the projected twenty-five-story building would house all headquarters functions. The American Motors Realty Corporation would own and manage the complex, designed by the Detroit architectural firm of Smith, Hinchman & Grylls. They sited the office tower, sheathed in reflective glass to reduce heat load, on an axis running northwest to southeast, to reduce the impact of the southern and western sun.[87]

The move to Southfield brought a reaction from Detroit mayor Coleman A. Young, who retaliated to the company's "abandoning Detroit" in December 1974 by barring AMC from bidding on city purchasing contracts. Detroit City Council president Carl Levin criticized Young's decision as shortsighted and self-destructive. The first office workers moved into the new building at the end of December 1975 and the transfer continued into February 1976. American Motors occupied the sixteenth floor and floors 19–25, with the rest of the building leased. By mid-September 1977, the American Motors Realty Corporation had leased 93 percent of the American Center.[88]

AMC's top management changed in 1977 and 1978 with the departure of Luneburg and Chapin from active management roles. The transition began on 24 May 1977, when the AMC board of directors named Gerald C. Meyers president and chief operating officer, replacing Luneburg, who retired. Chapin remained chairman and CEO, but only until 21 October 1977, when he stepped down as CEO and Meyers took over that position.

The transition to new management was not entirely without conflict or controversy. Meyers, who had been an executive vice president at AMC, became president at the end of May 1977, replacing Luneburg, who gave up his post but continued to work for American Motors. Luneburg stayed on as a consultant, with a $600,000, five-year contract that required him to work full-time for three years and then part-time after that. Meyers did not inherit all of Luneburg's power and authority. Rather than report to chairman and CEO Chapin, Meyers reported to R. William McNealy Jr., the vice chairman of the AMC board of directors. Meyers and McNealy were rivals to succeed Chapin as chairman.[89]

A surprise candidate also appeared in the summer of 1977, when John Z. DeLorean, former vice president of General Motors, proposed a merger of AMC and the DeLorean Motor Company, which was planning a two-door sports car. DeLorean would become chairman of AMC as part of the deal. Gerald Meyers recalled that

Gerald C. Meyers. *Courtesy DCHC.*

DeLorean made a formal presentation to the AMC board in the fall of 1976 in New York City, so there may have been more than one proposal. In a confidential memo to the AMC Policy Committee in June 1977, McNealy argued that DeLorean Motor Company offered AMC nothing that would help the latter fulfill its long-term objectives. McNealy stated his position: "Based on these criteria, and putting aside the question of Mr. DeLorean's personal qualifications to take over the role as Chief Executive Officer, the DMC proposal offers no apparent benefits to AMC." The AMC board rejected any affiliation with DeLorean as too risky.[90]

In late October 1977, Chapin relinquished his power as CEO to forty-nine-year-old Gerald C. Meyers but remained as chairman, a largely ceremonial post. McNealy, having lost the power struggle with Meyers, resigned from AMC almost immediately. McNealy lost out largely because he had directed AMC's marketing efforts, which many directors viewed as ineffective.[91]

Roy D. Chapin Jr. in Retrospect

Roy D. Chapin Jr. announced in mid-September 1978 that he would retire as chairman of AMC at the end of the month. Chapin ended forty years of work for American Motors and the Hudson Motor Car Company, where he began as an experimental engineer in 1938. His retirement marked the end of an era that began when Roy

D. Chapin first worked in the automobile industry in 1901 for Ransom E. Olds at the Olds Motor Works in Detroit. Roy D. Chapin Jr. would continue as a consultant for AMC for another five years, working on a half-time basis for half pay for three years and then on a quarter-time basis and pay for the last two years. The American Motors directors appointed Meyers chairman of the board on 20 October 1978 and named W. Paul Tippett Jr. to replace Meyers as president.[92]

Assessing the life and career of Roy D. Chapin Jr. is difficult. He worked for Hudson and American Motors for forty years, garnering more power and responsibility along the way, but when he finally had effective control in 1967, he inherited a company in a sales crisis as serious as the one George Romney faced in 1954. Shortly after taking the posts of chairman and CEO, Chapin told an interviewer, "I've been lucky in the past to have been dropped into situations where there's trouble. And that's the only way you get to produce." Business observers who wrote about Chapin made similar observations about him. They all mentioned that he easily delegated authority to others, in sharp contrast to Roy Abernethy, who did not. A *New York Times* article about Chapin suggested that his management style allowed his talented executives to do their jobs more easily than they had been able to under Abernethy. The same article described Chapin as a "somewhat retiring, reflective problem-solver who carefully considers each move before going ahead with it." He was a quiet, thoughtful leader who believed in teamwork.[93]

Before Chapin led American Motors to a recovery during the difficult years of 1967–78, he had already served the company productively in a variety of capacities. His success in building overseas sales in the 1960s was perhaps his most important early accomplishment. When he finally came to power, he led the way to several strategic decisions—the sale of the Kelvinator appliance business and the purchase of Kaiser Jeep—which helped American Motors survive, if not prosper. Chapin had a good sense of the market and the products he supported—Javelin, Hornet, Gremlin, and Pacer, among others—helped AMC survive. Given the plight American Motors faced most of the time he was at the helm, he was an energetic, bold, thoughtful, and generally effective leader. He died on 5 August 2001 at age eighty-five in Nantucket, Massachusetts, where he maintained a summer home.[94]

Roy D. Chapin Jr. was also instrumental in fostering the alliance between American Motors and Renault that began in January 1979 and led to Renault's investing heavily in AMC and, in time, gaining a controlling interest in the American automaker. Renault's partnership with American Motors, which will be considered in the next chapter, allowed the American company to survive, admittedly limping along, for nearly a decade before Renault sold its interest to the Chrysler Corporation in 1987. Chapin remained a director at AMC until the sale to Chrysler.

NINE

American Motors, Renault, and Chrysler

The Final Decade, 1978–87

> We are rifling our way into spots in the market where we can present
> a product that will be well-received and sold at a profit. Well, we can
> live in the cracks. There aren't many people there.
>
> American Motors chairman Gerald C. Meyers
> in an interview with the *Detroit News*, December 1978

American Motors earned profits in only four of its last eleven years of operation, in part the victim of the depressed American auto market of 1979–82. The company signed a sales and marketing agreement with the state-owned French automaker Renault in January 1979, and within nine months Renault owned 22.5 percent of AMC stock. By September 1980, this stake had grown to 46 percent, giving AMC badly needed capital and giving Renault effective control. American Motors assembled the Renault-designed Alliance starting in the 1983 model year and other models followed, but the financial losses did not end. Renault sold the ailing company to the Chrysler Corporation in 1987, ending American Motors' thirty-three-year independent existence.

The Meyers-Tippett Management Team and the Coming of Renault, 1978–82

The management team of Gerald C. Meyers and W. Paul Tippett Jr. served as a bridge between the Roy Chapin Jr.-William Luneburg administration and the final years of American Motors' independence, when Renault was the principal owner.

Chapin did not disappear from the scene, but kept a substantial advisory role to the AMC board and remained a director until 1987. Gerald Meyers served as CEO from October 1977 and as chairman from October 1978 until January 1982. W. Paul Tippett Jr. then held the same positions until 1985. An ambitious, aggressive, and confident man, Meyers admitted in a newspaper interview to having made only two mistakes in his life—he failed the first grade and he opposed AMC's purchase of Kaiser Jeep.[1]

Gerald C. Meyers was born in Buffalo, New York, where he attended public schools. He earned an engineering degree from the Carnegie Institute of Technology in 1950 and a master's degree in Industrial Administration from Carnegie in 1954, following three years as an air force officer. Meyers went to work for Chrysler in 1954 in the forward planning department and managed Chrysler's Twinsburg, Ohio stamping plant in 1957–59. He then moved to Geneva, Switzerland, working for Chrysler International and managed Chrysler's overseas plants in 1960–62. After coming to AMC as director of purchasing analysis in 1962, he became director of automotive manufacturing in 1965 and then vice president of automotive manufacturing in January 1967. Meyers became group vice president of product in June 1972 and executive vice president in November 1975. In late May 1977, he became president and chief operating officer for AMC and less than six months later became the CEO. At age forty-nine, he was the youngest top executive in the auto industry.[2]

When Meyers became chairman of AMC's board of directors in October 1978, the company needed to replace him as president and went outside the company to do so. They hired W. Paul Tippett Jr., who was president of the Sewing Products Group of the Singer Corporation. Tippett, age forty-five, brought with him a wealth of experience in marketing in several industries, including automobiles. Born in Cincinnati, Tippett earned an economics degree from Wabash College in 1953, served four years as an intelligence officer in the U.S. Navy, and then worked for five years (1959–64) at Proctor & Gamble in marketing. He held various marketing positions at Ford Motor Company in 1964–75. Tippett left Ford for the STP Corporation, where he served as president. After a year at STP, he worked as executive vice president and director of the Singer Company, the post he held when AMC enticed him to become its president. Outside observers of American Motors believed that Meyers and Tippett were a good combination because Meyers had manufacturing experience and Tippett was primarily interested in marketing and sales.[3]

Meyers explained his approach to returning AMC to profitability in an interview shortly after he became chairman. Unlike the other automakers who were downsizing their cars, he was downsizing American Motors. He dropped the slow-selling Matador from the product line, abandoned the production of passenger buses, and sold an unneeded stamping plant in Charleston, South Carolina, to Volkswagen for $18 million. He converted the Brampton, Ontario, plant to the production of Jeeps, turned the Milwaukee body plant into a stamping plant, and focused car production at Kenosha. Instead of building a two-liter, four-cylinder engine designed by Volkswagen, Meyers arranged to buy Pontiac's 2.5-liter four, giving AMC a better engine and saving $50 million in capital expenditures. AMC would become smaller, leaner, and more efficient. In describing their product strategy, he explained, "We are rifling our way into spots in the market where we can present a product that will be well-received and sold at a profit. Well, we can live in the cracks. There aren't many people there."[4]

Despite new leadership, American Motors continued to struggle, as Table 9.1 demonstrates. Although American Motors enjoyed some sales successes with new models such as Concord (1978 model year), Spirit (1979), and Eagle (1980), even the new models quickly became stale and sales stagnated. More important, a disastrous drop in Jeep sales from 1980 through 1983 negatively affected the overall sales results. The last hope for AMC came from several models designed by Renault and built in Kenosha using a substantial volume of Renault parts—the Alliance (1983) and the Encore (1984).

American Motors refreshed its lineup beginning with the Concord, first offered as a 1978 model. Concord underwent only minor styling changes in the years that followed and sales (predictably) fell off from 121,293 for the 1978 model year to

1979 Spirit Liftback. *Courtesy NAHC.*

Table 9.1. American Motors Wholesale Unit Sales in North America and Profits, Net of Taxes ($ Millions), by Fiscal Year Ending 30 September 1978–80 and by Calendar Year, 1979–85

Fiscal Year	Wholesale Unit Sales	Sales ($ Millions)	Net Profits ($ Millions)	Profit as Share of Sales (%)
1978	346,199	2,585.4	36.7	1.4
1979	360,103	3,117.1	83.9	2.7
1980	292,997	2,684.0	(155.7)	–
Calendar Year				
1979	360,428	3,191.7	70.6	2.2
1980	270,563	2,552.6	(200.8)	–
1981	243,050	2,588.9	(136.6)	–
1982	254,603	2,878.4	(153.5)	–
1983	359,168	3,271.7	(258.3)	–
1984	408,345	4,215.2	15.5	0.4
1985	354,795	4,039.9	(125.3)	–

Source: American Motors Corporation, Annual Reports, 1978–85, NAHC.

55,097 for the 1981 models. AMC introduced the Spirit as a 1979 model, replacing the Gremlin. Spirit sales peaked in the 1980 model year at 71,037 units, then fell to 20,186 units in the 1982 model year.[5]

The AMC offerings for 1980 were largely unchanged from the 1979 models, but with one important exception—the Eagle. This was a four-wheel-drive luxury automobile based on the Concord. Although Subaru offered a four-wheel-drive station wagon, the Eagle was the only American example of this technology in an automobile. The base Eagle carried a sticker price of $6,999, roughly $1,100 more than the base Concord. Test drivers noted that the Eagle felt like a car but acted like a four-wheel-drive truck in mud, snow, and ice. Model year production for 1980 was a robust 46,379 units, an impressive start for such a specialized vehicle.

With this one exception, American Motors offered nothing new for 1981 and 1982. The introduction of the front-wheel-drive Renault Alliance for the 1983 model year and the Renault Encore for 1984 ended the drought—but too late to save American

1980 Eagle. *Courtesy DCHC.*

Motors. The Renault partnership at least brought some short-term benefits to the ailing American automaker.[6]

At the end of March 1978, Meyers revealed that American Motors and Renault had signed a "proposed arrangement" whereby AMC would distribute and eventually manufacture Renault vehicles. In early January 1979, American Motors and Regie National des Usines Renault, the state-owned French automaker, announced a sales agreement whereby AMC would distribute Renault cars in the United States and Renault would sell Jeeps in Europe and South America. Although Renault was the world's sixth largest vehicle maker and sold 1.1 million cars and 175,000 trucks in 1977, it managed to sell only 13,200 vehicles in the United States through a tiny network of 330 sales outlets. AMC would distribute Renault's Le Car, a high-mileage minicar (26 miles per gallon city, 41 miles per gallon highway), through its network of 2,500 dealerships.[7]

The two automakers would partner to develop a new series of Renault passenger cars to be built in the United States, possibly as early as 1982. Gerald Meyers and Bernard Hanon, president of Regie National des Usines Renault, pointed out that the agreement involved no exchange of money, no purchase of AMC stock by Renault, and no plans for Renault to sell AMC passenger cars.[8] Less than nine months after the initial AMC-Renault agreement, Renault announced plans in mid-October 1979 to invest directly in American Motors. Renault would provide capital for the new line of Renault-designed cars that they would build in Kenosha for the 1983 model year. Renault would immediately buy 1.5 million shares of AMC stock (5 percent of the total) for $15 million, but would provide an additional $135 million in loans. With the eventual conversion of the loans into shares, Renault would own 22.5 percent of AMC's stock. Renault would also make available to AMC roughly $50 million to bolster AMC's working capital. Renault's CEO, Bernard Vernier-Palliez, immediately joined the AMC board of directors. Without Renault's help, AMC would not have survived the early 1980s. With losses mounting, they needed an infusion of outside funds if the company were to put any new products on the market.[9]

Within a year after the announcement of Renault's initial purchase of AMC stock, the French automaker revealed in late September 1980 its plan to purchase an additional $200 million in stock, giving it a 46 percent ownership stake. In February 1980, Paul Percie du Sert, deputy vice president of finance at Renault, joined the AMC board of directors, replacing Robert B. Evans. At Renault's request, additional new directors joined the AMC board—Pierre Semerena, the director of Renault's international business; Rudolph Lambert, the head of the French automaker's North American operations; and Felix Rohatyn, a New York City investment banker. In mid-December 1980, a consortium of American and French banks gave AMC a five-year unsecured credit line of $250 million. Once Renault completed its stock purchases, it was clearly in control of American Motors.[10]

AMC's losses continued through the early 1980s (see Table 9.1), but Renault continued with its plans to produce a new front-wheel-drive car in Kenosha for the 1983 model year. For its part, American Motors put into effect stringent cost-cutting programs in 1981 and 1982. Renault bought warrants for 4.6 million additional shares of common stock in February 1982, giving it a potential ownership of 55 percent of the shares. By this time, most observers considered American Motors to be merely a division of Renault, but AMC and Renault officials insisted that the two firms were equal partners.[11]

A shift in AMC's top management in January 1982 reflected the new realities at the automaker. Gerald C. Meyers resigned as chairman and CEO, replaced by W. Paul Tippett Jr., the former president and COO. The new president and COO was Jose J. Dedeurwaerder, who had come from Renault to manage the launch of the new Renault-designed car. As part of the management shake-up, Roy D. Chapin Jr. became the chairman of a new executive committee of the board of directors, which included Tippett and Dedeurwaerder. Chapin would serve as the liaison between AMC and Renault.[12]

As American Motors began to suffer losses starting with the 1980 fiscal year, the company's contractual relationship with the UAW began to change. In mid-September 1980, the two sides reached a tentative contract agreement after wildcat strikes closed the Kenosha plant for two days. The three-year contract included pay and benefits comparable to those in the Big Three labor agreements.[13]

Jose J. Dedeurwaerder.
Courtesy DCHC.

In mid-November 1981, American Motors proposed that UAW workers "invest" about 10 percent of their wages and benefits, roughly $150 million, in the company over the next twenty-two months. The workers' contributions would allow AMC to continue its $1 billion program to develop new products, including a new line of Jeeps for 1983. The investments would earn 10 percent interest, compounded annually, and AMC would begin repaying the workers in 1984. In mid-April 1982, the two sides reached a tentative agreement in which the AMC workers gave up six quarterly cost-of-living adjustments (COLAS), three "annual improvement factor" raises, and twenty-eight paid days off, which made up their investment in American Motors. The concessions, worth about $115 million, would translate into $150 million in investment because of the annual 10 percent interest the contributions would earn. Repayment of these "loans" would begin in 1985. After several votes at the UAW locals, the AMC workers approved the agreement.[14]

Renault and American Motors: A Failed Marriage, 1983–87

The 1983 Renault Alliance was the first offspring of the AMC-Renault marriage. Renault initially made the drivetrain (engine and transaxle) for this front-wheel-drive car in France (later, in Mexico) and American Motors built the rest of the vehicle in Wisconsin. Introduced in late September 1982, the Alliance was a remarkable economy sedan. Its fuel-injected 85.2 CID (1.4-liter) engine produced 56 horsepower, more than adequate for a car with a 97-inch wheelbase that weighed less than 2,000 pounds. The new compact car delivered 37 miles per gallon in city driving and 52 miles per gallon on the highway. This was the first all-new model from AMC since the 1975 Pacer and AMC dealers were wildly optimistic about the new product. Fortunately for American Motors, the car-buying public and automotive magazines shared this enthusiasm.[15]

Road & Track road-tested the Alliance and gave the new model a very positive review. The styling was dull, but the car offered plenty of interior room and good fuel economy. The review stated, "In the steering, suspension, and braking departments, we found the car to be impressive under all circumstances. It's a good freeway cruiser and it sticks very well under rough going in the best French tradition." *Motor Trend* named the Alliance "Car of the Year" for 1983. Six judges considered seven nominees and all six chose the Alliance as the top car. They cited Alliance's roominess, good fuel economy, and excellent handling. In discussing the competition, the editor noted: "With the well-thought-out engineering and design that went into the Alliance, from both Renault and AMC, the car emerged the clear winner in this year's competition. One's appreciation for the combined effort the American and French companies have put into the Alliance is increased the more you drive the car. Put simply, the Alliance

First 1983 Renault Alliance off the assembly line at
Kenosha, Wisconsin, June 1982. *Courtesy DCHC.*

may well be the best assembled first-year car we've ever seen." The Alliance received more critical acclaim than anyone at American Motors could have expected.[16]

AMC dropped the Spirit and Concord after the 1983 model year and in 1984 introduced the Encore, a sporty hatchback built on the same 98-inch wheelbase as the Alliance. Encore was mechanically identical to the Alliance, but with different bodies. The 1984 offerings consisted of the Alliance, Encore, and Eagle. However, the new models enjoyed only brief success. Alliance enjoyed robust sales of 124,687 for the 1983 model year, but then dropped to 105,340 for 1984, 75,208 for 1985, and only 55,603 units for 1986. Encore sold a promising 72,076 units in 1984, only 49,923 in 1985, and then sales fell to a disastrous 17,671 the following year.[17]

Starting in the late 1970s, the Jeep portion of American Motors went into a steep decline, as the figures in Table 9.2 show. The Mideast oil crisis of 1979 sent gasoline prices skyrocketing and pushed the U.S. economy into a serious recession that severely hurt all of the car companies in 1980–82. There were few changes to the Jeep offerings until 1984, when Jeep brought out all-new Cherokee and Wagoneer models. The 1980 CJ-5 and CJ-7 models were 200 pounds lighter than their 1979 counterparts, but the weight reduction did nothing to slow the sales slide.[18]

Table 9.2. American Motors Passenger Car and Jeep Sales,
by Calendar Year, 1977–84, and Production,
by Calendar Year, 1985–86

	Passenger Cars	Jeeps	Jeeps as Share of Total (%)
1977	184,361	115,079	38.4
1978	170,739	161,912	48.7
1979	162,057	140,431	46.4
1980	149,438	77,852	34.2
1981	136,682	63,275	31.6
1982	112,433	63,761	36.2
1983	193,351	82,140	29.8
1984	190,255	153,801	44.7
1985	111,138	236,277	68.0
1986	49,435	243,406	83.1

Source: 1985 Almanac: U.S. Marketing Data, Vehicle Distribution, AMC/Jeep/Renault, Corporate Files, NAHC; John A. Gunnell, Standard Catalog American Motors, 1902–1987 (Iola, WI: Krause, 1993), 269, 271, 296, 297.

Jeep's competitors moved toward more fuel-efficient, four-wheel-drive vehicles in 1983, temporarily leaving Jeep in the dust. Ford introduced a smaller Bronco II, powered by a small V-6 engine, and Chevrolet brought out its S-10 Blazer, a four-wheel-drive wagon with a stingy four-cylinder engine. Jeep discontinued the CJ-5 for 1984 and introduced all-new Cherokee and Wagoneer models, dubbed the XJ series. Both used unibody construction instead of body-on-frame design and both incorporated Jeep's new Quadra-Link suspension using coil springs and locator arms rather than an independent front suspension. The base Cherokee was 947 pounds lighter than its predecessor and the Wagoneer shed 822 pounds. With a four-cylinder engine, the Cherokee provided 24 miles per gallon in the city and 33 miles per gallon on the highway.[19]

One reviewer ranked Cherokee as superior to the Ford Bronco and the Chevy Blazer, in part because Cherokee could seat five passengers versus only four for the competition. The reviewer gushed, "What we have here is the first all-new Jeep since baby boomers got out of high school, and it seems a winner right out of the box." For the 1984 model year, Jeep produced 55,596 Cherokee XJs and 20,940 Wagoneer XJs. Jeep 1984 calendar year sales jumped to 153,801 units, the highest level in five years.[20]

The successes continued in the years that followed. Jeep introduced a two-wheel-drive Cherokee in 1985 at midyear, the first two-wheel-drive Cherokee in Jeep's history. The CJ-7 disappeared in mid-1986, replaced by the 1987 Wrangler. In 1986,

1987 Jeep Wrangler. *Courtesy NAHC.*

Jeep also introduced a new compact pickup truck, the Comanche, which a *Detroit News* review gave high marks for acceleration, handling, and interior space. For 1985 and 1986, Jeep substantially exceeded all previous sales records and accounted for more unit sales than American Motors passenger cars. What made American Motors an attractive buyout target for the Chrysler Corporation were its Jeeps, not the company's passenger cars.[21]

One of AMC's most interesting business experiments of this period was its unsuccessful effort to manufacture Jeeps in China. In early May 1983, American Motors announced an agreement with the Peoples Republic of China to create a joint venture, Beijing Jeep Corporation, to build Jeeps at an existing plant in Beijing (Peking). AMC would contribute $16 million to this $51 million joint venture and planned to build 40,000 Jeeps a year in Beijing. The operation faced multiple problems including vast cultural differences, the Chinese government's regulations, and the shortage of foreign exchange needed to import American-made components. The plant finally began assembling Jeep Cherokees in September 1985 from kits shipped from Brampton, Ontario, but managed to assemble only 1,081 in the first eight months of operations. In June 1986, the plant shut down for two months because of lack of foreign currency. The Chrysler Corporation, which inherited Beijing Jeep when it purchased American Motors, faced continuing problems there.[22]

American Motors faced the same chronic problems nearly every year of the 1980s until Chrysler bought it in March 1987. Poor sales meant large losses, which in turn created short-term cash-flow problems and made investment in new products extremely hard to finance. AMC liquidated many of its assets to raise operating funds. In October 1983, the company sold its headquarters building to a private real estate development company for $51 million. This followed on the heels of the sale of AM General to the LTV Corporation in June 1983 for $170 million. AMC also disposed of Windsor Plastics in 1982 for $11 million, along with its garden tractor subsidiary, Wheelhorse, for $8 million.[23]

On the eve of the introduction of the 1984 AMC models, company management remained publicly optimistic. Marketing vice president Joseph E. Cappy forecasted strong sales of AMC cars and Jeeps in the upcoming year. The company earned a small profit in the fourth quarter of 1983, the first in nearly four years, but still lost $258 million for the year. A small profit of $15.5 million in 1984 was the first since 1979. In September 1984, Cappy predicted combined sales of 200,000 Alliance and Encore cars in the 1985 model year, but actual sales amounted to 125,000. The downward spiral continued in the years that followed.[24]

The company's poor performance in sales and profits made labor relations more difficult. AMC's employees contributed about $10,000 each in concessions through the Employee Investment Plan negotiated between the union and the company in 1982. American Motors had agreed to restore the annual pay raises by 1985 and to repay the contributions, approximately $150 million, with 10 percent interest. The agreement gave the union the option of taking the repayments as profit sharing or in the form of a "wheel tax" of $100 per vehicle produced in North America for four years starting in 1985. The wheel tax would give each worker about $2,800 per year versus only $300 from profit sharing. The company estimated that the wheel tax would cost it $40 million a year, funds it simply did not have.[25]

The UAW agreed in mid-April 1985 to accept profit sharing in 1985, but kept the door open for a wheel tax in later years. Workers at AMC's Toledo Jeep plant engaged in wildcat strikes in mid-April to protest this agreement. Some workers engaged in acts of sabotage, denting vehicle bodies, putting sugar in gas tanks, and deliberately wrecking conveyor belts. AMC went to court and received a five-day injunction blocking the vandalism, which brought it to an end. Ultimately, the Toledo workers received the wheel tax for 1985, so the wildcat strikes worked.[26]

No sooner had the UAW agreed to a much smaller repayment of the workers "investment" in American Motors than the company came to the union asking for further concessions. AMC wanted wage parity, but it also asked its workers to give up one week of vacation pay and one paid holiday per year. AMC also demanded the same reductions in job classifications that the UAW had granted Mazda at its Flat Rock, Michigan, plant and General Motors/Toyota at their joint venture at Fremont, California. The company's threat was also clear—it gave official notice to the union that it would close the Milwaukee and Kenosha plants by mid-1986, if not earlier.[27]

American Motors gave the union a 24 May deadline to agree to the concessions. In mid-July 1985, after earlier negative votes, the two Wisconsin locals approved concessions that included a rollback of wages of 37 cents per hour and the loss of forty hours of paid vacation and nine paid days off per year. The agreement was to run through August 1988. American Motors immediately withdrew its plant-closing notices for the two Wisconsin factories.[28]

As the company struggled in the early 1980s, the top executive positions changed hands. Paul Tippett, who had served as chairman and CEO since January 1982, stepped down as CEO in September 1984. Jose J. Dedeurwaerder replaced him and remained the CEO until March 1986. In December 1985, Tippett also stepped down as chairman. His replacement, Pierre Semerena, executive vice president at Renault, remained as chairman until the Chrysler purchase. Joseph E. Cappy, a relatively new face at American Motors, became executive vice president for operations in June 1985 and chief operating officer in mid-December 1985. Cappy, who had held the post of general marketing manager at the Lincoln-Mercury Division of

Ford Motor Company, joined AMC in 1982 as vice president for marketing. In late March 1986, Cappy replaced Dedeurwaerder as president and CEO of American Motors and held those posts until the Chrysler purchase of AMC a year later.[29]

American Motors continued to rely on Renault's cash to survive. The company borrowed another $50 million from Renault in late December 1985, bringing the French automaker's investment in American Motors to $645 million—$405 million in stock and $240 million in loans. In late July 1986, AMC announced plans to issue an additional eight million shares of stock, which they hoped would raise $187 million. By November 1986, Renault had invested a total of $785 million in American Motors.[30]

Renault appeared willing to keep its investment in American Motors despite the American automaker's staggering losses starting in 1980 (Table 9.2). American Motors gave the French company a presence in North America and provided about 8,500 jobs in France. New products were on the way, including a compact car, the Medallion, to be made in France, and the mid-sized Renault Premier to be built in fall 1987 at the Brampton, Ontario, factory. Unfortunately Renault also had large losses in its European operations by the mid-1980s ($1.6 billion in 1985 alone). Changes in the French government brought additional pressures. Premier Jacques Chirac, elected in 1986 to replace socialist Francois Mitterand, promised to return many state-owned enterprises to the private sector.[31]

The American Motors-Renault alliance ultimately failed. According to former AMC officials who reflected on the failed partnership a decade later, the two sides represented quite different corporate and national cultures and had significantly different goals. As a government-controlled venture, Renault was mainly interested in creating jobs in France and the company answered to the French parliament and not to stockholders. Renault ignored and neglected the Jeep brand, AMC's most profitable vehicles, while Renault-designed cars satisfied European customers but did not match Americans' expectations.[32]

The greatest problem that AMC continued to face, even with Renault as its partner, was its inability to compete with the wide range of high-quality, fuel-efficient models offered by the Japanese automakers. The Japanese took over the small-car niche market that AMC had dominated since the late 1950s. Except for Jeep, AMC's products had very little appeal to American customers.

Chrysler's Purchase of American Motors

Well before Chrysler offered to buy American Motors it had established a working relationship with the struggling number four automaker. Chrysler and AMC reached an agreement in June 1986 whereby AMC would assemble the full-size rear-wheel-drive M-body cars—the Chrysler Fifth Avenue, Dodge Diplomat, and Plymouth Gran Fury—at its Kenosha assembly plant. As part of the agreement to bring production of the large cars to Kenosha, the State of Wisconsin provided more than $3 million to help Chrysler train the 2,700 workers who assembled the new product. The company produced these cars at Kenosha through September 1988, when it discontinued these models.[33]

Chrysler also had discussions with AMC about assembling its L-body front-wheel-drive subcompact cars (Dodge Omni/Plymouth Horizon) at AMC's idle Kenosha Lake Front plant starting in November 1987. The plan was to produce the 1988 through 1992 model Omni/Horizon cars at Kenosha at a rate of about 200,000 per year. The negotiations dragged on for nearly five months, in part because AMC was trying to gain concessions from the UAW and the State of Wisconsin for two interrelated projects—Chrysler subcompact car assembly and an entirely new Jeep model. The UAW had agreed, in a "Letter of Understanding on Assembly of Future Vehicles" (27 June 1985), to renegotiate its labor agreements in return for new products and job guarantees.[34]

The discussions began in October 1986 with a series of letters between Richard A. Calmes, AMC's vice president for industrial relations, and Marc Stepp, the director of the American Motors Department of the UAW. Calmes extended the deadline for reaching a new contract from 26 November 1986 to 25 January 1987. The negotiations temporarily blew up on 10 December 1986 when Stepp and AMC president Joseph Cappy exchanged a series of nasty letters accusing each other of being unreasonable and unrealistic in their demands. Meanwhile, Chrysler sat impatiently on the sidelines waiting for AMC and the UAW to resolve their differences.[35]

In January 1987, Wisconsin governor Tommy Thompson intervened in the negotiations. Following a meeting between Thompson and Cappy in mid-January, the two held a press conference in Kenosha outlining the status of negotiations. Cappy issued a statement calling for a "three-legged partnership" of AMC, the UAW, and the State of Wisconsin to modernize the Kenosha plant. Cappy asked for $200–250 million in assistance from the state, along with concessions from the UAW. Chrysler's proposal for L-body production called for a $70 million investment from AMC and a $130 million contribution from Wisconsin for plant renovations. Chrysler would spend $60 million for tooling.

Keeping the Kenosha plant running required a complex set of agreements involving AMC, Chrysler, the State of Wisconsin, the UAW, and the county and local governments. Chrysler was willing to bring L-body assembly to Kenosha only if AMC promised to operate the Kenosha plant through 1992. On its part, AMC would keep the plant operating only if it brought a new Jeep model there and produced it for seven years. The new investment required for the combined L-body/Jeep production was about $600 million. AMC and Chrysler together would pay $400 million of the total, with the State of Wisconsin contributing $200 million. AMC also demanded that the UAW agree to a new contract, which included pay cuts of 15 percent, which AMC would restore very slowly over the life of the contract. Kenosha workers would wait forty-two months before their pay rates returned to their original levels.[36]

Well before the negotiations about L-body production began, Chrysler had secret discussions with Renault about buying part or all of AMC. In the summer of 1986, Chrysler sold its stock in Peugeot, which it had received in August 1978 when it sold its European operations to the French company. The stock sale brought Chrysler $144 million ($132 million after taxes) and freed it to talk with Renault. Lee Iacocca had met with Renault chairman Georges Besse in June 1986 to discuss cooperative ventures and this meeting led to talks code-named "Titan," whereby Chrysler pursued Renault.

Chrysler initially expressed an interest in buying only the Jeep part of AMC's business, but Renault wanted to discuss selling the AMC operation as a whole. Renault kept these talks with Chrysler secret from the top AMC officials, including Joseph Cappy. When French terrorists assassinated Renault chairman Georges Besse on 17 November 1986, the talks stopped. His replacement, Raymond Levy, who resumed negotiations with Chrysler in February 1987, also refused to consider selling Jeep apart from AMC. The talks inevitably focused on Chrysler's possible purchase of Renault's AMC shares and ultimately the remaining shares as well.[37]

After Iacocca met with Levy in New York on 5 February, talks resumed and then produced an agreement in only a month's time. Around-the-clock marathon negotiations began in Paris on 6 March and produced an agreement three days later. In a letter dated 9 March 1987, Bennett Bidwell, Chrysler's vice chairman, informed AMC's Joseph Cappy of the merger agreement with Renault and gave Cappy a copy of the letter of intent of 9 March 1987 signed by Chrysler and Renault.[38]

The agreement was subject to Chrysler's completing a thorough examination of AMC's books, products, and facilities, but other nettlesome problems could have derailed the process. Ron Glantz, an analyst with Montgomery Securities in San Francisco, pointed out the major problems in an investment newsletter he issued in November 1986. Any company taking over AMC would have to deal with the aging facilities at Kenosha and Toledo; militant and uncooperative UAW locals at both plants; an unfunded pension liability of more than $600 million; and, most important, $1.9 billion in pending lawsuits resulting from rollovers of the Jeep CJ model.[39]

Chrysler took on the pension liabilities, and Renault and Chrysler agreed to share equally the costs of the rollover lawsuits. Another complication arose from the difficulty in placing a dollar value on Renault's stake in AMC because the American company was about to introduce new lines of Renault cars. Steve Miller, Chrysler's financial genius, developed a side agreement whereby Chrysler would pay Renault up to $350 million more for the buyout based on the 1987–91 sales volumes of the Jeep and Eagle lines.[40]

The American Motors management moved cautiously in dealing with the Chrysler proposal. They held a series of meetings in early and mid-March 1987 in which they defined "due diligence" in narrow terms. They agreed to give Chrysler only minimal information on new products, market projections, and AMC's executive corps. For its part, Chrysler established a coordinating committee and named thirty-four of its officials to serve as contacts for the AMC management. Bidwell and Richard Goodyear, Chrysler's general counsel, issued a detailed memo to their own managers strictly laying out "due diligence" guidelines they would follow in handling confidential information from AMC.[41]

In late March, AMC officials informed the New York Stock Exchange that, because of the Chrysler merger proposal, they would postpone the annual stockholders meeting scheduled for 29 April and would delay issuing the annual report for 1986. The AMC board of directors tentatively rescheduled the stockholders meeting for 24 June, but it did not take place until 9 August. The AMC board of directors' proxy statement regarding the merger, dated 2 July 1987, unanimously recommended that the stockholders approve the merger. At the special stockholders meeting held on 5 August 1987, the stockholders concurred, making the merger official.[42]

The minutes of the American Motors Corporation board of directors meetings reveal their nearly impossible situation once Renault and Chrysler had come to an agreement to merge. The non-Renault board members suspected that Renault was getting a better deal than the AMC stockholders, in part because no AMC representatives participated in the negotiations over the merger. At the AMC board meeting of 14 April 1987, Jose Dedeurwaerder disputed the charges of unfair treatment of the AMC stockholders, but also insisted that if the Chrysler deal failed, Renault would not give AMC additional financing.[43]

At the AMC board meeting of 19 May 1987, Shearson Lehman presented its findings regarding the issue of "fairness" and concluded that Renault was not receiving a better deal from Chrysler than the AMC stockholders. The AMC board conducted a final review of its options, including financial restructuring, sale to a third party, and continuing its current operations with no changes. They had no alternative, especially in light of Renault's unwillingness to invest any further in their struggling company. The AMC board of directors formally adopted the resolutions needed to consummate the deal.[44]

The initial announcement in March of the Chrysler proposal to buy AMC brought enthusiastic responses bordering on euphoria from most quarters. UAW leaders at Kenosha and Toledo hoped plants in both cities would keep jobs without workers having to grant additional concessions. AMC dealers assumed they would benefit from Chrysler's size and proven ability to sell vehicles. *Detroit News* columnist Marjorie Sorge was more cautious, pointing out that Chrysler was not likely to keep all of AMC's products on the market or all of its factories in operation. The obsolete plants at Kenosha and Toledo were both potential targets for closure, but Toledo was more likely to survive because the Jeeps made there were profitable.[45]

Chrysler for its part tried to reassure AMC employees that they would treat them fairly after the merger and that their future would be determined only by their performance. The company hired an outside consulting firm—Towers, Perrin, Forster & Crosby—to develop letters and other means of communication between Chrysler and the AMC executives and salaried employees. The plan was to send out common letters to all AMC *and* Chrysler employees, with Iacocca and Cappy cosigning them.[46]

Within months of the AMC purchase, with sales of its own vehicles doing poorly, Chrysler began to cut its overhead by laying off salaried workers. Iacocca announced in late October that he planned to reduce the combined salaried workforce of 38,000 by at least 9 percent (3,500 workers) before the end of the year and then by 3 percent per year after that. Most of the layoffs came from the AMC salaried force of 5,700. Employees at AMC's technical center in Detroit, including engineers and technicians, took the brunt of the first wave of layoffs.[47]

At the end of October 1987, Chrysler laid off one shift at Kenosha that made its rear-wheel-drive vehicles, a loss of 1,400 jobs, but said they would rehire 1,000 of these workers within a month to staff a second shift producing the Omni/Horizon twins. In late January 1988, in the dead of Wisconsin's winter, Chrysler announced it would close the Kenosha assembly plant, permanently idling 5,500 workers. Production would continue at Kenosha until August or September, when they would shift Omni/Horizon assembly to the Jefferson Avenue plant in Detroit. State and local officials in Wisconsin, along with governor Tommy Thompson, accused Chrysler of breaking its word to keep the plant open for five years.[48]

The UAW international union and its Local 72 at Kenosha appealed to Chrysler to reconsider the closing. Rudy Kuzel, the president of the local, threatened to "make the plant closing the most expensive in history if Chrysler did not reconsider." In mid-March, the Kenosha local rented a billboard near the Chrysler headquarters in Highland Park and posted the notice, "Iacocca, Keep Your Word to Kenosha."[49]

Iacocca held a press conference in Milwaukee on 16 February 1988 to announce a program to help the families of Kenosha auto workers who would lose their jobs because of the plant closing. He was clearly engaged in "damage control," trying to reduce the negative publicity Chrysler was receiving and to discourage Governor Thompson from suing Chrysler for violating its agreement to keep the plant open for five years. Iacocca announced that Chrysler would donate all of its profits from selling cars in Wisconsin for a full year, some $20 million, to a trust fund to aid unemployed Kenosha workers. The local UAW leaders rejected this as a public relations ploy and as totally inadequate.[50]

The Kenosha workers received a more generous compensation package from Chrysler in early May. The company had already announced that it would extend production of the Omni/Horizon models at Kenosha until January 1989. In essence, Chrysler agreed to repay the workers most of the $60 million in concessions that they had granted American Motors. Each worker would get a lump sum ranging between $5,000 and $10,000. They would also receive twenty-four weeks of Supplemental Unemployment Benefits (SUB). Because the American Motors SUB Fund was bankrupt, they would not have received any benefits without this agreement. Both the local and national UAW leadership accepted this package as the best possible agreement, given all the circumstances.[51]

The Kenosha local dropped a federal lawsuit against Chrysler that it had filed earlier in the year. Governor Tommy Thompson nevertheless promised that the state would sue Chrysler if Kenosha County and the City of Kenosha also sued. In September 1988, Chrysler offered the city administration a package of aid and reimbursements worth about $200 million, under the condition that Kenosha would not sue Chrysler. The city accepted Chrysler's offer.[52]

American Motors: The Last Independent Automaker

AMC's struggle to survive during the last decade of its existence reflected the fundamental problems the number four automaker faced since its birth in 1954. The company made a small profit in the fourth quarter of 1986, but the long-term outlook remained grim. AMC's share of the market dipped below 1 percent in 1986 and only the Jeep line seemed to have a promising future. American Motors had succeeded in the late 1950s by focusing on small cars, a part of the market ignored by the Big Three. The company mistakenly tried to become a full-line automaker in the 1960s and simply did not have the resources (or the design sense) to match the offerings of General Motors, Ford, and Chrysler. When it refocused its product line on smaller cars, AMC's sales went through a roller-coaster ride reflecting the wild fluctuations in gasoline prices in the 1970s.

The coming of new investments and new car models from Renault helped delay certain bankruptcy in the early 1980s. The Renault models did no better in the market than the AMC models they replaced. The widely held perception that AMC was on the verge of bankruptcy did not help sales. Throughout AMC's history, the automotive and business press routinely characterized the automaker as "struggling," "troubled," or "beleaguered." These negative perceptions of the company did not give potential buyers much confidence in American Motors. Nobody wanted to be the owner of an "orphan" car.

Was the disappearance of American Motors as an independent automobile manufacturer inevitable? Probably not, but its failure was a likely outcome, given the disadvantages of AMC's small size. The company largely overcame the inherently higher design and tooling costs per car by cleverly using the same chassis and mechanical parts for multiple models and simply using different bodies to create new models. Richard Teague deserves most of the credit for their success in following that strategy. However, most of AMC's customers probably recognized the true nature of this "rebadging" strategy. The company's small size and chronic losses made major new investments in updated plants extremely difficult to finance. The one major exception was the new Bramalea, Ontario, plant that opened in 1987. Otherwise, American Motors was wed to ancient and inefficient factories in Kenosha, Milwaukee, and Toledo. Substantial parts of all of those facilities dated from the first decade of the twentieth century.

AMC's inability to earn profits on a consistent basis made long-term investment in products or plants problematic. Over the period 1965–86, the company earned profits in eleven years and had losses in twelve, but the losses far exceeded the profits. Product missteps, such as the Marlin, were disastrous for a small, struggling company. Ford could absorb the losses from the Edsel because of the success of its other high-volume offerings, but American Motors did not enjoy that luxury.

Even AMC's most competent managers, including Romney and the Chapin-Luneberg team, had little margin for error. Roy Abernethy inherited a healthy American Motors and made the company sickly through his decision to compete with General Motors. The last set of managers before Renault took control—Gerald Meyers and Paul Tippett—were in many respects held hostage by the continuing crises that American Motors faced. By the time the Renault executives took over, AMC was trying simply to remain afloat and there was not much they could do to stave off the company's end. It was not surprising that American Motors went out of business in 1987. The company's survival for a third of a century was more remarkable.

Nash, Hudson, and American Motors

A Retrospective

In many significant respects, the Nash Motor Company and the Hudson Motor Car Company operated in a business environment that became increasingly competitive well before the Great Depression. The number of producers fell from 253 in 1908 to 108 in 1920 and then to only 44 in 1929. Following the rapid growth of the Ford Motor Company to a dominant position in the 1910s with the remarkable Model T, General Motors overtook Ford in the late 1920s. The newcomer, the Chrysler Corporation (1925), became a significant force following its purchase of Dodge Brothers Company and its introduction of the Plymouth and DeSoto nameplates in 1928. At that point, the Big Three already accounted for 75 percent of American automobile production.[1]

Only fifteen American automobile manufacturers remained in business in 1933 and only ten were left after World War II. Substantial independent producers such as Hupp, Pierce-Arrow, Franklin, Auburn, Willys-Overland, and Durant Motors did not survive the Depression or decided not to attempt to make cars when the war ended. Besides the Big Three, the remaining companies were Nash, Hudson, Packard, Studebaker, Willys, Crosely, and Kaiser-Frazer.[2]

How did the independents manage to survive as long as they did? The record of

Nash Motors and the Hudson Motor Car Company clearly show that there was no single path to success. Nash Motors earned profits in seventeen out of twenty years between 1917 and 1936, the Depression years of 1933–35 being the exception. Nash cars produced during the active management of Charles W. Nash were solid and reliable, if sometimes stodgy. Charles Nash's expertise was in manufacturing and in cost-cutting, not in styling or promotion, and the cars reflected the owner's strengths. Following the lead of Thomas Jeffery, Charles Nash emphasized vertical integration so he could better control the quality and costs of the components he used. This was also necessary because Kenosha was a long way from the principal component suppliers in Michigan, Ohio, and Indiana. Gaining control of the Seaman Body Corporation in 1919 was one example of this effort.

Customers best knew Nash cars as durable, reliable, mid-priced vehicles not notable for daring styling or "cutting-edge" mechanical advances or features. The first cars bearing the Nash name, the 1918 models, featured "perfected valve-in-head" (overhead valve) six-cylinder engines, a design that Buick had pioneered in 1904. The 1922 Nash Four featured rubber engine mounts, an industry first. Nash introduced medium-priced, closed-body models in 1922, in tune with Hudson, Dodge, and others. The 1929 Nash 400 series came with twin ignition, which featured two spark plugs in each cylinder, a technological advance according to the automaker. Nash Motors introduced its first eight-cylinder car in 1930, when most competitors were doing the same. Nash first used hydraulic brakes on its 1935 models, eleven years after Walter Chrysler used the system on his 1924 Chrysler Six and after most other U.S. automakers had made the transition.

Charles Nash tried to expand the company's range of offerings, recognizing the hazards of focusing on the crowded mid-priced segment of the market. Nash briefly entered the luxury car market with the Lafayette (1920–24), a large, heavy, expensive car with an eight-cylinder engine. After offering only six-cylinder cars in 1918–20, the company brought out the Nash Four in 1921. A lighter-weight, less expensive six, the Ajax Six, followed in 1925, soon re-badged as the Nash Light Six. Nash's first eight, introduced in 1930, came at a bad time in the car market. In response to its dealers' wishes, Nash reincarnated the LaFayette in 1934 as a lower-priced offering than the standard Nash Sixes. Nash Motors was not able to imitate General Motors, Chrysler, and, to a lesser extent, Ford, in offering a wide range of models in terms of size and cost.

The Nash cars reflected the personality and character of the company's founder and guiding light—they were steady and reliable, but not stylish or flashy. Charles Nash maintained tight control over his company's operations, kept costs under control, and spent few resources on promoting and advertising his cars. He embodied old-fashioned paternalism regarding his employees and the city of Kenosha. Charles Nash enjoyed occasional hunting and fishing trips and golf outings, but he was not a cosmopolitan world traveler. He was most at ease in the factory. The contrast between Nash Motors and the Hudson Motor Car Company is striking and instructive, as is the contrast between Charles W. Nash and Roy D. Chapin.

The Hudson Motor Car Company was also successful from 1909 through 1936, when Roy Chapin died. The company earned profits in twenty-three of those years and losses in only four years, 1931–34, during the worst part of the Depression. The contrast between Hudson and Nash in other respects was stark. Hudson was often at the leading edge of introducing new features on its cars, but more important, it redefined the automobile market on two separate occasions. The 1909 Hudson Twenty, while only $50 more expensive than a comparable Model T Ford, was in most respects a better car, in terms of features and interior roominess. The company, however, quickly moved "upmarket" with its offerings, conceding the low end of the market to Ford. Hudson was an industry leader in selling its 1912 models with electric self-starters as standard equipment. The Super-Six engine that went into the 1916 Hudsons was an engineering breakthrough. The company reentered the lower-price market with its 1919 Essex, but then redefined the automobile market with the industry's first low-priced closed car, the 1922 Essex Coach. Hudson's last major car introduction during Chapin's time was the 1933 Terraplane, priced to compete with Ford, Chevrolet, and Plymouth.

In contrast to Nash Motors, the Hudson Motor Car Company spent lavishly on advertising and promotion. One of the company's strategies involved a commitment to racing, beginning with endurance and economy races, but with the coming of the Super-Six, speed racing as well. The company supported and sponsored racing and then featured its racing achievements in its advertising. Hudson, Essex, and Terraplane models appeared everywhere from the Bonneville Salt Flats to Pike's Peak to Daytona Beach. The company unabashedly used Amelia Earhart and Orville Wright to promote the Terraplane.

Hudson's engineering, styling, and marketing strategies were far more aggressive than Nash's and reflected the personalities of the dominant figures at Hudson. Unlike Nash Motors, which was a one-man operation, Hudson was a partnership of Roy Chapin, Howard Coffin, and Roscoe Jackson. Coffin, arguably one of the leading automotive engineers of the early twentieth century, kept Hudson's cars at the leading edge of innovative engineering. Chapin's greatest interest and talent lay in advertising and marketing and Hudson's emphasis on those areas reflects his strengths. Jackson became the "inside man," managing the day-to-day factory operations. Their collective history together starting with the Olds Motor Works gave them more of an entrepreneurial, risk-taking mentality than Charles Nash had when he ran Nash Motors. By the late 1920s, we can see the longer-term results of the diverging styles and strategies of the two firms, when all the car companies prospered. Between 1925 and 1929, Nash production ranged from 96,000 vehicles to a peak of 138,000 units, while Hudson's output ranged from 227,500 vehicles to 301,000.

From 1937 to 1953, before the merger of Nash and Hudson to form American Motors, the fortunes and performances of the two companies were reversed. Nash earned profits in fifteen of those seventeen years, whereas Hudson earned profits in only twelve years. We can see the true "tale of the tape" when we compare the net profits of the two over this time. Hudson's net profits amounted to $40.3 million, while Nash's profits totaled $130 million. To be sure, most of the Nash-Kelvinator profits came from Kelvinator appliance sales, which were consistently profitable. The two companies had similar levels of production before World War II, but by the early 1950s, Hudson was suffering from declining sales. Nash production in 1951 and 1952 stood at 178,000 and 137,000 units, respectively, whereas Hudson's was a more anemic 93,000 and 79,000.

The merger of Nash and Kelvinator in 1936 rejuvenated Nash Motors. The Kelvinator managers including George Mason quickly took control of the Nash operations. Mason was a visionary more akin to Roy D. Chapin than to A. E. Barit, who ran Hudson during this period. Nash cars incorporated more innovative engineering and design features than had been the case before Mason came on the scene. Nash was the first U.S. automaker to use a unit-body or unitized body/frame construction in a low-priced car, the 1941 Ambassador 600. Unfortunately for Nash, the wartime cancellation of automobile production came just as sales of the new models were skyrocketing. The all-new 1948 Nash Airflyte models used the unit-body design exclusively. The company also moved ahead of the competition when it introduced the compact 1950 Nash Rambler and the subcompact 1954 Nash Metropolitan.

The contrast between Nash-Kelvinator and Hudson during World War II is also instructive. Nash took on several production challenges including making Hamilton Standard hydromatic variable pitch propellers, Pratt & Whitney 18-cylinder radial aircraft engines, and Sikorsky helicopters. Its Lansing, Michigan plants received the coveted Army-Navy "E" Award in September 1943 for propeller blade production. Nash reached or exceeded its delivery schedules throughout the war. Hudson also performed well in the first two years of the war and won the Army-Navy "E" Award twice, in January 1943 and November 1943, in both cases for aircraft component production. However, in October 1943, the navy canceled Hudson's contract to manage the Naval Ordnance Plant in Center Line, Michigan, and awarded the work to Westinghouse. During the last two years of the war, Hudson struggled without much success to meet delivery deadlines for B-29 wing and tail sections and Curtiss-Wright Helldiver wings.

Hudson's automotive offerings did not remain stagnant during A. Edward Barit's regime (1936–54). The 1948 "Step-down" Hudson was a drastic departure from earlier models and gave Hudson a low, sleek, stylish, roomy car to offer the public. The company introduced a dual carburetor system with dual-intake manifolds, the Twin H Power package, in 1952 and remained active and successful in racing throughout the postwar period. The last new model the company introduced, the 1953 Hudson Jet, was a sales disaster and forced Barit to agree to merge with Nash-Kelvinator. Barit made most of the key decisions regarding the Hudson Jet, disregarding the views of his stylists and other advisors.

The contrast between the management styles and abilities of Nash-Kelvinator's Mason and Hudson's Barit are striking and explain much of the poor performance of Hudson in the postwar years. Mason hired George Romney, intending to groom him to take his place. Barit, in contrast, actively blocked new leadership from Hudson, whether that leadership was Henry J. Kaiser, the Fisher brothers, or Roy D. Chapin Jr. He ignored his own well-established stylist Frank Spring in making styling decisions on new products. At times, Barit was more concerned about preserving his control over Hudson than anything else. Unlike Mason, Barit lacked vision.

The merger of Nash and Hudson to form American Motors only multiplied the problems the two independent producers endured in the early 1950s. Faced with what was the imminent failure of the new company, George Romney took drastic actions that George Mason would have found difficult to carry out—he eliminated the "Step-down" Hudson and the Hudson Jet in 1954 and closed the Hudson factory in Detroit. Following the 1957 model year, Romney dropped the Nash and Hudson marques and focused AMC's efforts on the compact Rambler. George Romney was an inspirational leader and a crusader who led American Motors back to profitability. He was a visionary who had the good fortune to deliver compact cars to a receptive market at a time when the Big Three had little to offer.

The successful years American Motors enjoyed at the end of Romney's tenure resulted from the company's capture of a market niche ignored by the other companies. Roy Abernethy's decision to abandon Romney's strategy and turn AMC into a full-line automaker probably guaranteed that the company would eventually fail. Despite Roy D. Chapin Jr.'s daring business decisions, especially the purchase of Kaiser Jeep, and some innovative vehicles such as the Hornet, Gremlin, and Pacer, American Motors faced an uphill battle for survival from the mid-1960s on. The company could not escape the fundamental economic disadvantage it faced in trying to compete against the other automakers with their large economies of scale. The partnership with Renault was perhaps as successful as possible, given AMC's grave market position. The alliance brought needed outside capital and new products, but it did not do enough to overcome American Motors' cost disadvantages and the volatile car market in the 1980s. The Chrysler purchase of American Motors brought an "official" end to the last independent automobile manufacturer in the United States as a separate corporation.

However, the contributions made by Nash, Hudson, and American Motors to automobile design, including mechanical features, are still embodied in most American cars. Advances such as balanced crankshafts, inexpensive closed bodies, and unit-body construction live on in millions of automobiles on the road today. Although two decades have passed since Chrysler took over American Motors, the independent automaker's personnel and products contributed greatly to Chrysler's successes in the 1990s and beyond. American Motors refined and popularized Jeep vehicles, which to this day serve as a mainstay of Chrysler's sales. Nash, Hudson, and American Motors long served as an antidote to the dominant market power of the Big Three automakers. Nash showed that an automaker could avoid making regular styling changes and offer a wide variety of models and still make respectable profits. Hudson's many engineering innovations forced the larger car companies to follow its lead. American Motors showed the rest of the industry that, given the choice, many consumers preferred smaller automobiles. The demise of the independent automakers left automobile buyers with fewer choices and laid the groundwork for the enormous success of Japanese cars in the American market starting in the late 1970s.

The Nash Family in Genesee County, Michigan, 1870–1910

The U.S. Census of Population manuscript census tracts make it possible to follow the lives of many of Charles Nash's relatives who remained in Genesee County, including his parents, David and Anna Nash, and younger sibling George Nash. For example, the census listing for Forest Township in 1870 also shows a Frank Nash (age 26), a farm laborer, born in New York, his wife, Sarah (25), and three daughters, Mazovia (6), Francis (4), and Emma (1). Sarah Nash and all three daughters were born in Michigan. Frank Nash and David Nash may have been brothers.[1]

The 1880 census also offers additional evidence of the fate of David Nash's family. Robert Lapworth (40), a farmer living in Flushing Township, appears with his wife, Sabrina (33), sons William (4) and George (2), and a thirteen-year-old stepdaughter. This was the family Charles Nash ran away from at age twelve. Flushing Township was also the home of farmer George Lapworth (49), his wife, Francis (40), and no children other than George Nash (age 14), identified as "adopted son." In 1871, the court apparently placed George Nash, the younger brother of Charles Nash, with George Lapworth, almost certainly the brother of Robert Lapworth. Anna Nash was still living in Forest Township, shown as "keeping house," but with two boarders,

Francis McComb (age 16) and McComb's daughter Anabelle (age two months), clearly born out of wedlock.[2]

David Nash, father of Charles, does not appear in the 1880 U.S. Census, at least not under that name, and there are no surviving enumeration sheets for 1890. He is, however, listed in the 1900 census in Richfield Township, in the northeast part of Genesee County. He was sixty-five years old, worked as a day laborer, and admitted working only seven months in the previous year. His wife of forty-five years, Anna Nash, was seventy-two years old and told the census enumerator that she was the mother of four children, with three still living. David and Anna Nash lived in a rented home. Appearing next to them on the census enumeration form was their son George Nash (age 34) with wife, Matti, and three children including Anna (age 5) and Charley (age 4). At least part of the Nash family that split in 1871 reunited some thirty years later.[3]

Notes

INTRODUCTION

1. Donald T. Critchlow, *Studebaker: The Life and Death of an American Corporation* (Bloomington: Indiana University Press, 1996); Thomas E. Bonsall, *More Than They Promised: The Studebaker Story* (Stanford: Stanford University Press, 2000); James A. Ward, *The Fall of the Packard Motor Car Company* (Stanford: Stanford University Press, 1995).
2. Richard M. Langworth, *Kaiser-Frazer, The Last Onslaught on Detroit: An Intimate Behind the Scenes Study of the Postwar American Car Industry* (Kutztown, PA: Automobile Quarterly, 1975).
3. E. D. Kennedy, *The Automobile Industry: The Coming of Age of Capitalism's Favorite Child* (New York: Reynal and Hitchcock, 1941); John B. Rae, *American Automobile Manufacturers: The First Forty Years* (Philadelphia: Chilton, 1959); John B. Rae, *The American Automobile: A Brief History* (Chicago: University of Chicago Press, 1965); James J. Flink, *The Automobile Age* (Cambridge, MA: MIT Press, 1988); Charles E. Edwards, *Dynamics of the United States Automobile Industry* (Columbia: University of South Carolina Press, 1965).
4. Two of the most recent and detailed biographies of Henry Ford are Douglas Brinkley, *Wheels for the World: Henry Ford, His Company, and a Century of Progress* (New York: Viking, 2003), and Steven Watts, *The People's Tycoon: Henry Ford and the American Century* (New York: Alfred A. Knopf, 2005). Notable biographies of Billy Durant and Alfred Sloan include Lawrence R. Gustin, *Billy Durant: Creator of General Motors* (Flushing, MI: Craneshaw, 1984); Barnard A. Weisberger, *The Dream Maker: William C. Durant, Founder of General Motors* (Boston: Little, Brown, 1979); David Farber, *Sloan Rules: Alfred P. Sloan and the Triumph of General Motors* (Chicago: University of Chicago Press, 2002); William Pelfrey, *Billy, Alfred, and General Motors: The Story of Two Unique Men, a Legendary Company, and a Remarkable Time in American History* (New York: American Management Association, 2006). The only biography of Walter Chrysler is Vincent Curcio, *Chrysler: The Life and Times of an Automotive Genius* (New York: Oxford University Press, 2000).
5. J. C. Long, *Roy D. Chapin* (Privately published, 1945).
6. American Motors Corporation, *Nash Family Album: A Pictorial Roll Call of the Passenger Cars Manufactured by Nash Motors and Its Predecessor Companies since 1902*, 3rd ed. (Detroit: American Motors Corporation, 1954); American Motors Corporation, *Rambler Family Album: A Pictorial Roll Call of the Passenger Cars and Trucks Produced by American Motors and Its Predecessor*

Companies (Detroit: American Motors Corporation, 1961); John A. Conde, *The American Motors Family Album: A Pictorial Roll Call of the Passenger Cars, Commercial Vehicles, and Trucks Produced by American Motors and Its Predecessor Companies* (Detroit: American Motors Corporation, 1976); John A. Conde, *The Cars That Hudson Built* (Keego Harbor, MI: Arnold-Porter Publishing, 1980); Don Butler, *The History of Hudson* (Sarasota, FL: Crestline Publishing, 1982); Patrick R. Foster, *American Motors: The Last Independent* (Iola, WI: Krause, 1993).

CHAPTER ONE

1. Clifford Sklarek, "Thomas B. Jeffery Historical," *Antique Motor News,* April 1975, 19, 20; Beverly Rae Kimes, "A Family in Kenosha: The Story of the Rambler and the Jeffery," *Automobile Quarterly* 61 (second quarter 1978): 130. Sklarek claims that Jeffery emigrated to the United States with his parents, while Kimes states that he came alone.

2. Sklarek asserts that Gormully came to the United States after Jeffery's 1878 trip to England, while Kimes claims that Gormully came to America before Jeffries emigrated in 1863.

3. David V. Herlihy, *Bicycle: The History* (New Haven: Yale University Press, 2004), 75–76, 86–87, 102–4, 108, 190.

4. Ibid., 192, 208–10; Stephen B. Goddard, *Colonel Albert Pope and His Dream Machine: The Life and Times of a Bicycle Tycoon Turned Automotive Pioneer* (Jefferson, NC: McFarland, 2000), 67–71.

5. "T. B. Jeffery Expires in Italy: Death Comes Suddenly While on Pleasure Tour—His Remarkable Career as an Inventor and Manufacturer," *Motor World* 23 (7 April 1910), 3; Kimes, "A Family in Kenosha," 130; Herlihy, *Bicycle,* 229.

6. Herlihy, *Bicycle,* 229; Goddard, *Colonel Albert Pope,* 87; *The Wheel, A Journal of Cycling* 10 (18 June 1886).

7. Herlihy, *Bicycle,* 235–50 passim.

8. Gormully & Jeffery Mfg. Company, *American Bicycles, 1889,* found in the Benson Ford Research Center, the Henry Ford, Dearborn, Michigan.

9. Miscellaneous Rambler bicycle advertisements, found in folder "Rambler Bicycles," box "Jeffery, 1846–1901," DCHC; Herlihy, *Bicycle*, 290, 292–94; Kimes, "A Family in Kenosha," 132, 133; "T. B. Jeffery Expires in Italy," 23; Rae, *American Automobile Manufacturers, 1889,* 14; Glenn Norcliffe, *The Ride to Modernity: The Bicycle in Canada, 1869–1900* (Toronto: University of Toronto Press, 2001), 107. An American Bicycle Company sales brochure for Rambler and Ideal bicycles for 1901 is found in the collection of bicycle industry papers held by the NAHC.

10. Kimes, "A Family in Kenosha," 132, 133; Hayward, "Thomas B. Jeffery," 14; John A. Conde, "Rambler-Chicago Debutante," *Bulb Horn* 18 (April 1957): 4.

11. Patent 661,697, carburetor, Thomas B. Jeffery, Chicago, Ill., file August 11, 1899, serial no. 726,852 (no model).

12. Kimes, "A Family in Kenosha," 132, 133; "New York Automobile Exhibition," *The Motor Age* 3 (8 November 1900): 383; Gregg D. Merksamer, *A History of the New York International Auto Show, 1900–2000* (Atlanta: Lionheart Books, 2000), 8; "Chicago Had a Big Role in the Development of Auto," *Chicago Sun-Times*, 9 February 1964, V-8; E. C. Oliver, "The Inter-Ocean Tournament," *Horseless Age* 6 (26 September 1900): 11; "Minor Mention," *Horseless Age* 7 (17 October 1900): 15.

13. George S. May, ed., *Encyclopedia of American Business History and Biography: The Automobile Industry, 1896–1920* (New York: Bruccoli Clark Layman, 1990), 393–97; Hiram Percy Maxim, *Horseless Carriage Days* (New York: Harper and Brothers, 1937), 4–5.

14. May, *The Automobile Industry, 1896–1920*, 8–11, 126, 165–67, 176–77, 383, 389–90, 393–97, 452, 462, 468.

15. "T. B. Jeffery Expires in Italy," 24; "Comes to Kenosha: Thomas J. [*sic*] Jeffery, the Well Known Chicago Manufacturer, to Live in This City. Has He Purchased Sterling?" *Kenosha Evening News,*

5 December 1900, 1; "It Brought $65,000: Papers in the Sale of the Sterling Plant Were Passed on Monday Afternoon; For an Automobile Factory," *Kenosha Evening News*, 6 December 1900, 1; *Horseless Age* 6 (12 December 1900): 32; "Trade News from Many Centers," *Motor Vehicle Review* 3 (13 December 1900): 5.

16. Kimes, "A Family in Kenosha," 133. The company letterhead is found in folder 4, box 50, collections of the Kenosha History Center.

17. "Will Be Leaders: What the Plans, Plant and Product of a Kenosha Company Promise," *Motor World* 2 (2 May 1901): 95.

18. Floyd Clymer, "Fifty Years of Progress by Nash," *Automobile Topics*, Nash Golden Anniversary Issue (September 1952): 19; Kimes, "A Family in Kenosha," 133, 135.

19. "What Was Shown at Chicago," *Motor World* 3 (6 March 1902): 599.

20. Rambler advertisement, *Saturday Evening Post*, 17 January 1903; *Rambler Automobile*, Thomas B. Jeffery & Co., General Office and Works, Kenosha, Wisconsin, folder "First Catalog of Rambler automobiles, 1902," box "Jeffery, 1902–1904," DCHC.

21. Kimes, "A Family in Kenosha," 135; John A. Conde, *The American Motors Family Album: A Pictorial Roll Call of the Passenger Cars, Commercial Vehicles, and Trucks Produced by American Motors and Its Predecessor Companies* (Detroit: American Motors Corporation, 1976), 8; "New York to Boston Reliability Test—The First Day's Trip," *Scientific American*, 18 October 1902, 255–56.

22. Beverly Rae Kimes, *Pioneers, Engineers and Scoundrels: The Dawn of the Automobile in America* (Warrendale, PA: SAE International, 2005), 137–39; "Minor Mention," *Horseless Age* 12 (21 October 1903): 444. For the definitive history of the Selden patent, see William Greenleaf, *Monopoly on Wheels: Henry Ford and the Selden Automobile Patent* (Detroit: Wayne State University Press, 1961).

23. "Jeffery and Selden: Kenosha Maker Announced a New Car and Lets Fall Some Remarks Bearing on His Much Discussed Attitude," *Motor World* 6 (3 September 1903): 843.

24. "A Climax Is Near: Action by the License Association Guaranteed—Position of Jeffery and Ford Defined," *Motor World* 7 (1 October 1903): 11–12; "Jeffery's Policy: Will 'Go It Alone' with a Line of Seven Cars at Popular Prices, $650 to $1250—Many Innovations Promised," *Motor World* 7 (8 October 1903): 47–48.

25. Kimes, *Pioneers, Engineers and Scoundrels*, 179, 226, 256–58; Greenleaf, *Monopoly on Wheels*, 233.

26. Thomas Jeffery & Company, *A Little History or A Test of Endurance* (Chicago: Fine Arts Press, 1904), 24. This booklet, which is thirty-two pages long and includes three pages of customers' testimonials in support of the Rambler, is found in folder "1904 Rambler," box "Jeffery, 1904–1906," DCHC.

27. Kimes, "A Family in Kenosha," 135; John A. Gunnell, ed., *Standard Catalog of American Motors, 1902–1987* (Iola, WI: Krause, 1993), 139–40; Kenosha County Historical Society, *Moving Forward: A Transportation Legacy* (Kenosha, WI: Kenosha County Historical Society, 1998), 8.

28. *The Rambler Line in 1906* (product catalog), NAHC; Kimes, "A Family in Kenosha," 138; Gunnell, *Standard Catalog of American Motors*, 140–42; Kenosha County Historical Society, *Moving Forward*, 8.

29. Kimes, "A Family in Kenosha," 135, 138, 145; "Early Auto Maker E. S. Jordan Dies," *Detroit Free Press*, 31 December 1958, 5; "Edward Jordan, Auto-Maker, Dies: Head of Motor Car Concern, 1916–1931, Was a Leader in Industry's Advertising," *New York Times*, 31 December 1958, C-38.

30. Charles K. Hyde, *The Dodge Brothers: The Men, the Motor Cars, and the Legacy* (Detroit: Wayne State University Press, 2005), 67; Allan Nevins and Frank Hill, *Ford: Decline and Rebirth, 1933–1962* (New York: Charles Scribner's Sons, 1962), 71.

31. "The Making of a Motor Car as Seen by a Trip through a Great American Factory," *Motor* 3 (January 1905): 49–52.

32. Thomas B. Jeffery & Company, *A Pictorial Story of the Rambler Factory* (Kenosha, WI, 1907); "Body Building in the Thomas B. Jeffery Automobile Factory," *Carriage Monthly* 16 (February

1911): 90. The Ford Motor Company Piquette Avenue plant in Detroit had a primitive oval test track in 1905, but this was quickly replaced with buildings.

33. Kimes, "A Family in Kenosha," 141–42; "T. B. Jeffery Expires in Italy," 23; "Jeffery Estate Accounting," *Motor Age* 21 (23 May 1912): 44.

34. Jeffery Carqueville to F. L. Black, director of public relations, Nash-Kelvinator, 10 February 1946, folder "Jeffery History," box "Jeffery/Nash, 1917–1919," DCHC.

35. Kimes, "A Family in Kenosha," 141, 143, 145; Gunnell, *Standard Catalog of American Motors*, 142–45; *The Demountable Rim* 3 (5 October 1911): 1–4, found in folder "1912 Rambler (2)," box "Jeffery, 1911–1913," DCHC; "Rambler Drops All But the Cross Country Model," *The Automobile* (21 November 1912): 1080–83.

36. *The Automobile* 29 (30 October 1913): 91.

37. Ibid., 92–96.

38. "The Things Made the Jeffery Four and Six Possible," *Jeffery Circle* (ca. Fall 1913): 20–22, found in folder "Jeffery, 1914," box "Jeffery 1913–1916," DCHC; "Car, Truck and Accessory Plants Plan Increased Production," *The Automobile* 30 (21 May 1914): 1056; Kimes, "A Family in Kenosha," 145; Gunnell, *Standard Catalog of American Motors*, 1435.

39. "Establishing a New Standard of Value at a $1000 Price," *Saturday Evening Post*, 25 September 1915, 51; "A New Standard of Value," *The American Chauffeur—An Automobile Digest* 4 (February 1916): 74; *The Jeffery Four: "America's Standard Automobile at a Thousand Dollar Price"* (Kenosha, WI: Thomas B. Jeffery Company, 1916), found in the archives of the Historical Society of Wisconsin; Alan Nevins and Frank Hill, *Ford: The Times, the Man, the Company* (New York: Charles Scribner's Sons, 1954), 647; Helen Jones Early and James R. Walkinshaw, *Setting the Pace: Oldsmobile's First 100 Years* (Lansing, MI: Oldsmobile Division of General Motors, 1996), 462; Terry B. Dunham and Lawrence R. Gustin, *The Buick: A Complete History*, 6th ed. (New Albany, IN: Automobile Quarterly, 2002), 570.

40. "Giant Jeffery Factory Runs Night and Day to Meet Demand: Army of Employees Increased by 2000—24 Hour Schedule in for Past Two Months," *Chicago Examiner*, 26 January 1916, 16; "Some Class to New Jeffery Buildings," *Jeffery Circle* 1 (29 June 1916): 3; *Jeffery Six, The Car of Mechanical Precision, $1,365* (Kenosha, WI: Nash Motors Company, 1916), 15, found in the archives of the Historical Society of Wisconsin; Gunnell, *Standard Catalog of American Motors*, 146.

41. James C. Mays, *From Kenosha to the World: The Rambler, Jeffery & Nash Truck Story, 1904–1955* (Yellow Springs, OH: Antique Power, 2003), 1, 6–8, 12–14; Conde, *The American Motors Family Album*, 18; Thomas B. Jeffery Company, *The Jeffery Motor Truck* (Kenosha, WI, 1914), found in box "Jeffery, 1913–1916," DCHC.

42. Frederick I. Olson, "Four Wheel Drive Auto Company," in George S. May, ed., *The Automobile Industry, 1896–1920* (New York: Bruccoli Clark Layman, 1990), 226. An in-depth history of this company can be found in Howard William Troyer, *The Four Wheel Drive Story: A Chapter in Cooperative Enterprise* (New York: McGraw-Hill, 1954).

43. Kimes, "A Family in Kenosha," 145; Martin P. Winther, *Eddy-Currents* (Cleveland, OH: Eaton Corporation, 1976), 22. James C. Mays, *From Kenosha to the World*, 15–16, accepts the Kimes chronology.

44. Thomas B. Jeffery Company, *The Jeffery Quad: Drives, Brakes and Steers on All Four Wheels, Efficient in War—Economical in Peace* (Kenosha, WI: Thomas B. Jeffery Company, 1915), 5.

45. *The Story of the Jeffery Quad* (ca. January 1916), 4–6 and J. K. Bond to the truck department of the Thomas B. Jeffery Company, 25 June 1915, both in folder 1, box 50, archives of the Kenosha History Center.

46. "Charles T. Jeffery Tells of Disaster," *Kenosha Evening News*, 15 May 1915; Kimes, "A Family in Kenosha," 145; "The Month in the Motor Industry: Charles W. Nash and Lee Higginson & Co. Buy Thomas B. Jeffery Co.," *Motor* 26 (August 1916): 103.

47. Statistics and rankings are from *The American Car since 1775* (Kutztown, PA: Automobile Quarterly, 1971), 138–39.

CHAPTER TWO

1. I found valuable materials in far-flung archives including the National Automotive History Collection and the Burton Historical Collection at the Detroit Public Library; the DaimlerChrysler Historical Collection; the Richard P. Scharchburg Archives, Kettering University, Flint, Michigan; the Buick Gallery and Research Center at the Alfred P. Sloan Museum in Flint, Michigan; and the Flint Public Library.

2. U.S. Census of Population, 1870, Michigan, Genesee County, Forest Township, 237. The standard national biographical dictionaries devote little space to Charles Nash's life before he entered the automobile industry. See John A. Garraty and Edward T. James, eds., *Dictionary of American Biography, Supplement Four, 1946–1950* (New York: Charles Scribner's Sons, 1950), 620–21; *The National Cyclopaedia of American Biography,* vol. 36 (New York: James T. White, 1950), 50–51; and John A. Garraty and Mark C. Carnes, eds., *American National Biography,* vol. 16 (New York: Oxford University Press, 1999), 235–36. The two most detailed accounts of Nash's early life are a long article, "Fellow Townsmen of Charles W. Nash Pay Him Marked Tribute," *Flint Daily Journal,* 30 November 1912, 1, 2, which describes a banquet in Flint to celebrate Nash's appointment as president of General Motors, and W. A. P. John, "A Dollar Saved Is Worth Two Earned," *Motor* 37 (February 1922): 32–33, 76, 78, based on a lengthy interview John had with Nash.

3. John, "A Dollar Saved," 33; U.S. Census of Population, 1870, Michigan, Genesee County, Flushing Township, 221R; U.S. Census of Population, 1880, Michigan, Genesee County, Flushing Township, 21. The farmer is sometimes identified as "Lathrop," but "Lapworth" is correct. The 1870 census lists a Robert Lapworth, farmer (age 31) living with wife, Mary (30), with no children. By the 1880 census, he has a new wife, Sabrina (33), and sons William (4) and George (2), both born in Michigan. What is more interesting is that the 1880 census shows a George Lapworth in Flushing Township with an adopted son, David Nash (age 14), living with his family. David Nash must be Charles Nash's younger brother, also "orphaned" by the breakup of their parents' marriage.

4. U.S. Population Census, 1870, Genesee County, Grand Blanc, 301, and City of Flint, First Ward, 134; U.S. Population Census, Genesee County, City of Flint, 144; *Polk's Flint City and Genesee County Directory, 1888–9* (Detroit: R. L. Polk, 1889), 116, 318.

5. "Fellow Townsmen of Charles W. Nash," 2; John, "A Dollar Saved," 33; Norman G. Shidle, "To Succeed, Deal Sincerely with Men, Watch Factory Overhead—Says Chas. W. Nash," *Automotive Industries* 52 (11 June 1925): 1012; "Charles W. Nash Started Famous Career from Deal in Ten Sheep on Farm," *Old Timers News* 3 (October 1945): 13.

6. Charles B. Glasscock, *The Gasoline Age: The Story of the Men Who Made It* (New York: Bobbs-Merrill, 1937), 152.

7. "Merger Spotlight Centered on C. W. Nash and G. W. Mason," *Kenosha Telegraph-Courier,* 29 October 1936, 7.

8. John, "A Dollar Saved," 33.

9. Thomas J. Noer, "Charles W. Nash: Self-Made Man," in Nicholas C. Burckel and John A. Neuenschwander, eds., *Kenosha Retrospective: A Biographical Approach* (Kenosha, WI: Kenosha County Bicentennial Commission, 1981), 114; "Fellow Townsmen of Charles Nash," 2; U.S. Population Census, 1880, Genesee County, Burton Township, 12, and Mt. Morris, 21; *Polk's Flint City and Genesee County Directory, 1881–2* (Detroit: R. L. Polk, 1882), 218; *Polk's Flint City and Genesee County Directory, 1888–9,* 134, 144, 334, 344.

10. "Fellow Townsmen of Charles W. Nash," 2; John, "A Dollar Saved," 76; "Charles Nash Started Famous Career," 13; *Flint City and Genesee County Directory, 1892–3* (Detroit: R. L. Polk, 1893), 71, 199.

11. W. C. Durant to Charles W. Nash, 29 January 1942, folder D74-2.10, William C. Durant Papers, SA/KU. Lawrence R. Gustin, *Billy Durant, Creator of General Motors* (Grand Rapids, MI: Eerdmans, 1973), 39–40, accepts Durant's account.

12. "Fellow Townsmen of Charles W. Nash," 2; Shidle, "To Succeed, Deal Sincerely with Men," 1012; "Charles Nash Started Famous Career," 13. An article in *Carriage Monthly* 48 (January 1913): 53, confirms the plum story.

13. Gustin, *Billy Durant,* 17–25, 38–39, 41.

14. Frank Rodolf, "An Industrial History of Flint," unpublished book manuscript (1949), 78; Gustin, *Billy Durant,* 45, 49; *Flint Journal,* 9 June 1898. The Rodolf manuscript is in the Automotive History Collection of the Flint Public Library. The photograph of 9 June 1898 is in the private automotive history collection of Leroy D. Cole.

15. Gustin, *Billy Durant,* 41–48.

16. Durant-Dort Carriage Company, minutes of the board of directors meetings, 21 October 1900, and minutes of subsequent annual stockholders' meetings, 1901–12, SM; Gustin, *Billy Durant,* 45, 49–50; Rodolf, "Industrial History of Flint," 78, 120.

17. Durant-Dort Carriage Company minutes, 9 July 1901, 17 August 1901, and 8 February 1902, SM.

18. Rodolf, "Industrial History of Flint," 96–97; Durant-Dort Carriage Company minutes, 14 September 1900, 14 September 1901, 8 September 1903, 11 September 1909, 12 September 1912, 24 May 1913, and 29 August 1913, SM; Robert G. Schafer, *J. Dallas Dort: Citizen Compleat* (Flint: University of Michigan-Flint Archives, 1986), 10–11.

19. Untitled account book, Charles Nash biography file, NAHC.

20. Scottish-born David Dunbar Buick (1854–1929) came to the United States at age two and made a fortune in Detroit in the manufacturing of plumbing fixtures. He invented and patented a method for getting porcelain to adhere to cast iron sinks, tubs, and toilets. In the late 1890s, Buick began tinkering with gasoline engines for small boats and then larger engines for automobiles. He launched the Buick Auto-Vim and Power Company (1900–1902) and the Buick Manufacturing Company (1902–3) to make engines and automobiles. He built his first experimental automobile in April 1901, but kept experimenting with various engines over the next several years without producing a car he could sell. See Gustin, *Billy Durant,* 56–58.

21. Ibid., 58–61.

22. Ibid., 62–77; Bernard A. Weisberger, *The Dream Maker: William C. Durant, Founder of General Motors* (Boston: Little, Brown, 1979), 83–97; Arthur Pound, *The Turning Wheel: The Story of General Motors through Twenty-Five Years, 1908–1933* (Garden City, NY: Doubleday, Doran, 1934), 79–80; Carl Crowe, *The City of Flint Grows Up: The Success Story of an American Community* (New York: Harper and Brothers, 1945), 62–63; George Humphrey Maines, *Men . . . a City . . . and Buick* (Flint: Advertisers Press, 1953), 9.

23. Gustin, *Billy Durant,* 111–23; Weisberger, *The Dream Maker,* 132–42.

24. Gustin, *Billy Durant,* 136–44; Weisberger, *The Dream Maker,* 147–52.

25. Storrow, the son of a notable Boston attorney, graduated from Harvard Law School in 1889 and worked for eleven years for the law firm of Fish, Richardson & Storrow, which took care of the legal affairs of Lee, Higginson & Company. Storrow became a partner in Lee Higginson in 1900. He became an active force in the management of General Motors in 1910–16 and in Nash Motors thereafter. See "James J. Storrow," *Automobile Topics* 81 (20 March 1926): 504.

26. Pearson, *Son of New England,* 128; John, "A Dollar Saved," 76; Terry B. Dunham and Lawrence R. Gustin, *The Buick: A Complete History,* 6th ed. (New Albany, IN: Automobile Quarterly Publications, 2002), 84; James J. Storrow to C. W. Nash, 27 May 1912, Leroy Cole Collection.

27. Dunham and Gustin, *The Buick,* 84, 86; "Fellow Townsmen of Charles W. Nash," 2.

28. Dunham and Gustin, *The Buick,* 86, 551; Walter P. Chrysler, in collaboration with Boyden Sparkes, *Life of an American Workman* (New York: Dodd, Mead and Company, 1950), 117–27, 134–36, 141–43. For a more detailed discussion of Chrysler's improvements at the Buick factory, see Dunham and Gustin, *The Buick,* 89, and Charles K. Hyde, *Riding the Roller Coaster: A History of the Chrysler Corporation* (Detroit: Wayne State University Press, 2003), 6–7.

29. Rae, *American Automobile Manufacturers,* 89; Albert N. Marquis, ed., *The Book of Detroiters: A Biographical Dictionary of the Leading Living Men of the City of Detroit* (Chicago: A. N. Marquis,

1908), 341; Pearson, *Son of New England*, 135–36; Rodolf, "Industrial History of Flint," 257; *New York World*, 12 July 1912; "C. W. Nash Succeeded Thomas Neal as President of the General Motors Company," *Automobile Trade Journal* 17 (1 December 1912): 79b.

30. Found in folder "C. W. Nash Biography," box "C .W. Nash," DaimlerChrysler Archives.
31. Rae, *American Automobile Manufacturers*, 94–97.
32. "Fellow Townsmen of Charles W. Nash," 2.
33. Chrysler, *Life of an American Workman*, 138 (quote), 140–41.
34. "Branch Managers at Country Club: Dinner Marks Close of Annual Meeting; Discuss Future of Buick; 'Buick Six' Is Advocated for 1914 Season," *Flint Journal*, 10 July 1912, 7; Dunham and Gustin, *The Buick*, 96–98, 551.
35. James J. Storrow to Richard H. Collins, Esq., general sales manager, Buick Motor Company, 18 May 1915, Leroy Cole Collection.
36. James J. Storrow to Charles W. Nash, president, General Motors Company, 9 July 1915, Leroy Cole Collection.
37. Gustin, *Billy Durant*, 145–81 passim; Weisberger, *The Dream Maker*, 153–77, 185–95 passim.
38. James J. Storrow to Hugh G. Levick, 24 September 1915, Leroy Cole Collection.
39. Dr. Edwin R. Campbell to W. C. Durant, 12 September 1915; W. C. Durant to Dr. E. R. Campbell, 16 September 1915; and Edward R. Campbell to W. C. Durant, undated but ca. 24 September 1915, all in folder D74-2.7B, William C. Durant Papers, SA/KU.
40. Weisberger, *The Dream Maker*, 195–99; series of telegrams between Durant and Nash, 13–15 March 1916; telegram, Emory Clark to W. C. Durant, 17 March 1916; W. C. Durant to Dr. E. R. Campbell, 26 March 1916, folders D74-2.7B and 2.8B, all in William C. Durant Papers, SA/KU.
41. General Motors Company, minutes of the meeting of the board of directors, 1 June 1916, copy in the Leroy Cole Collection; Dunham and Gustin, *The Buick*, 101–3; "Nash's Resignation Credibly Reported: President of General Motors Said to Have Retired Last Week—News Not Unexpected in View of Recent Shift in Control," *Automobile Topics* 42 (20 May 1916): 42; "Durant President of General Motors: Nash to Fill Out Year in Advisory Capacity," *Automobile Topics* 42 (3 June 1916): 320, 326.
42. Memorandum, "The Chrysler Incident," folder D74-2.1A, William Durant Papers, SA/KU; Chrysler, *Life of an American Workman*, 143–45; Gustin, *Billy Durant*, 177–78, 181–83; Weisberger, *The Dream Maker*, 200–201.
43. Chrysler, *Life of an American Workman*, 137.
44. Pearson, *Son of New England*, 142–44.
45. James J. Storrow to Walter P. Chrysler, 27 July 1916, reprinted in Pearson, *Son of New England*, 143.
46. *Automobile Topics* 116 (29 December 1934): 460; Beverly Rae Kimes, "Blueprints and Balance Sheets—The Company That Charlie Built," *Automobile Quarterly* 15 (second quarter 1977): 119; Karla A. Rosenbusch, "Climbing His Own Ladder: The Elevation of Charles Nash," *Automobile Quarterly* 35 (July 1996): 22.
47. "Nash Takes Over Jeffery Company: Former General Motors Head Buys Out Jeffery Family, Assuming Full Control—Lee, Higginson & Co. Join in Big Business Operation," *Automobile Topics* 42 (22 July 1916): 1061, 1068.
48. "The Month in the Motor Industry," *Motor* 26 (August 1916): 103; "Nash Motors Co. Forming in Maryland: Takes Over Business of Jeffery Motor Company of Kenosha, Wis.," *Flint Journal*, 3 August 1916.
49. "Gentlemen, Meet Mr. C. W. Nash—Our New Executive Head," *Jeffery Circle* 1, no. 1 (3 August 1916), n.p., folder "Jeffery, 1913–1916," box "Jeffery, 1913–1916," DCHC.

CHAPTER THREE

1. *The American Car since 1775* (Kutztown, PA: Automobile Quarterly, 1971), 138, 141.
2. "In Seventeen Years Nash Motors Grew and Prospered," *Automobile Topics* 116 (29 December

1934): 461; Beverly Rae Kimes, "Blueprints and Balance Sheets—The Company That Charlie Built," *Automobile Quarterly* 15 (second quarter 1977): 120.

3. Ibid.

4. "An Important Announcement by C. W. Nash, President, The Nash Motors Company, *Cleveland Plain Dealer*, 11 March 1917, 5-B.

5. "Nash Motors," *Motor World* 50 (28 March 1917): 4.

6. "Factory Chiefs Powwow for Bigger Production: Output Boosters Meet Once Weekly; Foremen and Others Get Together and Work Out Production Plans and Solve Problems," *Jeffery Circle* 1, no. 6 (October 1916): 1; "Story of Nash Goes Deep into Kenosha History: Pioneer Ramblers, Jeffery Cars Preceded Famous Nash Models," *Kenosha Evening News*, 17 September 1946, 1.

7. Kimes, "Blueprints and Balance Sheets," 120; "In Seventeen Years Nash Motors Grew and Prospered," 461–62; summaries of Jeffery and Nash production found in the DCHC.

8. *Full Speed Ahead! The Story of the Nash Idea at Work in the Great Nash Factory,* copyright, the Nash Motors Company, found in folder "1917 Nash," box "Jeffery/Nash, 1917–19," DCHC.

9. For Henry Ford's production practices and his use of specialized machines at the Highland Park plant, see Horace Lucien Arnold and Fay Leone Faurote, *Ford Methods and the Ford Shops* (New York: Engineering Magazine, 1915); and David A. Hounshell, *From the American System to Mass Production, 1800–1932: The Development of Manufacturing in the United States* (Baltimore: Johns Hopkins University Press, 1984).

10. John A. Gunnell, ed., *Standard Catalog of American Motors, 1902–1987* (Iola, WI: Krause, 1993), 147, 154; Kimes, "Blueprints and Balance Sheets," 120; "Nash Announce [*sic*]—Perfected Valve-in-Head—Known as 'The Nash Six,'" *The American Chauffeur—An Automobile Digest* (5 October 1917): 552–53.

11. Gunnell, *Standard Catalog of American Motors*, 154–56; Kimes, "Blueprints and Balance Sheets," 124.

12. Kimes, "Blueprints and Balance Sheets," 120; "Nash Dealers Have Big Meeting," *Automobile Topics* 52 (18 January 1919): 1097; "In Seventeen Years Nash Motors Grew and Prospered," 462; James C. Mays, *From Kenosha to the World: The Rambler, Jeffery & Nash Truck Story, 1904–1955* (Yellow Springs, OH: Antique Power, 2003), 48. Mays gives a total of 9,277 Quads in his text, but adding the individual Quad model figures yields a total of 9,721.

13. "No Quad Royalties," *Automotive Industries* 39 (4 July 1918): 42. Contract information regarding the Nash Quad truck includes "Contract, Nash Motors Company and the U.S.A.," 13 April 1918; "License to Manufacture Nash Quad Trucks and Parts Thereof, Made by the Chief of Ordnance with the Nash Motors Company," 25 April 1918, found in files 1 and 15, respectively, box 15, Jeffery/Nash Papers, Seaver Center for Western History Research, Natural History Museum of Los Angeles County, Los Angeles; contracts for Paige-Detroit Motor Car Company (27 May 1918), Hudson Motor Car Company (28 May 1918), and National Motor and Vehicle Corporation (27 June 1918) to manufacture Nash Quad trucks for the U.S. government, found in files 23 and 24, box 22, Jeffery/Nash Papers, Seaver Center. The fourth licensee, the Premier Motor Corporation, is identified in Mays, *From Kenosha to the World,* 31.

14. "Nash Plows Acres of Gardens: Head of Big Motors Plant Shows Personal Interest in Boosting Conservation Movement, Asks Employees to Farm," *Kenosha Telegraph-Courier*, 26 April 1917, 7; "Nash Sounds Call for Patriotic Duty: President of Great Motors Co. Calls for the Highest Form of Patriotic Actions as Thousands Cheer at Patriotic Demonstration Incidental to the Raising of Old Glory," *Kenosha Telegraph-Courier*, 3 May 1917, 2; Thomas J. Noer, "Charles W. Nash: Self-Made Man," in Nicholas C. Burckel and John A. Neuenschwander, eds., *Kenosha Retrospective: A Biographical Approach* (Kenosha, WI: Kenosha County Bicentennial Commission, 1981), 120, 121.

15. "Motor Executive and Wife Observe 50th Anniversary, *Kenosha Telegraph-Courier,* 26 April 1934, 3; "C. W. Nash to Aid Ryan in Aircraft," *Automobile Topics* 50 (20 July 1918): 1083; "Government Picks Executives Wisely: Nash Motors Progress Factor in Selecting Its Head for Important Post—Men of Trust Considered Trustworthy—Accustomed to Big Things," *Automobile Topics* 51 (10

August 1918): 26; "Charles W. Nash Returns to His Own at Kenosha," *Automobile Topics* 52 (23 November 1918): 214.

16. Benedict Crowell and Robert Forrest Wilson, *The Armies of Industry: Our Nation's Manufacture of Munitions for a World in Arms, 1917–1918*, 2 vols. (New Haven: Yale University Press, 1921) passim; Michael W. R. Davis, *Detroit's Wartime Industry: Arsenal of Democracy* (Charleston, SC: Arcadia, 2007), 9–16; Charles K. Hyde, *The Dodge Brothers: The Men, the Motor Cars and the Legacy* (Detroit: Wayne State University Press, 2005), 92–94, 96–104.

17. *Nash News* 1, no. 2 (April 1917); Nash Motors Company, *Buy Your Truck to Fit Your Individual Needs; Saturday Evening Post,* 24 November 1917, 87; Nash Motors Company, *Nash Motor Trucks* (1918), folder "1917 Jeffery/Nash and 1918 Nash trucks," box "Jeffery/Nash, 1917–19," DCHC.

18. Kimes, "Blueprints and Balance Sheets," 120; Winther, *Eddy-Currents*, 24; Mays, *From Kenosha to the World*, 38–39, 51, 54–57.

19. "One Hundred Years of Craftsmanship: The Story behind the Seaman Body Division, Nash-Kelvinator Corporation," folder "Seaman History, 1846–91," box "Jeffery, 1846–1901," DCHC.

20. Ibid.; "New Sedan Completes Closed Car Line," *The Nash Times, A Newspaper Devoted to the Interests of Nash Dealers* 1 (September 1922): 1; "The Craftsman Spirit Prevails in the Seaman Organization," *Automobile Topics* 116 (29 December 1934): 436; Harold H. Seaman to Charles W. Nash, 16 July 1936 (offer to sell Seaman shares), folder "Seaman History," box "Seaman Body History, 1846–1954," DCHC; "Seaman Bros. Leave Nash Body Division: Retire to Private Affairs; Weiland Heads Plant," *Automobile Topics* 130 (16 May 1938): 95.

21. Kimes, "Blueprints and Balance Sheets," 122; "Lafayette Motors New Nash Project: Six Million Dollar Concern to Make Car Developed by Howard and McCall White—Lee Higginson Backs Company to Build High Grade Car," *Automobile Topics* 55 (October 1919): 1059, 1070.

22. "Lafayette Built for the Particular Buyer: Advanced Features Produce Lasting Design—Body Offerings Feature Elaborate Equipment," *Automobile Topics* 56 (24 January 1920): 1489–92; Kimes, "Blueprints and Balance Sheets," 124. Production figures are from Gunnell, *The Standard Catalog of American Motors*, 148–50.

23. "New Sedan Completes Closed Car Line," 1–3; John A. Conde, *The Cars That Hudson Built* (Keego Harbor, MI: Arnold-Porter Publishing, 1980), 44; Kimes, "Blueprints and Balance Sheets," 124–25.

24. "Nash Adds Smaller Six and Drops Four Cylinder Models," *Automotive Industries* 51 (31 July 1924): 231–36; "Nash Advances with Strong New Line: Offers Complete String of Sixes at Competitive Prices—Four Wheel Brakes and Balloon Tires Featured," *Automobile Topics* 74 (2 August 1924): 1136–39; "Nash Brings out New Model Sixes: Eleven Body Styles Offered on Special and Advanced Chassis—New Line of Seaman Bodies a Striking Attraction," *Automobile Topics* 74 (25 July 1925): 1027–28; "Nash Has 'Enclosed Car' Engine: Made More Powerful to Take Care of Heavier Demands—New Advanced Sedan, Roadster and Special Coupe Offered," *Automobile Topics* 80 (9 January 1926): 841, 846.

25. Terry B. Dunham and Lawrence R. Gustin, *The Buick: A Complete History*, 6th ed. (New Albany, IN: Automobile Quarterly, 2002), 571; Helen Jones Early and James R. Walkinshaw, *Setting the Pace: Oldsmobile's First 100 Years* (Lansing, MI: General Motors Corporation, 1996), 464; James T. Lenzke, ed., *Standard Catalog of Chrysler, 1914–2000* (Iola, WI: Krause, 200), 188; "Nash Advances with Strong New Line," 1136; "$1,000,000 Extension Approved by Nash: Huge Program Arranged for Enlarging Factory at Kenosha, Wis.—Plants Running at Full Tilt—New Record for November Is Expected," *Automobile Topics* 76 (22 November 1924): 115.

26. "Receiver Appointed to Act for Mitchell: Appointment Follows Bankruptcy Petition by Three Creditors," *Automotive Industries* 48 (19 April 1923): 901; "Nash to Build Cars in the Mitchell Plant in Racine: $405,000 Is Price Paid by C. W. Nash for Entire Mitchell Holdings," *Motor Age* 45 (7 February 1924): 44.

27. "Ajax Car Will Make Its Bow on May 27: Racine, Wis. Declares Holiday in Honor of the Event—First Sedan to Lead Street Parade and Be Awarded as Prize—Public to Inspect Plant," *Automobile Topics* 78 (16 May 1925): 19; "Ajax Car Unveiled," *Automobile Topics* 78 (16 May 1925): 221;

W. L. Carver, "Nash-Built Ajax Announced," *Automotive Industries* 52 (28 May 1925): 931–35; "Racine Papers Present Special 'Ajax' Editions: C. W. Nash and New Car Lauded by Press and Officials," *Automobile Topics* 78 (20 June 1925): 506; Kimes, "Blueprints and Balance Sheets," 128, 130; Gunnell, *Standard Catalog of American Motors,* 156.

28. *The American Car since 1975* (Kutztown, PA: Automobile Quarterly, 1971), 141; Rudolph Hokanson, *What Nash Motors Means to Wisconsin: Facts Worth Knowing about Our Great State* (Milwaukee: Nash Motors, 1926).

29. John C. Gourlie, "Financial History of Nash Motors Is Impressive," *Automotive Industries* 57 (10 December 1927): 858–60.

30. "Nash Will Add to His Plants: Auto Maker Orders $1,200,000 Expansion; Will Build Up Output at Racine," *Detroit News*, 25 September 1927, sec. 10, p. 1; "Nash Reaches a New Peak: Daily Production of New Series Is Now More Than 1,000 Cars," *Detroit News*, 2 September 1928, sec. 10, p. 2.

31. Kimes, "Blueprints and Balance Sheets," 133–35; Gunnell, *Standard Catalog of American Motors,* 158–59; "Nash 400 Series Offers Two Sixes and One Eight," *Automotive Daily News* 10 (27 January 1930): 35; "Nash Introduces Its First Twin-Ignition 8 Phaeton," *Automotive Daily News* 10 (4 March 1930): 1.

32. "James J. Storrow," *Automobile Topics* 81 (20 March 1926): 504; Kimes, "Blueprints and Balance Sheets," 134; "Nash Motors Elects New Vice-President," *Detroit News*, 28 February 1928, sec. 10, p. 2; "McCarty President of Nash Motors Co.," *Automobile Topics* 104 (16 January 1932): 829, 835; "E. H. McCarty Worked Up through the Selling End," *Automobile Topics* 116 (29 December 1934): 404, 420. The quotation is from Pearson, *Son of New England*, 144.

33. "Nash Offers Four Distinctive Engine Designs in Four 1931 Models," *Automotive Industries* 63 (11 October 1930): 524–26; "Nash Adopts Synchronizing Clutches and Oil Temperature Control," *Automotive Industries* 64 (27 June 1931): 1001, 1012, 1014.

34. "Nash Makes Best of a Poor Market: Begins Third Quarter on a Profit Basis," *Automobile Topics* 105 (25 June 1932): 409; "Nash Dividend Cut Improves Its Position," *Automobile Topics* 105 (16 July 1932): 575; "Nash Co. Follows a Conservative Policy," *Automobile Topics* 107 (1 October 1932): 414; "Nash Controlled Operations Closely," *Automobile Topics* 107 (8 October 1932): 470; "Nash Cars Built to ORDER," *Automobile Topics* 166 (29 December 1934): 455, 469.

35. Alfred P. Sloan Jr., *My Years with General Motors* (Garden City, NY: Doubleday, 1964), 127–32.

36. Kimes, "Blueprints and Balance Sheets," 136–38; Gunnell, *Standard Catalog of American Motors,* 161–62.

37. "The LaFayette Makes Debut: Nash-Built Car Enters Low-Priced Field—Only New Name of Year," *Detroit News*, 21 January 1934, sec. 8, p. 13; "LaFayette Has New Springing: Friction-Controlling Inserts Rid Car of Bouncing and Pitching," *Detroit News*, 13 January 1935, sec. 6, p. 15; "Looking to the Future in LaFayette," *Automobile Topics* 116 (29 December 1934): 429, 430; "Nash-LaFayette Progress," 1935, folder "1935 Nash and Lafayette," box "Nash, 1929–1935," DCHC; Kimes, "Blueprints and Balance Sheets," 138.

38. "McCarty President of Nash Motors Co.: Promotion of Vice-President Follows Long Record of Success with Company; Charles W. Nash Continues as Chairman of Board," *Automobile Topics* 104 (16 January 1932): 829, 835.

39. "'Men and Methods' Management Methods Used by Two Corporation Presidents to Pilot Their Businesses to Positions of Recognized Leadership," *System* 49 (April 1926): 526; Norman G. Shidle, "To Succeed, Deal Sincerely with Men, Watch Factory Overhead—Says Chas. W. Nash," *Automotive Industries* 52 (11 June 1925): 1015; "Motor Executive and Wife Observe 50th Anniversary."

40. "Nash and His Methods," *System and Business Management* 5 (September 1935): 11–13.

41. C. W. Nash, "Purchasing for a Fast Rate of Turnover in the Plant," *Factory and Industrial Management* 75 (January 1928): 51.

42. Charles W. Nash, "The Dealer Takes the Limelight: Bankers' Confidence and Sound Policies Mark the Trade's Established Position," *Automobile Topics* 53 (8 February 1919): 89, 90; Charles

W. Nash, "The Automobile Dealer Has Rights: He Should Be Regarded as a Partner by the Factory; He Is the Industry's Greatest Asset; The Saturation Point Is Discussed; Production Must Be Limited to Fit the Demand," *Motor* 43 (March 1925): 30, 31.

43. Shidle, "To Succeed, Deal Sincerely with Men," 1014; "Nash Cars Built to ORDER," 455; "Nash Gives Dealers Increased Profits: Discount on Four-Cylinder Models Increased Three Per Cent— Made Retroactive to July 1, 1923—Increase Is Given Dealers Voluntarily," *Automobile Topics* 72 (12 January 1924): 929.

44. "Kenasha Club Starts with Rousing Send-Off: President C. W. Nash Promises His Employees Help," *Automobile Topics* 62 (6 August 1921): 1064; "Nash Gives Baseball Stadium," *Automobile Topics* 70 (26 May 1923): 125; "Scenes from Our Opening Day, May 12, 1923: Park Opening One Big Day," *Ke-Nash-A Club News* 2 (May 1923): 1; B. C. Forbes, "Nash Knew What He Wanted— and He Got It," *Forbes* 17 (15 January 1926): 46; Noer, "Charles W. Nash," 125; Karla A. Rosenbusch, "Climbing His Own Ladder: The Elevation of Charles Nash," *Automobile Quarterly* 35 (July 1996): 27; *Ke-Nash-A Club News* 4 (June 1925): 8, and 7 (July 1928): 10.

45. "25,000 Factory Folk at Picnic: Nash Annual Outing Largest Ever Held—Milwaukee and Racine Divisions Participate," *Ke-Nash-A Club News* 5 (August 1926): 1.

46. Noer, "Charles W. Nash," 124, 135.

47. Angela Howard Zophy, "UAW Local 72: Assertive Union," in Burckel and Neuenschwander, *Kenosha Retrospective*, 298–301.

48. Steve Babson, *Working Detroit* (Detroit: Wayne State University Press, 1985), 61–63, 75–77, 84–86.

49. Noer, "Charles W. Nash," 135.

50. Ibid., 136, 138; Kimes, "Blueprints and Balance Sheets," 138.

51. "Nash-Kelvinator," *Fortune* 15 (April 1937): 95.

52. Ibid.

53. Ibid., 140; Christy Borth, "Corporate Durability Is an Old Tradition," *Ward's Quarterly* 1 (Spring 1965): 98.

54. Borth, "Corporate Durability Is an Old Tradition."

55. Ibid.; Kelvinator Corporation and Subsidiaries, *Second Annual Report, Fiscal Year Ending September 30, 1928* and *Third Annual Report, Fiscal Year Ending September 30, 1929,* NAHC; "Woodbridge Quits Kelvinator Offices: George W. Mason Succeeds Him as President," *Detroit News,* 22 January 1929, 35; "Merger of Nash and Kelvinator Approved; Mason New President: Capital Stock of Motors Firm Will Be Increased," *Milwaukee Sentinel,* 29 October 1936, 1.

56. Kelvinator Corporation and Subsidiaries, *Annual Report* for years 1929–36, DCHC; "Nash-Kelvinator," *Fortune* 15 (April 1937): 97, 99, 140, 142; "2 Kelvinator Units Planned: $600,000 for Expansion, Company Announces," *Detroit News,* 9 September 1936, 19; "Kelvinator to Enter Washing Machine Field," *Detroit News,* 21 September 1936, 29.

57. Alfred P. Sloan Jr., *My Years with General Motors* (Garden City, NY: Doubleday, 1964), 354–61.

58. "Kelvinator Merger to Unite $55,000,000 Assets," *Michigan Manufacturing and Financial Record* 58 (31 October 1936): 3, 4; "Nash-Kelvinator Merger in Offing: Stockholders Expected to Vote Speedy Approval of Plan," *Automobile Topics* 124 (2 November 1936): 3, 7; "Nash-Kelvinator Merger in Offing: Biggest Undertaking of Its Kind since the Depression," *Automobile Topics* 124 (21 December 1936): 389, 397; "Nash-Kelvinator Merger Approved: Stockholders of Both Companies Vote Ratification," *Automobile Topics* 124 (28 December 1936): 423.

59. "Nash-Kelvinator Names Directors," *Detroit News,* 14 January 1937, 39; "Nash-Kelvinator Directors Named," *Michigan Manufacturer and Financial Record* 59 (16 January 1937): 4; "Nash Dealers Greet the New President: Mason Inspires Distributing Organization with New Confidence," *Automobile Topics* 124 (25 January 1937): 583; "Kelvinator Men Dominate Merger," *Detroit News,* 26 February 1937, 38; "Nash-Kelvinator Corp. Elects 7 Directors: Two Former Nash Men Included," *Automobile Topics* 125 (1 March 1937): 154; "Staff of Nash Has Moved to Detroit," *Detroit News,* 2 January 1938, sec. 1, p. 8.

60. Rosenbusch, "Climbing His Own Ladder," 28, 29; "Death Takes Wife of Charles W. Nash,"

Detroit News, 19 August 1947, 1; "C. W. Nash Dies at 84 on Coast: Auto Pioneer Was Production Genius," *Detroit News,* 7 June 1948, 1, 7; "Nash Funds Left to G. P. Daughter," *Detroit News,* 15 June 1948, 1.

61. "Charles Nash Notebook of European Trip," folder "1910 notebook," box "Charles Nash," DCHC; "C. W. Nash Takes Family Abroad: General Manager of Buick Combines Business with Pleasure," *The Buick Bulletin* 1 (5 June 1913): 1, Leroy Cole Collection; "Nash Goes after Grizzlies," *Automobile Topics* 74 (2 August 1924): 114, 1136; "When Indoor Jobs Give Way to Outdoor Minds," *Automobile Topics* 68 (16 December 1922): 441; photograph of Nash with walleye pike, *Automobile Topics* 98 (5 July 1930): 698.

62. Noer, "Charles W. Nash," 127; Rosenbusch, "Climbing His Own Ladder," 29; "Motor Executive and Wife Observe 50th Anniversary." Several sources claim that Nash purchased Thomas Jeffery's house, but the house Nash occupied by 1918 (512 Durkee Avenue, later 6221 Third Avenue) was built for Charles Jeffery in 1904 and he is listed in the Kenosha city directories as living in the house until 1916. Thomas Jeffery's house was listed as vacant in 1918.

63. Noer, "Charles W. Nash," 127–28.

64. "Nash Blackmailer Meets with Arrest: Sought to Extort $10,000 from C. W. Nash," *Automobile Topics* 80 (19 December 1925): 509; "Nash Undergoes Operation," *Automobile Topics* 82 (22 May 1926): 128.

65. Shidle, "To Succeed, Deal Sincerely with Men," 1014; Noer, "Charles W. Nash," 122; John, "A Dollar Saved," 78.

66. "Gift of $400,000 to YMCA Is Kenosha's Biggest: Nash Gift to YMCA Brings Joy to Many; With Mrs. Nash He Has Given Over Half Million Dollars," *Kenosha Evening News,* 29 July 1936, 28; "Boy Scout Camp Presented to Kenosha: Scout Camp Is Gift of Nash to City's Boys; 70-Acre Site Presented to Kenosha Council by Nash in 1929," *Kenosha Evening News,* 29 July 1936, 30; Father Edward J. Flanagan to C. W. Nash, 21 July 1947, Charles Nash biography file, NAHC.

67. "Fellow Townsmen of Charles W. Nash Pay Him Marked Tribute," *Flint Daily Journal,* 30 November 1912, 2; Clarence H. Young and William A. Quinn, *Foundation for Living: The Story of Charles Stewart Mott and Flint* (New York: McGraw-Hill, 1963), 57–58.

68. "Charles W. Nash," *Detroit News,* 8 June 1948, 22.

CHAPTER FOUR

1. Nash-Kelvinator Corporation, *Annual Report for 1938,* NAHC.

2. John A. Gunnell, ed., *Standard Catalog of American Motors, 1902–1987* (Iola, WI: Krause, 1993), 163, 169; 1940 Nash advertisement.

3. Kathleen Franz, *Tinkering: Consumers Reinvent the Early Automobile* (Philadelphia: University of Pennsylvania Press, 2005), 32–37, 85–91; Warren James Belasco, *Americans on the Road: From Autocamp to Motel, 1910–1945* (Cambridge, MA: MIT Press, 1979), 41–127 passim.

4. Nash-Kelvinator Corporation, *Annual Report for 1940,* NAHC; American Motors Corporation, *Nash Family Album* (Detroit: American Motors Corporation, 1954), 58; Gunnell, *Standard Catalog of American Motors,* 166.

5. Allan Nevins and Frank Ernest Hill, *Ford: Decline and Rebirth, 1933–1962* (New York: Charles Scribner's Sons, 1962), 131; Gunnell, *Standard Catalog of American Motors,* 418; John Gunnell, ed., *Standard Catalog of Chevrolet, 1912–2003* (Iola, WI: Krause, 2003), 45.

6. H. D. Beutlich, Nash Motors director of personnel, to George Kiebler, UAW International Representative, 9 February, 15 February, and 2 March 1938; George Kiebler to H. D. Beutlich, 14 and 24 February 1938; Nash Motors to all employees, 1 February and 2 March 1938; announcement made to UAW Local 72 by the Executive Board, International Union, UAW Local 72, found in folder "1938 Nash," box "Nash, 1922–1938," DCHC; "Settlement Sends 6,000 Back at Nash," *Detroit News,* 21 October 1939, 5; "Production Is Resumed at Nash Motors," *Detroit News,* 24 October 1939, 27.

7. "Nash Sales Program Outlined to Dealers: 2,615 Car Driveway Sets 24 Year Record," *Automobile*

Topics 135 (4 September 1939): 169; "Important Instructions on Biggest Drive-Away in Nash History, Kenosha, Tuesday, August 29, 1939," folder "Nash, 1939," box 4, "Nash-Kelvinator, 1939," DCHC; "Nash-Kelvinator Expanding Plant," *Detroit News*, 10 July 1940, 27.

8. "Nash Reports Record Profit: 1941 Earnings Are Largest since Merger," *Detroit News*, 5 December 1941, 42; "Nash-Kelvinator to Spend $10,000,000 for Reconversion," *Michigan Manufacturer and Financial Record* 76 (8 December 1945): 5; "The Nash Tunes Up: The Automobile Race Is On, to Get Up Ahead, Nash Banks on Its Good Name, Low Eight, Fewer Dealers, and Its Corporate Half-Sister, Kelvinator," *Fortune* 32 (September 1945): 250.

9. "Introduction to the World War II History of the Nash-Kelvinator Corporation," p. 2, folder "World War II History," World War II Production Series, box 4, "Nash-Kelvinator War Production, 1942–1945," DCHC; Charles K. Hyde, *Riding the Roller Coaster: A History of the Chrysler Corporation* (Detroit: Wayne State University Press, 2003), 134.

10. "Introduction," 3.

11. Ibid., 17–19; "Nash Makes Flying Boats: Navy Air Transport Latest Undertaking," *Detroit News*, 4 June 1942, 44; "Pacific Air Drive Hinted: Navy Cancels Nash Cargo Plane Contract," *Detroit News*, 22 November 1942, sec. 1, p. 8.

12. "Introduction," 4, 5.

13. Ibid., 5, 6; "U.S. Buys REO Building for Defense Work: Nash to Build Propellers in Part of Plant," *Lansing State Journal*, 19 May 1941, 1.

14. "Lansing Plant About Ready: Old REO Factory to Make Bomber Propellers," *Detroit News*, 22 September 1941, 6.

15. Nomination of Nash-Kelvinator Corporation Propeller Division for the Army-Navy "E" Production Award, 28 January 1943, folder "World War II History," World War II Production Series, box 4, "Nash-Kelvinator War Production, 1942–1945," DCHC; "New Defense Job to Nash-Kelvinator," *Detroit News*, 29 September 1941, 5; "Grand Rapids Plant to Make Propeller," *Detroit News*, 22 December 1942, 35.

16. The description of Nash-Kelvinator's work on aircraft engines in the next few paragraphs comes mostly from "Introduction," 8–14.

17. Ibid.; "Narrative of Navy Program at Nash-Kelvinator, Kenosha, Wisconsin," folder "World War II History," World War II Production Series, box 4, "Nash-Kelvinator War Production, 1942–1945," DCHC, pp. 2–3.

18. "Introduction," 11; "Narrative of Navy Program," 6.

19. "Narrative of Navy Program," 8–10.

20. "Introduction," 12–14; Wesley Frank Craven and James Lea Cate, *The Army Air Forces in World War II* (Washington, DC: Office of Air Force History, 1983), 356.

21. Introduction," 23–25; "Contract for Army Helicopters: Big Output Is Proposed, Production to Pass Sikorsky Plants," *Detroit News*, 13 June 1943, sec. 1, p. 12; "Nash Retools for Helicopter: Quantity Production Planned for U.S. Army," *Detroit News*, 15 July 1943, 21.

22. "Introduction," 26–28; "Completes Helicopter Tests," *Michigan Manufacturer and Financial Record* 74 (16 September 1944): 11.

23. Michael W. R. Davis, *Detroit's Wartime Industry: Arsenal of Democracy* (Charleston, SC: Arcadia, 2007), 83–94; Hyde, *Riding the Roller Coaster*, 140–44.

24. "Nash Gets $75,000,000 Credit," *Detroit News*, 24 September 1943, 38; "WPB Authorize Nash Postwar Car Planning," *Detroit News*, 1 October 1944, sec. 4, p. 7.

25. See Nelson Lichtenstein, *Labor's War at Home: The CIO in World War II* (Cambridge: Cambridge University Press, 1982); Martin Glaberman, *Wartime Strikes: The Struggle against the No-Strike Pledge in the UAW during World War II* (Detroit: Berwick Editions, 1980).

26. "Propeller Plant Idle in 'Cutback' Strike," *Detroit News*, 3 October 1944, 4; "Truce Halts Cutback Row: 6,500 Back on Jobs; Give WLB until Monday," *Detroit News*, 4 October 1944, 2; "Production Is Resumed as 'Union Meeting' Ends," *Detroit News*, 19 October 1944, 25.

27. Nash-Kelvinator Corporation, *Annual Report for 1949*, NAHC, 10.

28. *Looking Ahead with Nash* (1942), Nash-Kelvinator corporate files, NAHC; V. Dennis Wrynn,

Detroit Goes to War: The American Automobile Industry in World War II (Osceola, WI: Motorbooks International, 1993).

29. Nash-Kelvinator Corporation, *Annual Report for 1945*, NAHC, 10; "Nash-Kelvinator Gets Non-war Loan," *Detroit News*, 1 February 1945, 36.

30. "Huge Expansion Planned by Nash," *Detroit News*, 22 August 1945, 5; Nash-Kelvinator Corporation, *Annual Report for 1945*, 6–8.

31. "The Nash Tunes Up," *Fortune* 32 (September 1945): 252.

32. Nash-Kelvinator Corporation, *Annual Report for 1945*, 7; "Supplier Strikes Halt Nash Output," *Detroit News*, 10 October 1945, 9; Nash-Kelvinator Corporation, *Annual Report for 1946*, NAHC, 6, 7; "Nash-Kelvinator Offer of 18 1/2 Cents Is O.K.'d," *Detroit News*, 9 March 1946, 2.

33. "Nash Submits Bid for Kenosha Plant," *Detroit News*, 29 August 1946, 49; "Nash Bid Excludes Surplus Machinery," *Detroit News*, 30 August 1946; "Nash-Kelvinator Buys War Plant," *Detroit News*, 23 October 1946, 35; Nash-Kelvinator Corporation, *Annual Report for 1946*, 7, 8.

34. "Mason Chairman of Nash-Kelvinator," *Detroit News*, 1 July 1948, 51; Nash-Kelvinator Corporation, *Annual Report for 1942*, NAHC, 4; Nash-Kelvinator Corporation, *Annual Report for 1946*, 3; "Proxy Statement, Annual Meeting of Stockholders of Nash-Kelvinator Corporation, February 4, 1953," 5 January 1953, 4–5.

35. James C. Mays, *From Kenosha to the World: The Rambler, Jeffery & Nash Truck Story, 1904–1955* (Yellow Springs, OH: Antique Power, 2003), 99, 101–3.

36. Ibid., 103, 105; "Commence Nash Dealer Service Truck Deliveries," *Nash News*, December 1948, 4; "Nash Haul Thrift Service Truck, *Nash News*, March 1949, 9; "Kenosha Truck Production—Nash," folder "Nash Towing Truck," box "Nash, 1947–1949," DCHC.

37. Nash-Kelvinator Corporation, *Annual Report for 1948*, NAHC, n.p.; Gunnell, *Standard Catalog of American Motors*, 169.

38. "Many Improvements on 1950 Nash Models," *Automotive Industries* 101 (1 October 1949): 24–26; Nash-Kelvinator Corporation, *Annual Report for 1950*, NAHC, 4–5; communication from Don Loper to the author regarding the Weather Eye heater sales to General Motors, 18 June 2007.

39. Joseph Geschelin, "New 2400-Lb. Nash Rambler Powered by 82-Hp Engine," *Automotive Industries* 102 (15 April 1950): 42–45, 102; Gunnell, *Standard Catalog of American Motors*, 170, 171; American Automobile Association Contest Board, "Certificate of Stock Status and Performance," folder "1951 Nash (2)," box "Nash, 1951," Series II, DCHC.

40. *The American Car since 1775* (Kutztown, PA: Automobile Quarterly, 1971), 142, 143.

41. Asher Lauren, "Nash Signs Accord on Pensions: Ching May Urge Keller to Join Talks," *Detroit News*, 16 March 1950, 1; Nash-Kelvinator Corporation, *Annual Report for 1952*, NAHC, 5; "Back at Kelvinator," *Detroit News*, 13 November 1951, 42; "Nash Body Union Votes to Walk Out," *Detroit News*, 13 November 1953, 63.

42. Nash-Kelvinator Corporation, *Annual Report for 1951*, NAHC, 6; "Nash Plants to Cut Output: 25 Pct. Reduction to Cost 4,500 Jobs," *Detroit News*, 21 December 1950, 21; "Nash to Cut Output," *Detroit News*, 22 December 1950, 26.

43. Gunnell, *Standard Catalog of American Motors*, 178.

44. Ibid., 178–80; Earl L. Munson, "British-American Hybrid," *SAE Journal* 60 (March 1952): 62, 63; "The Story of Nash-Healey," box "Nash-Healey," DCHC.

45. Hyde, *Riding the Roller Coaster*, 272.

46. Floyd Clymer, "Fifty Years Progress by Nash, 1902–1952," *Automobile Topics*, Nash Golden Anniversary Issue (September 1952): 41; "'52 Nashes Get European Look, More Power," *Popular Science* 160 (April 1952): 102–3; Gunnell, *Standard Catalog of American Motors*, 171–72.

47. Michael Lamm and Dave Holls, *A Century of Automotive Style: 100 Years of American Car Design* (Stockton, CA: Lamm-Morada, 1996), 199–200; Bob Thomas, *Confessions of an Automotive Stylist: An Inside Look at What Goes on behind the Locked Doors of Detroit's Car Styling Studios* (R. M. Thomas, 1995), 24–25.

48. Gunnell, *Standard Catalog of American Motors,* 173–74; "New Nash Rambler Sedan on 108-Inch Wheelbase," *Automotive Industries* 109 (1 December 1953): 61, 100, 102.

49. Patrick Foster, "A Little Style from Kenosha: Nash Metropolitan," *Automobile Quarterly* 32 (October 1993): 4, 6; Patrick Foster, "Developing the Metropolitan," *Hemmings Classic Car* 2 (October 2005): 62–63; Sam Medway, "Refrigerators and Two Georges—From Nash-Kelvinator to American Motors," *Automobile Quarterly* 15 (second quarter 1977): 154.

50. Foster, "A Little Style from Kenosha," 7, 8; Nash-Kelvinator Corporation, minutes of the board of directors meeting, 1 November 1951, DCHC; Nash-Kelvinator Corporation, *Annual Report for 1952,* 4; Gunnell, *Standard Catalog of American Motors,* 181.

51. Nash-Kelvinator Corporation, *Annual Report for 1953,* NAHC, 5.

52. "Say Packard Eyes Merger: Report Nance Seeks Combine with Nash," *Detroit News,* 16 May 1952, 1; Ralph R. Watts, "Report Talks on Merger by Hudson, Nash," *Detroit News,* 7 October 1953, 17; Ralph R. Watts, "Merger of Hudson and Nash Builds No. 4 Auto Company," *Detroit News,* 15 January 1954, 1, 4.

53. Nash-Kelvinator Corporation, annual reports for 1947–53; "Nash Sales at Record: Net Higher," *Detroit News,* 4 December 1953, 42.

54. Charles E. Edwards, *Dynamics of the United States Automobile Industry* (Columbia: University of South Carolina Press, 1965), 13, 15, 106–7.

55. Donald T. Critchlow, *Studebaker: The Life and Death of a Corporation* (Bloomington: Indiana University Press, 1996), 140; *The American Car since 1775,* 143.

56. Lawrence J. White, *The Automobile Industry since 1945* (Cambridge, MA: Harvard University Press, 1971), 13–15, 40–41, 271–72, 290–95; Edwards, *Dynamics of the United States Automobile Industry,* 112, 123–24, 220, 231.

57. White, *The Automobile Industry since 1945,* 70, 207–8, 216, 219, 271–72. A recent full-length study on the Kaiser-Frazer Corporation is Jack Mueller, *Built to Better the Best: The Kaiser-Frazer Corporation History* (Evansville, IN: M.T. Publishing, 2005). The histories of Studebaker and Packard are found in Critchlow, *Studebaker;* Thomas E. Bonsall, *More Than They Promised: The Studebaker Story* (Stanford: Stanford University Press, 2000); and James A. Ward, *The Fall of the Packard Motor Car Company* (Stanford: Stanford University Press, 1995).

58. William B. Harris, "Last Stand of the Auto Independents?" *Fortune* 50 (December 1954): 204, 206.

59. Ibid., 206, 208.

60. Tom Mahoney, *The Story of George Romney: Builder, Salesman, Crusader* (New York: Harper and Brothers, 1960), 168–69.

61. Ward, *Fall of the Packard Motor Car Company,* 56–59.

62. Mahoney, *The Story of George Romney,* 132–35.

63. "Say Packard Eyes Merger"; Mahoney, *The Story of George Romney,* 169; Ward, *Fall of the Packard Motor Car Company,* 101, 128.

64. Ward, *Fall of the Packard Motor Car Company,* 141–44, 150, 157; Mahoney, *The Story of George Romney,* 170–71.

65. "Hudson Shipments, Calendar Years 1909–1957," DCHC.

66. Don Butler, *The History of Hudson* (Sarasota, FL: Crestline, 1982), 306; *The American Car since 1775,* 142–43; Mahoney, *The Story of George Romney,* 169–70.

67. Watts, "Report Talks on Merger by Hudson, Nash"; "Color Styling Rules '54 Cars," *Detroit News,* 5 November 1953; "Nash Looks to the Future: A Special Message to Nash Dealers from George W. Mason," ca. 1953, NAHC.

68. Watts, "Merger of Hudson and Nash Builds No. 4 Auto Company," 1, 4; "Hudson-Nash Plan Sent to Stockholders," *Detroit News,* 20 February 1954, 17; "Hudson, Nash Stockholders Vote Merger," *Detroit News,* 25 March 1954, 54; "Suit Opposes Hudson-Nash Merger Plan," *Detroit News,* 12 April 1954, 35; "Nash, Hudson Merger OK'd," *Detroit News,* 23 April 1954, 14; "Hudson Stock Value Set at $9.81 Share," *Detroit News,* 26 February 1957, 32.

69. Mahoney, *The Story of George Romney*, 181; John Treen, "700 from All Walks of Life Pay Tribute to George Mason," *Detroit News*, 12 October 1954, 15; "My Work and My Glory," remarks by George Romney at the funeral services for George Mason at Christ Church Cranbrook, 11 October 1954, DCHC; "George W. Mason," *Detroit News*, 11 October 1954, 22.

70. "Round Table to Offer George Mason Tribute," *Detroit News*, 1 November 1954, 9; Philip Workman, "George Mason's Memory Honored by Round Table," *Detroit News*, 19 November 1954, 16.

71. James A. Crowe, "14-Mile Au Sable River Stretch Sought for George Mason Park," *Detroit News*, 21 November 1954, B-3; "Way Cleared for State to Accept Mason's Gift," *Detroit News*, 1 November 1955, 6.

72. "Six Awarded Honorary Degrees," *Detroit News*, 18 June 1950, sec. 1, p. 4.

73. Statement summarizing Mason's life, issued by the American Motors Public Relations Department following his death, found in Mason biography file, DCHC; "Mason Is Chairman for Juniors' Banquet," *Detroit News*, 13 April 1952, 11; "Torch Picks 2 Executives," *Detroit News*, 27 July 1952, sec. 1, p. 19; "Ford, Webber, Mason Named UF Co-Chairmen," *Detroit News*, 26 August 1954, 56; William T. Noble, "Mason's First Love Was Motorcycle," *Detroit News*, 5 August 1954, 46.

CHAPTER FIVE

1. J. C. Long, *Roy D. Chapin: The Man behind the Hudson Motor Car Company* (1945; reprint, Detroit: Wayne State University Press, 1984), 69–72; Louise Webber O'Brien, "J. L. Hudson and the Hudson Car," *Detroit News*, 19 January 1958.

2. Beverly Rae Kimes and Henry Austin Clark Jr., *The Standard Catalog of American Cars, 1805–1942*, 3rd ed. (Iola, WI: Krause, 1996), 398.

3. Long, *Roy D. Chapin*, 23, 24; George S. May, "The Detroit–New York Odyssey of Roy D. Chapin," *Detroit in Perspective: A Journal of Regional History* 2 (Autumn 1973): 8.

4. Long, *Roy D. Chapin*, 9–22 passim. Long's biography of Chapin is detailed and accurate. Unfortunately, there are no similar biographies for any of the remaining partners who established Hudson.

5. Albert Nelson Marquis, ed., *The Book of Detroiters: A Biographical Dictionary of Living Men of the City of Detroit*, 2nd ed. (Chicago: A. N. Marquis, 1914), 116; Helen Jones Earley and James R. Walkinshaw, *Setting the Pace: Oldsmobile's First 100 Years* (Lansing, MI: Oldsmobile Division of the General Motors Corporation, 1996), 47; "H. E. Coffin, Pioneer Motor Builder, Dies: Long Identified with Hudson Company," *Automobile Topics* 128 (29 November 1937): 212; "H. E. Coffin Dies from Bullet Wound," *American Machinist* 81 (1 December 1937): 1160g.

6. Clarence E. Burton, ed., *The City of Detroit, Michigan, 1701–1922*, vol. 3 (Chicago: S. J. Clarke, 1922), 419–20; Earley and Walkinshaw, *Setting the Pace*, 25–26; George S. May, *Ransom E. Olds, Auto Industry Pioneer* (Grand Rapids, MI: Eerdmans, 1977), 148–49.

7. Marquis, *The Book of Detroiters* (1914), 51.

8. Ibid., 263; Earley and Walkinshaw, *Setting the Pace*, 459.

9. O. D. Foster, "Chapin Got an Early Start and Kept Ahead," *Forbes* 14 (10 May 1924): 151; Long, *Roy D. Chapin*, 24–28, 31–33; George W. Stark, "Auto World Loses Chapin: Head of Hudson Motors Dies of Pneumonia," *Detroit News*, 17 February 1936, 4; telegram, Roy D. Chapin to Olds Motor Works, 5 November 1901, box 1, Roy D. Chapin Sr. Papers, BHL. For a detailed account of the Detroit–New York City run, see May, "The Detroit–New York Odyssey of Roy D. Chapin," 5–25.

10. Foster, "Chapin Got an Early Start," 153; Long, *Roy D. Chapin*, 36–38; May, *Ransom E. Olds*, 219–20; Fred L. Smith to Mrs. E. C. Chapin, 6 June 1902, box 1, Roy D. Chapin Sr. Papers, BHL.

11. May, *Ransom E. Olds*, 111–13, 235–37.

12. Long, *Roy D. Chapin*, 38–41; Angus Smith, secretary-treasurer, Olds Motor Works, to Roy D. Chapin, 29 December 1904, box 1, Roy D. Chapin Sr. Papers, BHL.

13. Earley and Walkinshaw, *Setting the Pace*, 461.

14. Ibid., 56.

15. Long, *Roy D. Chapin*, 42–46; Olds Motor Works colleagues to Roy D. Chapin, 1 March 1906, Scrapbook, 1886–1911, Roy D. Chapin Sr. Papers, BHL.

16. Long, *Roy D. Chapin*, 47, 49–51; Michael J. Kollins, *Pioneers of the U.S. Automobile Industry*, vol. 2, *The Small Independents* (Warrendale, PA: Society of Automotive Engineers, 2002), 197–99; "Articles of Association of E. R. Thomas-Detroit Company," Chalmers Motor Company corporate files, NAHC.

17. Long, *Roy D. Chapin*, 51–58 passim.

18. John A. Conde, *The Cars That Hudson Built* (Keego Harbor, MI: Arnold-Porter Publishing, 1980), 3.

19. Ibid.; "Minneapolis Mud Pilgrimage Captured by Thomas-Detroit," *Motor Age* 13 (4 June 1908): 6–9; "Denver Race Is Won by Thomas-Detroit," *Motor Age* 13 (4 June 1908): 20–21.

20. Long, *Roy D. Chapin*, 61–64 passim.

21. Ibid., 64–66; David Chalmers Hammond, *Hugh Chalmers: The Man and His Car* (Mountain View, CA: Shoreline Printing and Graphics, 2005), 6–9, 49–51; E. R. Thomas-Detroit Company, minutes of meetings of the board of directors, meeting of 3 December 1907; E. R. Thomas Company, minutes of stockholders meetings, meeting of 15 June 1908, DCHC.

22. Marquis, *The Book of Detroiters* (1914), 103; Long, *Roy D. Chapin*, 68.

23. *Pyramid Plan of Organization, Chalmers-Detroit Motor Co., Detroit, Michigan* [1908], Chalmers-Detroit Motor Company corporate files, NAHC.

24. Advertisement, "Chalmers-Detroit Thirty: This Astounding Car for $1,500," *Detroit News*, 12 July 1908, 6; George S. May, "Hugh Chalmers," in George S. May, ed., *The Automobile Industry, 1896–1920* (New York: Bruccoli Clark Layman, 1989), 76–77; Chalmers-Detroit Motor Company, *Annual Report for Fiscal Year Ending June 30, 1909*, box 1, Roy D. Chapin Sr. Papers, BHL.

25. Long, *Roy D. Chapin*, 69–71.

26. Hudson Account Book, entry of 28 October 1908, box "Roy D. Chapin Biography," DCHC; Conde, *The Cars That Hudson Built*, 4, 6.

27. Conde, *The Cars That Hudson Built*, 7–8; John A. Gunnell, ed., *Standard Catalog of American Motors, 1902–1987* (Iola, WI: Krause, 1993), 183.

28. J. C. Long, *Roy D. Chapin* (presentation copy, privately printed, 1945), 74; Don Butler, *The History of Hudson* (Sarasota, FL: Crestline, 1982), 16; Hudson Motor Car Company, *Finishing the Triangle: A Book of Facts and Experiences* (n.p., ca. 1910), n.p., courtesy of Ken Poynter.

29. Long, *Roy D. Chapin*, 75–88 passim.

30. "Memorandum of Agreement, December 6, 1909, between Hugh Chalmers and Roy D. Chapin, Howard E. Coffin and Frederick O. Bezner," box 1, Roy D. Chapin Sr. Papers, BHL; Burton, *The City of Detroit*, 3:420; Long, *Roy D. Chapin*, 87–92.

31. Chalmers-Detroit Motor Company, "Minutes of the Special Meeting of the Directors," and "Minutes of the Special Stockholders Meeting," 5 January 1910, DCHC; "Certificate of Amendment to the Articles of Association of the Chalmers-Detroit Motor Company," 14 February 1910, Chalmers Motor Company corporate files, NAHC; "Chalmers Gets Control of Big Motor Company: Deal Means Separation of Chalmers-Detroit and Hudson Plants—Coffin, Bezner, and Chapin to Conduct Destinies of Latter," *Detroit News*, 18 December 1909, 1, 2.

32. "Dinner Tendered to Mr. Hugh Chalmers by His Fellow Directors of the Detroit Athletic Club," DCHC; Hugh Chalmers to Roy D. Chapin, 19 January 1917, and Roy D. Chapin to Hugh Chalmers, 23 January 1917, box 3, Roy D. Chapin Sr. Papers, BHL.

33. "Hudson Auto Company to Build New $400,000 Plant: Close Big Deal; Propose Making an 'Auto City' of Old Fairview," *Detroit News*, 27 January 1910, 1, 2; Long, *Roy D. Chapin*, 93.

34. "Work on the New Hudson Factory Started Last Week," *The Hudson Triangle* 1 (May 1910): 1; "This Is Moving Day for Hudson Motor: New Factory Out Jefferson a Model of Modern Equipment," *Detroit News*, 27 October 1910, 7.

35. "The Hudson Twenty," *Horseless Age* 23 (9 June 1909): 789; "The Hudson Twenty," *The Automobile* 20 (8 July 1909): 73; Butler, *History of Hudson,* 16.

36. Long, *Roy D. Chapin,* 97–101, 106; *Hudson Motor Car Company Stock Ledger, 1909–1922,* DCHC.

37. *The American Car since 1775* (Kutztown, PA: Automobile Quarterly, 1971), 138–41.

38. Butler, *History of Hudson,* 22–25; Gunnell, *Standard Catalog of American Motors,* 185–86; Ralph C. Epstein, *The Automobile Industry: Its Economic and Commercial Development* (Chicago: A. W. Shaw, 1928), 110, 342.

39. Butler, *History of Hudson,* 26–32; Gunnell, *Standard Catalog of American Motors,* 186–87.

40. Conde, *The Cars That Hudson Built,* 9; William Wagner, *Continental! Its Motors and Its People* (Fallbrook, CA: Aero, 1983), 10–11.

41. "The 48 Engineers Who Designed the Hudson," *Saturday Evening Post,* 28 September 1912, 46–47; Conde, *The Cars That Hudson Built,* 21–23; Long, *Roy D. Chapin,* 109–13; "The 48 Engineers Who Designed the New Hudsons," *The Hudson Triangle* 2 (24 August 1912): 1. Long provides transcripts of parts of six of the letters.

42. Howard E. Coffin, *Critical Analysis of Motor Cars of 1914* (Detroit: Hudson Motor Car Company, 1913), 7–8.

43. Epstein, *The Automobile Industry,* 339, 343–44.

44. Long, *Roy D. Chapin,* 129–31; "Summary of Hudson Motor Car Company Performance, Year Ended 31 May 1915," box 2, Roy D. Chapin Jr. Papers, BHL; Charles K. Hyde, *The Dodge Brothers: The Men, the Motor Cars, and the Legacy* (Detroit: Wayne State University Press, 2005), 113.

45. Long, *Roy D. Chapin,* 133; letter, "Private & Confidential," Henry B. Joy to Roy D. Chapin, 23 November 1915, box 2, Roy D. Chapin Sr. Papers, BHL.

46. "Hudson and Chalmers in Big Combine: Local Motor Car Companies Included in $200,000,000 Merger," *Detroit News*, 3 June 1916, 1; "Auto Combine Ford's Rival, Street Hears: Willys Merger Backed by Duponts, Advocates of Preparedness," *Detroit News*, 4 June 1916, 1, 2. Two undated documents confirm the seriousness of this effort: "Consolidation of the Willys-Overland Company, Chalmers Motor Company, Hudson Motor Car Company, and the Autolite Company" and "Proposed Plan of Protecting Voting Common Stock Held by Messrs. Willys, Chalmers and Chapin," found in folder "Miscellaneous, 1916," box 3, Roy D. Chapin Sr. Papers, BHL.

47. George Tiedeman to Roy D. Chapin, 9 June 1916; announcements of special meetings of the Hudson Motor Car Company directors and shareholders; Roy D. Chapin to Sydney Gardiner, 17 June 1916, all in box 2, Roy D. Chapin Sr. Papers, BHL; statement in *The Hudson Triangle* 5 (17 June 1916), 1.

48. Roscoe B. Jackson to Roy D. Chapin, 23 November 1918, box 6, Roy D. Chapin Sr. Papers, BHL.

49. Butler, *History of Hudson,* 37–41.

50. Gunnell, *Standard Catalog of American Motors,* 186–88; Conde, *The Cars That Hudson Built,* 29; "Nothing Can Stop a Factory That Grows Like This," folder "1915 Hudson General," box "Hudson 1914/1916," DCHC.

51. *Hudson Super-Six: It Solved Motordom's Knottiest Problem: Holds All Worth-While Records,* folder "1917 Hudson Super-Six," box "Hudson, 1916/1918," DCHC; Butler, *History of Hudson,* 50–51; "Hudson Quits Racing Because of the War," *The Hudson Triangle* 7 (11 August 1917): 2.

52. Kollins, *Pioneers of the U.S. Automobile Industry,* 2:352; "H. E. Coffin, Pioneer Motor Builder Dies," *Automobile Topics* 128 (29 November 1937), 212; Long, *Roy D. Chapin,* 141–44, 151–66 passim.

53. Benedict Crowell, *America's Munitions, 1917–1918* (Washington, DC: GPO, 1919), 504.

54. Conde, *The Cars That Hudson Built,* 33; Butler, *History of Hudson,* 52, 58; Kollins, *Pioneers of the*

U.S. Automobile Industry, 2:352. According to Benedict Crowell and Robert Forrest Wilson, *The Armies of Industry: Our Nation's Manufacture of Munitions for a World in Arms, 1917–1918* (New Haven: Yale University Press, 1921), 2:384–85, all of the Curtiss O-X engines were made in the Curtiss plant in Hammondsport, New York, and in the Willys-Morrow factory in Elmira, New York.

55. "Automobiles Must Now Be Delivered under Their Own Power: Drive-aways the Only Method by Which Deliveries Can Be Made—Freight Equipment Shortage Continues," *The Hudson Triangle* 7 (9 March 1918): 1.

56. R. B. Jackson to Roy D. Chapin, 15 November 1918, box 6, Roy D. Chapin Sr. Papers, BHL; "Just So That You May Know," *The Hudson Triangle* 8 (22 February 1919): 2, 3.

57. "Hudson Men to Make a Car," *Automobile Topics* 47 (29 September 1917): 843.

58. Butler, *History of Hudson,* 52; Long, *Roy D. Chapin,* 170; Roscoe B. Jackson to Roy D. Chapin, 1 March 1918, box 5, Roy D. Chapin Sr. Papers, BHL.

59. Butler, *History of Hudson,* 59; Kimes and Clark, *Standard Catalog of American Cars,* 541; "Nothing Can Stop a Factory That Grows Like This."

60. Butler, *History of Hudson,* 64–66; Gunnell, *Standard Catalog of American Motors,* 189; Kimes and Clark, *Standard Catalog of American Cars,* 542.

61. Kimes and Clark, *Standard Catalog of American Cars,* 541–42; Kit Foster, "Terraplane: Flying by Land," *Automobile Quarterly* 39 (May 1999): 66.

62. "Essex Sets World's Long Distance Endurance Mark," *The Hudson Triangle* 9 (20 December 1919): 1; "Essex Again Triumphs—Sets New Transcontinental Record," *The Hudson Triangle* 9 (21 August 1920): 1–5.

63. Epstein, *The Automobile Industry,* 144; Maurice D. Hendry, "Hudson: The Car Named for Jackson's Wife's Uncle," *Automobile Quarterly* 11 (Summer 1971): 368–69; Kimes and Clark, *Standard Catalog of American Cars,* 543–44.

64. "Hudson Introduces the New Essex Six: Super-Model Is the 'Big Surprise,' Long Held in Store—Coach Sells for $975 Fully Equipped," *Automobile Topics* 72 (15 December 1923): 442–47.

65. Butler, *History of Hudson,* 90; Kimes and Clark, *Standard Catalog of American Cars,* 544.

66. Hendry, "Hudson: The Car Named for Jackson's Wife's Uncle," 369; *The American Car since 1775,* 141.

67. Alfred P. Sloan Jr., *My Years with General Motors* (New York: Doubleday, 1964), 158–59.

68. Epstein, *The Automobile Industry,* 110–15, 343.

69. Long, *Roy D. Chapin,* 191–93.

70. Ibid., 196; Hudson Motor Car Company, *Report for the Year Ended November 30, 1922–1924,* NAHC.

71. Long, *Roy D. Chapin,* 100; Hendry, "Hudson: The Car Named for Jackson's Wife's Uncle," 369. For more information on the Amesbury, Massachusetts, automobile body companies, see K. Doubleday, *The Automobile Bodybuilders of Amesbury, Massachusetts* (Amesbury, MA: Whittier Press, 2006).

72. Hendry, "Hudson: The Car Named for Jackson's Wife's Uncle," 369; Conde, *The Cars That Hudson Built,* 48–49; Michael Lamm and Dave Holls, *A Century of Automotive Style: 100 Years of American Car Design* (Stockton, CA: Lamm-Morada Publishing, 1996), 65–66.

73. Gunnell, *Standard Catalog of American Motors,* 195, 197; Kimes and Clark, *Standard Catalog of American Cars,* 548, 1458–59. The model-by-model changes are spelled out in detail in the two sources listed above and in Butler, *History of Hudson,* and Conde, *The Cars That Hudson Built.*

74. Butler, *History of Hudson,* 129–30, 137–38, 156, 168; Gunnell, *Standard Catalog of American Motors,* 192–96; "Hudson Leaves 6-Cylinder Field: New L-Head 8 Engine Delivers 80 H.P. at Brakes," *Automotive Daily News* 19 (4 January 1930): 3; Hendry, "Hudson: The Car Named for Jackson's Wife's Uncle," 374.

75. Butler, *History of Hudson,* 107; "Hudson's Half Year Largest: First 6 Months Output Reached 180,000 Total; 30,000 for June," *Detroit News,* 1 July 1928, sec. 10, p. 2; "Hudson Using $1,000,000 Plant to Apply Lacquer," *Detroit News,* 22 July 1928, sec. 10, p. 1; E. Y. Watson,

"Hudson Shows a New System: Synchronizes Production of Parts, Gives Variety to 1,900 Cars a Day," *Detroit News*, 24 March 1929, sec. 6, p. 1.

76. "Hudson Brings Out the 'Dover': New Commercial Car Line Is Three-Quarter Ton Size in Five Body Types," *Detroit News*, 30 June 1929, sec. 6, p. 3; Butler, *History of Hudson*, 120, 127–28, 135; Conde, *The Cars That Hudson Built,* 153–54.

77. "Hudson's New President," *The Hudson Triangle and Essex Topics* 17 (15 April 1929): 1; Kollins, *Pioneers of the U.S. Automobile Industry,* 2:348–49; Hendry, "Hudson: The Car Named for Jackson's Wife's Uncle," 382.

78. "Report to the Stockholders by R. B. Jackson, President and General Manager, 26 January 1929," Hudson Motor Car Company, *Annual Report for the Year Ended December 31, 1929,* NAHC.

79. Ibid.

80. Ibid.

81. Guardian Detroit Company, *Hudson Motors: An Investment Analysis* (Detroit: Guardian Detroit Company, September 1929), 11.

82. "5,700 Hudson Men Are Returning to Jobs at Hudson Plant," *Detroit News*, 16 December 1930, 12; Hudson Motor Car Company, *Annual Report for the Year Ended December 31, 1929,* NAHC.

83. Foster, "Terraplane," 67–69.

84. Quoted in ibid., 69.

85. See especially Joseph J. Corn, *The Winged Gospel: America's Romance with Aviation, 1900–1950* (New York: Oxford University Press, 1983).

86. Ibid., 69–71; E. V. Watson, "The New Essex Shown Today: Amelia Earhart Christens First 'Terraplane' at Public Ceremonies," *Detroit News*, 21 July 1932, 1–2; "Essex Prices as Low as $425: Newly Introduced Series Ranges up to $610; 2,000 New Ones Driven Away," *Detroit News*, 22 July 1932, 7.

87. Norman G. Shidle, quoting Ethel Denham, "Just among Friends," *Automotive Industries* 67 (30 July 1932): 132.

88. Hendry, "Hudson: The Car Named for Jackson's Wife's Uncle," 374–75; Foster, "Terraplane," 74.

89. Hendry, "Hudson: The Car Named for Jackson's Wife's Uncle," 375; Foster, "Terraplane," 73; "'Terraplanes' Continue to Take Hill Climb Marks," *Detroit News*, 16 April 1933, sec. 1, p. 14; "Terraplane Winner in Trial in the Alps," *Detroit News*, 16 September 1934, sec. 4, p. 9; "'Flyer' Begins Tri-State Run: 'Terraplane' Sent away from City Hall after Ceremony and a Presentation," *Detroit News*, 23 September 1934, sec. 4, p. 9; "Run by 'Flyer' Is 11,452 Miles: Hudson-Terraplane Completes Two Weeks Drive over a Tri-State Route," *Detroit News*, 7 October 1934, sec. 4, p. 11; "Economy Trial by Terraplane: Under Eyes of A.A.A., Car Makes Two 100-Mile Runs on Dry Lake," *Detroit News*, 21 July 1935, sec. 1, p. 8.

90. Hendry, "Hudson: The Car Named for Jackson's Wife's Uncle," 375, 376; Butler, *The History of Hudson*, 168, 180; Gunnell, *Standard Catalog of American Motors,* 197, 198; "'Knee Action' in Front End of Car as Hudson Will Offer It," *Detroit News*, 10 December 1933, sec. 10, p. 12; "Hudson Offers Electric Shift: Automatic Gear Change and Steel Roofs Features of Both Its Lines," *Detroit News*, 13 January 1935, sec. 6, p. 7. For more detailed coverage of the changes to the Hudson-Essex models in the 1930s, see Butler, *History of Hudson,* and Gunnell, *Standard Catalog of American Motors.*

91. Lamm and Holls, *A Century of Automotive Style,* 190–91, 193.

92. Hendry, "Hudson: The Car Named for Jackson's Wife's Uncle," 382; Long, *Roy D. Chapin*, 253; "Barit and Baits Get Hudson Co. Promotions: Become General Manager and Assistant General Manager," *Automobile Topics* 114 (23 June 1934): 306.

93. Long, *Roy D. Chapin*, 255–60.

94. Ibid., 260–61; *The American Car since 1775*, 140, 141.

95. George W. Stark, "Auto World Loses Chapin: Head of Hudson Motors Dies of Pneumonia," *Detroit News*, 17 February 1936, 1; "Chapin Post Goes to Barit: Executive Flies Here for Rites

Wednesday," *Detroit News*, 18 February 1936, 10; "A. E. Barit Succeeds Chapin at Hudson: Has Been with the Company Ever since Its Inception," *Automobile Topics* 121 (2 March 1936): 167.

96. "Chapin Rites Held at Home: Friends, Business Associates at Services," *Detroit News*, 19 February 1936, 28; "Service Held for Chapin: Hundreds of Friends in Final Tribute," *Detroit News*, 20 February 1936, 9.

97. "Chapin Post Goes to Barit"; editorial, "Roy Dikeman Chapin," *Detroit News*, 18 February 1936, 10, 18.

98. Jerry M. Fisher, *The Pacesetter: The Untold Story of Carl G. Fisher* (Fort Bragg, CA: Lost Coast Press, 1998), 115–17; Drake Hokanson, *The Lincoln Highway: Main Street across America* (Iowa City: University of Iowa Press, 1988), 109–10; Lincoln Highway Association, *The Lincoln Highway: The Story of a Crusade That Made Transportation History* (New York: Dodd, Mead, 1935), 81, 125–37, 277, 293; Long, *Roy D. Chapin*, 103–4, 131–32, 176, 194–95, 205–42 passim; "Roy D. Chapin—A Man of Service to His Country and His Industry," *Automotive Industries* 74 (22 February 1936): 304–6, 318.

99. Long, *Roy D. Chapin*, 207–10, 222, 223.

100. Ibid., 212–15.

101. Ibid., 229–32, 238–42.

102. Resolution, Detroit Board of Commerce to Charles H. Ziegler, state highway commissioner, 4 April 1946, Scrapbook, 1932–46, Roy D. Chapin Sr. Papers, BHL; "Roy D. Chapin or Edsel Ford? Both Names Up for Highway," *Detroit News*, 10 April 1946, 6.

CHAPTER SIX

1. "A. E. Barit Succeeds Chapin at Hudson: Has Been with the Company Ever since Its Inception," *Automobile Topics* 121 (2 March 1936): 167; "A. Barit Is Elected Vice-President and Treasurer," *The Hudson Triangle and Essex Topics* 17 (15 April 1929): 2; "Biographical Sketch of Mr. A. E. Barit," Hudson Motor Car Company press release, 17 November 1946, DCHC; "Barit and Baits Get Hudson Co. Promotions: Become General Manager and Assistant General Manager," *Automobile Topics* 114 (23 June 1934): 306; A. E. Barit obituary, *Detroit Free Press*, 17 July 1974, B-16.

2. "Three Thousand Hudson Men on Strike: Body Plant Employees Walk Out Demanding Higher Pay Scale," *Detroit News*, 7 February 1933, 1; "Hudson Invites Men to Confer: Meeting Expected Today to Talk Over Demands by Strikers," *Detroit News*, 8 February 1933, 1, 4; "Pickets Block Hudson Work: Present Resumption of Body Plant Operations by Turning Back Men," *Detroit News*, 9 February 1933, 1, 4; "Hudson Plant Gate Cleared: Police Prevent Pickets from Blocking Return of Workers," *Detroit News*, 9 February 1933, 3; "Hudson Work at Standstill: Plant Officials Expect Large Turnout of Workers Monday Morning," *Detroit News*, 11 February 1933, 4; "Hudson Body Plant Reopens: Workers Return, and Company Expects Full Operation to Start Tuesday," *Detroit News*, 13 February 1933, 4; "Pickets Drop Hudson Vigil: Workers Not Molested as Normal Force Returns to Both Plants," *Detroit News*, 14 February 1933, 2.

3. "Hudson Motor Strike Off, Too: Union Men Favor Walkout, But Agree to Let Labor Board Hear Their Case," *Detroit News*, 8 March 1934, 40; "Hudson Official Makes Statement to Board," *Detroit News*, 16 March 1934, 13.

4. "Hudson Union Deserts AFL: 7,000 Workers Vote to Join New Organization of Auto Employees," *Detroit News*, 5 August 1934, sec. 1, p. 13; "Hudson Plant Vote Assailed: Head of Independent Union Group Goes to Auto Labor Board," *Detroit News*, 30 August 1934, 11; "Workers Electing at Hudson Plant: Independent Union Chairman Voices Protest," *Detroit News*, 6 September 1934, 31; "Hudson Motor Car Company Employees Ballot in Rain," *Detroit News*, 7 September 1934, 12; "Plant Ballot Ruling Scored: Workers' Chairman Attacks Automobile Labor Board in Hudson Case," *Detroit News*, 19 September 1934, 9; "Hudson Plant Voting Starts: 2 Rival Organizations End Spirited Drives for Bargaining Posts," *Detroit News*, 1 February 1935, 38; "Non-Unionists

Lead Auto Vote: 40,953 of 53,771 Employees Who Have Voted So Far Indicate No Affiliation; Hudson Workers Elect," *Detroit News*, 2 February 1935, 1, 15; "Hudson Groups Seek Control: Independent, Company Unions Compete; Unaffiliated Men Win at Chevrolet," *Detroit News*, 15 February 1935, 27; "Hudson Unions Vote Deadlock: Unaffiliated Candidates Will Hold Balance of Power in Employee Agency," *Detroit News*, 16 February 1935, 21.

5. Steve Babson, *Working Detroit* (Detroit: Wayne State University Press, 1985), 68–86 passim.

6. "Weighty Problem Solved in Hudson Plant Sit-Down," *Detroit News*, 21 March 1937, sec. 5, p. 10; "Hudson States Stand," *Detroit News*, 3 April 1937, 1; "Union at Hudson Motor Spurns Company Offer," *Detroit News*, 4 April 1937, sec. 1, p. 10; "Hudson Motor Talks Resume: Conferees Meet Again at Murphy Office in Lansing; Auto Labor Troubles Practically at an End," *Detroit News*, 8 April 1937, 1; "Back-to-Work Parade Begins: 1,500 Dodge Employees Are First in Line as Strike Siege Is Lifted; Hudson Pact Is Put to Vote," *Detroit News*, 9 April 1937, 1; "U.S. Auto Business Strikeless: Hudson Motor Plants Are Evacuated," *Detroit News*, 10 April 1937, 1; "Hudson Auto Pact Signed: Post-Strike Agreement Is Supplemented," *Detroit News*, 2 May 1937, sec. 1, p. 1.

7. "Hudson UAW without Pact: Union and Company in Clash Over Contract," *Detroit News*, 9 April 1938, 3; "Hudson Strike Is Voted Down: New Contract Restores Union Confidence," *Detroit News*, 15 November 1938, 1; "Hudson Auto Pact Accepted: Workers Vote Approval at Local Meeting," *Detroit News*, 28 November 1938, 4; "UAW Signs with Hudson: Contract Leaves 75-Cent Base Unchanged," *Detroit News*, 30 November 1938, 29; "Hudson Motor and UAW Sign Contract for Year," *Detroit News*, 19 December 1939, 14; "Hudson Pact to Go to Men: Union Shop, Vacations, Protection Cited," *Detroit News*, 12 December 1940, 4; "Auto Unions Ratify Pacts: Chrysler, Hudson Votes Almost Unanimous," *Detroit News*, 16 December 1940, 2.

8. "Hudson Strike Delay Sought: Company, CIO to Confer Late Today," *Detroit News*, 8 May 1941, 28; "Hudson Poll Tallied by CIO: State to Check Effect of Strike on Defense," *Detroit News*, 9 May 1941, 33; "Hudson Motor Strike Authorized by Union," *Detroit News*, 10 May 1941, 2; "Hudson Gets an Ultimatum: Strike Tuesday Morning Threatened," *Detroit News*, 11 May 1941, sec. 1, p. 13; "Agreement Is Reached at Hudson: Strike Terms Placed with Workers," *Detroit News*, 21 May 1941, 1; "Hudson Plant Back at Work: Strike Ended by 8 Cent Increase in Wage," *Detroit News*, 22 May 1941, 23.

9. Don Butler, *The History of Hudson* (Sarasota, FL: Crestline Publishing, 1982), 221, 251.

10. Ibid., 196–97; Maurice D. Hendry, "Hudson: The Car Named for Jackson's Wife's Uncle," *Automobile Quarterly* 11 (Summer 1971): 383; John A. Gunnell, ed., *Standard Catalog of American Motors, 1902–1987* (Iola, WI: Krause, 1993), 199.

11. Kit Foster, "Terraplane: Flying by Land," *Automobile Quarterly* 39 (May 1999): 79; Hendry, "Hudson: The Car Named for Jackson's Wife's Uncle," 383; Beverly Rae Kimes and Henry Austin Clark Jr., *The Standard Catalog of American Cars, 1805–1942*, 3rd ed. (Iola, WI: Krause, 1996), 1461; Gunnell, *Standard Catalog of American Motors*, 200–201.

12. Gunnell, *Standard Catalogue of American Motors*, 201–2.

13. Hendry, "Hudson: The Car Named for Jackson's Wife's Uncle," 383.

14. Butler, *History of Hudson*, 251, 259.

15. There is no detailed history of Hudson's war work, but an excellent summary is found in Jim Donnelly, "Detroit Goes to War, Part IV: Independents Day; America Called for War Materiel Galore and Hudson Answered with Pride," *Hemmings Classic Car*, no. 19 (April 2006): 46–53.

16. Ibid., 49; "Hudson Signs New Contract: $13,000,000 Arsenal Will Employ 4,000," *Detroit News*, 11 January 1941, 1; "Steel Work Rises for $20,000,000 Arsenal Here," *Detroit News*, sec. 1, p. 9; "Navy Gives Hudson $14,038,500 Order," *Detroit News*, 31 July 1941, 16.

17. Hudson Motor Car Company, directors' meetings, 21 July 1941, 19 September 1941, 20 February 1942, and 20 May 1942, DCHC. A monthly summary of production is found with the minutes of the Hudson directors' meetings.

18. "Hudson Aircraft Plant Is Now in Production," *Detroit News*, 6 February 1941, 36; "Hudson Air Head," *Detroit News*, 16 February 1941, sec. 5, p. 24.

19. Hudson Motor Car Company, directors' meetings, 19 September 1941, 20 May 1942, 20 September 1943, and 27 February 1945.

20. Hudson Motor Car Company, directors' meetings, 27 June 1941, 21 July 1941, 20 May 1942, 20 August 1942, 20 April 1943, 3 August 1943, and 25 April 1944; memorandum, Roy Chapin Jr. to Lt. W. Long, 29 June 1942, box 1, Roy D. Chapin Jr. Papers, BHL; report, Dennis Mulligan, Lt. Colonel, Air Corps to the Chief, Production Division, Wright Field, 30 December 1942, box 1, Roy D. Chapin Jr. Papers, BHL.

21. Donnelly, "Detroit Goes to War," 52; "Curtiss Dive-Bomber for Which Hudson Will Produce Wings," *Detroit News,* 20 September 1942, sec. 1, p. 12; memorandum, Van C. Loewe to Paul Pierce, 31 December 1942, box 1, Roy D. Chapin Jr. Papers, BHL; "Hudson Produces Wings for Dive Bombers," *Detroit News,* 2 January 1944, sec. 4, p. 5; Hudson Motor Car Company, directors' meetings, 20 February 1942, 21 September 1942, 20 February 1943, 21 June 1943, and 22 November 1943.

22. Hudson Motor Car Company, directors' meetings, 20 September 1943, 25 February 1944, 20 March 1944, 25 April 1944, and 31 August 1944.

23. Hudson Motor Car Company, directors' meetings, 20 December 1943, 20 June 1944, 24 July 1944, 31 August 1944, 20 December 1944, 20 January 1945, 21 May 1945, and 20 June 1945.

24. Hudson Motor Car Company, directors' meetings, 20 February 1942, 6 April 1942, 20 July 1942, 20 August 1942, and 28 October 1942.

25. "Hudson Produces Power for Invasion Fleet," *Detroit News,* 4 April 1943, sec. 4, p. 6; Hudson Motor Car Company, directors' meetings, 25 November 1942, 20 January 1943, 20 April 1943, and 20 October 1944.

26. The employment figures come from the minutes of various Hudson Motor Car Company directors' meetings.

27. "Ride-Sharing Drive Is Near: Will Be Based on Factory Survey," *Detroit News,* 31 May 1942, sec. 1, p. 2; "Night Workers Get a Break," *Detroit News,* 10 July 1942, 4.

28. "Women Plant Guards Prove Successful," *Detroit News,* 11 August 1942, 15; "Women Demonstrate Ability as Ordnance Plant Guards," *Detroit News,* 22 November 1942, sec. 1, p. 1; "Women Guard Naval Plant under Coast Guard Banner," *Detroit News,* 10 February 1943, 14; "War Working Mothers Get Child Care Center," *Detroit News,* 12 December 1943, sec. 4, p. 9.

29. Nelson Lichtenstein, *Labor's War at Home: The CIO in World War II* (Cambridge: Cambridge University Press, 1982), 98–102; Robert C. Weaver, "Detroit and Negro Skill," *Phylon* 4 (second quarter 1943): 138.

30. Weaver, "Detroit and Negro Skill," 140–41; "Walkout Ends in Gun Plant: Schedule Is Normal at Hudson Arsenal," *Detroit News,* 19 June 1942, 1; "Discharges Approved by Union: Plant Resumes Full Operation," *Detroit News,* 20 June 1942, 1; "Knox Cracks Down on War Plant Strikers," *Detroit News,* 20 June 1942, 12; "Arsenal Runs at Full Speed: 4 Linked with Strike Are Ousted," *Detroit News,* 21 June 1942, sec. 1, p. 5.

31. "Hudson Pay Boost Denied by WLB," *Detroit News,* 9 January 1943, 19; "4,000 at Hudson Granted Increase in Vacation Pay," *Detroit News,* 4 February 1944, 4.

32. "Men Quit at Conner and Hudson," *Detroit News,* 1 May 1944, 1; "Foremen Spurn U.S. Order to End Strike: WLB Talks Demanded by Union," *Detroit News,* 2 May 1944, 1; "Packard, Hudson, Briggs Recall Men," *Detroit News,* 18 May 1944, 1, 2; "Plant and Foremen Argue over Status," *Detroit News,* 19 May 1944, 1, 2.

33. "7,000 Idle at Hudson Plant: Production of Fighters Is Held Up; Shutdown Caused by 110 Inspectors," *Detroit News,* 29 March 1945, 1; "13,000 Idle in B-29 Parts Plant Strike: WLB Asks for Peace at Hudson; Army and Navy Demand Work," *Detroit News,* 30 March 1945, 1, 4; "Order Hudson Strike Ended: Union Board to Meet on WLB Directive," *Detroit News,* 31 March 1945, 1, 2; "Hudson Finds Strike Accord: Union Urges Workers to Return on Monday," *Detroit News,* 1 April 1945, sec. 1, p. 5; "Strike Shuts Down Hudson B-29 Parts Unit," *Detroit News,* 26 June 1945, 1; "Secret CIO Parley Fights to End Strikes: 11,400 Go Back to Job at Hudson," *Detroit News,* 28 June 1945, 1, 2.

34. "Win Production Award," *Detroit News*, 7 January 1943, 3; "Hudson Aircraft Workers Praised at E Flag Rally," *Detroit News*, 9 January 1943, 16; "Aviation Division Wins 2nd 'E' Award: White Star Added to Army-Navy 'E' Flag Flying over Hudson Plants," *Hudson Triangle* 1 (December 1943), 2.

35. "Naval Ordnance Plant to Switch Pilots," *Detroit News*, 7 October 1943, 1, 11; "A Letter from the Navy," *Detroit Times*, 7 October 1943, 4; "Navy Silent on Cause for Change at Arsenal," *Detroit Free Press*, 8 October 1943, 21.

36. "Hudson Co. Loses Reins at Arsenal: Navy Terminates Contract; Gives Job to Westinghouse; Rift Is Reported," *Detroit Free Press*, 7 October 1943, 1, 9; "Inside Story: How Hudson Lost Arsenal," *Detroit Times*, 10 October 1943, part 1, p. 2.

37. Memorandum, 10 September 1951, J. J. Murphy to Paul E. West, "Meeting Wright-Patterson Air Force Base, Dayton, Ohio, September 6–7," Hudson Motor Car Company corporate files, NAHC.

38. Confidential memorandum, H. M. Northrup to A. E. Barit, 4 October 1951, Hudson Motor Car Company corporate files, NAHC.

39. "Statistical Summary since 1917, Hudson Motor Car Company," DCHC; "Statistical Summary, 1937–1953, Nash-Kelvinator Corporation," DCHC; Charles K. Hyde, *Riding the Roller Coaster: A History of the Chrysler Corporation* (Detroit: Wayne State University Press, 2003), 120.

40. The minutes of the directors' meetings cover the period from 21 July 1941 through 20 June 1945, are all signed or initialed by Carsten Tiedeman, and are in a looseleaf binder with "Roy D. Chapin, Jr." inscribed on the cover. The collection, found in the DCHC, includes minutes from four meetings in 1946 written by Roy Chapin Jr. Tiedeman's call for new outside directors is found in the minutes of the Hudson Motor Car Company directors' meeting of 21 July 1941.

41. Hudson Motor Car Company, directors' meetings, 6 April 1942, 20 July 1942, 5 April 1943, 3 August 1943, and 20 January 1944.

42. Hudson Motor Car Company, directors' meetings, 22 November 1943, 20 December 1943, and 23 February 1944.

43. "Venture by Fisher: Rumor Piles on Rumor as Detroit Speculates on Plans of Famed Brothers after They Quit General Motors Positions," *Business Week*, 12 August 1944, 64, 66, 68; Carl Muller, "Fishers Liken Hudson 'Deal' to Small Town Flirtation," *Detroit News*, 20 May 1945, sec. 1, pp. 1, 2; "Flirting Fishers," *Business Week*, 26 May 1945, 80, 83.

44. "Flirting Fishers," 80, 83; George B. Hassett, "Hudson Deal Claim Denied: Whether Fisher Brothers Seek Control Moot Issue," *Detroit News*, 22 May 1945, 4; "Rumblings at Hudson," *Investor's Reader* 4 (6 June 1945): 10, 11.

45. Hudson Motor Car Company, directors' meetings, 21 May 1945 and 20 June 1945; "Hudson Motor Offers Rights: Subscription Rate Is One for Seven," *Detroit News*, 31 March 1946, sec. 4, p. 11.

46. "Biographical Reference, American Motors Corporation," 18 April 1955, DCHC; H. M. Northrup, vice president, Hudson Motor Car Company, to Local Board No. 57, Grosse Pointe, Michigan, 15 June 1945, box 1, Roy D. Chapin Jr. Papers, BHL. Materials on Chapin's studies at the Hotchkiss School and Yale University, including transcripts of his grades, are found in box 1, Roy D. Chapin Jr. Papers, BHL.

47. Gunnell, *Standard Catalog of American Motors*, 205; Butler, *History of Hudson*, 269–70, 273; "1946 Hudson Makes Bow: New Model Appears Much Like '42 Car," *Detroit News*, 30 August 1945, 2; "Mile-Long Assembly," *Detroit News*, 31 August 1945, 28; "Hudson's Preview," *Detroit News*, 24 October 1946, 29.

48. "Ford, Hudson Lines Halted by Strikes," *Detroit News*, 1 September 1945, 1; "Hudson, Briggs Output Stalled," *Detroit News*, 4 September 1945, 1, 2; "Ford Workers Back: Others Idle," *Detroit News*, 10 September 1945, 1, 2; "Ford Unit in Windsor Shut Tight: Power Crew Balks at Picket Lines," *Detroit News*, 8 October 1945, 1, 2; "Hudson Opens Wage Parley: UAW to Ask Increase Similar to Ford Grant," *Detroit News*, 31 January 1946, 2; "Hudson Signs with UAW: 18½-Ct. Raise Awaits Union Ratification," *Detroit News*, 3 March 1946, sec. 1, p. 18; "Wage Board O.K.'s

Raises: Way Paved for Action on Higher Car Prices," *Detroit News*, 10 March 1946, sec. 1, p. 1; "500 Hudson Foremen Will Vote on FAA," *Detroit News*, 5 May 1946, sec. 1, p. 11; "Foremen Win Hudson Union," *Detroit News*, 29 October 1946, 15.

49. "Hudson Plant Shut by Parts Shortage," *Detroit News*, 31 July 1946, 3; "Hudson Motor to Resume Monday," *Detroit News*, 4 October 1946, 1; "Lack of Steel Idles 13,000 at Hudson," *Detroit News*, 11 October 1946, 1; "Hudson Plant Back at Work," *Detroit News,* 25 November 1946, 2; "Hudson to Be Shut by Steel Shortage," *Detroit News*, 21 December 1946, 2; Ralph Watts, "Production Underway on Hudson 1947 Models," *Detroit News*, 3 January 1947, 29; "Hudson Sales Ratio Larger," *Detroit News*, 21 May 1947, 37; "Across the Years—The 3,000,000th Hudson and Old No. 1," *Detroit News*, 17 September 1947, 52.

50. Michael Lamm and Dave Holls, *A Century of Automotive Style: 100 Years of American Car Design* (Stockton, CA: Lamm-Morada, 1996), 194, 195.

51. Bob Hall, "Step-Down in Style: Hudson's Last Hurrah," *Automobile Quarterly* 34 (October 1995): 90–99. For personal reminiscences about the designers associated with the Step-down Hudson by one of the stylists, see Robert F. Andrews, "On Designing the 'Step-Down' Hudson," *Automobile Quarterly* 9 (Summer 1971): 392–97.

52. United States Patent Nos. 2,627,426 and 2,627,437 for "Motor Vehicle Body Frame," granted 3 February 1953.

53. Lamm and Holls, *A Century of Automotive Style*, 194–95.

54. Hall, "Step-Down in Style," 101.

55. E-mail communication, Bob Elton to the author, 2 September 2007.

56. E-mail communication, Ed Ostrowski to the author, 5 November 2007.

57. Butler, *History of Hudson*, 284–85.

58. Hall, "Step-Down in Style," 99; Gunnell, *Standard Catalog of American Motors,* 206–8; Ralph R. Watts, "New Convertible Brougham Introduced Here by Hudson," *Detroit News*, 2 September 1948, 29; Ralph R. Watts, "Lower-Priced Hudson Six to Be Introduced Monday," *Detroit News*, 20 November 1949, sec. 4, p. 21; Ralph R. Watts, "New Hudson Models Appear; Price Cut," *Detroit News*, 10 February 1950, 16; Ralph R. Watts, "Hudson Announces Custom Convertible," *Detroit News*, 20 April 1950, 34.

59. Hall, "Step-Down in Style," 104; Ralph R. Watts, "'51 Hudson to Have New L-Head Engine," *Detroit News*, 22 September 1950, 54; "Hornet Leads 1951 Parade of Hudson Cars," *Detroit News*, 15 October 1950, sec. 4, p. 16.

60. Gunnell, *Standard Catalog of American Motors*, 209–11; Ralph R. Watts, "2 More Join New Model Parade," *Detroit News*, 18 January 1952, 6.

61. Hendry, "Hudson: The Car Named for Jackson's Wife's Uncle," 387, 390; Hall, "Step-Down in Style," 102–3. For a complete listing of Hudson finishes in NASCAR and stock car races, see Butler, *History of Hudson*, 293, 299, 307, 315. The recent (2006) animated feature film *Cars* (Disney/Pixar) "starred" a car, Doc Hudson, which was really a retired 1951 Hudson Hornet race car, a "Fabulous Hudson Hornet." Paul Newman served as the voice of Doc Hudson, who revealed that he had ended his racing career in 1954 after winning scores of "meaningless" trophies. He retired after seeing a major crash during a race.

62. Hendry, "Hudson: The Car Named for Jackson's Wife's Uncle," 390; Hall, "Step-Down in Style," 107–8.

63. Lamm and Holls, *A Century of Automotive Style,* 195.

64. Richard M. Langworth, *Hudson, 1946–1957: The Classic Postwar Years* (Osceola, WI: Motorbooks International, 1993), 78–85; Richard M. Langworth, "1953–54 Hudson Jet: The Car That Torpedoed Hudson," *Collectable Automobile* 11 (April 1995): 47–55; Hall, "Step-Down in Style," 108.

65. John A. Conde, *The Cars That Hudson Built* (Keego Harbor, MI: Arnold-Porter Publishing, 1980), 165–68.

66. "Hudson Gets Bomber Job: To Build Fuselage, Tail of Canberra Jet," *Detroit News*, 30 August 1951, 27; "Hudson Gets B-57 Contract," *Detroit News*, 11 February 1954, 1; "Hudson Gets Jet Contract: To Make Forward Sections of B-47," *Detroit News*, 20 September 1951, 36; "Hudson

Gets Jet Fuselage Order," *Detroit News*, 1 November 1951, 30; "Hudson Car Boost Due in Plane Shift," *Detroit News*, 24 October 1953, 1.

67. "14,000 Remain Out at Hudson: Steward's Suspension Brings UAW Walkout," *Detroit News*, 28 January 1947, 4; "Strikers Back at Hudson's: Auto Plant Resumes after 2 Stoppages," *Detroit News*, 30 January 1947, 2; "Hudson Shut, 14,000 Idled: Steward's Layoff Brings 60-Man Strike," *Detroit News*, 1 April 1947, p. 1; "Hudson Auto Row Settled: Strike of 51 Drivers Makes 14,000 Idle," *Detroit News*, 10 April 1947, 55; "Hudson Raised 15 Cents: Wage Hike Negotiated for 14,000," *Detroit News*, 13 May 1947, 1; "15,000 Idle as Pickets Halt Entry," *Detroit News*, 11 June 1947, 1, 2; "Hudson Plant Shut as 9,000 Walk," *Detroit News*, 1 August 1947, 1; "18,000 Back at 2 Plants: Union Action Reopens Hudson, Kaiser Units," *Detroit News*, 4 August 1947, 4; "Hudson Plant Hums Again: Welders Go Back; 12,000 Are Recalled," *Detroit News*, 2 December 1947, 4.

68. "Hudson Sends 10,000 Home," *Detroit News*, 11 June 1951, 1; "Hudson Local Votes to Quit: UAW Leaders Advise They Hunt Other Jobs," *Detroit News*, 25 July 1951, 3; "Hudson Rally Asks Seizure: Proposes U.S. Take Plant for War Work," *Detroit News*, 4 August 1951, 8; Asher Lauren, "Workers O.K. Pact at Hudson: 3,000 to Resume Work by Friday," *Detroit News*, 14 August 1951, 1, 2; "UAW Sues Hudson for $500,000 on Layoffs: Charges Breach of Contract; Blasts Shutdowns as 'Manufactured,'" *Detroit News*, 24 September 1951, 1; "Hudson Tops UAW's Sum: Suit Asks $1,500,000 for Contract Violations," *Detroit* News, 27 October 1951, 16.

69. Hendry, "Hudson: The Car Named for Jackson's Wife's Uncle," 391.

70. Biography files, Roy Dikeman Chapin Jr., 18 April 1955, DCHC; "3 New Directors Named by Hudson," *Detroit News*, 21 May 1946, 22; "Chapin Promoted," *Detroit News*, 11 January 1948, sec. 4, p. 12; "Appointments," *Detroit News*, 9 August 1948, 26; Butler, *History of Hudson*, 293.

71. "Barit's Notes Recall Hotel Room Talk That Sparked Merger of Nash, Hudson; Both Were Fretting Over Credit Shortage," *Wall Street Journal*, 18 April 1953, 14.

72. "Proxy Statement, Special Meeting of Stockholders of Hudson Motor Car Company, March 24, 1954," DCHC; "Hudson, Nash-Kelvinator Agree to Merge; New Firm Will be 4th Largest Auto Maker: American Motors Corp. to Be Name; Holders Vote in March on Proposal," *Wall Street Journal*, 15 January 1954, 1.

CHAPTER SEVEN

1. American Motors Corporation, directors' meetings, 12 October 1954, 18 November 1954, and 24 November 1958, DCHC; "Romney Paid $200,000 by AMC in 1958," *Detroit News*, 20 January 1959, 32.

2. The only full-length biographies of George Romney were prepared to support his candidacy for governor of Michigan and for president of the United States. Tom Mahoney, *The Story of George Romney: Builder, Statesman, Crusader* (New York: Harper and Brothers, 1960), and Clark R. Mollenhoff, *George Romney: Mormon in Politics* (New York: Meredith Press, 1968). National newspapers and business magazines focused almost entirely on Romney's maverick positions regarding the auto industry but were seldom critical of his management of American Motors.

3. Mahoney, *The Story of George Romney*, 51–54, 59–68; Mollenhoff, *George Romney*, 25–33.

4. Department of Defense Personal Security Questionnaire, 3 October 1960, biography file, box 1-A, George Romney Papers, BHL; Mahoney, *The Story of George Romney*, 67–69.

5. Mahoney, *The Story of George Romney*, 73–87 passim.

6. Mollenhoff, *George Romney*, 40–45.

7. Mahoney, *The Story of George Romney*, 96–102, 106.

8. Ibid., 104–9.

9. Ibid., 110–15.

10. Mollenhoff, *George Romney*, 64–85 passim.

11. Mahoney, *The Story of George Romney*, 122–26.

12. Ibid., 132–36.

13. Ibid., 153–55; Mollenhoff, *George Romney,* 100–101.

14. "Personal Report to Mr. Mason, February 8, 1949," Nash-Kelvinator Corporation, General Information, box 13-E, George W. Romney Papers, BHL.

15. Mahoney, *The Story of George Romney,* 156–60; Mollenhoff, *George Romney,* 102–3; "Vice President," *Detroit News,* 3 February 1950, 38.

16. Mahoney, *The Story of George Romney,* 160–61; "American Motors Fills New Post of Management Chief," *Detroit News,* 25 November 1954, 72.

17. Mahoney, *The Story of George Romney,* 152, 154.

18. "Barit's Notes Recall Hotel Room Talk That Sparked Merger of Nash, Hudson; Both Were Fretting Over Credit Shortage," *Wall Street Journal,* 18 April 1955, 14; Hudson Motor Car Company, *Annual Report for 1953,* NAHC; American Motors Corporation, annual reports for 1954 and 1955.

19. Maurice D. Hendry, "Hudson: The Car Named for Jackson's Wife's Uncle," *Automobile Quarterly* 11 (Summer 1971): 391; "Barit's Notes Recall Hotel Room Talk," 14; Stuart G. Baits to Hudson employees, 27 May 1954, Hudson Motor Car Company corporate records, NAHC.

20. "AMC Priority for Hudson Idle," *Detroit News,* 31 January 1955, 1, 2; "1st Hudson Men Ask to Transfer," *Detroit News,* 10 March 1955, 4; "Hudson Men Get Seniority in Wisconsin," *Detroit News,* 1 April 1955, 20; "Kenosha Waits Shift of Detroit Workers," *Detroit News,* 9 March 1955, 1, 4.

21. "4,300 to Lose Jobs as Hudson Moves: Assembly Shifted to Wisconsin," *Detroit News,* 28 May 1954, 1, 2; John H. Gill, "Hudson Area Gloomy But Looks to Future," *Detroit News,* 28 May 1954, 7; Jerry Ter Horst, "Loss of Millions in Hudson Taxes Visioned by City," *Detroit News,* 30 May 1954, A-8.

22. "Dealers See Benefits in Hudson Transfer," *Detroit News,* 30 May 1954, A-8; letter to Stuart Baits, 27 February 1955, box "Series II, Hudson, 1954–56," folder "1955 Hudson," DCHC.

23. Louis Rugani, "When Hudson Came to Kenosha," *Midwest Bulletin* 8 (March 22, 1988), and "Wisconsin Welcomes Hudson Celebration Banquet" program, both in the vertical files "Industry, AMC" at the Kenosha, Wisconsin, Public Library.

24. Thomas E. Bonsall, *More Than They Promised: The Studebaker Story* (Stanford: Stanford University Press, 2000), 278–80, 285, 287, 290.

25. "Agreement between Packard Motor Car Company and American Motors Corporation," 27 August 1954, box "AMC 1954," DCHC.

26. Bonsall, *More Than They Promised,* 187–290; Mahoney, *The Story of George Romney,* 187; James A. Ward, *The Fall of the Packard Motor Car Company* (Stanford: Stanford University Press, 1995), 205, 206.

27. "Hope Raised for Defense Jobs in City," *Detroit News,* 29 August 1954, A-9; "More Hudson Contracts," *Detroit News,* 21 November 1954, B-13; "New Vehicle to Be Built at Hudson Plant," *Detroit News,* 18 November 1954, 62; "Merger Merits: American Motors Sales Up, Costs Down after Year," *Wall Street Journal,* 18 April 1955, 14.

28. Ralph R. Watts, "American Motors Set to Shut Special Plant: Shrinking Defense Contracts Hold Fate," *Detroit News,* 2 February 1958, D-16; "$33 Million Contracts to Boost State Jobs," *Detroit News,* 30 March 1958, A-7; "'Mite' Models," *Detroit News,* 9 January 1959, 36; "State Gets $19 Million in U.S. Jobs," *Detroit News,* 1 July 1960, A-4; "Army Work to Add 1,000 Jobs Here," *Detroit News,* 3 July 1960, A-7; "$2.4 Million Job for AMC," *Detroit News,* 22 December 1960, D-7; "2 Firms Get $5 Million in Contracts," *Detroit News,* 2 March 1961, D-7; "Local Firms Get 2 Army Orders," *Detroit News,* 23 November 1961, C-15; "AMC Gets Truck Award," *Detroit News,* 18 January 1962, C-12.

29. "Barit's Notes Recall Hotel Room Talk," 14; Sam Medway, "Refrigerators and the Two Georges—From Nash-Kelvinator to American Motors," *Automobile Quarterly* 15 (second quarter 1977): 157; Don Butler, *The History of Hudson* (Sarasota, FL: Crestline Publishing, 1982), 322.

30. "Detroit Stockholders View All American Motors Show," *Detroit News,* 8 December 1954, 32; Ralph R. Watts, "Nash to Put Rambler on View Friday," *Detroit News,* 23 November 1954, 1;

"Nash, Hudson to Use Same Body in 1955," *Detroit News,* 22 September 1954, 70; "One Car But Two Looks," *Business Week,* 6 November 1954, 32; "Driving the Nash," *Motor Life* 4 (Spring 1955): 13; "Nash-Hudson," *Automotive Service Digest* 43 (March 1955): 52–53; "Hudson Completely Restyled for 1955," *Northern Automotive Journal* 64 (January 1955): 6, 54; "The New Hudson: Most Complete Model Changeover in Company History," *Automobile Topics* 55 (January 1955): 16–17; "Nash Develops Entirely New Model Series," *Northern Automotive Journal* 64 (January 1955): 11, 32, 56; Mahoney, *The Story of George Romney,* 16.

31. "1956 Nash," *Automobile Topics* 55 (December 1955): 22, 23, 35; "Hudson, 1956," *Automobile Topics* 55 (December 1955): 26, 27, 35; "Nash Road Test," *Motor Life* 6 (April 1957): 64, 65; Ralph R. Watts, "V-Line Wasp and Hornet Make Debut," *Detroit News,* 30 November 1955, 1,2; Butler, *History of Hudson,* 327, 328, 332; Hyde, *Riding the Roller Coaster,* 173–77.

32. Ralph R. Watts, "1956 Rambler Begins Run on Own Line," *Detroit News,* 10 October 1955, 1, 18; Ralph R. Watts, "Rambler Slated as Separate Line," *Detroit News,* 14 June 1956, 61; Butler, *History of Hudson,* 332.

33. Foster, "A Little Style from Kenosha," 8; John A. Gunnell, ed., *Standard Catalog of American Motors, 1902–1987* (Iola, WI: Krause, 1993), 174, 182; A. G. Koepfgen, "Metropolitan Shipments from Inception," 20 December 1963, box "Metropolitan," DCHC.

34. Foster, "A Little Style from Kenosha," 13; Ralph R. Watts, "AMC Revamps Metropolitan," *Detroit News,* 9 April 1956, 32; Koepfgen, "Metropolitan Shipments from Inception."

35. American Motors Corporation, Public Relations Department, press releases, 15 December 1955 and 23 December 1963, both in the Roy Abernethy biography file, NAHC; "Rambler Genius Abernethy Dies," *Detroit News,* 1 March 1977, A-6.

36. Mahoney, *The Story of George Romney,* 185–86, 249; Hendry, "Hudson: The Car Named for Jackson's Wife's Uncle," 391; Butler, *History of Hudson,* 333.

37. "Chapin in New Post," *Detroit News,* 7 November 1954, B-14; "American Motors Elevates Chapin to Treasurer," *Detroit News,* 26 April 1955, 24; American Motors Corporation, directors' meeting, 6 December 1955, DCHC; "Business Shorts," *Detroit News,* 17 January 1956, 58; American Motors Corporation, *Annual Report for 1956,* 16.

38. American Motors Corporation, directors' meeting, 6 December 1955, DCHC; Ralph R. Watts, "Hudson Plant Here Bought by Cadillac," *Detroit News,* 5 August 1956, sec. 1, p. 7.

39. "Plan Stores on Hudson Plant Site," *Detroit News,* 15 December 1957, A-1, A-2; John C. Treen, "Trains to Haul away Hudson Power Plant," *Detroit News,* 20 December 1957, 1, 17, 32; "City Sues to Speed Wrecking," *Detroit News,* 27 September 1960, B-9.

40. "AMC Offers to Clean Up Hudson Site," *Detroit News,* 4 November 1960, B-11; "Hudson Plant Demolition to Be Resumed Dec. 15," *Detroit News,* 2 December 1960, A-3; "Old Hudson's Plant's Last Gasp," *Detroit News,* 8 January 1961, B-6; "200-Footer Bites the Dust," *Detroit News,* 18 October 1961, D-16.

41. "Barit's Notes Recall Hotel Room Talk," 14; Mahoney, *The Story of George Romney,* 11–14; Tom Joyce, "Reach Accord at AMC: Brief Walkout Ends; Layoff Pay Plan, Raises Included," *Detroit News,* 2 September 1955, 1, 2; "Milwaukee Plant Rejects American Motors Pact," *Detroit News,* 4 October 1955, 19; "AMC Pact Is Approved in Kenosha," *Detroit News,* 5 October 1955, 75; "Milwaukee UAW Says Unions' Employees Have Approved Pact," *Detroit News,* 28 November 1955.

42. Patrick R. Foster, "George Romney: On the Path of Persistence," *Automobile Quarterly* 35 (October 1996): 25.

43. "'We Are the David,' Says President of American Motors on 1956 Plans," *Southern Automotive Journal* 35 (November 1955): 13; "American Motors Meets the Press," transcript of press conference with George Romney, president, on occasion of the company's second anniversary, 24 April 1956, Hotel Statler-Detroit, Kenosha, Wisconsin, Public Library, vertical files, "Industry," AMC.

44. Foster, "George Romney," 23, 26.

45. Ibid., 25; Mahoney, *The Story of George Romney,* 190–91.

46. Mahoney, *The Story of George Romney,* 28–35; "Wolfson in AMC Deal: Becomes Firm's Largest

Shareholder; Financier Has 'Ideas of Own' about Operation, Romney Says," *Detroit News*, 11 March 1957, 1, 4; "Wolfson Rules Out AMC Proxy Battle," *Detroit News*, 12 March 1957, 10; Edgar C. Greene, "Wolfson Surprised by Stir; Intends to Make AMC 'Healthy,'" *Detroit News*, 13 March 1957, 70; Ralph R. Watts, "More Stock Purchased by Wolfson," *Detroit News*, 22 March 1957, 50.

47. Mahoney, *The Story of George Romney*, 38–43; "Wolfson Sells 100,000 Shares of AMC Stock," *Detroit News*, 20 June 1958, 1, 2; "Court Slaps Wolfson: U.S. Investigates Deals in AMC Stock; Deceitful Reports Charged; Ordered to Halt Alleged Violation of Security Act," *Detroit News*, 24 June 1958, 1, 2; "Ailing Wolfson Denies Fraud in AMC Stock," *Detroit News*, 25 June 1958, 33.

48. Bruce M. Tuttle, "AMC Given $67 Million Credit Line," *Detroit News*, 28 August 1956, 1; "American Motors Retires Bank Debt," *Detroit News*, 18 July 1958, 38; "AMC Given Warning to Gain or Die," *Detroit News*, 16 September 1957, 1; "Confident AMC Stakes All on Success of '58 Cars," *Detroit News*, 29 September 1957, A-14.

49. Lawrence J. White, *The Automobile Industry since 1945* (Cambridge, MA: Harvard University Press, 1971), 295.

50. "The Dinosaur in the Driveway: A Talk Presented by George Romney, President, American Motors Corporation, Delivered before the Motor City Traffic Club of Detroit, January 27, 1955," box "George Romney's Speeches," DCHC; Mahoney, *The Story of George Romney*, 20–24; James Playsted Wood, "Leaders in Marketing: George Romney," *Journal of Marketing* 27 (July 1963): 78, 79.

51. Wood, "Leaders in Marketing," 79; Mahoney, *The Story of George Romney*, 202–8; John Keats, *The Insolent Chariots* (New York: J. B. Lippincott, 1958).

52. "Statement by George Romney, President, American Motors Corporation before Subcommittee on Antitrust and Monopoly of the Committee on the Judiciary, United States Senate, February 7, 1958," George Romney biography file, NAHC.

53. Mahoney, *The Story of George Romney*, 9, 10; "Drop Nash, Hudson as Car Names," *Detroit News*, 28 September 1957, 1; Earl F. Wegmann, "Rambler Takes Over as 2 Names Vanish," *Detroit News*, 2 October 1957, 62; "A Tear in Parting" (editorial), *Detroit News*, 5 October 1957, 4.

54. Ralph R. Watts, "AM Tells Plan for Smaller Car: 100-Inch Wheelbase," *Detroit News*, 2 August 1957, 19; "New Rambler Out Soon: AMC Gets Set for 100-Inch Car," *Detroit News*, 14 November 1957, 61; Ralph R. Watts, "Reveal Details of News Rambler: 100-Inch Wheelbase," *Detroit News*, 3 January 1958, 31; "Rust-Proof Bodies," *Detroit News*, 16 August 1957, 37; Gunnell, *Standard Catalog of American Motors*, 218, 220–21.

55. Ralph R. Watts, "Rambler Sets Record: Coast-to-Coast Gas Bill of $26," *Detroit News*, 29 June 1956, 47; Ralph R. Watts, "Detroit Use Told: Rambler Woos Taxicab Drivers," *Detroit News*, 31 July 1957, 53.

56. "Why AMC Can Gamble on Its Small Cars," *Business Week*, 11 January 1958, 78–82; Richard Austin Smith, "Will Success Spoil American Motors?" *Fortune* 59 (January 1959): 97–99, 176, 184.

57. American Motors Corporation, directors' meetings, 18 June 1959 and 30 November 1959, DCHC.

58. Patrick R. Foster, *American Motors: The Last Independent* (Iola, WI: Krause, 1993), 58–70; Ralph R. Watts, "AMC Goal Is 550,000 Car Sales," *Detroit News*, 17 August 1960, A-7; Ralph R. Watts, "Rambler Cuts Compact's Size in 1961 Models," *Detroit News*, 18 August 1960, A-38; Ralph R. Watts, "AMC's New Classic to Bow Oct. 12," *Detroit News*, 6 October 1960, A-1, A-13.

59. White, *The Automobile Industry since 1945*, 296–306; Walter Henry Nelson, *Small Wonder: The Amazing Story of the Volkswagen* (Boston: Little, Brown, 1967), 307; Terry Shular with Griffith Bordeson and Jerry Sloniger, *The Origin and Evolution of the VW Beetle* (Princeton, NJ: Princeton Publishing, 1985), 171–73.

60. White, *The Automobile Industry since 1945*, 182–85.

61. Asher Lauren, "AMC Seeks Freeze for 2 Years," *Detroit News*, 2 April 1958, 1, 2; Tom Joyce, "Oct. 17 Deadline Spurs AMC-UAW Bargaining," *Detroit News*, 8 October 1958, 22; Herb Levitt

and Jack Crellin, "Profit-Sharing OK's in AMC-UAW Agreement: Stock Included in 3-Year Pact; 23,000 Workers to Share 10 Per Cent of Earnings," *Detroit News,* 17 August 1961, A-1; Herb Levitt, "Tell Detail of AMC Contract: Workers Get Control over Stock Shares," *Detroit News,* 31 August 1961, A-1, A-10.

62. "'No' Vote May Kill AMC Pact: Biggest Local Turns down Agreement," *Detroit News,* 9 October 1961, A-1, A-2; "UAW Nears Showdown on Kenosha AMC Vote," *Detroit News,* 10 October 1961, A-1, A-15; "AMC Local 'No' Vote Overruled," *Detroit News,* 12 October 1961, A-1, A-2; "Woodcock at Kenosha to Push AMC Pact Vote," *Detroit News,* 26 October 1961, B-3; "Profit-Sharing Pact Approved by Rebel Local: Kenosha UAW Reverses Itself; AMC Workers Pass Contract on Second Vote by 2–1 Margin," *Detroit News,* 4 November 1961, A-1, A-2.

63. Ralph R. Watts, "AMC Shuffles Top Officers," *Detroit News,* 2 December 1960, A-1, A-2; "AMC Elects Abernethy as Manager," *Detroit News,* 17 November 1961, A-1, A-2; "AMC Picks Executives for Exports," *Detroit News,* 29 November 1961, A-1.

64. Mahoney, *The Story of George Romney,* 1–4, 228–38.

65.Ibid., 240–47; Foster, "George Romney," 27–28.

66. Jack Crellin, "Romney Will Pray Tonight for 'Guidance' on Decision," *Detroit News,* 9 February 1962, A-1, A-16; Glenn Engle, "Romney Promises to Finish Con-Con before Campaign," *Detroit News,* 10 February 1962, A-1, A-2; American Motors Corporation, directors' special meeting, 12 February 1962; telegram, Bentley G. Burns to George W. Romney, 12 February 1962, DCHC; Jack Crellin, "Abernethy, Cross Split Romney's Job," *Detroit News,* 12 February 1962, A-1, A-3.

67. J. A. Livingstone, "Will AMC Miss Romney's Fanfare?" *Detroit News,* 21 February 1962, C-12.

CHAPTER EIGHT

1. Jack Crellin, "AMC Sets Sales Goal at 500,000: New Executives Voice Confidence on Firm's Future," *Detroit News,* 13 February 1962, A-1, A-23; Anthony Ripley, "Romney Successors Plan Big Year for AMC in '63," *Detroit News,* 16 November 1962, A-4.

2. Patrick R. Foster, *American Motors: The Last Independent* (Iola, WI: Krause, 1993), 87–90, 105; Lawrence J. White, *The Automobile Industry since 1945* (Cambridge, MA: Harvard University Press, 1971), 298, 301, 304, 306.

3. John A. Gunnell, ed., *Standard Catalog of American Motors, 1907–1987* (Iola, WI: Krause, 1993), 223–24; Ralph R. Watts, "Rambler Makes Styling Changes," *Detroit News,* 14 September 1962, C-15; Ralph R. Watts, "'63 Rambler Is Lower after Rare Redesigning," *Detroit News,* 1 October 1962, B-9; Ralph R. Watts, "New Hardtop in AMC Models," *Detroit News,* 27 September 1962, C-14; Ralph R. Watts, "V-8 Added to Rambler Classic Line," *Detroit News,* 21 February 1963, C-19.

4. Jim Wright, "Motor Trend's Car of the Year: Classic and Ambassador," *Motor Trend* 15 (February 1963): 20–28; "AMC Joins in 2-Year Warranties," *Detroit News,* 29 September 1962, A-3.

5. Gunnell, *Standard Catalog of American Motors,* 226–27; Ralph W. Watts, "Rambler's '64 Lineup Streamlined," *Detroit News,* 20 September 1963, A-1, A-10; Jack Crellin, "AMC 'Idea Car' Unveiled," *Detroit News,* 6 February 1964, D-13.

6. Gunnell, *Standard Catalog of American Motors,* 228–29; Jack Crellin, "AMC Eyes Rebound with Sporty '65 Cars," *Detroit News,* 10 May 1964, A-1, A-2; Ralph W. Watts, "Sports Car by AMC—the Marlin," *Detroit News,* 6 December 1964, A-1, A-4; Jack Crellin, "AMC to Introduce Marlin, Sporty Fastback, on March 1," *Detroit News,* 5 February 1965, D-10; Michael Lamm and Dave Holls, *A Century of Automotive Style: 100 Years of American Car Design* (Stockton, CA: Lamm-Morada, 1996), 203.

7. Malcolm J. Brooks, "A Strike at the Marlin," *Automobile Quarterly* 4 (Fall 1965): 146–49; Gunnell, *Standard Catalog of American Motors,* 229, 230, 233; Charles K. Hyde, *Riding the Roller Coaster: A History of the Chrysler Corporation* (Detroit: Wayne State University Press, 2003), 213.

8. Gunnell, *Standard Catalog of American Motors,* 229–30; "AMC Bids for 'Cushy' Car Market," *Detroit News,* 6 August 1965, A-15; Ralph W. Watts, "'66 AMC Models Street Luxury, Sporty Styling," *Detroit News,* 10 September 1965, D-7; Robert W. Irvin, "AMC Brings Out Small Powerhouse," *Detroit News,* 7 April 1966, D-9.

9. "AMC Goes Shopping for Ad Agency," *Detroit News,* 20 February 1965, A-6; Ralph R. Watts, "Will New Ad Approach Help Lift AMC Sales?" *Detroit News,* 16 March 1965, B-8; "New Ad Firm Named by AMC in Move to Bolster '66 Sales," *Detroit News,* 5 April 1965, A-3.

10. Robert W. Irvin, "3 Firms Boost Car Warranty: 5-Yr. Protection for '67 Models of GM, Ford, AMC," *Detroit News,* 1 September 1966, A-1, A-18.

11. "Abernethy Rebuked by Racer: Blames Drivers, Not Fast Cars for Accidents," *Detroit News,* 7 February 1963, A-3; "Rambler to Debut in Stock Car Race," *Detroit News,* 12 February 1966, B-5; Robert W. Irvin, "AMC Ads *Switch* Gears, Talk Up Daytona Showing," *Detroit News,* 15 May 1966, B-6.

12. Richard E. Cross to Roy D, Chapin Jr., 27 May 1966, folder "General History," box "AMC, 1966," DCHC.

13. American Motors Corporation, annual reports for 1962–74; Robert Irvin, "AMC Sells 25 Percent of Output Outside U.S.," *Detroit News,* 10 January 1966, C-4.

14. "How AMC Profit Fund Is Split for Employees," *Detroit News,* 16 November 1962, A-16; Asher Lauren, "Share Plan Lifts AMC Efficiency: 27,000 Workers Get Stock Valued at $3.4 Million," *Detroit News,* 16 November 1962, A-1, A-16.

15. Jim Crellin, "Worker Confusion Still Plagues AMC Profit-Sharing Plan," *Detroit News,* 22 March 1964, A-25; Asher Lauren, "AMC Profit Sharing Up for Decision," *Detroit News,* 5 June 1964, B-9.

16. Asher Lauren, "1st Talks to Open at AMC: UAW Bargaining Huddle Brings Quick Accord," *Detroit News,* 27 April 1963, A-3; Asher Lauren, "Last Auto Strike Over; Full Output Due Monday," *Detroit News,* 26 November 1964, C-18; "New AMC Talks Asked by Union," *Detroit News,* 2 December 1964, A-3; "UAW Presses Local to Ratify AMC Pact," *Detroit News,* 3 December 1964, A-12.

17. "Board Gets OK to Call AMC Strike," *Detroit News,* 19 January 1965, A-12; "5,000 Halt AMC Lines in Kenosha," *Detroit News,* 3 June 1965, B-13; "17,000 Out at AMC as Talks Fail," *Detroit News,* 23 August 1965, A-1, A-28; "AMC Walkout Laid to Short Work Weeks," *Detroit News,* 24 August 1965, A-6; Jim Crellin, "Mediators Talk to Both Sides as Strike Keeps AMC Closed," *Detroit News,* 26 August 1965, A-21; Jim Crellin, "1st AMC Talks since Strike Fail to Point Way to Settlement," *Detroit News,* 27 August 1965, C-8; "UAW Seeks 'Extras' in Strike, AMC Says," *Detroit News,* 3 September 1965, A-4; "AMC, Union Reach Pact: Local Meets to Ratify; Every Grievance Reported Settled," *Detroit News,* 11 September 1965, A-1; "Rehiring of Steward by AMC Key to Pact," *Detroit News,* 12 September 1965, A-4; Jim Crellin, "Order 2nd AMC Vote on Contract," *Detroit News,* 17 September 1965, A-6; "AMC Local Approved Pact Again," *Detroit News,* 24 September 1965, A-13.

18. White, *The Automobile Industry since 1945,* 295, 301, 306; Walter B. Smith, "2 Form AMC Stockholder Committee," *Detroit News,* 1 June 1965, A-1, A-15; Alfred W. Lowman, "What's Next for AMC? Wall Street Awaits Word on Dividends and Earnings," *Detroit News,* 1 August 1965, D-10; Walter B. Smith, "American Motors' $50 Million Borrowing Disclosed," *Detroit News,* 5 January 1966, C-17; "AMC Reportedly Negotiating Big New Credit Line," *Detroit News,* 17 March 1966, C-23.

19. Walter B. Smith, "Will Evans' Big Holdings Give Him Voice in AMC Affairs?" *Detroit News,* 30 January 1966, B-14; Robert W. Irvin, "No AMC Take-Over Sought, Says Evans," *Detroit News,* 2 February 1966, A-1; Robert W. Irvin, "Big Stockholder Evans Still Mum on Plans for American Motors," *Detroit News,* 3 February 1966, C-6; Robert W. Irvin, "Evans Put on Board of AMC," *Detroit News,* 7 March 1966, A-1, A-2; "AMC Names Robt. Evans to New Executive Unit," *Detroit News,* 5 April 1966, B-6.

20. Jim Crellin, "Cushman Quits AMC for High WSU Post: Sees Bright Outlook for Auto Firm," *Detroit News,* 22 March 1966, A-1, A-4; Jim Crellin, "WSU Hires 2nd Official from AMC," *Detroit News*, 16 August 1966, A-1, A-8; Jim Crellin, "Ex-Burroughs VP Seen as Cushman's Successor," *Detroit News*, 1 May 1966, B-8.

21. Richard E. Cross to Roy D. Chapin Jr., 27 May 1966, folder "General History," box "AMC, 1966," DCHC; American Motors Corporation, board of directors meeting, 6 June 1966, DCHC; Robert W. Irvin, "Evans Takes AMC Helm, Pledges 'Action and Results' to End Slump," *Detroit News,* 7 June 1966, D-9; Robert W. Irvin, "AMC Names Chapin Auto Chief: Firm Ties Success to '67 Line; New Manager Is Heir-Apparent to Abernethy," *Detroit News*, 13 September 1966, A-1, A-13.

22. American Motors Corporation, board of directors meeting, 9 January 1967, DCHC; Laurence G. O'Donnell, "Roy D. Chapin, Jr. Is Named AMC's Chief Executive: He Succeeds Roy Abernethy; Chapin Elected Chairman in Top Realignment; Luneburg Becomes President," *Wall Street Journal*, 10 January 1967, 1.

23. Robert W. Irvin, "Comeback Pledged at AMC," *Detroit News*, 10 January 1967, A-1, A-8; Robert W. Irwin, "AMC's 'New Strategy' Has a Familiar Sound," *Detroit News*, 11 January 1967, B-12; Tom Kleene, "Holder Goads Ex-Chairman into Bitter Review of Past," *Detroit Free Press*, 3 February 1972, B-8; Walter B. Smith, "Evans Blames AMC Woes on Ex-Officers," *Detroit News*, 3 February 1972, C-4.

24. "Biography, William V. Luneburg, President, American Motors Corporation," American Motors Public Relations Department press release, 9 January 1967, box "Luneburg," DCHC; Fred Girard, "A Tough Boss Shoved AMC Into High Gear," *Detroit Free Press*, 24 March 1974.

25. James J. Flink, *The Automobile Age* (Cambridge, MA: MIT Press, 1988), 384–87; B. Bruce-Briggs, *The War against the Automobile* (New York: E. P. Dutton, 1977), 85; Robert B. Reich and John D. Donahue, *New Deals: The Chrysler Revival and the American System* (New York: Times Books, 1985), 28.

26. Hyde, *Riding the Roller Coaster*, 217–18; Flink, *The Automobile Age*, 388.

27. "Agreement between General Motors Corporation (AC Spark Plug Division) and American Motors Corporation, July 12, 1974," folder "General Motors," box "AMC Agreements and Contracts," DCHC.

28. L. A. Kintigh, vice president, General Motors Corporation to John F. Anderson, vice president, Engineering and Research, American Motors Corporation, 7 November 1969; Bruce B. Wilson, deputy assistant attorney general, Antitrust Division, U.S. Department of Justice, to Forrest A. Hainline Jr., general counsel, American Motors Corporation, 9 October 1973; Thomas E. Kauper, assistant attorney general, Antitrust Division, U.S. Department of Justice, to Forrest A. Hainline, 4 December 1975; "Report, October 14, 1980 Consultation, Pursuant to the May 2, 1972 American Motors–General Motors Agreement," all found in folder "General Motors," box "AMC Agreements and Contracts," DCHC.

29. "Notes for RDC Remarks, Meeting with Banks, 1/12/67," folder "AMC Steering Committee," box 11, Roy D. Chapin Jr. Papers, BHL; American Motors Corporation, board of directors meeting, 20 January 1967, DCHC; Walter B. Smith, "Stockholders Hear AMC's Woes," *Detroit News*, 2 February 1967, C-5; "AMC's Bankers Agree to Extend Repayment Date: Debt May Be Cut by $25 Million before May 31 by Proceeds from Redisco Unit's Sale," *Wall Street Journal*, 1 May 1967, 24; Robert C. Gurvin, "AMC Wins Extension on $95 Million Loan," *Detroit News*, 2 May 1967, C-13.

30. "Memo to File, J. C. Secrest, 7 June 1968," folder "White Consolidated Industries," box 14, Roy D. Chapin Jr. Papers, BHL; American Motors Corporation, directors' meetings, 28 June 1968, 3 July 1968, DCHC; American Motors Corporation, *Annual Report for 1968*, 5; Robert W. Irvin, "AMC Shareholders Get Rosy Forecast for '69," *Detroit News*, 6 February 1969, C-7.

31. Ralph R. Watts, "AMC Unveils Its 'AMX,' and Experimental Show Car," *Detroit News*, 5 January 1966, C-17; Robert W. Irvin, "AMC Puts Experiments on Display," *Detroit News*, 20 June 1966,

A-1, A-10; Robert C. Ackerson, "Changing of an Image: Behind the Scenes at AMC with the AMX and the Javelin," *Automobile Quarterly* 19 (first quarter 1981): 8, 9.

32. Michael Lamm and Dave Holls, *A Century of Automotive Style: 100 Years of American Car Design* (Stockton, CA: Lamm-Morada, 1996), 202; Julian G. Schmidt, "Dick Teague," *Motor Trend*, November 1968, 76–77.

33. Lamm and Holls, *A Century of Automotive Style*, 202; Tom Kleene, "His Challenge: Small-Car Design," *Detroit Free Press*, 29 September 1969, B-1, B-3.

34. Foster, *American Motors, The Last Independent*, 128; Gunnell, *Standard Catalog of American Motors*, 235–37; Beverly Rae Kimes, "AMX, Javelin; The New Look of American Motors," *Automobile Quarterly* 6 (Winter 1968): 278.

35. Robert W. Irvin, "New AMC Sportscar Due in '68," *Detroit News*, 8 July 1966, A-1, A-4; "Background on 1968 AMX," American Motors public relations release, undated (ca. January 1968), folder "Press Releases," box "AMX," DCHC; Gunnell, *Standard Catalog of American Motors*, 235, 236; Foster, *American Motors, The Last Independent*, 130; Ackerson, "Changing of an Image," 16.

36. Brock Yates, *The Decline and Fall of the American Automobile Industry* (New York: Random House, 1983), 96–97; Leon Mandel, *American Cars* (New York: Stewart, Tabori & Chang, 1982), 305, 308, 319; Flink, *The Automobile Age*, 288–89; Hyde, *Riding the Roller Coaster*, 212–16, 228.

37. "AMC Again Switching Ad Agencies," *Detroit News*, 13 June 1967, B-9; Linda LaMarre, "Mary Wells: Scrambler Wins Rambler Account," *Detroit News*, 14 June 1967, C-23; Richard A. Wright, "'Non-Average' Ad Agency Appointed by AMC," *Automotive News*, 19 June 1967, 6, 66.

38. "AMC in Race," *Detroit News*, 4 February 1967, A-10; Robert W. Irvin, "'Funny Car' AMC Answer," *Detroit News*, 26 August 1967, B-3; Ackerson, "Changing of an Image," 16; "Racing Boss Set at AMC," *Detroit News*, 30 September 1967, B-5.

39. Ackerson, "Changing of an Image," 17, 22, 23, 28; Robert W. Irvin, "AMC Building Car for Land Speed Bid," *Detroit News*, 17 August 1968, B-3; Joe Dowdall, "AMC Plans to Go All Out with Auto Racing Program: Company to Challenge, Ford, Chrysler," *Detroit News*, 7 September 1968, B-3; "Speed Model," *Detroit News*, 18 October 1968, D-7.

40. Gunnell, *Standard Catalog of American Motors*, 236–38; Foster, *American Motors, The Last Independent*, 136; Robert W. Irvin, "1969 Ambassador to Be Biggest AMC Car Ever," *Detroit News*, 13 August 1968, B-11; Robert W. Irvin, "Sales of AMC's Scrambler Outracing Production," *Detroit News*, 9 March 1969, F-1.

41. Schmidt, "Dick Teague," 77; "Hot Rodder to Hot Designer: Dick Teague's Boyhood Auto Mania Drove Him into Design," *Business Week*, 4 October 1969, 134, 136; Kleene, "His Challenge: Small-Car Design."

42. Robert W. Irvin, "Hornet AMC's Answer to Imports, Maverick," *Detroit News*, 13 August 1969, C-18; Robert W. Irvin, "AMC Expecting Big Things from Its New Little Hornet," *Detroit News*, 13 August 1969, C-18; "AMC Hornet Is $1 Below the Maverick," *Detroit News*, 4 September 1969, C-7; William V. Luneburg, "AM's Hornet: A New Concept in Compacts," *Automotive Industries* 141 (10 November 1969): 58.

43. Robert W. Irvin, "AMC's New Gremlin: Anti-Beetle Machine," *Detroit News*, 13 January 1970, A-1, A-6; Robert W. Irvin, "AMC Takes Wraps off Gremlin," *Detroit News*, 12 February 1970, C-10; Robert W. Irvin, "AMC's Gremlin Costs $40 to $120 More Than 'Beetle,'" *Detroit News*, 10 March 1970, B-6.

44. William S. Rukeyser, "Detroit's Reluctant Ride into Smallsville," *Fortune* 79 (March 1969): 110–14, 164, 167, 168; Foster, *American Motors: The Last Independent*, 145; Hyde, *Riding the Roller Coaster*, 225–26.

45. Flink, *The Automobile Age*, 327, 339–43; Wanda James, *Driving from Japan: Japanese Cars in America* (Jefferson, NC: McFarland, 2005), 115–23, 216.

46. Greg Conderacci, "When Richard Teague Thinks Up a New Car, It's a 'Make-Do' Effort: American Motors Designer, Holding Costs Low, Puts a New Face on Old Parts," *Wall Street Journal*, 18 June 1975, 15; Gunnell, *Standard Catalog of American Motors*, 134–35.

47. Robert W. Irvin, "AMC's Gremlin Turns on a Dime," *Detroit News*, 13 February 1970, A-7; Kleene, "His Challenge: Small-Car Design."

48. Foster, *American Motors: The Last Independent*, 155–58.

49. For a detailed history of the "birth" of the Jeep and its service in World War II, see Patrick R. Foster, *The Story of Jeep*, 2nd ed. (Iola, WI: Krause, 2004), 34–65. The production figures are from John A. Conde, *The American Motors Family Album: A Pictorial Roll Call of the Passenger Cars, Commercial Vehicles, and Trucks Produced by American Motors and Its Predecessor Companies* (Detroit: American Motors Corporation, 1976), 63.

50. Foster, *The Story of Jeep*, 76–81, 89–91.

51. Ibid., 94, 96–98, 101–2, 112–16, 124–26, 132.

52. "American Motors Corporation, Kaiser-Jeep Acquisition Study, Book I—Background Data," 25 April 1969, folder "Kaiser Jeep Corporation," box "AMC, 1969/1970," DCHC; Foster, *The Story of Jeep*, 132–33.

53. American Motors Corporation, board of directors meeting, 2 June 1969, DCHC; Robert W. Irvin, "Jeep Corp., AMC in Deal," *Detroit News*, 20 October 1969, A-1, A-8; Robert W. Irvin, "AMC-Jeep Deal Seen as Good for Both," *Detroit News*, 21 October 1969, B-3; Robert W. Irvin, "AMC Signs Purchase Deal for Kaiser Jeep," *Detroit News*, 2 December 1969, C-6; "U.S. Eyes AMC Deal with Jeep," *Detroit News*, 27 October 1969, D-7; Robert W. Irvin, "AMC Stock Sale Expected," *Detroit News*, 27 February 1972, B-4.

54. Robert W. Irvin, "AMC Signs Switch to a New Identity," *Detroit News*, 21 September 1969, C-16; Robert W. Irvin, "Why American Motors Changed Its Symbol," *Detroit News*, 24 September 1969, C-16.

55. Walter B. Smith, "AMC Profit Report Surprises Analysts," *Detroit News*, 20 July 1971, C-6; Robert W. Irvin, "AMC Is Making Money, But for How Long?" *Detroit News*, 8 August 1971, E-6, E-11.

56. Joseph M. Callahan, "AMC Lowers Break-Even Point," *Automotive Industries* 149 (1 November 1971): 33–37; "Find the Problems—Fix Them: Here's What American Motors Executives Are Doing about It," *Quality Assurance* 9 (March 1970): 34–42.

57. Robert W. Irvin, "AMC to Offer New 'Buyer Protection Plan,'" *Detroit News*, 10 August 1971, C-7; Walter B. Smith, "Here's What AMC '72 Warranty Offers," *Detroit News*, 11 August 1971, C-5; Robert W. Irvin, "AMC Warranty—Not Only Fine Print," *Detroit News*, 14 November 1971, E-7; Robert W. Irvin, "AMC Counters Skeptics of Warranty Plan," *Detroit News*, 8 February 1972, C-5; Robert W. Irvin, "Warranty Plan Boosts AMC Market Share by 20 Pct.," *Detroit News*, 9 May 1972, A-16.

58. Denise Shere, "AMC Warranty Outpaces Rest of Industry," *Detroit News*, 9 May 1972, A-16; Robert W. Irvin, "Few Buyers Seek AMC 'Super' Protection," *Detroit News*, 19 October 1972, D-13; Lou Mleczko, "AMC's Car Warranty Best of Big 3, Survey Says," *Detroit News*, 2 August 1973, E-1, E-2.

59. Gunnell, *Standard Catalog of American Motors*, 241–48.

60. Christopher Willcox, "Motor World Drives the AMC Hornet," *Detroit News*, 4 April 1974, C-1, C-4; Christopher Willcox, "Test Drive: Sportabout," *Detroit News*, 13 June 1974, F-3; Vincent R. Courtenay, "Testing the Matador Wagon," *Detroit News*, 20 June 1974, E-2.

61. Robert W. Irvin, "Another AMC Gamble: A New Small Car for '75," *Detroit News*, 5 January 1975, A-1, A-2; Irvin, "AMC Introduced Pacer," *Detroit News*, 9 January 1975, E-1; Irvin, "AMC—An Innovator," *Detroit News*, 9 January 1975, E-1, E-3; Irvin, "Testing AMC Pacer," *Detroit News*, 9 January 1975, E-2.

62. Paul Gainer, "Big Ad Budget for AMC Pacer," *Detroit News*, 5 February 1975, C-8; Robert W. Irvin, "Pacer Pulls: AMC Ups Output to Meet Early *Demand*," *Detroit News*, 11 March 1975, C-9; Robert L. Wells, "Pacer Sales Boom," *Detroit News*, 27 March 1975, E-1: Robert W. Irvin, "Pacer Start of Revolution?" *Detroit News*, 7 August 1975, D-2; Robert W. Irvin, "Pacer Featured as AMC Unveils Its 1976 Models," *Detroit News*, 8 August 1975, D-4; Gunnell, *Standard Catalog*

of American Motors, 246–49; American Motors Corporation, Public Relations Department, press release, 23 February 1976, DCHC.

63. Gunnell, *Standard Catalog of American Motors,* 250–57; Ted Kade, "AMC to Drop the Matador," *Detroit News,* 15 April 1978, A-17.

64. Robert W. Irvin, "AMC Views Pacer as Comeback Key," *Detroit News,* 22 August 1976, *Detroit News,* E-1, E-3; Robert W. Irvin, "Pacer Wagon Unveiled," *Detroit News,* 1 September 1976, C-20; Tom Kleene, "AMC's Chapin to Retire," *Detroit Free Press,* 19 September 1978, A-5; Charles G. Burck, "A Fresh Start—Again—For American Motors: The Perennially Ailing Baby of the Auto Industry Suddenly Looks Healthy, and Its New Management Has a Clear Design for the Future," *Fortune* 79 (16 July 1979): 68; Gunnell, *Standard Catalog of American Motors,* 249, 251, 253, 256.

65. "AMC Unveils 1978 Car Lines," *Detroit News,* 26 August 1977, A-11; "AMC's Concord: Most Say They Like It; Some Say It's Overpriced," *Detroit News,* 25 September 1977, E-1, E-2; Ted Goczkowski, "Motor World Tests the AMC Concord," *Detroit News,* 6 October 1977, D-1; Gunnell, *Standard Catalog of American Motors,* 253, 256.

66. Gunnell, *Standard Catalog of American Motors,* 273, 274.

67. Ibid., 272; Foster, *The Story of Jeep,* 151.

68. Gunnell, *Standard Catalog of American Motors,* 279; "Jeep for Spring," *Detroit News,* 8 June 1971, C-8; Christopher Willcox, "Testing Jeep Cherokee," *Detroit News,* 29 August 1974, C-2.

69. Gunnell, *Standard Catalog of American Motors,* 281; Robert W. Irvin, "1976 Rundown by AMC Shows Minor Changes," *Detroit News,* 7 August 1975, D-1; "AMC Offers New Model in Jeep Lines," *Detroit News,* 14 August 1975, G-2; Robert W. Irvin, "Reporters Test New Jeeps on Mountain Trails," *Detroit News,* 28 August 1975, E-1; Vince Courtenay, "Motor World Tests CJ-7 Jeep," *Detroit News,* 26 February 1976, E-2; Foster, *The Story of Jeep,* 170–73.

70. American Motors Corporation, annual reports, 1970–78; Clark Hallas, "AMC Rides Jeep Sales to a Profit," *Detroit News,* 10 November 1978, A-1, A-4.

71. *AM General: A Story of Capability,* folder "AM General History," box "AM General History, 1977–1982," DCHC, 6–9; Patrick R. Foster, *AM General: Hummers, Mutts, Buses & Postal Jeeps* (Hudson, WI: Iconografix, 2005), 6, 14.

72. Irvin, "AMC-Jeep Deal Seen as Good for Both"; *AM General: A Story of Capability,* 10, 11; "AM General Formed by AMC," *Detroit News,* 4 April 1971, E-12.

73. *AM General: A Story of Capability,* 15, 24, 25; Foster, *AM General,* 9, 13, 16–18, 36, 52, 53.

74. American Motors Corporation, press release, 20 May 1975, and AM General Corporation, *New Electruck Now Available,* both in folder "Electric Truck," box "AM General History, 1974–1977," DCHC; Richard Willing, "Jeeps Past Test: Postal Service Denies Giving Up on AMC Electric Vehicles," *Detroit News,* 21 January 1976, D-1.

75. Foster, *AM General,* 10–12, 43–51.

76. Robert W. Irvin, "AMC Will Build Buses," *Detroit News,* 6 October 1971, C-10; "AM General Corporation, Bus Marketing Program, 5 October 1971," folder "AM General Bus," box 12, Roy D. Chapin Jr. Papers, BHL.

77. Foster, *AM General,* 19; Robert W. Irvin, "AMC Jumps into Bus Business," *Detroit News,* 22 February 1974, F-5; Robert W. Irvin, "American Motors Builds Luxury Buses," *Detroit News,* 24 February 1974, F-1.

78. Foster, *AM General,* 21, 29; "Transbus—Interim Bus Briefing," folder "Transbus, Interim Bus Briefing," box 12, Roy D. Chapin Jr. Papers, BHL.

79. Foster, *AM General,* 26, 32–35.

80. Ibid., 6, 7.

81. Robert W. Irvin, "American Motors Back in Big League," *Detroit News,* 8 February 1973, C-12; Robert W. Irvin, "AMC Expects Big 1973 Profit Gains," *Detroit News,* 6 March 1973, C-17; Robert W. Irvin, "AMC Returns to 'Big Four' Status," *Detroit News,* 11 April 1973, E-7; Robert W. Irvin, "AMC Takes Success, Looks to the Future," *Detroit News,* 7 February 1974, A-13.

82. AMC, Jeep, Renault, *1985 Almanac: U.S. Market Data, Vehicle Distribution,* p. 3, American Motors Corporate File, NAHC. The figures are the share of AMC passenger car penetration of the U.S. market, including foreign manufacturers, based on calendar year sales.

83. "AMC Shifting Brampton Plant to Jeep Production," *Detroit News,* 28 March 1978, B-4; "Ohio Offers Loans to American Motors," *Detroit News,* 17 October 1978, B-2; American Motors Corporation, Public Relations Department press release, 7 February 1979; "AMC Notes Increased Output of Jeeps, Cars," *Detroit News,* 11 April 1979.

84. "Accord Is Reached in AMC Strike," *Detroit News,* 17 October 1969, A-2; "AMC Plant Settles, 2 Still Out," *Detroit News,* 20 October 1969, A-7; "Strikers and AMC Talk Again," *Detroit News,* 24 October 1969, A-8; "AMC Workers Ratify Pact," *Detroit News,* 5 November 1969, A-16.

85. Jack Crellin, "AMC Gets Same Terms from UAW," *Detroit News,* 18 August 1970, A-6; "AMC Builds 'Strike Bank' of GM and Chrysler Parts," *Detroit News,* 5 September 1970, A-10; "AMC to Halt Jeep Output," *Detroit News,* 10 November 1970, C-12; Jack Crellin, "UAW Sets Deadline for AMC," *Detroit News,* 11 March 1971, A-12; Darwin Bennett, "UAW Works without Contract at AMC," *Detroit News,* 2 April 1971, A-10; John Gill, "National AMC Pact Reached," *Detroit News,* 13 April 1971, A-13.

86. Jack Crellin, "AMC Bargaining Pace Stepped Up," *Detroit News,* 26 July 1974, F-8; "UAW Hails AMC Settlement," *Detroit News,* 1 October 1974, A-5; "UAW Ratifies Pact at AMC," *Detroit News,* 4 October 1974, F-6; "AMC-UAW Pact Runs Out Today," *Detroit News,* 15 February 1977, A-18; "UAW Extends AMC Contract for 7 Months," *Detroit News,* 16 February 1977, A-6; "American Motors Bargaining Starts," *Detroit News,* 29 July 1977, A-5; Avi Lank, "Accord Reached at AMC; Union Chiefs Elated," *Detroit News,* 16 September 1977, A-3; "AMC Workers Ratify 1-Year Pact," *Detroit News,* 21 September 1977, B-9; Mark Lett, "AMC Plans Catch-Up in AMC Talks," *Detroit News,* 20 August 1978, A-1, A-13; "AMC Workers Ratify New Pact," *Detroit News,* 22 September 1978, A-2.

87. Robert W. Irvin, "American Motors Hints at Moving HQ to Southfield," *Detroit News,* 26 May 1973, A-3; Clark Hallas, "Not Quitting Detroit, AMC Tells Gribbs: Chapin Explains Southfield Land Purchase," *Detroit News,* 31 May 1973, A-28; Clark Hallas, "AMC Complex Reported Planned for Southfield," *Detroit News,* 3 June 1973, A-1, A-27; "October Start Planned for New AMC Building," *Detroit News,* 7 July 1974, B-4; "Tower in Southfield For American Motors," *Detroit News,* 24 May 1974, B-4.

88. Paul Bernstein, "Young Says Detroit Won't Buy AMC Cars: Firm's Move to Southfield Cited," *Detroit News,* 6 December 1974, A-3; Paul Bernstein, "Levin Criticizes Ban on AMC," *Detroit News,* 7 December 1974, A-3; "AMC Begins Shift," *Detroit News,* 30 December 1975, C-4; "Moving Time For AMC," *Detroit News,* 3 February 1976, A-13; memo, J. P. Tierney to Roy D. Chapin Jr. and I. M. Anderson, 15 September 1977, folder "AMC Headquarters," box 11, Roy D. Chapin Jr. Papers, BHL.

89. Robert B. Smith, "Gerald Meyers Named New President of AMC," *Detroit News,* 25 May 1977, E-1; Robert W. Irvin, "Officially He's Retired, But Luneburg Keeps Working," *Detroit News,* 1 June 1977, E-1.

90. Memorandum, "R. W. McNealy to the American Motors Policy Committee, Personal; & Confidential, Subject: The DeLorean Motor Company Proposal, 7 June 1977," folder "Miscellaneous," box "Agreements and Contracts," DCHC; Robert W. Irvin, "AMC Turns Down DeLorean for Job," *Detroit News,* 25 August 1977, D-2; Gerald C. Meyers, with John Holusha, *When It Hits the Fan: Managing the Nine Crises of Business* (Boston: Houghton Mifflin, 1986), 43–44.

91. Clark Hallas, "Chapin Quits as AMC Boss," *Detroit News,* 22 October 1977, A-1, A-7; "AMC Shuffles Top Execs, Plans 4 More '78 Models," *Detroit News,* 19 November 1977, A-1, A-23; American Motors Corporation, minutes of the board of directors meeting, 21 October 1977, DCHC.

92. Clark Hallas, "Chapin Announces Retirement; Ends Long Family Reign at AMC," *Detroit News,* 19 September 1978, A-16; Tom Kleene, "Roy D. Chapin, AMC Chairman, to Retire Sept. 30," *Detroit*

Free Press, 19 September 1978, A-5; Bob Luke, "New Wheel at AMC: Company Appoints Outsider President as Meyers Moves to Chairmanship," *Detroit News*, 21 October 1978, A-1, A-6.

93. "Quiet Man at American Motors; Roy Chapin Leading Recovery Program for the Rambler; Executive Is Known as a Reflective Problem Solver," *New York Times*, 13 November 1966, 42; Laurence G. O'Donnell, "Roy D. Chapin Is Named AMC's Chief Executive: He Succeeds Roy Abernethy; Chapin Elected Chairman in Top Level Realignment; Luneburg Becomes President," *Wall Street Journal*, 10 January 1967, 1; John J. Green, "Chapin: New Man at AMC Wheel: He Holds the 'Ignition Key,'" *Detroit News Magazine*, 26 February 1967, 10–12, 14, 40.

94. Keith Bradsher, "Roy D. Chapin, Jr., 85; Ran American Motors," *New York Times*, 7 August 2001; Hawke Fracassa, "Roy D. Chapin Jr., Ex-AMC Chairman Gambled to Save Jeep," *Detroit News*, 7 August 2001; Jeanne May, "Roy Chapin Jr.: Former AMC Head Loved Hunting," *Detroit Free Press*, 7 August 2001.

CHAPTER NINE

1. Charles W. Theisen, "New AMC Boss Admits 2 Errors, 1 in 1st Grade," *Detroit News*, 2 October 1977, A-7.

2. American Motors Corporation, Public Relations Department, press release, 24 May 1977, AMC corporate files, NAHC.

3. Gregory Swira, "AMC Hires a Marketing Pro," *Detroit Free Press*, 21 October 1978, C-6; Michael J. Trojanowski, "AMC Getting a Fresh Perspective: Ex–Sewing Machine Exec Leads Auto Firm," *Detroit News*, 22 October 1979, A-14; James V. Higgins, "Paul Tippett AMC's Own Diplomatic Corps," *Detroit News*, 8 November 1981, L-1, L-2.

4. Ted Kade, "AMC's Meyers: Downsizing," *Detroit News*, 10 December 1978, F-1; Charles G. Burck, "A Fresh Start—Again—For American Motors: The Perennially Ailing Baby of the Auto Industry Suddenly Looks Healthy, and Its New Management Has a Clear Design for the Future," *Fortune* 79 (16 July 1979): 68, 72.

5. John A. Gunnell, ed., *Standard Catalog of American Motors, 1902–1987* (Iola, WI: Krause, 1993), 255–64; Michael J. Trojanowski, "That's the Spirit: Pleasant Ride and Several Extras," *Detroit News*, 12 December 1979, C-1; Ted Kade, "Pacer Loses: Chubby Model with Slim Sales Falls Prey to Soaring Eagle," *Detroit News*, 13 November 1979, C-4.

6. Michael J. Trojanowski, "AMC Hopes to Soar with Eagle," *Detroit News*, 17 May 1979, D-17; "4-Wheel-Drive Eagle Unveiled," *Detroit News*, 24 August 1979, D-8; "Eagle Appeals to the 'Closet 4-Wheeler,'" *Detroit News*, 27 August 1979, B-6; "Car Test: The Eagle Has Landed, Dealers' Hopes Soar," *Detroit News*, 31 October 1979, C-1, C-2; "Eagle Revs Up Auto Show," *Detroit News*, 13 January 1980, A-1, A-5; "AMC Plans to Introduce 'Eaglet,'" *Detroit News*, 7 February 1980, C-8.

7. Walter B. Smith, "AMC Is Considering Possible Merger," *Detroit News*, 2 February 1978, C-11; "AMC Confirms Plan for Foreign-Car Tie," *Detroit News*, 21 February 1978, A-11.

8. "AMC, Renault Plan Ties," *Detroit News*, 31 March 1978, A-1; Ted Kade, "Renault Says 'Oui' to AMC," *Detroit News*, 1 April 1978, A-1, A-5; Clark Hallas, "AMC, Renault—Marriage of Need; Their Hopes Ride on 'Le Car,'" *Detroit News*, 1 April 1978, A-3; "Renault Deal Should Help AMC" (editorial), *Detroit News*, 4 April 1978, A-16; Clark Hallas, "Viva AMC 'Ray for Renault," *Detroit News*, 10 April 1978, A-15; "Meyers: Renault Deal Will Help," *Detroit News*, 20 April 1978, F-10; Ted Kade, "AMC Joins Renault in Sales Pact," *Detroit News*, 10 January 1979, A-1, A-17; Jeffrey Hadden and Ted Kade, "AMC, Renault Sign Marketing Pact: New Line Predicted," *Detroit News*, 11 January 1979, D-10, D-11.

9. Michael J. Trojanowski, "AMC, Renault Tighten Bond," *Detroit News*, 13 October 1979, A-17; "Renault's Top Executive Becomes AMC Director," *Detroit News*, 20 October 1979, A-17; Michael J. Trojanowski, "2 Car Companies Rendezvous at High Speed," *Detroit News*, 22 October 1979, A-14.

10. Michael J. Trojanowski, "AMC's Hot Streak Cools a Bit before Stockholder Meeting," *Detroit News,* 3 February 1980, L-1, L-2; "Renault to Own 46% of AMC Stock," *Detroit News*, 25 September 1980, D-13; "'Felix the Fixer' to Join AMC as Director," *Detroit News*, 19 November 1980, E-8; "AMC Bank Deal Aims at Renault," *Detroit News*, 10 December 1980, C-11; "It's Official: Renault 'Takes Over' AMC," *Detroit News*, 17 December 1980, E-3.

11. "Renault's Plans Still Include Joint Production with AMC," *Detroit News*, 25 December 1981, C-12, C-13; "Business Journal," *Detroit News,* 10 February 1982, D-9; James V. Higgins, "It's Still American Motors," *Detroit News*, 25 April 1982, J-1; James V. Higgins, "Renault, AMC 'Partners': French Firm Owns 46%," *Detroit News*, 29 April 1982, B-9, B-13.

12. James V. Higgins, "AMC Replaces Meyers in Shake-Up," *Detroit News*, 16 January 1982, A-4; "Chapin Forges Link between AMC-Renault," *Detroit News*, 3 March 1982, C-7, C-10.

13. Mark Lett, "UAW, AMC Get Down to Money Issues," *Detroit News*, 11 September 1980, D-10; "UAW Offer of Board Seat in AMC Talks," *Detroit News*, 16 September 1980, A-1; "Strike Shuts Plant, Halts AMC Output," *Detroit News*, 17 September 1980, A-3, A-12; "UAW Reaches Accord on 3-Year AMC Pact," *Detroit News*, 18 September 1980, A-3.

14. John F. Nehman, "AMC Asks Employees for Help: Capital for Product Program," *Detroit News*, 12 November 1981, D-14; "UAW Will Talk Over AMC Plan: Company Seeks Workers' Loans," *Detroit News*, 2 December 1981, D-1; "AMC, UAW Near Deal on Investment Plan," *Detroit News*, 29 March 1982, A-1, A-2; Richard Willing, "AMC Wins New Accord with UAW," *Detroit News*, 19 April 1982, A-1, A-2; John F. Nehman, "UAW Vote Puts AMC Pact Over," *Detroit News*, 19 May 1982, A-1, A-5; "Renault Role Grows at AMC," *Detroit News*, 4 June 1983, A-1, A-4.

15. Gunnell, *Standard Catalog of American Motors*, 264–66; James V. Higgins, "AMC-Renault Unveil Their New Alliance: Designed in France, Built in America," *Detroit News*, 31 August 1982, B-5; Melinda Grenier, "Alliance Pays Off for AMC," *Detroit News*, 15 December 1982, E-2, E-7.

16. "Renault Alliance: An Efficient Sedan That Lives Up to Its Name," *Road & Track*, September 1982, 44–47; "Car of the Year, 1983, or Perhaps We Should Say, 'Voiture de l'année,'" *Motor Trend,* February 1983, 24–36.

17. Gunnell, *Standard Catalogue of American Motors,* 265, 267, 269–71.

18. Ibid., 287–89; Foster, *The Story of Jeep*, 176, 183–87.

19. Gunnell, *Standard Catalog of American Motors*, 292, 294; Foster, *The Story of Jeep*, 187, 190–93.

20. Gary Witzenburg, "Jeep Cherokee: Downsized Utility Vehicle Offers Comfort, Convenience," *Detroit News,* 12 October 1983, B-1, B-2.

21. Foster, *The Story of Jeep*, 196–201; Chris Singer, "Jeep's Comanche a No-Nonsense Fooler," *Detroit News*, 13 November 1985, D-1, D-2.

22. James V. Higgins, "AMC, China Plan to Build Utility Truck: Tippett in China to Sign $51 Million Joint Venture," *Detroit News*, 3 May 1983, B-5; "AMC, China Agreement to Build Jeeps," *Detroit News,* 5 May 1983, A-4; James V. Higgins and Jacquelyn Swearingen, "AMC's China Connection: Similar Strategies Led to Jeep Joint Venture," *Detroit News*, 1 June 1983, C-1, C-2; "Jeep Plant in Peking Resumes Work," *Detroit News*, 17 August 1986, A-8; Jim Mann, *Beijing Jeep: The Short, Unhappy Romance of American Business in China* (New York: Simon and Schuster, 1989) passim.

23. "Sold!: Developer to Buy AMC Headquarters," *Detroit News*, 19 August 1983, A-10; "Development Group Buys AMC Building, Land," *Detroit News*, 22 October 1983, C-1.

24. James V. Higgins, "AMC Out to Compete with the Big Three," *Detroit News*, 24 August 1983, B-1; "AMC Back in the Black: Larger Car, Smaller Pickup under Development," *Detroit News*, 5 January 1984, B-5; "AMC Expects to Hold Share," *Detroit News*, 6 September 1984, D-3.

25. Ann M. Job, "AMC Plans Concession Repayments," *Detroit News*, 17 December 1984, A-1, A-10; "AMC Warns of Shutdown," *Detroit News*, 19 March 1985, C-4; "AMC Warns of Damaging Reductions," *Detroit News*, 20 March 1985, A-8; "No Wheel Tax, AMC Insists," *Detroit News*, 16 April 1985, D-1, D-2.

26. Ann M. Job, "Profit Sharing Accepted at AMC," *Detroit News*, 11 April 1985, F-1; "Workers Again

Shut Toledo Jeep Plants," *Detroit News*, 14 April 1985, B-2; Marjorie Sorge, "AMC Keeps Cranking Out Jeeps in 70-Year-Old Plant—For Now," *Detroit News*, 22 December 1985, E-1, E-4.

27. Ann M. Job, "AMC to Seek 'Mazda Deal,'" *Detroit News*, 12 April 1985, A-15; Ann M. Job, "AMC Seeks New Givebacks," *Detroit News*, 7 May 1985, D-1.

28. Ann M. Job, "AMC Sets Deadline on UAW Givebacks," *Detroit News*, 8 May 1985, A-11; Ann M. Job, "'No' Vote Expected by AMC Workers," *Detroit News*, 16 May 1985, D-14; John Nehman, "AMC Workers Ratify Pact to Preserve Jobs," *Detroit News*, 13 July 1985, A-1, A-2; "AMC Withdraws Plant-Closing Notices," *Detroit News*, 14 July 1985, A-16.

29. "AMC Chief Takes New Job," *Detroit News*, 29 September 1984, A-10; Ann M. Job, "AMC Chairman Tippett Steps Aside," *Detroit News*, 15 April 1985, F-1; James V. Higgins and John Nehman, "AMC Elects No. 2 Man, Union Talks Continue," *Detroit News*, 22 June 1985, B-1; Marjorie Sorge, "AMC Shuffles Executives at Top Level," *Detroit News*, 14 December 1985, B-1; James V. Higgins, "Cappy Gets Top AMC Post," *Detroit News*, 22 March 1986, B-1; James V. Higgins, "AMC Chief Renault's Man for Job," *Detroit News*, 30 March 1986, D-1.

30. James V. Higgins, "Big Plans Spur New Loan for AMC," *Detroit News*, 25 December 1985, B-7.

31. George S. May, "American Motors Corporation," in George S. May, ed., *Encyclopedia of American Business History and Biography: The Automobile Industry, 1920–1980* (New York: Bruccoli Clark Layman, 1989), 6–8; "Renault Hangs on to AMC and Its 'Global' Position," *Detroit News*, 24 April 1985, D-1, D-2; Edward Miller, "AMC, Renault Future Etched on Medallion," *Detroit News*, 22 February 1987, D-1, D-3; Ann M. Job, Helen Fogel, and Tim Kiska, "Chrysler May Buy Big Part of AMC," *Detroit Free Press*, 6 November 1986, A-15; Ann M. Job, "Inside the Chrysler-Renault-AMC Talks," *Detroit Free Press*, 17 November 1986, C-14; James V. Higgins and Eric Starkman, "Proposed Chrysler-AMC Merger: End of Era?" *Detroit News*, 10 March 1987, A-9.

32. Katherine Yung, "Recalling a Failed Merger: Former American Motors Corp. Officials Tell of Potential Problems in Chrysler Deal," *Detroit News*, 2 June 1998, B-1, B-3.

33. Chrysler Corporation, *1986 Report to Shareholders*, 10; Marjorie Sorge, "Kenosha Eyed for New Jeeps: Decision Could Hurt AMC's Toledo Plant," *Detroit News*, 7 January 1987, C-7; "Wisconsin Employment Statistics," 23 January 1987, box "Chrysler/AMC 1," DCHC.

34. Jim Mateja, "UAW Concessions Sought by AMC in Chrysler Deal," *Chicago Tribune*, 11 December 1986, sec. 3, p. 4; Richard A. Calmes, vice president, personnel and industrial relations, to Marc Stepp, director, American Motors Department, UAW, 26 December 1986, box "Chrysler/AMC 1," DCHC; "Chrysler L-Body Contract Assembly Proposal," 9 January 1987, box "Chrysler/AMC 1," DCHC.

35. Richard A. Calmes to Raymond E. Majerus, director, American Motors Department, UAW, 16 October 1986; Calmes to Marc Stepp, director, American Motors Department, UAW, 7 November 1986, 3 and 26 December 1986; "UAW Leaders Lambaste AMC Statement on Kenosha," UAW press release, 10 December 1986; Joseph A. Cappy, president and chief executive officer, American Motors Corporation, to Marc Stepp, 11 December 1986, all found in box "Chrysler/AMC 1," DCHC.

36. AMC memorandum, T. R. Adams to eight officers, "AMC/Chrysler Kenosha Development Proposal, 23 December 1986"; *Wisconsin Financial Assistance*, 21 January 1987; (draft) *Agreement, Assembly of New Model Vehicle, Kenosha and Milwaukee Plants,* 21 January 1987, all in box "Chrysler/AMC 1," DCHC.

37. Chrysler Corporation, *1986 Report to Shareholders*, NAHC, 25; Doron P. Levin, *Behind the Wheel at Chrysler: The Iacocca Legacy* (New York: Harcourt Brace, 1995), 101–3; Marjorie Sorge, "Chrysler-AMC Discuss New Venture," *Detroit News*, 7 November 1986, E-2; John Bussey, "Chrysler's Miller and Bidwell Kept 'Titan' Bid for AMC from Sinking," *Wall Street Journal*, 13 March 1987, 1.

38. Bussey, "Chrysler's Miller and Bidwell Kept 'Titan' Bid for AMC from Sinking"; Bennett E. Bidwell, vice chairman, Chrysler Corporation, to Joseph E. Cappy, president and chief executive officer, American Motors Corporation, 9 March 1987, box "AMC/Chrysler 1," DCHC.

39. Job, "Inside the Chrysler-Renault-AMC Talks."

40. Edward Miller, "Chrysler's Deal Hailed: Talks on Deal Got Serious in Summer," *Detroit News*, 10 March 1987, A-9; Brian Gruley, "Chrysler Deal Hailed: $1 Billion Bid for AMC Is a Smart Move, Analysts Say," *Detroit News*, 10 March 1987, A-6; Bussey, "Chrysler's Miller and Bidwell Kept 'Titan' Bid for AMC from Sinking."

41. Transcripts of AMC officers' meetings, 9, 13, 18, and 23 March 1987; memorandum, *Due Diligence Guidelines*, B. E. Bidwell, R. S. Miller Jr., and Richard Goodyear to Chrysler Management, 11 March 1987; "Chrysler Contact List Re: American Motors," 12 March 1987, all in box "Chrysler/AMC 1," DCHC.

42. R. D. Houtman, assistant general counsel, American Motors Corporation, to Thomas McGivern, listing representative, New York Stock Exchange, 23 March 1987; *Confidential American Motors Corporate Calendar,* 18 March 1987; American Motors Corporation, proxy statement for stockholders, 2 July 1987, all found in box "Chrysler/AMC 1," DCHC; "Presentation to the Board of Directors, American Motors Corporation, by Shearson Lehman Brothers, May 19, 1987," box "Chrysler/AMC 3," DCHC.

43. American Motors Corporation, minutes of the board of directors meeting, 14 April 1987, 3–4, DCHC.

44. Ibid., 19 May 1987, 2–9, DCHC.

45. Jon F. Nehman, "UAW Leaders Voice Relief: Kenosha, Toledo Union Spokesmen Express Cautious Optimism at Sale," *Detroit News,* 10 March 1987, A-7; Carol Cain and Kathleen Kerwin, "Dealers Are Elated: 'Nothing But Good,' Says One; Chrysler Sellers Not Worried," *Detroit News*, 10 March 1987, A-7; Marjorie Sorge, "Future Uncertain: Fate of Plants, Models Up in the Air," *Detroit News*, 10 March 1987, A-6.

46. American Motors Corporation, "Salaried Employee Retention Program," 2 June 1987, and Towers, Perrin, Forster & Crosby, "Chrysler Corporation, Chrysler-AMC Employee Communication," 10 June 1987, both in box "Chrysler/AMC 1," DCHC.

47. Edward Miller and Marjorie Sorge, "Chrysler, AMC Workers Feel Ax: Firings Could Grow to 4,500; Amtek Staff Is Hardest Hit," *Detroit News,* 31 October 1987, A-1, A-8; Warren Brown, "Buyout Brings Pain to AMC: Merger with Chrysler Means Job Losses, Reassignments," *Washington Post*, 22 November 1987, 1.

48. Marjorie Sorge, "Chrysler to Lay Off 400 in Kenosha: Changes Start Next Week," *Detroit News*, 30 October 1987, E-2; Edward Miller, "5,500 Lose Jobs in Chrysler Closing," *Detroit News*, 28 January 1988, A-1, A-12; Marjorie Sorge, "Aged Facility Earns Place in Industrial History," *Detroit News,* 28 January 1988, F-1; Marjorie Sorge, "Officials Accuse Chrysler of Breaking Word," *Detroit News*, 28 January 1988, F-1, F-3.

49. Marjorie Sorge, "UAW Asks Chrysler to Keep Kenosha," *Detroit News,* 5 February 1988, E-1; "Kenosha Workers Send Chrysler a Big Message," *Detroit News*, 10 March 1988, F-1.

50. "Prepared Remarks by L. A. Iacocca, Chairman of the Board, Chrysler Corporation, at a Milwaukee Press Conference, Milwaukee, Wisconsin, February 16, 1988," box "LAI Speeches 10—1988," DCHC; James V. Higgins, "Chrysler to Aid Kenosha Workers Who Lose Jobs," *Detroit News*, 17 February 1988, A-3.

51. David Sedgwick and Helen Fogel, "Kenosha Deal May Give Workers Up to $10,000 Each," *Detroit News*, 3 May 1988, A-1, A-9.

52. Kathryn Marie Dudley, *The End of the Line: Lost Jobs, New Lives in Postindustrial America* (Chicago: University of Chicago Press, 1994), 24–26. This book is a detailed analysis of the Kenosha plant closing and its impact on factory workers there.

RETROSPECTIVE

1. John B. Rae, *American Automobile Manufacturers: The First Forty Years* (Philadelphia: Chilton, 1959), 173.

2. Lawrence J. White, *The Automobile Industry since 1945* (Cambridge, MA: Harvard University Press, 1971), 10.

APPENDIX

1. U.S. Census of Population, 1870, Genesee County, Forest Township, 238R.
2. U.S. Census of Population, 1870, Genesee County, Flushing Township, 221R; U.S. Census of Population, 1880, Genesee County, Flushing Village, 21, 22, and Forest Township, 20.
3. U.S. Census of Population, 1900, Genesee County, Richfield Township, 6.

Index